Work, Ideology, and Film under Socialism in Romania

Studies in Critical Social Sciences Book Series

Haymarket Books is proud to be working with Brill Academic Publishers (www.brill.nl) to republish the *Studies in Critical Social Sciences* book series in paperback editions. This peer-reviewed book series offers insights into our current reality by exploring the content and consequences of power relationships under capitalism, and by considering the spaces of opposition and resistance to these changes that have been defining our new age. Our full catalog of *SCSS* volumes can be viewed at https://www.haymarketbooks.org/series_collections/4-studies-in-critical-social-sciences.

Series Editor
David Fasenfest (York University, Canada)

Editorial Board
Eduardo Bonilla-Silva (Duke University)
Chris Chase-Dunn (University of California–Riverside)
William Carroll (University of Victoria)
Raewyn Connell (University of Sydney)
Kimberlé W. Crenshaw (University of California–LA and Columbia University)
Heidi Gottfried (Wayne State University)
Alfredo Saad-Filho (Queen's University, Belfast)
Chizuko Ueno (University of Tokyo)
Sylvia Walby (Lancaster University)
Raju Das (York University)

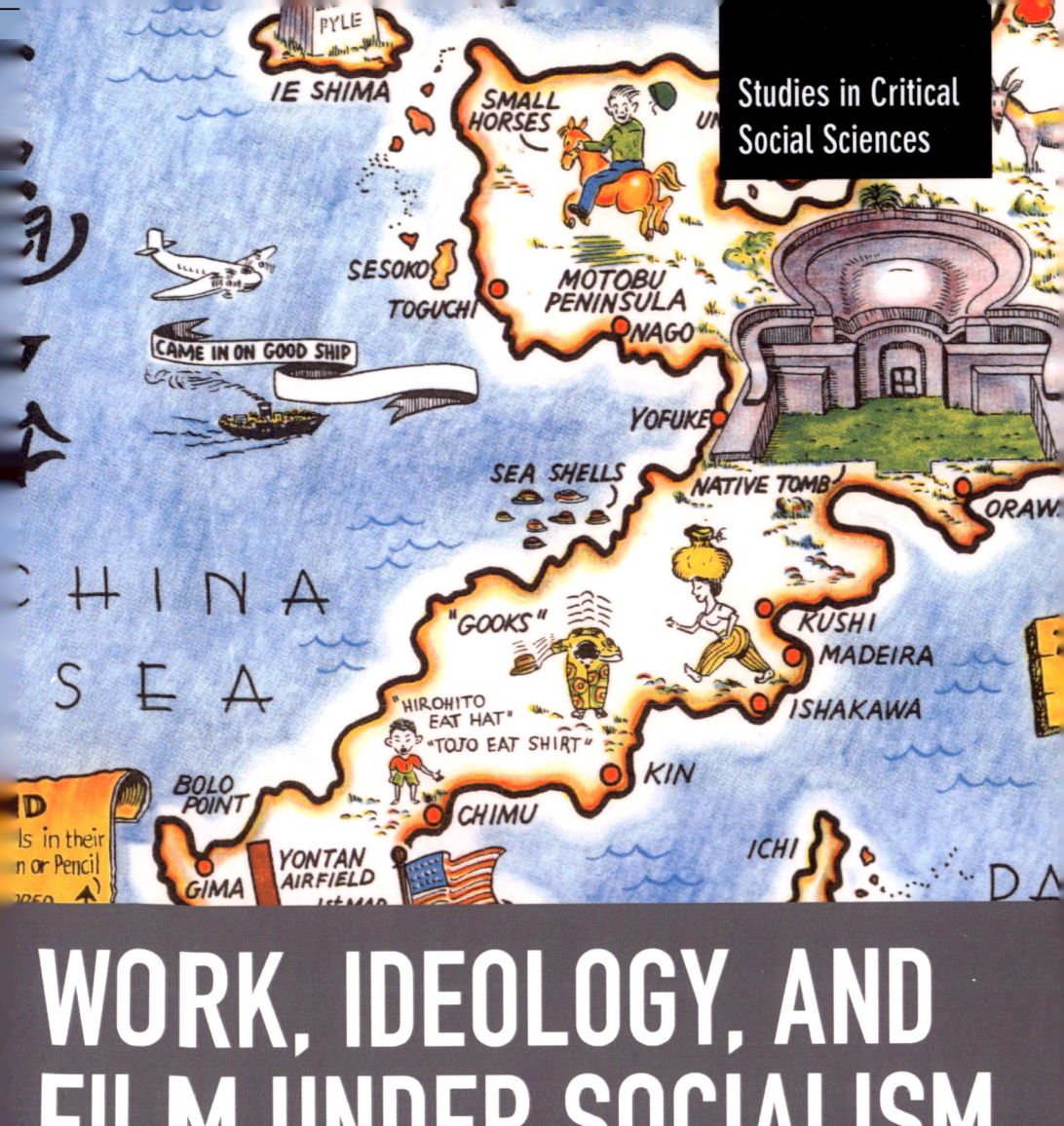

Studies in Critical Social Sciences

WORK, IDEOLOGY, AND FILM UNDER SOCIALISM IN ROMANIA
STUDIES IN THE SOCIOLOGY OF FILM

Roxana Cuciumeanu

Work, Ideology, and Film under Socialism in Romania

Studies in the Sociology of Film

Roxana Cuciumeanu

Haymarket Books
Chicago, IL

First published in 2024 by Brill Academic Publishers, The Netherlands
© 2024 Koninklijke Brill NV, Leiden, The Netherlands

Published in paperback in 2025 by
Haymarket Books
P.O. Box 180165
Chicago, IL 60618
773-583-7884
www.haymarketbooks.org

ISBN: 979-8-88890-544-9

Distributed to the trade in the US through Consortium Book Sales and Distribution (www.cbsd.com) and internationally through Ingram Publisher Services International (www.ingramcontent.com).

This book was published with the generous support of Lannan Foundation, Wallace Action Fund, and the Marguerite Casey Foundation.

Special discounts are available for bulk purchases by organizations and institutions. Please call 773-583-7884 or email info@haymarketbooks.org for more information.

Cover design by Jamie Kerry and Ragina Johnson.

Printed in the United States.

Library of Congress Cataloging-in-Publication data is available.

For Arghir

Contents

List of Figures and Tables XI
List of Films and Directors XIII

Introduction 1

1 **Work, Modernity, and Film** 6
  1 From Furniture on Fire to Image Reversibility 6
  2 Images of Work and Social Contexts That Produce Images of Work 12

2 **Film as Instrument of the Sociological Imagination** 17
  1 Film towards a Quality of the Mind 17
  2 The Dramatized Construction of Reality 19
  3 Structural Components of Film Mechanism 24

3 **Work and Ideology** 26
  1 Work: Etymological Roots, Semantic Structures, and Ideological Meanings 26
  2 Work at Marx: Historical Concept and Practical Reality 28
  3 Working People and Social Class(es) 31
  4 Workers, Social Class, and "Socialist" Urbanization 36
  5 Elements of Urbanization in Romania 52
  6 Elements of Work System 61

4 **Work and Socialist Realism** 65
  1 Social Value of Work: Preferable Modes and Desirable End-States 65
  2 Working People and the Role of Art in Socialism 67

5 **Image and Elements of Film Language** 71
  1 Image Concept and Cinematic Structure 71
  2 Filmic Narrative: A *What* and a *Way* 80

6 **Sociological Approaches to Film** 85
  1 Thinking the Film: Crystallised Images of the Real 85
  2 Sociology and Film: A Historical Perspective 94
  3 Film as Economic Production 95
  4 Film as Social Institution 97

5 Film as Cultural Industry 100
  6 Film and Representations of the Social 104
     6.1 *Siegfried Kracauer and the Discovery of the Non-visible Realities* 105
     6.2 *Marc Ferro and Film as Witness: A Counter-Analysis of Society* 109
     6.3 *Pierre Sorlin and the Filmic Construction* 114

7 **Theoretical Perspectives on Culture in Socialism** 117
  1 Marxist Foundations of Culture in Socialism. The Dominant Ideology 117
  2 Vladimir Ilici Lenin and the Theory of Reflection 121
  3 Antonio Gramsci and the Hegemonic Ideology 124
  4 Louis Althusser and the Theory of Interpellation 130

8 **Ideology, Art, and Culture in Socialism** 134
  1 Socialist Realism: From Cultural Doctrine to Political Strategy 134
  2 Socialist Realism in Romania: Elements of Sociopolitical Context 139
  3 Directions for Action in Film-Making Work 142
  4 Unfortunate Events and Social Consciousness. Mangalia Theses (August 1983) 149

9 **Actuality Film as a Matter of Realism** 153
  1 Here, Now, and the Future: Filmmakers as Historians 153
  2 The Political Nature of Actuality Film 157

10 **Film Culture and Its Economy** 160
   1 The Institution of Film in Post-war Romania. Elements of Film Repertoire 160
   2 Film Economy under the Spectrum of Profitability 171

11 **Cinematic Representations of Work** 174
   1 Physical Frames of Work 174
   2 Apparent Indolents and Working Leaders: The Cinematic Division of Work 176
      2.1 *Images of Workers and Engineers: Producers of Means of Productions* 177
      2.2 *Main Characters and Gender Configurations* 188

3   Work Attitudes and Evaluations: Two Ideological Hypostases
        of Work   195
    4   Working Subject and City Dweller between Hero and Marginal   198
    5   Work and Social Space: An Ideological Pattern of Job
        Distribution   203

12 Domination, Hegemony, and Interpellation. Film and the Impossibility
    of Getting Out of Ideology   209
    1   Film and Ideology: Two Constructions   211
        1.1   *Cave (Illusion): A Projection on Work and the City. The Mental
              Image of Work in the Context of the Visual Image of the City*   211
        1.2   *The Ideological State Apparatus and the Counter-Analysis
              of Socialist Education: Work and the Process of Socialization
              in a* Ciné-Verité *Style*   214

13 Evaluative Structures of Work in Seven Romanian Films   221
    1   *Diminețile unui băiat cuminte/The Mornings of a Good Boy*
        (Andrei Blaier, 1967)   221
        1.1   *Workers and Intellectuals. Meanings and Significances
              of Ideological Constructions*   221
        1.2   *Discourse on (Social) Other*   225
    2   *Filip cel bun/Filip the Kind* (Dan Pița, 1975)   228
        2.1   *It's Very Important to Get to Know the People at Work*   228
        2.2   *Housing, Administrative Bureaucracy, and Social
              Inequality*   231
    3   *Iarba verde de acasă/The Green Grass of Home*
        (Stere Gulea, 1977)   233
        3.1   *A Critical Commentary on Socialist Modernization*   234
        3.2   *Institutions and the People They Are Made Of*   239
    4   *Probă de microfon/Microphone Test* (Mircea Daneliuc, 1980)   242
        4.1   *Looking for a Job*   243
        4.2   *Figures of Work and Themes of Urban Centrality*   244
        4.3   *Elements of the Social Condition of the Marginal*   250
    5   *La capătul liniei/At the End of the Line* (Dinu Tănase, 1983)   255
        5.1   *Towards a Personal Definition of Work Ethics*   256
        5.2   *Human Element and Mechanical Sensitivity*   257
    6   *Faleze de nisip/Sand Cliffs* (Dan Pița, 1983)   260
        6.1   *"Young Trees" and the "Forest Rot"*   261
        6.2   *The Kid – A Young Worker at the Black Sea*   262
        6.3   *A Counter-Analysis of the Official Critique of the Film*   269

    6.4   *One Film. Multiple Discourses*   270
7   *Imposibila iubire/Impossible Love* (Constantin Vaeni, 1984)   273
    7.1   *The Project of a Town with No Name*   274
    7.2   *The Work Hero and the Cancellation of Reality*   276

14   **Conclusions / Open Ending**   279

    References   283
    Index   293

Figures and Tables

Figures

1. Theoretical model of the research   13
2. Dimensions and indicators used in the analysis of filmic representations of work   14
3. Conceptual model of a possible relationship between sociology and film   15
4. Film and sociological imagination   24
5. Work system/adaptation after Krasnaseschi, 1971: 14   63
6. Ideological displays: Bucharest and an industrial town   249
7. Elements of socio-spatial mobility under urbanization   252
8. Dramatization of the biography of work hero in *Impossible Love* (1984)   277

Tables

1. Distribution of Romania's *urban* population during socialism (1948–1985)   56
2. Factors of *urban* population growth (1948–1982)   57
3. Dialectic configuration of Marxist (socialist) materialism and philosophical materialism   121
4. Number of Romanian films within general film repertoire (1956–1975)   164
5. Cinema attendance in Romania in 1970 and 1980   165
6. Global cinema attendance (1977)   165
7. Number of viewers per film shown, by country of production (1970, 1980)   166
8. Total number of cinema-goers in Romania (1965–1980)   166
9. Number/sohare of films by country of production within national film repertoire (1960, 1981)   167
10. Professional and occupational categories in Romanian films (1960–1989)   178
11. Distribution of professional and occupational categories by branch of economic activity   185
12. Social characteristics of female characters in 36 films (1960–1989)   190
13. Socio-professional configuration of main female characters in "socialist" city (1960–1989)   193
14. Ideological economy of characters in *Hot Days* and *Microphone Test*   196
15. Professions and occupations of characters   222
16. Professions and occupations of characters   229
17. Professions and occupations of characters   235
18. Professions and occupations of characters   243

19	Urban profiles. The figure of the marginal	251
20	Professions and occupations of characters	256
21	Professions and occupations of characters	263
22	Professions and occupations of characters	275

Films and Directors

Aproape de soare/Close to the Sun (Savel Stiopul, 1960)
Post-Restant/Post Restante (Gheroghe Vitanidis, 1962)
Cerul n-are gratii/ The Sky Has No Bars (Francisc Munteanu, 1962)
Doi băieți ca pâinea caldă/Two Lads with a Heart of Gold (Andrei Călărașu, 1962)
Omul de lângă tine/The Man Next to You (Horea Popescu, 1962)
Puștiul/The Kid (Elisabeta Bostan, 1962)
A fost prietenul meu/He Was My Friend (Andrei Blaier, 1963)
Partea ta de vină/Your Share of the Blame (Mircea Mureșan, 1963)
Pisica de mare/Sea Cat (Gheorghe Turcu, 1963)
Casa neterminată/ The Unfinished House (Andrei Blaier, 1964)
Un surâs în plină vară/A Smile in the Middle of Summer (Geo Saizescu, 1964)
Diminețile unui băiat cuminte/Mornings of a Good Boy (Andrei Blaier, 1967)
Șeful sectorului de suflete/Head of the Soul Sector (Gheorghe Vitanidis, 1967)
Subteranul/The Underground (Virgil Calotescu, 1967)
Un film cu o fată fermecătoare/A Film with a Charming Girl (Lucian Bratu, 1967)
Meandre/Meanders (Mircea Săucan, 1967)
Reconstituirea/The Reenactment (Lucian Pintilie, 1968)
к.о./к.о. (Mircea Mureșan, 1968)
Gioconda fără surâs/Gioconda without a Smile (Malvina Urșianu, 1968)
Balul de sâmbătă seara/Saturday Night Ball (Geo Saizescu,1968)
Apoi s-a născut legenda/Then the Legend Was Born (Andrei Blaier, 1969)
Răutăciosul adolescent/The Mischievous Teenager (Gheorghe Vitanidis, 1969)
Pantoful cenușăresei/Cinderella's Shoe (Jean Georgescu, 1969)
Brigada Diverse intră în acțiune/ The Miscellaneous Brigade Gets into Action (Mircea Drăgan, 1970)
Brigada Diverse în alertă/ The Miscellaneous Brigade on Alert (Mircea Drăgan, 1971)
Brigada Diverse la munte și la mare/ The Miscellaneous Brigade to the Mountains and at the Seaside (Mircea Drăgan, 1971)
Așteptarea/The Waiting (Șerban Creangă, 1971)
Puterea și adevărul/The Power and the Truth (Manole Marcus, 1972)
100 de lei/100 lei (Mircea Săucan, 1973)
Dragostea începe vineri/Love Begins on Friday (Virgil Calotescu, 1973)
Proprietarii/The Owners (Șerban Creangă, 1974)
Trei scrisori secrete/Three Secret Letters (Virgil Calotescu, 1974)
Cursa/The Race (Mircea Daneliuc, 1975)
Filip cel bun/Filip the Kind (Dan Pița, 1975)

Tată de duminică/Sunday Father (Mihai Constantinescu, 1975)
Zile fierbinți/Hot Days (Sergiu Nicolaescu, 1975)
Toamna bobocilor/Freshmen Autumn (Mircea Moldovan, 1975)
Orașul văzut de sus/The City Seen from Above (Lucian Bratu, 1975)
Muntele ascuns/The Hidden Mountain (Andrei C. Băleanu, 1975)
Mere roșii/Red Apples (Alexandru Tatos, 1976)
Singurătatea florilor/The Loneliness of Flowers (Mihai Constantinescu, 1976)
Serenadă pentru etajul XII/Serenade for the XIIth Floor (Carol Corfanta, 1976)
Accident/Accident (Sergiu Nicolaescu, 1976)
Iarba verde de acasă/The Green Grass of Home (Stere Gulea, 1977)
Iarna bobocilor/Freshman Winter (Mircea Moldovan, 1977)
Trepte spre cer/Steps to the Sky (Andrei Blaier, 1978)
Din nou împreună/Together Again (George Cornea, 1978)
Gustul și culoarea fericirii/The Taste and Colour of Happiness (Felicia Cernăianu, 1978)
Probă de microfon/Microphone Test (Mircea Daneliuc, 1980)
Mijlocaș la deschidere/Midfielder at the Opening (Dinu Tănase, 1980)
Croaziera/The Cruise (Mircea Daneliuc, 1981)
Secvențe/Sequences (Alexandru Tatos, 1982)
La capătul liniei/At the End of the Line (Dinu Tănase, 1983)
Sfârșitul nopții/The End of the Night (Mircea Veroiu, 1983)
Faleze de nisip/Sand Cliffs (Dan Pița, 1983)
Buletin de București/Bucharest Identity Card (Virgil Calotescu, 1983)
Un petic de cer/A Patch of Sky (Francisc Munteanu, 1984)
Miezul fierbinte al pâinii/The Hot Crumb of Bread (Al. G. Croitoru, 1984)
Secretul lui Bachus/The Secret of Bachus (Geo Saizescu, 1984)
Imposibila iubire/Impossible Love (Constantin Vaeni, 1984)
O lumină la etajul zece/A Light on the Tenth Floor (Malvina Urșianu, 1984)
Pas în doi/Step in Two (Dan Pița, 1985)
Râdeți ca-n viață/Laugh as in Life (Andrei Blaier, 1985)
Căsătorie cu repetiție/Marriage with Repetition (Virgil Calotescu, 1985)
Promisiuni/Promisses (Elisabeta Bostan, 1985)
Anotimpul iubirii/The Season of Love (Iulian Mihu, 1986)
Clipa de răgaz/The Moment of Respite (Șerban Creangă, 1986)
Vară sentimentală/Sentimental Summer (Francisc Munteanu, 1986)
Declarație de dragoste/Declaration of Love (Nicolae Corjos, 1985)
Liceenii/The High School Students (Nicolae Corjos, 1986)
Secretul lui Nemesis/The Secret of Nemesis (Geo Saizescu, 1986)
Punct și de la capăt/Stop and from the Beginning (Alexa Visarion, 1987)
Liliacul înflorește a doua oară/The Lilac Blooms a Second Time (Cristina Nichituș, 1988)

Introduction

This book provides a framework in which I have sketched some elements in order to organize a meaningful insight into Romanian film during socialist modernization (in the context of urbanization), and into the ways in which the value and social institution of work were reflected in films produced between 1960 and 1989. The book uses an interdisciplinary strategy at the incidence between social theory and film, bringing together approaches specific to visual sociology, sociology of work and urban sociology. Based on this strategy is structured the claim to a relatively novel approach in recent sociological research, a claim that I try to satisfy through relevant and significant theoretical and empirical means.

Texts on Romanian film in the context of socialism are relatively numerous after 1989 and most of them belong to the field of film studies. A common denominator is their historical orientation and strong anchoring in a national dimension with specific temporal and spatial variables. A constant element in these texts is a binary view which often trenchantly displays classic oppositions between elements of film system and the socialist state: propaganda films – films of social critique, filmmakers – state power/political party, official discourse – subversive discourse, conformity – dissidence. Such oppositions are dominant in reflections on Romanian socialist film, lacking a reflective, nuanced orientation that would question not only elements that faithfully reproduce a highly rigid determinism in analysis and interpretation of (socialist) film – nation, socialist realism, propaganda, censorship – but also alternative approaches to filmic cultural production that deconstruct these limits and thick lines drawn over a much broader and geographically and temporally diverse experience. Such a view is partly tributary to the way in which in the Eastern Bloc, to a greater extent than in Western Europe, understanding of history has been structured: before socialism/communism – during socialism/communism (and after socialism/communism).

The compulsive preoccupation with delivering the "true" history or historical "truth" has developed a more or less diffuse binary representational mechanism that has been constantly reproduced in other spheres of cultural production as well. Thinking of socialist film production in a dihotomic logic, coupled with often sterile and uninteresting rhetorical practices of ideological exclusivity, significantly limits a comprehensive and realistic view of film under socialism. Challenging such boundaries – ideological, national, methodological – can only be beneficial and has the advantage of developing possibilities of building an alternative vision of different imageries that populate the history of film under socialism.

What and how one thinks about films, ideology, cultural and socio-economic contexts in which films are produced, seen, discussed and written about are elements that constitute the architectonics of a cinematic sophistication understood as individual's willingness and ability to incorporate, filter, process and integrate information and data about cinematic phenomenon into a coherent value system. The difference between the possible perspectives of reading and assigning meanings is given by the nature of methods and tools used in analysing data about these categories of the cinematic fact. Just as a film director deconstructs and recomposes, in a creative vision of his or her own, a given social world (placing it in the "actuality" of an epoch), the reality of work being a hypostasis of it, the sociologist also deconstructs and recomposes the forms and experiences of filmed work, not so much with the aim of reconstructing them, as with the aim of restoring and, above all, establishing new ways of seeing and understanding the realities of work, ways that become a constitutive part of the very dynamics of the subjective experience of urban reality. I do not consider film only in its primary quality of reflecting more or less faithfully a reality of a time and of the experiences of work attached to it (in a so-called *external* approach to film), but as a social fact and, therefore, as a reality examined as thing, as a constitutive part and form of the experience of work itself, in its quality and at the same time in its function of updating ideas about work which, transposed into the perceptual tools specific to the art of film, become sources in the articulation of new ways of approaching, living, and understanding the material and human universe of work. Work is understood both in terms of its physical morphology and in terms of the way of life it embodies, work understood as subjective experience (an approach to film that I call *internal*). By *novel ways* I understand those forms of knowledge endowed with function of drawing attention to elements and aspects of work life that are worth noticing and that otherwise escape common sight and knowledge.

The importance of this approach also derives from the fact that it allows the perceptive and interpretative angles of films of an epoch to be broadened in relation to the *present* reality of that epoch, bringing together perspectives, images, and narratives that are not directly or manifestly accessible to immediate visible, in the sense of a common knowledge structure. Such a vision structures an instrumental value of film for sociological imagination, in the sense that the interference space between social theory and film becomes fertile in articulating ways of knowing external reality, on the one hand, and relationships between individuals and the historical sequence in which they are placed, on the other. This space of interference is structured at the border between reality and imagination. By imagination I understand the ability to make visible what is not (perceived as) present, having a knowledge function. In this sense, imagination is a specific tool of both sociology and film art. In the case of the former, we are dealing with a scientific type of instrumentalization, in the case of the latter, with a creative, artistic type.

Film is understood not only as medium for conveying ideas about work that are susceptible to sociological insights, but as an autonomous producer of ways of thinking and knowing work in audiovisual terms and which, by doing so, makes important contribution to the diversification of sociological ways of thinking about reality of work, and not merely reflecting it. Elements of visual thinking embody sociological conceptual forms: it is the workspace of visual sociology. Both theoretical and empirical approaches of the research are based on the importance attributed to visual perspective on social, in general, and on urban (socialist) hypostasis of work, in particular. There are two premises I use in defining the theoretical model of the research: 1. work (the representation of work) is to a large extent also a product of the visual culture of an epoch and 2. the films produced in an epoch provide vast and prolific resources in articulating a matrix of the visual culture of that epoch. From this follows an intimate connection between film and the imaginary of work, on the one hand, and the theoretical and practical usefulness of doing sociology visually, on the other. In order to clarify the structure of the methodological toolkit used, I state that the research approach – circumscribed to the broader field of visual sociology – is not one of *visual methods*, but one of *visual studies*. I do not use a visual methodology in order to investigate elements of work life in its "socialist" contexts, but I use sociological methods in order to analyse films about work produced under socialism.

I have chosen to analyze the films in a sociological perspective based on the premise that film is susceptible to multiple readings; it is not just a story constructed using elements of cinematic language, thus reduced to the manifestation of its narrative and aesthetic functions. Film provides, first and foremost, a means of expression and communication of feelings and thoughts. From the point of view of the intentions that a director, scriptwriter, or producer may have, the instrumentalization of film for the purposes of sociological knowledge remains a claim without means. Possible contribution of films to social knowledge is not conditioned by the spectrum of the spoken or unspoken intentions of those who conceive and make them (directors, actors, screenwriters, camera operators, producers, etc.), but by the final product itself that constitutes the *film work*, whether it is an art film, a historical film or an actuality film, to the extent that "Everything, in a film, is potentially describable" (Aumont, 2007: 35). Significant elements in a sociological analysis of film are neither the intentions nor the people, in their particular, personal, or professional circumstances, who produced that good, but what is important is how we can be able to scrutinize the social mechanism that made it readable and effective. The fact that one director was considered an evader by the regime after making some of his films or that another director was a political prisoner is not a strong criterion in the selection and analysis of the films they made, in an approach focused on the sociological meanings and significance of such an investigation. Possibly, such aspects can be used as incidental criteria in the case of the films that have been subject to censorship, that is, they are justified on the basis of an institutional context that allows the practice and legitimisation of certain forms of intervention in the production of a cultural good in a given society at a given time, influencing its content and the manifestation of its function. This hypostasis is significant because it implies an institutional dimension of the relationship between product and social and political context in which it was conceived and produced.

Cinematic representations of work are a form of subjective experience of work. The core of (mental) image of work given by ideas, principles, abstract constructs related to this institution and the experience associated with these cognitive and symbolic elements are structured in a multidimensional matrix, which constantly configures and recalibrates the meanings collectively shared. Cinematic images of work, workers and work contexts provide images of society and of the relationship between individuals and society, between individuals and political power. The living conditions and cultural-artistic activities of non-family women workers at the "Romlux" light bulb factory in Târgoviște, the working rhythm of the workers at "Eugenia" factory in Constanța, who prepared and packed "Eugenia" biscuits by hand, the workers finishing their work hours and coming out of the gates of Fieni cement factory (in *Probă de microfon/Microphone Test*, Mircea Daneliuc, 1980), the group of workers from "Republica" factory in Bucharest and the forms of sociability at work (in *Pas în doi/Step in Two*, Dan Pița, 1985), the informal relations between employees at "Meteor" warehouse in Bucharest, the workers in the halls of Reșița steelworks (in *Filip cel bun/Filip the Kind*, Dan Pița, 1975), the anonymous workers working at the smelting furnaces in the foundry at the Constanța shipyard to manufacture a Romanian propeller for a new minelayer ship, the labour protection rules for young workers on shipyard (in *Zile fierbinți/Hot Days*, Sergiu Nicolaescu, 1975), the researcher at Oltchim chemical plant in Râmnicu Vâlcea interviewed by journalists, wanting to make a product superior to nitrogen (in *Gioconda fără surâs/Gioconda without a Smile*, Malvina Urșianu, 1968), the driver transporting food for the canteen at the Iron Gates 1 construction site, in search of romantic adventures (in *Balul de sâmbătă seara/The Saturday Night*

Ball, Geo Saizescu, 1968), the line worker from Râmnicu Vâlcea Plant and the precariousness of being a working class hero (in *O iubire imposibilă/Impossible Love*, Constantin Vaeni, 1984), the workers who print electrical circuits on pertinax plates at Electronica and I.P.R.S. Băneasa (in *Dragostea începe vineri/ Love Starts on Friday*, Virgil Calotescu, 1973) – these cinematic hypostases of (industrial) work and workers compose a visual archive of great documentary value, not so much representative as significant of the (representations of) work life, of institutional frameworks of work in the context of socialist industrialization and urbanization, on the one hand, and in the context of socialist realism, on the other hand.

CHAPTER 1

Work, Modernity, and Film

1   From Furniture on Fire to Image Reversibility

The first film known in the history of moving image belongs to Lumière brothers and is called *La sortie des usines Lumière/Employees Leaving the Lumière Factory*. The film shows men and women leaving the Lumière factory in Lyon after the working hours. We don't see people at work, in the concrete performance of the production activities. The context that is part of the filmic object suggests the experience of work. And not just any kind of work, but industrial work, one essential element of modern life. It is the first cinematic representation of people, and the hypostasis in which they are presented is that of (industrial) working people. The film was first shown to the public in Paris on 28 December 1859 at the *Salon Indien de Grand Café* (Boulevard des Capucins) and had thirty-three spectators. The images in the film are anthological for the history of cinema, not only because they mark the early stage of this form of culture, but also because they provide premises for the articulation of the character and functions of this art throughout the following century, particularly striking in the ideologically oriented cinematic movements. The images depict people coming out of the factory gates, establishing *avant la lettre* the relationship between film and industrial work in the context of capitalism: "Working women in cloche skirts and feather hats, working men pushing their bicycles give today a naive charm to this simple parade. After the staff came the patrons, in a "Victoria" coach pulled by two horses. At the end, the gatekeeper closed the gates" (Sadoul, 1961: 16). The Lumière brothers' production marks the beginning of an age, that of early cinema, described as a "cinema of attractions" (Abel, 2005: lx), whose defining characteristic was not so much the story or the narrative, but rather the attractions, that is, forms of spectacle or display. A function of industrial development and the cultural prefaces that accompanied it, early cinema was "inextricably bound up with other forms and practices of mass culture", it emerged "as a *combinatoire* of existing and innovative elements (audio as well as visual)", it was "a hybrid medium which only gradually coalesced into something more or less distinct as *cinema*" (Abel, 2005: lxi).

Film has become a mass art through the development of the film industry, and is one of the most expressive social institutions of modern society.

Cinematography is a product of industrial development, of the reconfiguration of thinking of work and of the role of people in the industrial working process:

> Cinema is a fenomenon to which most people feel some connection if they are at all caught up in the mood of our modern times: it lacks significance only for those who remain rooted in an earlier period of economic organization on account of their occupation. [...] Cinema exists, then, primarily for modern people who are simply carried along by the current of the times. [...] With the new demands placed on people by a century of work and mechanization, with the greater use and abuse of people's energies bringing with it for some individuals a struggle for survival, the other side of everyday life – relaxing doing something purposeless, being preoccupied with some aimless pursuit – had to offer some counterweight. The thousands of picture houses could never had emerged had the need for such entertainments not been engendered for the broad mass of the population by precisely such an intensification of work and consequent concentration of work into fewer hours of the day. as industrialization has progressed, moreover, people found they had more money in their pockets. Increased leisure time and higher wages for the working classes are two of the factors crucial to any undestanding of this characteristically modern medium.
> ALTENLOH, 1914 [2001]: 287–288

In socio-historical perspective, the cultural phenomenon of film can be described as a system of equations in two variables: 1. on the one hand, the relationship between industrial work and modernity, on the other hand, the relationship between modernity and film (film production is industrial activity); 2. on the one hand, the relationship between social representations and dominant value system, on the other hand, the relationship between dominant value system and film (cinematic representation as function of value system taken as reference); 3. on the one hand, the relationship between reception and membership of social category/class, on the other hand, the relationship between (consumption of) films and social class (values in film reception are distributed according to the social class of the receiver/audience).

Film is a cultural form related to the diversification of phenomena associated with urban life in the context of early 20th century modernity. Film seen from the point of view of "production, representation, and reception" (Mennel, 2008: 19) is one of most spectacular forms, by nature of its means of expression, of modern life. Modernity has generated specific forms of manifestation of mass culture and film is one of them. Cinematography is "naturally and naively modern", born "from a technique without particular artistic intentions", from the need for capitalist transformation of art, by bringing it to the market of everyday life. Cinematography was discovered and functioned as a result of the discovery and functioning of a new technique and is "of modern essence as it embodies that very modern value which is the New" (Lipovetsky, Serroy, 2008: 30–35). Cinematography is the result of two processes of modernity: on the one hand, the development of photographic techniques and the reproduction of movement and, on the other, the persistence of symbolic structures in the social imaginary. The idea of capturing expressions of existence in images and constructing a different, visual perspective on them is an intellectual construction and therefore symbolic by its nature. The idea could be materialized in the context of the evolution of visual arts from the time of the first cave paintings and then developed with the evolution of photographic technology. This tandem defines the context in which a technical process and a form of visual thinking made the reality of cinema possible. The cinema was born "from the mith of the *total cinema*" (Bazin, 2014: 17), a mith I understand as a symbolic form, as a structure, as an explanatory pattern for a human experience or condition, and can use real or fictitious or real and fictitious material at the same time. Cinematic thinking as a form of visual thinking, as film has a *"first of all visual"* character (Faure, 1971: 91), is the expression of an instance of the imagination (an imagination much older than industrial revolution), that is, the ability to structure (visual) perception and thought in novel ways compared to previous representations of the image.

> The fanatics, the maniacs, the disinterested pioneers, capable, like Bernard Pallisy, of setting their furniture on fire in order to obtain a few seconds of flickering images, are neither industrialists nor scientists, but men possessed by their imagination. Cinema was born from the convergence of their obsession [...] In this way, both Plateau's delay in applying the optical principle of retinal persistence and the constant progress of motion synthesis in relation to the state of photographic techniques are explained. The truth is that both were dominated by the imaginary of the century.
> BAZIN, 2014: 17

The novel experiences of modernity and the development of new photographic and cinematic techniques have structured the potential for the articulation of new socio-aesthetic representations, incorporating new forms, compositions, narratives and structures of visual perception. Cinematography "comes out of scientific culture and technical evolution", "is aimed at all possible viewers of any age, of any gender and in any country, by the universality of its language, by the countless number of places where the *same film* is or can be shown" (Faure, 1971: 84). The intimate relationship between cinema and modern urbanity in the early 20th century (1920s) is based on the dual role of cinema as part of mass culture, considered both "product of urban modernity", and "producer of urban culture" (Weihsmann, 1997: 10). In the context of industrial modernity, work has constantly provided a generous raw material for film narratives, regardless of the form of its ideological insight. More importantly for "our material and cultural survival", work is also "a privileged topic for cinema" (Mazierska, 2013: 1). Cinema literally uses people's work (in the production and distribution system), and work provides themes and subjects for cinematic representations, which in turn reconstruct mental images of work for viewers, for those who work.

The reflections and screen reproductions of the social experiences of work generate a fertile space for the representation in various forms and expressions of what Marx and Engels called "the first historical act" (Marx, Engels, 1998: 47), namely the production of material goods necessary to satisfy the basic needs of life. Experiences of working life become objects of filmed experiences, while people's modes of action, interaction and communication in the context of work become replicas of pre-defined historical modes of representation on the screen. The experience of work in film is not a common experience of any work, but of work dependent on the language of film, that is, on its spatio-temporal structure. Film is a type of language with a high degree of conventionality that needs to be learned. The reality of film is socially established. Film is a social institution, and the explanations attached to an approach to analysing the theme of work in films are sociological only insofar as these explanations (of the researcher) make exclusive use of social conditions and institutions.

Cinematic hypostases of work and working people compose a distinct visual space for representing the various forms of operationalization of the concept of work, understood as a social institution. Film involves the elaboration of visual paradigms of work, of its precise cultural, social, political physiognomies, it has a stable logic in the context of interpretive readings. Unlike documentary film, in fiction film work is only a context, represented by stereotypical symbols, in which narratives of social relations unfold. Representations of work in cinematic images have a documentary value in that they offer a unique perspective in the investigation of the social imaginary of work (that of the director, the producer, the actors, each contributing, due to the social division of cinematic work, to the articulation of representational forms of work that may be more or less close to real work they ideologically illustrate).

Film is source of information, an instrument of introspection on the social valorisation of work, direct testimony and evaluative construction of work. Unlike literature, photography or painting, it allows us to observe the physical frameworks of work, work activities in their processuality, the human dimension of work, the sensitive relationship between individual and work, the alienating contexts of work, the ideologization of work. Work is not a static object, it is thought of as an organ in relation to other organs of a social whole, in a fluid dynamic that allows the probing of real and potential dimensions of work in present reality. Through montage, film develops structures of binary oppositions: work seen as a beneficial activity, in its spectacular dimension, in highly aestheticising aspects, and wage labour seen as form of alienation, hostile, oppressive and degrading to human being. Film can help to the reading of various manifestations of work: experience of work, work practices, social conditions of work, work relations, terminal and instrumental values of work, social functions of work, be it manual, mechanical, industrial, intellectual, or artistic work.

Cinematic images of work bring together multiple displays and critical commentaries: work seen as a framework of human time and social change, work in the material frameworks of socialist construction, a context of reflexivity, individualization and identity questioning, work in utopian or dystopian expressions, the relationship between work and the spatial order, between work and the body, the political ideologization of work, the instrumental value of work in the life projects of individuals.

Aspects of working life in the context of postmodernity, relating to the phenomenon of individualization, conflicts, and the diversification of experiences and social interactions are found especially in representations of Western cinema. The differences in the representation of work and different aspects of working life between films produced in capitalist societies and those produced in socialism shape specific architectonics in filmic imagery of work, resulting from different cultural patterns, reflected in ideological constructions of cinematic type. Dramatized patterns of work produce developments, movements, contrasts that generate the means by which reality can be known and dominated, by which action can be stimulated, by which people can understand the nature and aims of social transformations. The space in which film decomposes and then recomposes the materials of which social life and its problems are made up is that of overlaps and mergers. Documentary and fiction overlap in views that are new in a neo-realist perspective: the premise of social change, of radical transformations, is the one on which the cinematic construction is based, aiming to provide people with the broad frameworks of social existence and sources for activating imagination. John Grierson advances a discourse that draws attention to the mechanisms of information and the construction of popular education, referring to documentary, but the same premises are equally effective in the case of realistic fiction film, film as social document: film passes

> from the "dramatization" of the worker and his everyday work, to the "dramatization" of modern organization and the new collective factors of society, that is to the "dramatization" of social problems, and in this way it advances step by step to capture the significance of the rough matter that forms the fabric of modern social life, to "embolden" the heart and the will of the people to dominate it.
> ARISTARCO, 1965: 291

In both Western and East-Socialist cinematic traditions, work is an important theme, with various evaluative perspectives depending on the dominant ideological orientation. Work is a specific category of main character, a theme that structures narratives and political discourses about modern society. The working conditions, the division of work, the industrial context of labor and the working class (components of labour production) are facets of the same ideological character in films such as *The Man with a Movie Camera* (Dziga Vertov, 1929, USSR) and *Metropolis* (Fritz Lang, 1929, Germany), two reference films in classical cinema for modern urbanity and the question of work and social classes, time and the ideologically structured rhythms of economic and social life. By modern urbanity I understand "a generic description of the social, economic and political developments structuring the development of twentieth century urban life" (Brooker, 2002: 2). Forms of consumption, metal figures, the dynamic rhythm of human and machine energy, the electric body and the human intervention, architecture and its ideological meanings, class identity, the complex processes of work in Metropolis make up a "fetish-image of all city and cyborg futures" (Elsaesser, 2000: 7), offers a "fluorescent" architecture in the visual culture of this form of social life. Flows of activities that fill time and shape subjective perception of time, repetitiveness, work rhythms, social division of labour, multiplicity of urban spaces, housing, spatial overlaps and ideological division of views on industrial, cultural, economic everyday, urban infrastructure, orderly movement of people within conceived frameworks of the city, human body on film, situated between symbolic, ideological forms and practical use, the attractions and sensuality embedded in the aesthetics of the modern urban in *The Man with a Movie Camera* make this of this film a cinematic manifesto of work and the city in which reality is seen as it is (life as it is), but how it cannot be seen in certain forms of its presence by the human eye. Eliminating any form of language specific to theatre or literature, Vertov explores ideological underpinnings of montage and constructs a sum of captured facts that result into a unique discourse on the relationship between reality and film, between truth and the film. Both films build an idea of what a city of the future looks like, and what it could look like, the result of a fabric that brings together various classes of work and categories of actions. City is a pretext for exploring the nature of technology that allows for the ideological domination of space and time, coagulating fragmentations and discontinuities that are brought together in a novel cultural experience, with the aim of rationalizing perceptions of sociality, frameworks of socio-historical identities, belonging to industrial urbanity. Filmic metropolis is a symbolic construction that has the capacity to discipline and order social representations of space and of the relationship between space and politics, imbuing a collective meaning to presences of urban, working communities, providing contents susceptible to new ideologies, new dynamics in (Simmelian) terms of distance, proximity, separation, and connection: "the fact of a spatial framework for a group is by no means limited formally and sociologically to its political boundary" (Simmel, 1997: 145). Both films experiment with the relationship between camera and human ocular device, creating theoretical and methodological premises for the cinematic construction of reality(ies), objectivating the experience of bringing the recorded elements in their present processuality into the specific function and character of cinematic art, not only of representing reality, but also of constructing reality.

2 Images of Work and Social Contexts That Produce Images of Work

The sociological analysis of cinematic representations of work in actuality films produced between 1960 and 1989 is based on data of a visual research carried out with the aim of identifying the status, character and meaning of work in the cinematic discourses under socialism (Fig. 1). The films made during socialism are seen as cultural products that can be analysed as forms of manifestation of ideological, aesthetic and social possibilities, which bear the imprint (regardless of the conformist or critical rperspective) of the socialist project and which, beyond the historical context, can be discovered by both ordinary consumers and academic researchers, new forms of knowledge of how social change can occur, how social institutions are articulated or dismantled according to ideological orientations, the capacity and willingness of individuals and social groups to produce and reproduce elements of a socio-cultural identity in a more or less critical way, the potential for deconstruction and reconstruction of the meanings associated with these social processes.

What are the manifest and latent expressions and meanings attached to work? What are the characters' attitudes towards work? What are the social hypostases of the working subjects? What elements describe the characters according to their professional category? To what extent are the relationships between individuals and society ideologically structured in the context of work? What are the relationships between work/workers and the spatial order in which they are placed? What are the forms of filmic deconstruction of ideological imperatives of working subjects? What are the elements of official film criticism that problematize the condition of work?

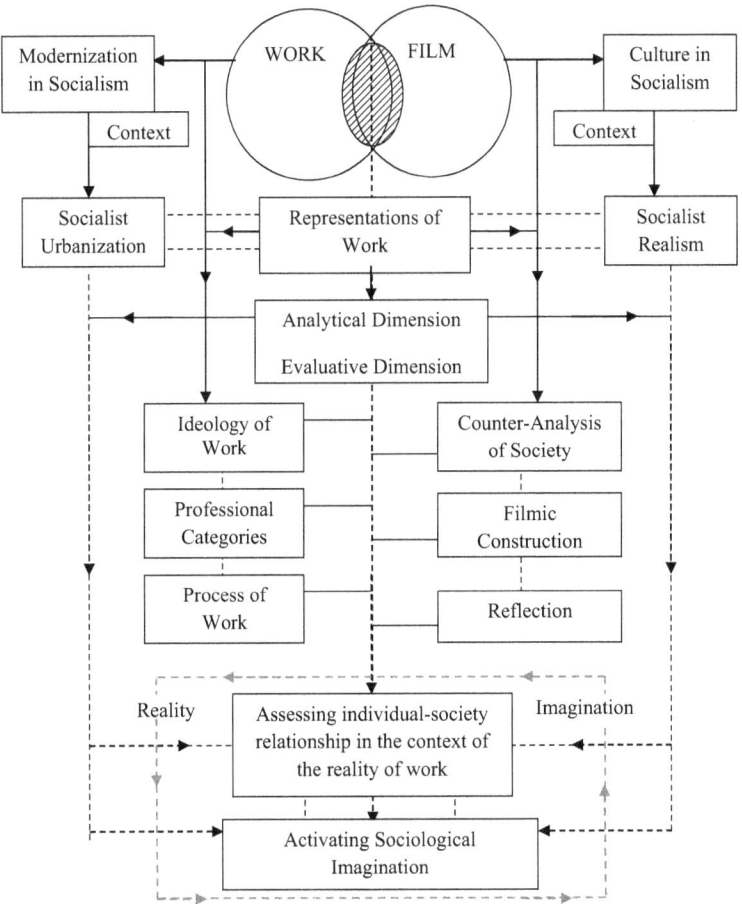

FIGURE 1   Theoretical model of the research

These are the questions that guide the analysis of the "internal" and "external narratives" of the selected films. The internal narrative refers to "the content of an image", and the external narrative to "the social context that produced the image" (Banks, 2001: 11).

The social imaginary of work is shaped at the intersection of actual practices of work that can be identified and recognized in present reality, at empirical level, and the ideologies constructed about work in the context of a broader cultural pattern (Fig. 2). They are two facets of the same thing understood as object of knowledge, each belonging to a different order of reality: the first belong to concrete or present reality, the others belong to imagined or virtual reality. Between these two dimensions lies the universe of research and reflection on work in socialist cinematic representations, in an approach that instruments the relationship between sociology and film in order to identify the forms of activation of sociological ideas in film, on the one hand, and the activation of the sociological imagination through film, on the other hand (Fig. 3). We can represent the significant approximations between the two fields by analogy with the physical phenomenon of reflection, which involves reversing the direction of propagation of light, light rays, waves at the separating surface of two different media. In the same way, the interference between sociology and film (or in other words, when light "strikes" a different surface) produces an explanation through the actualization of the sociological imagination (in analogy, the "refracted ray") as a result of the conveyance of sociological ideas, meanings

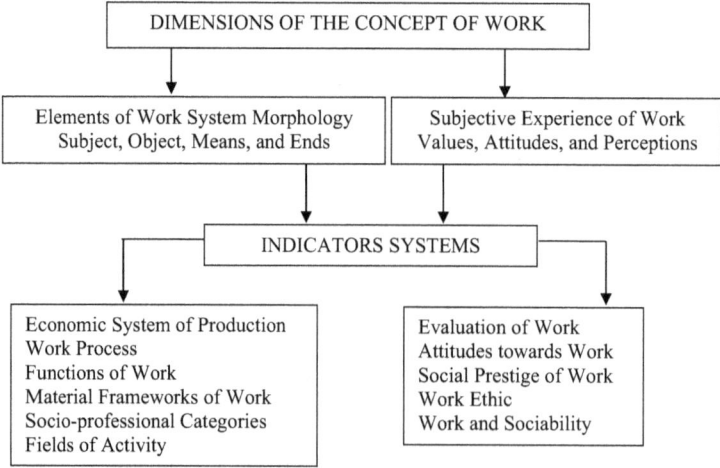

FIGURE 2   Dimensions and indicators used in the analysis of filmic representations of work

and significance generated by the application (propagation) of the specific conceptual and methodological tools of sociology to film.

The analysis includes: on the one hand, the specific sub-themes related to work placed at the manifest level of cinematic representations (of visual and auditory images), on the other hand, the relationship with contextual elements or information, a component placed at the latent level of the content to be analysed. The methodology is based predominantly on a qualitative strategy, the methodological kit including: qualitative and quantitative content analysis components, interviews with Romanian actors and filmmakers who worked in film production at the time and participated directly in the making of some of the films analyzed or have relevant information on the cultural and political contexts in which films were produced under socialism, case studies used to illustrate ideological dynamics of mechanisms of social representations of work in films.

Both theoretically and methodologically, the research is based on an interdisciplinary strategy, bringing together approaches and perspectives specific to sociology of work, urban sociology, and visual sociology. The research has an exploratory character and proposes a niche field within the broader space of social research of film, especially as the interest for sociology of film are still poorly articulated among researchers in both the social sciences and film studies. The approach I use to analyse actuality films produced between 1960 and 1989 is one in which investigation follows sociological aims, the films being a raw material explored on the basis of a sociological toolkit with the aim of providing descriptions of convergence and/or divergences of discourses on work in the films analysed in the socio-historical context in which their were produced.

In a strictly methodological perspective, I will operate with two major components: on the one hand, sociological concepts, on the other hand, narratives

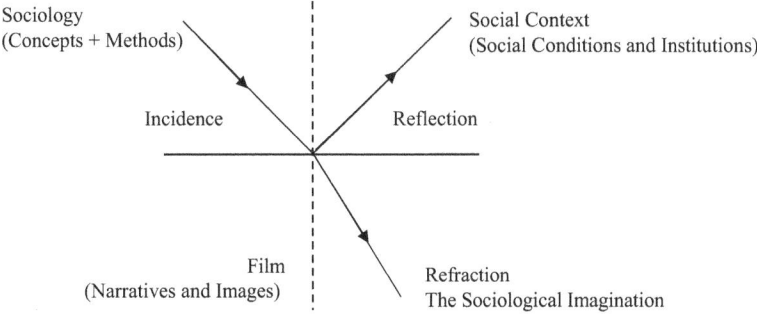

FIGURE 3   Conceptual model of a possible relationship between sociology and film

and cinematic images. The aim of this book is to develop an interpretative framework rather than an explanatory model. The approach to researching cinematic work is based on placing it in a perspective that I call *images of work*, that is, a complex that includes: the identity of the (visual) object of work, the relationship between it and the receiver, and the meaning that the object has for the receiver. The three components of work are described using contents of films – empirical data – using analytical units of content given by visual and narrative units corresponding to structure and organization of film material: narrative material or content (the script with its subcomponents – sequences of events, relationships between characters, conflicts, set of information) and the discursive component (elements and expressive techniques specific to filmic language: types of shots, of framing, of camera angles, of camera movements, scenes and sequences according to script parameters (interior/exterior, visual/dialogue, day/night, action, movement, tension/inaction, stillness, intimate/collective/public, one-character/two-character/group).

CHAPTER 2

Film as Instrument of the Sociological Imagination

1   Film towards a Quality of the Mind

In this chapter, I propose an attempt at theoretical reflection on the relationship between film and sociology, in general, and between film and sociological imagination, in particular. I present a pattern for the determining relationship between film and sociological imagination, a relationship identified in the hypostasis in which film is understood as a factor of activation, that is, of setting the sociological imagination *in motion*.

Just as the individual has a biography, society has a history. Just as the individual has a baggage of knowledge, values, norms, practices, memory, society has a specific culture. In such an equation, film represents a type of individual biography. The meaning of relationship between individual – film – society becomes significant in the perspective of placing it in the space of the conceptual construction proposed by the sociologist C. W. Mills in his work *The Sociological Imagination* ([1959] 2000). I refer, as the title of the chapter shows, to the concept of *sociological imagination*. According to Mills, the function of the sociological imagination is to help the individual, in the context of his or her individual existence and everyday life, to understand his or her position on the larger stage of the society of which he or she is a part, to understand the connection between the problems he or she faces in everyday social life and the larger context of the phenomena, processes and mechanisms by which a social, economic, political order manifests itself, by which social institutions and practices operate based on a system of values and norms.

Film acquires – in the context of its use in the perspective of sociological research approaches and film studies – an instrumental value for the sociological imagination, in the sense that the research of the raw material that it makes available to the sociologist produces a form of knowledge that allows us to understand both biography and history, as well as the relationship between them, understanding by biography a part of history and by society an actor of history. Film not only fulfils a representational, descriptive function, but above all a cognitive and explanatory one, thus creating the space for the articulation and development of the individual's capacity to think and understand the relationship between the individual and society, the connection between what happens in the individual's life and what happens in society, between a certain configuration of the individual's social condition and features of contemporary society. Film can be a hypostasis of placing the individual biography (of the character/social group/social class), elevated to an ideal type, in a specific socio-historical sequence.

Accessibility, attractiveness, expressiveness, ability to concentrate real raw material treated cinematically form the basis for massive borrowings that audiences make through film consumption. It follows that "the relationship between art/cinema and the social is one of contamination and irreducibility" (Diken, Laustsen, 2007: 7). Reality does not reduce itself to film. Reality is not a component of film. Film is reducible to reality because it is a component of reality. Films have the ability to create mental maps (alternative spaces of reality) that are easy to borrow and use in everyday life. Borrowings from films are nothing more than operationalizations in the space of cinematic art of various forms of manifestation of the social construction of reality and activation of the sociological imagination.

The relationship between film and sociology in the perspective of the contribution that film can bring to what is known as sociological imagination is defined at the interference of two spheres of reflection, two theoretical models that I associate in a new construction focused on the cinematic element and aiming at configuring a convergence between film and sociology. This construction brings together the method of dramatization (Gilles Deleuze) and the social construction of reality (Peter L. Berger and Thomas Luckman).

For a coherent and consistent picture of the theoretical construction approach that I advance, it is necessary to briefly present the main concepts and theoretical developments that I have gathered in this matrix of relations between film and sociology. In the following, I will present the concept of sociological imagination (C.W. Mills), describe some conceptual elements relevant to the present approach from the theory of the social construction of reality (Peter L. Berger and Thomas Luckman) and the method of dramatization (Gilles Deleuze), and then advance my own theoretical model of determinations between film and the sphere of sociological imagination, with the aim of clarifying the nature of film, on the one hand, as a form of empirical data and as an instrument of sociological interpretation, on the other.

Imagination, before any sociological understanding and/or use, reffers to (human) capacity to create new representations or ideas based on previously accumulated perceptions, representations or ideas. The aim of conceptual instrumentalization that C.W. Mills sets for the notion of imagination in a sociological perspective is extremely broad and susceptible to multiple interferences from other fields and/or disciplines, such as the field of film studies.

According to C.W. Mills ([1959] 2000), the sociological imagination "consists of the capacity to shift from one perspective to another, and in the process to build up an adequate view of a total society and of its components" (Mills, 2000: 211). It is based on the need to know the social and historical significance of the individual in society and in the time in which he or she lives and acts. The sociological imagination enables an understanding of both biography and history and the relationships between them, and is actualized through the ability to move from one perspective to another. The premise Mills starts from is the absence of a capacity (which may exist but be latent, or may not exist) to understand the relationship between individual and society, the fact that the individual cannot understand his own experience, his individual condition, and can only construct his identity by placing himself in the epoch in which he or she lives. The epoch in which he or she lives presupposes the existence of an external reality which the individual cannot understand through mere introspection. The sociological imagination helps the individual, from the context of his or her everyday life, to understand his or her position on the larger stage of the history of society, the implications of what happens on this stage for particular aspects of individual life, allows the biography to be placed in a particular historical sequence.

The problem to which Mills draws attention, with reference to the context marked by the development of mass communication sources of the age of action, is not that people do not have the necessary information, but that they do not have that "spiritual condition" (Mills, 2000: 41), as Mills calls it, to profit from the information they collect. Journalists, scholars, artists and publics, scientists and editors can help individuals form a way of thinking and understanding the connection between what happens in their individual lives and what happens in their society. Only information and skills of reason are not enough to understand the meaning of an epoch for one own's life. What is needed is "a quality of mind that will help them to use information and to develop reason in order to achieve lucid summations of what is going on in the world and of what may be happening within themselves" (Mills, 2000: 5). It is the playground of what is called the sociological imagination. Film is also part of this sphere of action, as it is a product whose function is to generate a particular capacity identified in the sociological imagination (through the expressive means specific to cinema apparatus).

2   The Dramatized Construction of Reality

Before looking at how film can be used as a factor in activating the sociological imagination, I will present what I call the processual components in the elaboration of such a function of film. These are the two theoretical constructs mentioned above: the method of dramatization and the theory of the social construction of reality. I will start with the latter.

According to the theory developed by Berger and Luckman, any reality is a socially established one. Institutions exist as a reality external to the individual, therefore they are not directly accessible, they cannot be understood based on one's own biography. To understand them, the individual must "go out" (Berger, Luckman, 1991: 78) and learn about the institution (process called *externalization*). The objectivity of social world, the authors argue, however massive it may seem to the individual, is a constructed, man-made objectivity. "The process by which the externalized products of human activity attain the character of objectivity is objectivation. The institutional world is objectivated human activity, and so is every single institution" (Berger, Luckman, 1991: 78). The relationship between man and the world is identified with the relationship between "producer" and "product" and it is a dialectical relationship in the sense that man and the social world "interact with each other". The main moments of this process are the "externalization", the "objectivation" and the "internalization", "three dialectical moments of social reality" (Berger, Luckman, 1991: 78–79). As for the third moment – through internalization, the objectified social world is redesigned, reflected in consciousness. The construction results in a tripartite relationship expressed in the following main statements of the theory: "1. *Soceity is a human product*. 2. *Society is an objective reality*. 3. *Man is a social product*" (Berger, Luckman, 1991: 79).

Using the conceptual elements of the social construction of reality, I place one of the fundamental premises of sociology, namely that any social reality is an established one, ans based on a double relationship: between the individual and society, on the one hand, and between film and society, on the other.

Film, through the referential categories (referents of reality) based on which it operates in the construction of filmic narrative, allows to shorten the distance between the individual – between his representations and social experience – and the historical course of the society in which he or she lives. This shortening of distance is possible as a result of the manifestation of one of the major functions of film, namely that of condensation: human types, social experiences, representations of life. Mills argues that sociological imagination is based on the need for knowledge and understanding of the relationship between the individual and society. Film, which incorporates images of reality outside the individual, through a *certain* sequence of events involving *certain* human and social types in *certain* contexts or hypostases (regardless of what aspect(s) of social life is/are taken as reference) is a factor in the awareness and/or creation of such structural need. How? By providing representations, that is, synthetic images (elaborated on two principles: dislocation and condensation) of reality, that is, essentialising social life, without being reduced to individual experiences and representations of it. By applying to the sphere of film, part of sociocultural reality, the definition formulated by Berger and Luckman according to which "society exists only as individuals are conscious of it" (Berger, Luckman, 1991: 96), it follows that the social reality that film contains (based on its construction in cinematic terms) exists only insofar as individuals become aware of it through the act of cinematic consumption. The authors argue that "individual consciousness is socially determined" (Berger, Luckman, 1991: 96). Film is a part of the social system represented by society, that is part of a set of interdependent cultural and social elements that can be thought of as a unit. Based on a such positioning, it follows that film is a factor of such a consciousness, which represents only one moment (t_1) in the continuum represented by social consciousness ($t \ldots n$), that is, a continuum on which awareness and understanding of the individual-society relationship is inscribed beyond moment t_1.

The knowledge that the film provides about subject X (an aspect of social life) in relationship to object Y (a certain social context) is structured exclusively according to certain elements and characteristics of the relationship between subject and object that are relevant only because they are found in the cinematic construction of the idea of the relationship between X and Y in the vision of the author (creator) R (director). The objectification of reality by means of the film is conditioned by an essential aspect in the construction of the vision of reality (first), namely *the arrangement* of the parts that make up the filmic whole, an arrangement according to which the whole is identified and its meaning understood, and not according to the characteristics as such of the parts.

Film generates the activation of a process of understanding and knowledge of the relationship between individual and society (of the space of manifestation of the sociological imagination) by allowing, due to the distinct features of the cinematic mode of operation, on the one hand, and of the conveyance of ideas on the basis of cinematic operation, on the other, a significant deformation of the perceptual view of reality, which it constructs, reconstructs and/or creates through a *novel arrangement* of internal elements to which correspond categories of ideological referents defined at the level of the actual social system (in the sense of present at the level of the social experience of individuals and groups), regardless of the form of the system in terms of size and complexity – which may be a collective of industrial workers, a family, a city, a society. How is the interpretation of reality or what Berger and Luckman call the objectification of social reality produced in film? One perspective is that of "dramatization" in the Deleuzian sense of the concept. Before developing the answer to the above question, an explanation of the parameters according to which I approach the reality of film is necessary.

On the one hand, there is current social reality (in the sense of present reality), on the other hand there is this cultural product/object and social fact that is film. On the one hand, film can be treated as a social fact in that it represents a structural feature of a system that we experience as external to us, while at the same time exerting a certain influence on us, having the capacity to shape people's lives to varying degrees through various forms of internalization of ideas, (moving) images conveyed through it. On the other hand, we can also treat film as a social system in itself, on a specific scale, representing a set of elements that are both cultural (in terms of content) and social (in terms of form, production system, etc.).

I start from the premise that film is virtual reality. It follows from this that the relationship I need to clarify is that between real and virtual in the context of cinematic reality, because reality can be both real and virtual. An explanation of both the nature and the relationship between the terms *virtual, real and possible* is provided by Gilles Deleuze in *The Method of Dramatization* (2004). Deleuze writes: "The virtual is not opposed to the real; it is the real that is opposed to the possible. Virtual is opposed ti actual, and therefore, possesses a full reality" (Deleuze, 2004: 101). Deleuze defines the virtual as an extension of the formulation that Proust developed to define certain states of his experience: *"real without being actual"*. Deleuze draws a series of opposition lines between the virtual and the possible. On the one hand, the possible is such that the real is constructed as its resemblance. Because of this defect, the possible looks suspiciously "retrospective" and "retroactive", it is suspected of being constructed after the fact, in resemblance to the real which it is supposed to precede. The possible is just the concept as principle of representation of the thing, under the following categories: identity of *what is representing* and the resemblance of what *is being represented*. On the other hand,

> the virtual belongs to the Idea and does not resemble the actual, no more than the actual resembles the virtual. The Idea is an image without resemblance; the virtual actualizes itself not through resemblance, but through divergence and differentiation. Differentiation or actualization is always reproductive or limiting. The difference between the virtual and the actual is no longer the difference of the Same insofar the Same is posited once in representation, and once again outside representation. Rather, it is the difference of the Other, insofar as the Other appears once

in Idea, and once again, though in a totally different manner, in the process of actualizing the Idea.
DELEUZE, 2004: 101

Etymologically, drama means staged, stylised action presented before an audience. Dramatization is actualization of an idea, of a fixed form, that is, its transposition into a form of a different nature, a concrete, material form. Through dramatization, Deleuze explains, "the Idea is incarnated or actualized (staged), *it differentiates itself*" (Deleuze, 2004:94), a differentiation involving two correlative aspects or forms: "species and parts, specification and organization" (Deleuze, 2004: 96), conditions of the representaion of things in general.

I take into consideration the premise that the virtual reality represented by the film is part of (social) reality, reality can be both virtual and present (*actual*). The social character is given by the fact that film as object is part and product of the social world in which is produced. Moreover, it is a producer of the reality from which it originates, in that it re-projects aspects of present reality into virtual forms, which are further projected back into the real world. This circuit is made possible by the very fact that ideas are constantly updated, that is, by the continuous dramatization of the elements that make social reality.

Dramatization in film is directly related to the nature of the means by which the two major components of film, the visual image and the aural image, corresponding to the two fundamental mechanisms of film, the characters and the actions, are produced. The relationship between dramatization and the cinematic image is a structural one because it incorporates "movement" and "time" as it fallows:

1. The film works with two complementary categories of data: "instantaneous sections which are called images" and "a movement or a time which is impersonal, uniform, abstract, invisible, or imperceptible, whic is "in" the apparatus, and "with" which the images are made to pass consecutively". (Deleuze, 1997: 1)
2. "The image itself is the system of the relationships between its elements, that is, a set of relationships of time from which the variable present only flows. [...] What is specific to the image, as soon as it creative, is to make perceptible, to make visible, relationships of time which cannot be seen in the represented object and do not allow themselves to be reduced to the present". (Deleuze, 1997: xii)

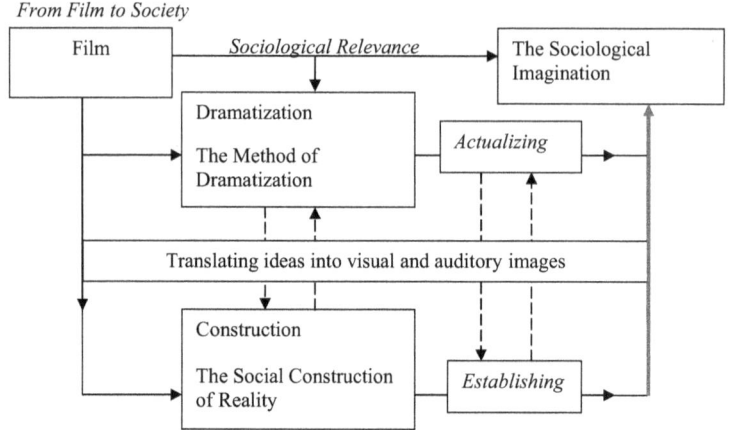

FIGURE 4   Film and sociological imagination
SOURCE: ACTIVATING SOCIOLOGICAL IMAGINATION THROUGH FILM

3   Structural Components of Film Mechanism

What is the process of dramatization, what is the actualization of ideas (embodied in what is called screenplay) in film? This process can be described in terms of a number of actional components which have the value of an organising principle, on the one hand, at the level of experience of social life, an experience which can take an indefinite number of forms and expressions, and, on the other hand, at the level of organization of the ideas according to which this space of representation is organised. From the perspective of the mechanism of dramatization, film performs the following structural operations:

1. *Dislocates* a space and a time from historical reality and organizes them according to a particular vision that gathers ideas about certain subjects and objects (real or imagined) attached to that time and that space;
2. *Organizes* space and time based on its own structure, which brings together categories of referents that correspond to reality and are represented based on the relationship between narrative content and filmic expression;
3. *Condenses* the relationships between the elements of the (filmic) representational structure by actualizing classes of objects with real referents, generating for the relationships between these classes meaning (which depends strictly on the context of the internal structure, that is, the content [or internal narrative]) and meanings, the latter of which can be multiple, being conditioned by the diversity of perceptual

apparatuses of the receivers; condensation is a function of the nature of cinematographic language which allows not only the recording, reproduction, rendering of reality, but also the conveyance of ideas about reality;
4. *Constructs a certain* image of the relationships between different classes of objects that constitute the material or the parts from which the new structure of representation is made (idea proposed by the film about class X, Y ...); this constructed image becomes the real object of real (subjective) perception;
5. *Actualizes* the ideas underlying the conception of subject of the film by translating them into concrete forms, that is, into actions, characters and relationships between characters; the ideas are initially expressed in the form of the screenplay, but most of the time the screenplay has no existence for the viewer, it exists only to the extent that the content becomes projected on the screen, that is, the ideas are set in motion, actualized, dramatized (the actualization of the idea results in the screen, virtual reality);
6. *Establishes* a novel (social) reality resulting from a particular organization of the elements and relationships between the ideational elements describing the chosen classes of objects, that is, a reality established through a novel arrangement not necessarily in relation to reality, but in relation to a pre-existing patterns of representation (including cinematographic) of reality.

Paraphrasing the sociologist and art critic Pierre Francastel in formulating one of his fundamental ideas about the relationship between art and society, it is not film that is explained by society, but film that partly explains the true springs of society. The aim of analysing films is to discover in the mass of films produced in a given epoch those that contain principles likely to give people the means to (know) themselves and (understand) themselves. By knowing and understanding the social and material foundations, the dominant value orientations and the structures of thought that result from them, it becomes possible to individualize the biography and to place it in a meaningful way in the context of the social history of which the individual is part.

CHAPTER 3

Work and Ideology

1   Work: Etymological Roots, Semantic Structures, and Ideological Meanings

What is work? What are the meanings historically attributed to work? How did the political and economic meanings of work emerge? A terminological clarification is necessary in order to shape a conceptual reflection on work. A refined clarification of the meanings and significances of work comes from Maurice Godelier in *Work and its Representations: A Research Proposal* (1980). According to Godelier, the terms "work", "to work", "worker" emerged at certain moments in history at the level of language and need to be analysed and interpreted within the socio-cultural contexts in which they were articulated and developed. Political economy is one of the first fields of science in which "the idea of work became a central concept in the 19th century" (Godelier, 1980: 164). The author refers to elements of the etymology of the term "work" described by Lucien Fevre. In France, the word "work" entered the vocabulary in the 16th century: *travailler*, derived from the Latin *tripaliare*

> which meant torturing with a *tripalium*, an instrument made of three stakes. [...] *travailler* meant to torture an offender on a tripalium and the *travailleur* in this case was not hte victim but the torturer. [...] *Travail* (the modern word for work) also meant a wooden device to which horses or cattle were tied when they were to be shod.
>   GODELIER, 1980: 165

The idea of wage labour is incorporated linguistically in new words that appeared in the mid-14th century: "they appeared one after another *salarié* (1450) (meaning a wage earner) and in 1840 *prolétaire* (proleterian, worker), both of which remained rare until the mid 18th century" (Godelier, 1980: 165). Other words related to the above were already in use a century earlier:

> In the 14th century, before *salarié* there was also *salaire* (salary, wage) from *salarium* meaning money to buy salt (*sal*). *Prolétaire* came from *proletarius,* which in antiquity had meant a poor man who was exempt from taxation and who only had rights to citizenship by virtue of the number of his offspring (*proles*). *Artisan* appear around 1546 and meant what we

mean today by the two words worker and artist. Artisans and workers practice trades (*métiers*), which derived from *ministerium*, an inferior activity (10th century) (*minis*, meaning less, and *sterium*, meaning the work of a servant); while master (*maître*) came from *magister*, ,the one who is the suprior' in a trade (1150), and *compagnon* (journeyman, co-worker) meant someone with whom you break bread (*cum pane*, with bread).

GODELIER, 1980: 165

Hannah Arendt develops similar and more refined etymological clarifications in *The Human Condition* (1998). We are familiar with various forms of work: wage labour, manual labour, physical labour, productive labour, non-productive labour, intellectual labour, artistic labour, etc. Etymologically, the word "labour" comes from the Proto-Slavic "moka", meaning "torture", "torment". The Latin "laborare" also indicates a sense of pain and trouble. The English forms "work" and "labour" indicate the semantic difference between the two terms. "Work" denotes work that does not necessarily involve physical effort, burden, or torment, but is characterized by certain degrees of freedom, is desirable, while "labour" implies physical effort, suffering, constraint, physical deterioration. The same etymological root and semantic structure is replicated in Greek, Latin, French and German equivalents: *ponein* and *ergazesthai*, *laborare* and *facere* or *fabricari*, *travailkr* and *ouvrer*, *arbeiten* and *werken* (Arendt, 1998: 80). The word "labour" never denotes a finished product, the result of work, while the product itself is invariably derived from the word "work". Wage labour is associated with the amount of physical effort put into the production of products. Hannah Arendt outlines a semantic delimitation between work and occupation. By work she means that activity performed with the hands, which gives objectivity to the world, while occupation denotes a physical activity whose purpose is survival and whose results are consumed almost immediately. At the end of the 5th century, occupations, which were associated with heavy deterioration of the body, began to be classified according to the amount of effort required to perform them.

In the modern Western tradition, work was generally understood as any activity that extracted from nature the means necessary to sustain existence. Further developments have led to the articulation of another criterion for defining work, which today refers to all activities for which individuals are paid. Work refers at the same time to "relations between people and nature and between people and their fellow beings" (Godelier, 1980: 167). Activities are based on different forms of division of work whereby individuals are assigned tasks according to certain individual and social characteristics: gender, age, social status, membership of a particular social category or class. In understanding the nature and function of work, Godelier draws attention to a confusion that must not be made between the labour process and the production process: "The production process means not only the relations between people and with nature within the work process, but also the relations (of external actors) to the work process itself and their rights over its product" (Godelier, 1980:168). Relationships of subordination or domination are not only reflected in the way work activities are organised and represented. They are also present beyond the performance of activities, in the relationships that exist between actors and the conditions and outcomes of their work.

2   Work at Marx: Historical Concept and Practical Reality

Labour, in Marx's view, is what determines all the essential changes in the modern world, a basic value that is the source of all social values. The whole of human history is based on work. One of the specific differences is the measurability of wage labour. Labour, in Marxist view, must be and can be measured, that is, abstracted, in relationship to the surplus value it produces. It is labour that produces value, but labour itself has no value. Of all the semantic delimitations in the etymological history of the word "labour", perhaps the most useful in terms of its political value is that between productive and nonproductive labour. Productivity is a strong criterion in defining work in the context of modern industrialization, which is structured on two basic constitutive elements: production and consumption. It is work that created man, work that distinguishes man from animal, man's most important activity. This is the ontological value that Marx and Engels attribute to work. In June 1876, Friedrich Engels wrote the article *The Part played by Labour in the Transition from Ape to Man*: "Labour is the source of all wealth, the political economists assert. And it really is the source – next to nature, which supplies it with the material that it converts into wealth. But it is even infinitely more than this. It is the prime basic condition for all human existence, and this to such an extent that, in a sense, we have to say that labour created man himself". (Marx, Engels, 1987: 452) The history of human existence is in Marx's and Engels' view a history of labour. The human being is essentially a *homo faber*, created and subject to the transforming force of labour.

> we must begin by stating the first premise of all human existence and, therefore, of all history, the premise, namely, that men must be in a

position to live in order to be able to "make history". But life involves before everything else eating and drinking, housing, clothing and various other things. The first historical act is thus the production of the means to satisfy these needs, the production of material life itself.
MARX, ENGELS, 1998: 47

According to Marx, labour is the "essence" of man, the typical activity of human species, a historical concept, a means for the creation of welfare in general, a practical reality and a nodal point of modern economy. It is work that distinguishes the human species from other forms of life. It is the most important human activity

as labour is a creator of use-value, is useful labour, it is a necessary condition, independent of all forms of society, for the existnce fo the human race; it is an eternal nature-imposed necessity, without which there can be no material exchanges between man and Nature, and therefore no life.
MARX, 1906: 50

Beyond providing the objects necessary to satisfy the needs, work has an essential function in the cultural development of the individual: "through labouring, through developing his productive powers, man comes to educate, civilize, and indeed, to create himself as a fully "human" being" (Berki, 1979: 36). Using the notion of labour, Marx refers to "*production*, to purposeful and rational but at the same time (and irreducibly) material activity, the human activity which constitutes the basis of wealth-creation and thus supplies the only ultimately valid explanation of socio-economic processes and institutions" (Berki, 1979: 36). Society constitues itself by work: from the moment people work in some way for each other, their work takes on a social form. Man's most important activity, work is necessarily prior to any economy, and any attempt by people to live together, to survive and to provide for basic and higher needs begins with and requires work. According to Marx, what makes man human is constraint, not freedom, and it is work that essentially distinguishes human life from animal life. The sphere of freedom arises only where work, understood as an essential human capacity, conditioned by external need and utility, ends.

What Marx understood was that labor itself had undergone a decisive change in the modern world: that it had not only become the source of all wealth, and consequently the origin of all social values, but that all man,

> independent of class origin, were sooner or later destined to become laborers, and that those who could not be adjusted into this process of labor would be seen and judged by society as mere parasites. To put it another way: while others were concerned with this or that right of the laboring class, Marx already foresaw the time when, not this class, but the consciousness that corresponded to it, and to its importance for society as a whole, would decree that no one would have any rights, not even the right to stay alive, who was not a laborer. The result of this process of course has not been the elimination of all other occupations, but the reinterpretation of all human activities as laboring activities.
> ARENDT, 2002: 278–9

In the Marxist "materialist" view, labour unifyingly links matter, nature and history. At the basis of all work is the specifically human form of consuming matter, by instrumentalizing the body in orderly activities. In society, nothing results from matter apart from the consuming activity that defines human nature, that is, work. The dynamics of any society are generated by the system of production: "men, developing their material production and their material intercourse, alter, along with this their actual world, also their thinking and the products of their thinking. It is not consciousness that determines life, but life that determines consciousness" (Marx, Engels, 1998: 42). The economic basis of modern society is industrial, in which the use of the forces of production generates the relations of production that form the economic structure of society. The origin of the term "industry" is Latin – "*industrius* (adj.) meaning active, ingenious, diligent, and *industry* (subs.) activity, skill" (Herseni, 1974: 45). Industry understood as "branch of economic activity engaged in the organised and large-scale manufacture of material goods", "production of material goods carried out by means of modern machinery, starting with the steam engine, irrespective of the degree of automation" (Herseni, 1974: 46) is the one that marked industrial revolutions and underlies industrialization. Industrialization, originally, therefore prior to socialism, is defined as "a complex process comprising mainly: the spread of machinery, large-scale production based on rationalization and technical division of work, the formation of an urban proletariat and the intensification of antagonisms between social classes"; in socialism, industrialization "increases the wealth of the masses and the working class becomes the ruling class", while in capitalism it "increases the number of capitalists and of the proletarians" (Herseni, 1974: 47). In Marxist-Leninist perspective, industrialization is a process of formation and development of the great machine industry.

3 Working People and Social Class(es)

In the historical context of early industrialization (18th century), the presence of workers becomes an important factor in political life, as a certain sense of belonging to a community of interests is articulated and develops, coupled with a sense of distancing from political leaders and employers. What we now call social class is an intellectual construct, designating a set of processes and phenomena describing certain human relationships. The concept of *work* and the term *workers* are intimately linked to that of social class, a phenomenon rooted in the contexts of industrialization, urbanization and political democracy, essential elements in defining modernity.

One way of understanding social class articulated in the context of industrialization is that defined by Karl Marx in *Capital*. The source of income and the position in the economic system are the two basic criteria that Marx uses in the definition of social class and at the same time sources of conflict between social classes. Working people existed even before industrialization, it is just that the problematization of their social condition in terms of social classes and inter-class conflict took root as this condition became the object of social analysis. Marx links the idea of social class to that of conflict. Disparities and inequalities between classes are an inevitable consequence of their economic conditions reflected in the living standards of individuals. The simplifying dimension in which Marx brings the two basic classes of society into a conflictual relationship implies a political instrumentation in the sense that the constitution of a category into a class necessarily implies its organization for political action. The organization of the proletarians into a class means its organization "into a political party" since "every class struggle is a political struggle" (Marx, 2008: 47). Friedrich Engels, in defining the social class of workers (in England), takes into consideration the emergence of elements in the differentiation of the means of production that took off in the context of industrial developments from the mid-18 century onwards: "The history of the English working classes begins in the second half of the eighteenth century with the invention of the steam engine and of machines for spinning and weaving cotton" (Engels, Henderson, Chaloner, 1968: 9).

Following Marx's understanding of social class, Ralph Dahrendorf develops a theoretical scenario constructed as a reflexive critique to Marx's defining elements of class, a scenario that opens a new framework of analysis and interpretation, taking into account the general dynamics of a multiple social differentiation generating resources for a differentiation also at the level of social representations (evaluation) of the relationships between categories according to their position in society. According to him, social class is rather defined by differentiated positions within the system of authority, the economic system being only a subtype of this system:

> this differential distribution of authority invariably becomes the determining factor of systematic social conflicts of a type that is germane to class conflicts in the traditional (Marxian) sense of this term. The structural origin of such group conflicts must be sought in the arrangemet of social roles endowed with expectations of domination or subjection. Wherever there are such roles, group conflict of the type in question are to be expected. Differentiation of groups engaged in such conflicts follows the lines of differentiation of roles that are relevant from the point of view of the exercise of the authority.
> DAHRENDORF, 1959: 165

The persistence of a structural conflict between main social classes, the bourgeoisie and the proletariat (which have replaced, in the polar terms of Marxist social theory, property owners and the nobility on the one hand, and workers and peasants on the other), becomes critical in the context of the evolution of industrialization, as industrial workers move from the status of proletariat, that is, workers living in poverty and oppression, to a higher status by the "bourgeoisification of the proletariat" (Dahrendorf, 1959: 253), by improving their economic situation on the basis of work done within the industrial system. However, class conflict does not disappear. According to Dahrendorf, group conflict theory does not postulate that there is necessarily a link between class conflict and economic conditions. Living standards are not relevant to the emergence of social conflict. Conflicts are "ultimately generated by relations of authority" (Dahrendorf, 1959: 253).

Within predefined frameworks of understanding the notion of social class in the context of modernity, elements of sociological analysis and philosophical speculation have developed in distinct traditions. In terms of sociological analysis, one type of approach is the static one. One such theoretical development belongs to Talcott Parsons, who considers social class a component of social structure, a static object, a category. The emphasis is on *classes*, not on *class*, on a series of categories that bring together certain characteristics on the basis of which classifications and delimitations can be made and that are useful in empirical research with aims of theoretical generalizations. In Parsons's view, social class is "an aggregate of kinship units of approximately equal status in the system of stratification" (Parsons, Turner, 1991: 119). Classes are forms of manifestation of an increasingly diverse social differentiation, in which emphasis is on adaptive modernization made possible by an increasing specialization of roles, forms of social organization and institutions. Differentiation is mapped in terms of social actors, groups, institutions, social movements, civilisations and states.

Contradiction, inequality, conflict are considered fundamental features of modernity. Class, along with gender and race, is one of the patterns of inequality in the context of modern developments. Neil Joseph Smelser and Hans Haferkamp, in *Social Change and Modernity*, describe a close link between class and inequality, in the sense that "Inequality plays a large role in shaping modernity because it generates class and group conflicts, which become the basis of the institutional inventions and innovation that come to constitute the structures of modernity" (Haferkamp, Smelser, 1992: 18). Although he places the idea of conflict at the heart of social classes and the articulation of modern institutions, Smelser makes a significant distinction when referring to certain socio-economic sequences of modernity, with reference to the role that class plays in the dynamics of this modernity. This is the specific difference he attributes to the working class, whose social movements are considered to be "the product of industrialization and urbanization" (Haferkamp, Smelser, 1992: 46) and also a reaction to modernity. Beyond the theoretical differences between progressives and conservatives on the principles of the social order, the strong criterion in the frequently reproduced polarization is a historical, temporal orientation: "The working class does not build its interests on old claims that have been disregarded in the past but on the societal order of the future" (Haferkamp, Smelser, 1992: 305). Smelser develops a novel definition of class in that it does not integrate the beneficial and revolutionary character of social consciousness from the Marxist theoretical tradition. In Smelser's conception, the working class is understood as a component of the social structure, but he attributes a negative role to social consciousness, considering that it rather disrupts the coexistence of different groups interpreting different social roles.

Another approach to the analysis of class is a dynamic one, according to which class is understood not as a phenomenon and in descriptive terms, bringing together manifestations of historical relations imbued with the fluidity of people's shared experiences in their real contexts. Edward Palmer Thompson, in *The Making of the English Working Class*, provides such an approach in dealing with the concept of class with reference to the history of British workers and the structuring of the notion of class in the context of the Industrial Revolution.

> By class I understand an historical phenomenon, unifying a number of disparate and seemingly unconnected events, both in the raw material

> of experience and in consciousness. I emphasize thai it is an *historical* phenomenon. I do not see class a "structure", nor even as a "category", but as something which in fact happens (and can be shown to have happend) in human relationships.
>
> THOMPSON, 1966: 9

According to him, "we cannot have two distinct classes, each with an independent being, and then bring them *into* relationship with each other" (Thompson, 1966: 9). In terms of a dynamic view, class is defined by belonging to common goals and ways of acting towards them, based on common experiences.

> class happens when some men, as result of common experiences (inherited or shared), feel and articulate the identity of their interests as between themselves, and as against other men whose interests are different from (and ususally opposed to) theirs. The class experience is largely determined by the productive relations into which men are born – or enter involuntarily. Class-consciousness is the way in which these experiences are handled in cultural terms: embodied in traditions, value-systems, ideas, and institutional forms.
>
> THOMPSON, 1966: 9–10

On the one hand, Marxists speak of a working class in a constant and inevitable state of degradation and social inequality; on the other hand, liberals invest this class with potential for social development and mobility and advocate a tendency towards equalisation. A critical perspective that reasonably integrates these contradictory positions belongs to André Gorz. He divides the working class into two distinct categories, depending on the degree of organization and on the level of income: a well-organised core in the labour markets, defined by high wages, job security, moderate trade unionism, and a lumpen proletariat located on the periphery of the labour market and taking the form of a new social movement that challenges the alliance based on economic growth and security between labour and capital. According to "scientific socialism", the proletariat was

> the potential subject of socialist revolution because each proletarian experienced a contradiction between sovereignty over his or her work and work relationships, and the negation of this sovereignty by capital. [...] The proletariat was the only class, and the first in history, which had no interest but to destroy its class being by destroying the external constraints by which it had been constituted.
>
> GORZ, 1982: 66

Temporary jobs, job insecurity, contingent work, lack of identification with the work done, "blank interval on the margins of life" (Gorz, 1982: 70) become the characteristics of a new proletariat, which, contrary to Marx's philosophical conviction, is not defined by work or by position in the social process of production. Those who carry out different kinds of work, in different fields of activity and with different sources of income, have no sense of belonging either to the social class of working people or to the social category of the unemployed. They form an intermediate, fluid social stratum, oscillating between different occupational levels, without the work they do having a stable meaning, but rather being a way of subordination to the mechanisms of a universal domination.

According to Zukin, the socialist philosophy of class relationships under socialism is rather understood in terms of similarities with those of the precapitalist society:

> These similarities include: the absence of the private property; a politically organized redistribution of the surplus; the priority of political and ideological over economic relations; a functional elite which may develop into a social class; the paralle existence of various means of exchange which have not been superseded by a single, uniform market; and, finally, the incomplete or partial nature of social classes, in constrast to capitalist social classes.
> ZUKIN, 1978: 392–393

Understanding social class in these terms implies understanding the socialist society itself not just as a response reaction to economic capitalist developments, "but also as a social formation with its own trajectory" for the study of which "both synchronic and diachronic analysis" is needed (Zukin, 1978: 393). The level of income, the relations to means of production, the status are not enough for a mass of people to emerge into a class. A class is "a human group that constituted itself, that actively organized itself into a commonality" (Poster, 1975: 169). A social class is not just a collectivity of persons united by participating in the process of production and playing the same role, therefore becoming the raw human material of a formal identity of diversity. According to Sartre, this would be a mechanistic definition pretending a unity of social class, but deliviring instead the "identity of the items in a collection" (Sartre, 1968: 93). It is the solidarity, the action, the movement, the degree of integration that gives existence to class, "a *real* unity of crowds and historical masses" (Sartre, 1968: 97), and not the formal statuses defined within the process of production, within collectivities: "it is by community of action and not in isolation that each would become a person" (Sartre, 1968: 94). That is why a more useful concept in understanding class is that of class practice or class struggle or the "concrete will which animates it" (Sartre, 1968: 97), much more fertile in uncovering the dynamics of class development under socialism:

> a conceptual link between the underlying structure which determines all social relations and those contradictions which engender class relations. The concept also has the potential to express three important aspects of social class: first, that the social classes are continually being constructed in ongoing social relations; second, that class relations may derive from the "superstructure" of politics, ideology, and culture, as well as from the economic "base" of the society; and, third, that through an interaction between the objective and the subjective aspects of social existence, the collectivities which co-exist in class relations create themselves.
>
> ZUKIN, 1978: 395–396

4   Workers, Social Class, and "Socialist" Urbanization

An important process that accompanied industrialization was urbanization, which took specific forms under socialism. The relationship between industrialization and urbanization is an important one, with multiple effects on both the economic and socio-political structure.

In the context of socialism, the question of labour is closely linked to the dynamics of complex processes which put into practice the ideas and principles of the development of society according to the model of "dialectical" and "historical" materialism. The development of the public wealth and the increasing political power of the proletariat could have only be achieved within specific material frameworks that had to be built. One such process of development and social construction was the industrialization. Labour culture in socialism is a result of the way in which production relations were politically instrumentalized in the context of economic and social change processes.

In the theoretical socialist toolkit of industrialization, city occupies a privileged place in the processes of building socialist society and its classes, functioning as a framework for the most important transformations intended at social, economic and political level. Urban life was considered the highest form of socialist life, in the sense that the city became "the place where socialist consciousness can best develop the environment necessary to achieve the perfection of a socialist society" (French, Hamilton, 1979: 7). The principles of Marxist theory are faithfully reflected in the socialist orientation towards the development of socio-spatial forms designed to meet the wider goals of urbanization in the socialist countries. This orientation is expressed in the resolution adopted in 1969 at the symposium organised by the Institute of the International Workers Movement of the Soviet Academy of Sciences, which expressed the fundamental dimensions of the urbanization process in socialism:

> Eliminating the differences between town and village, increasing labour productivity and the efficiency of social production, increasing the cultural and educational level of the population and the permanent development of the individual – all these things are closely associated with urbanisation.
> REINER, WILSON, 1979: 56

In the Marxist theoretical tradition, factories and plants were seen as the main stage for the manifestation of class struggle. In socialism, one of the major goals was to eliminate the endemic differences between village and town. This principle underpinned the justification for the policy of forced industrialization that took place after the communists took political power. One of the intermediate goals associated with this state policy was the transformation of existing rural settlements, villages, hamlets and isolated households into small towns with the facilities and social structures of urban settlements.

In *Cities under Socialism – and After* (1996), Iván Szelényi delivers a descriptive and explanatory pattern for the process of urbanization in Eastern European countries, identifying a number of specific features of urban dynamics, but he does not do that in evaluative terms, but rather in terms of essential differentiations from the specific features of urbanization in the capitalist societies. Szelényi considers that an evaluative approach to urbanization is not necessarily the most useful way of understanding how urban development occurred under socialism. What is important to see is not whether socialist urbanization was better or worse than capitalist urbanization, but in what ways it was different. Szelényi argues that many of the features labelled as socialist were not actually intended by the ideologues of socialism, many of them even undesirable. Hence the relevance of differentiating between what actually constituted socialist urban planning and other spontaneous elements that reconfigured the ways in which urban policies and practices were used in socialism. The question Szelényi tries to answer is to what extent socialism has generated differences in urban development, compared to corresponding patterns in Western countries. The answers he provides on different aspects of modes and practices of the urbanization process in socialist countries tend to assert consistent differences, according to the tradition of divergent theories of the urbanization process.

Referring to the three fundamental dimensions in defining urbanization (urban growth, quality of social relations and urban forms), Szelényi argues that socialist and capitalist countries differ in relationship to each other. The author adopts the neo-Weberian version of the historical approach to socialist urbanization and shows that *underurbanization* is the form of urban development specific to state socialism. He argues that there is a socialist model of urban development, taking a completely different position from Georgy Enyedi who argues that socialist urbanization merely reproduces certain stages of a process of urban development specific to Western countries.

The sociological interest is rather situated in the social effects of suburbanization. Chris Pickvance (2002) highlights three of these:

1. The city's housing stock was insufficient to meet the housing needs of those who worked in the city. This problem became widespread, even though the ideology and state policy of the 1950s and 1970s envisaged concentrating housing construction in the cities at the expense of rural areas in order to support primarily industrial growth. One of the direct effects of this housing shortage was that many young couples had to live in households with their parents before they could get their own homes. The waiting period for housing was as long as two, three or even four years.
2. Increased commuting from rural areas. This was the case for those who could not get housing in the city. Those who were in the commuter category enjoyed, on the one hand, the benefits of their own produce from cultivating their country gardens and, on the other, had access to some of the amenities of urban life.
3. Suburbanization policy involved a system of control to prevent rural residents from moving to urban areas. This control was made possible by requiring people to have a registered place of residence. It gave people the right to live only in certain places and was a very effective mechanism for the authorities to maintain control over the population. In fact, however, the practice of dealing with housing problems was quite different (French, 1995: 99–100). Thus, the mechanisms of escape were diverse. For example, enterprises had strong reasons to circumvent this registration system in order to provide the necessary workforce, because otherwise penalties would have arisen for failure to comply with the production plan. Fictitious marriages were another type of response to this problem. Another type of practice was that people living at other addresses than

those where they were registered in order to evade control. Checking documents involved lengthy checks, which would have led to too much work. Against the backdrop of these widespread housing control-avoidance practices, living in the city became a very strong attraction, since it implied access to better housing conditions, better infrastructure and more job opportunities (Pickvance, 2002: 186–187).

Suburbanization or partial urbanization is one of the four stages of development that Murray and Szelényi (1984) attribute to socialism. The identification of the four different stages is explained by a certain specificity of socialist countries and their different levels of development. The four stages are: "deurbanization" as a "response to neocolonialist 'overurbanization'" (Murray, Szelényi, 1984: 94), "zero-urban population growth" when "a particular economic growth policy is followed in which industrial growth can be achieved without any growth in urban industry" (Murray, Szelényi, 1984: 96), "partial urbanization" (*underurbanization*) understood as "a relatively delayed urban growth" (Murray, Szelényi, 1984: 98) and "socialist intensive urbanization", when "infrastructural growth is speeded up, but 'no urban population explosion' is occurring" (Murray, Szelényi, 1984: 101).

Deurbanization reffers to "a significant decline in urban population" (Szelényi, 1996: 297). This is explained by major transformations in class and property relations as the communist elites who came to power removed the bourgeoisie from the cities in order to consolidate power, state ownership and central planning.

Zero urban growth refers to that context of urbanization in which the urban population is not declining, but neither is growing. Such an effect is generated, Szelényi argues, by those industrialization strategies that create more jobs in industry, but which are not located in cities, but in rural communes. Examples given by the author are China from the early 1960s to the mid-1970s and Cuba in the late 1960s, where urban population growth was very low.

Szelényi defines the suburbanization by the relationship between two processes of urban development: industrialization and urban population growth. Under socialism, job growth in the urban industrial sector seems to have been much faster than urban (permanent) population growth. Countries that experienced such a situation therefore became "suburbanised". Szelényi 's hypothesis is that "underurbanization was a consequence of a socialist-type social and economic structure. It was the result of the elimination of the private property and the centrally planned or redistributive nature of the economic system" (Szelényi, 1996: 295). Alongside the two variables mentioned (growth in industrial employment and urban population growth), Szelényi introduces into the model the proportion of working-class commuters, those workers who lived in the countryside and worked in the city. He shows that the gap between the first two variables, together with the proportion of commuters, measures the degree of suburbanization. Suburbanization is temporally placed at the beginning of the socialist industrialization process (1950s, 1960s). The socialist intensive urbanization is situated in contrast to suburbanization phase: "industrial employment stops rising as a share and starts to decline and infrastructure investemnt increases" (Pickvance, 2002: 187). In Hungary, in the late 1960s, the population employed in industry stopped growing. Moreover, the proportion of workers in the industrial sector began to decline. On the one hand, this stage can be interpreted as a transition of state socialism from the stage of forced growth to a stage in which consumption and services become a priority, leading to what Murray and Szelényi have called "fully developed socialism". On the other hand, the same stage is considered by the same authors as a step towards capitalism, in that it allowed the development of a private economic sector based on small-scale activities, small properties and private firms, a process that allowed the restricted practice of the market economy and the manifestation of the private initiatives on which it was based.

Socialist societies produced a different kind of urbanism from the urbanism of Western countries. Szelényi takes into consideration three indicators of urbanism: the degree of diversity, the degree of space saving and the level of urban marginality. Applying the three indicators of the concept of urbanism to socialist countries in Eastern Europe, Szelényi shows that: "there was less urban diversity; there was less economizing with space and consequently lower inner-city urban density, including the density of social interaction in inner urban urban public spaces; and there was less urban marginality" (Szelényi, 1996: 300). Szelényi's premise is that the lower degree of urbanism in socialist countries is actually the consequence of socialist urban political and socio-economic organization.

When referring to the low degree of diversity in the socialist countries of Eastern Europe, Szelényi uses as indicator "the relative scarcity of urban services, such as shops, restaurants, advertisements and street vendors in socialist cities" (Szelényi, 1996: 300). The author acknowledges, however, that there have been differences between Eastern European countries on this indicator, pointing to the cases of Budapest and Prague, which were characterised by a higher degree of urbanism than, for example, East Berlin or Warsaw, the latter having been heavily rebuilt during the socialist period.

As far as socialist urban space management is concerned, given the fact that in socialism land had virtually no real market value, there being no free market in the capitalist sense of the term, urban planners in socialist cities enjoyed significantly more freedom in identifying the spaces needed to implement their plans and projects than did urban planners in the West.

> As a result, urban planners in socialist cities typically could be more generous in using space and could pay more attention to aesthetic rather than to narrow economic considerations in their urban design. One good example was Alexander Platz in East Berlin, indeed an impressive development, which expressed some kind of imperial grandeur and responded to certain ceremonial needs of a socialist society. Such a rather luxurious use of inner urban space is not unheard of in a capitalist city either, but the creation of such a public space in a market economy is very exceptional, while it appeared quite normal and functional in a socialist non-market economy.
> SZELÉNYI, 1996: 301

Less constrained by economic restrictions, urban planners in socialist cities had the privilege of using urban space in a rather aesthetic manner, with many of the projects developed under socialism serving symbolic and political needs.

Socialist cities produce less marginality, one of essential characteristics of urbanism and an expression of diversity. On the one hand, there is a positive meaning associated with the typology of the marginal, in that marginality is defined by the fact that individuals, in the context of the urban environment, are less controlled by existing norms, which further leads to a higher degree of innovation and creativity. Marginality can also be seen as a resource for the manifestation of dynamism and innovation in urban environments. On the other hand, there is also a negative dimension to the definition of marginality in the context of the city and this refers to the phenomena of urban deviance such as crime, prostitution, homelessness. Referring to marginality in a comparative perspective, Szelenyi argues that there is indeed a higher level of marginalization in capitalist cities than there was in socialist cities: "Other conditions being equal, the cities of socialist Eastern Europe were relatively safe from crime. There were relatively few of the extreme expressions of poverty, such as beggars or homeless people on the streets, in railway stations and under bridges. Ando ne had to search far longer than in similar cities of Western Europe to find prostitutes or drug dealers" (Szelényi, 1996: 302). The absence of these deviant aspects of urban life is also largely explained by the strict police control carried out in socialist cities. It was illegal for a person to be homeless or jobless. Police practices were effective in that the police were quick to deal with those who tried to sleep in parks or under bridges, or those who wandered around the city without their identity cards on them.

On the issue of urban forms in the socialist countries, Szelenyi starts from the premise that socialist cities, by limiting markets and regulating regional processes, primarily through central planning, "did produce and reproduced the asymmetrical allocation of social classes, occupational and ethnic groups in space" (Szelényi, 1996: 303). In analysing urban forms during socialist urbanization, Szelényi advances the hypothesis according to which "the redistributive character of a socialist economy had consequences [...] for the inner urban spatial distribution of social classes, occupational and ethnic groups, and economic, social and cultural institutions" (Szelényi, 1996: 304). This explanatory perspective takes into account two main elements: on the one hand, the classical model of state socialism, and on the other hand, the urban planning practices from the late 1940s to the mid-1970s. Urban growth under socialism was influenced by two elements of urban economics: the predominant role of the state in financing, building and allocating housing in urban areas and the high restrictions on the land market in the cities. In the first decades of the socialism, private housing construction was only possible in the villages, while all new housing in the city was to be built with state funding. Added to this was the nationalization of the housing stock, especially block apartment type housing. The high level of public ownership had important environmental consequences. Thus, the quality of housing has deteriorated, leading to physical and even social decay in central neighbourhoods. At the same time, all the newly built housing has been concentrated in large blocks of flats, usually located at considerable distances from the decaying old town centres. Housing construction was planned on a large scale, and when the housing industry faced labour shortages, a policy of reducing the amount of work on site and increasing investment in expensive technology was adopted, which again increased the attractiveness of large-scale construction projects. According to the new planning in the field of housing construction, a change in the activities and technological means specific to housing construction, involving the preparation of land for construction, the building of roads, the unloading of large quantities of prefabricated materials, the use of cranes to handle these materials, seemed much more rational when building sites were to be extended.

The main changes in the urban structure of socialist cities in Eastern Europe between the 1950s and the mid-1970s were the heavy deterioration of the old central districts and the development of new residential areas around them. These changes in urban form were linked to a succession of the population. Szelényi uses the term "succession" in the sense that Burgess describes the five concentric circles urban expansion. Succession is an aspect of population expansion consisting in "the tendency of each inner zone to extend its area by the invasion of the next outer zone" (Park, Burgess, 2019 50). For two decades, the urban middle class was overwhelmingly supported by the public sector. People in this category were willing to move into new homes either because they did not have a home before or because they wanted to move out of rundown neighbourhoods. For this reason, by the mid-1970s, newly developed residential areas had a strong middle-class character. On the other hand, inner-city neighbourhoods began to lose their social status, becoming attractive to "lower-class immigrants" (Szelényi, 1996: 306), such as the Roma. The situation changed with the beginning of the 1970s, when an expansion of private housing construction took place. After the 1970s, middle-class people tended to build condominiums in former middle-class neighbourhoods. On the one hand, because the newest residential areas were located at a significant distance from the city centre, the areas close to it being already occupied, and, on the other hand, because there was a reluctance to live in poor areas, close to the working class. This trend in urban mobility has been called by Szelenyi a "re-bourgeoisification of traditional bourgeois neighbourhoods" (Szelényi, 1996: 307).

One perspective of defining and understanding urbanization is that which focuses on the idea of spatial process. This perspective is used by Hungarian sociologist and geographer Gyorgy Enyedi in his study of urbanization in the socialist countries of Central and Eastern Europe. According to this approach, urbanization is

> the spatial reorganization of society by which, first, the geographical distribution of the population of a given country changes and (at least in the first stages of modern urbanization) gradually concentrates in cities and urban agglomerations; and second, the urban life style, urban social structure and technology diffuse into the countryside, so that a continuum urban/rural (or a unified settlement system) replaces the earlier sharp urban/rural dichotomy
> ENYEDI, 1996: 101

While Szelényi rather advocates for a divergence theories perspective, emphasizing the specific features and significant differences of urbanization in socialist countries, Enyedi embraces the convergent theories, insisting on aspects that demonstrate common features and similar tendencies of the urbanization patterns in socialist and capitalist countries. According to Enyedi, socialist urbanization did not represent a new model of modern urbanization, and was not fundamentally different from urbanization in capitalist societies. Urbanization in the socialist context was more a matter of reproducing the stages that defined the Western model of urbanization. According to his explanatory perspective, this model of modern urbanization includes the following stages: industrial and urban growth, increasing employment in industrial sector mainly through rural-urban migration and growth of urban areas; suburbanization, expansion and selective development of small and medium-sized towns; deconcentration of the urban population and its concentration in non-metropolitan areas. The economy is characterized by the rapid growth of the tertiary and especially the quaternary sectors, the internal reorganization of the production system and the introduction and spread of high technology (a stage that has also been called "counter-urbanization").

There were a number of specific characteristics that described each of these stages of urbanization. These differences were explained by reference to two types of sources: on the one hand, late economic and urban modernization, and on the other, the socialist political system. Most countries in Eastern Europe were "at a relatively low level of urbanization when socialist governments took over" (French, Hamilton, 1979: 2). The context in which socialist urbanization was introduced and developed was marked by late modernization, which was one of the main sources that generated elements of specificity in urbanization in Central and Eastern European countries. At the end of the 1950s, Romania was a predominantly rural country: the proportion of the rural population was over 70%, as in Poland, close to the average for other Central and Eastern European countries: rural population over 80% in Bulgaria and Yugoslavia and over 60% in Hungary. Socialist urbanization practices were introduced in an area which was poor in terms of urbanization, where modernization was more akin to a pre-industrial phase, and which marked the strong differentiation between the industrialised West and the peripheral East.

The communist parties' takeover of power in Central and Eastern Europe between 1945 and 1948 continued with a series of radical economic and political transformations. In pursuit of the fundamental political goal of building a socialist society, according to the Soviet model, industrial, financial and commercial enterprises were nationalized, with attempts to collectivise agriculture. Through massive nationalization, a shift has been made from a system of private ownership to one in which collective ownership became dominant. Collectivism became the basic principle of social relationships in the socialist order and of communist morality, proposing the replacement of private property by collective property. It implied solidarity, unity, the subordination of individual interests to the general, the pursuit of goals through common action, at the level of the nation as the most comprehensive collectivity, and used the state as an instrument. It was fundamentally opposed to individualism defined by self-interest and competition and was a core value of socialism, a core value meaning "an enduring belief that a specific mode of conduct or end-state of existance is personally or socially preferable to an opposite or converse mode of conduct or end-state of existence" (Rokeach, 1973: 5).

At the heart of many measures to redefine economic objectives and practices in the newly socialist countries was the aim of closing the significant gap between the industrialized West and the peripheral East. Agriculture and the rural population provided the resources for the process of industrialization and thus for the development of the first stage of modern urbanization which accelerated after 1950. According to the Soviet industrial model, energy production, mining and heavy industry were the basic sectors of economy. These components were organised in large, concentrated production units. According to Enyedi, only some cities were directly subject to major transformations in the context of the new model of economic organization. One of the key characteristics of these cities was the massive attraction of the rural population, as they became bastions of the working class, thereby attracting a number of privileges at the expense of rural communes and non-industrialized towns. Rural-urban migration became one of the key dimensions in the dynamics of socialist urbanization.

Some of the main features of the urbanization process, and which are found in both socialist and capitalist countries, are: 1. rural-to-urban migration and the urban concentration of the population, a consequence of urbanization 2. the spatial separation of working zones and residences 3. suburban development 4. the relative increase in the importance of small and medium-sized centers in urban development 5. the growing importance of tertiary and quaternary employment, which changes the locational pattern of workplaces (Enyedi, 1996: 103).

These fundamental features were conditioned, the author argues, by different mechanisms specific to the two types of societies, but the processes that generated these phenomena were largely similar. The different mechanisms of urbanization that operated in the two types of society were in fact different forms of manifestation of the same process. Enyedi argues that socialist urban policies were adapted to the complexity of social system, so that the urban system could not be planned and oriented in a strictly normative sense. He points out that too much emphasis has been placed on proper planning, which is seen as the key element in socialist urbanization. Such an observation allows us to identify a dynamic of urbanization under socialism, planning, as a crude intervention in physical morphology of the city, being no more than an operation of adjustment or, in Enyedi's terms, the role of planning is to "apply some 'corrections' to the spontaneous processes of urbanization" (Enyedi, 1996: 104). This spontaneous nature is one of the elements that have made socialist urban policies undergo important changes from its predefined goals. The idea that social processes can be changed by construction has been proven wrong, Enyedi points out, referring to assumptions of Soviet and Western European urban planners with radical views: "Built on a massive scale, standardized apartments did not make society more homogeneous; living at close quarters did not engender collectivism but rather social tension and neurosis" (Enyedi, 1996: 104).

Another argument in favour of this understanding of urbanization in socialist countries is that the state housing system and the centralised allocation of infrastructure investment only created the built environment, but not the social structures and relations that would generate a specific culture within the urbanization process. The planned and built urban environment did not fundamentally diminish the individual character of the decisions people made about where to settle, where to find a new job, in choosing a new apartment or in choosing education for their children. These different angles of urban fixed in a common framework of representation indicate precisely the differences between the three categories of space defined by Henri Lefebvre: objective, planned, "conceived" space (the representations of space), "perceived" space (the social practice) and "lived" space (the representational space) (Lefebvre, 1991: 38–39). This disjunction between the three spatial hypostases is generally valid, irrespective of ideology (political regime and/or economic system), justifying even the assumption that the average citizen set his goals in virtually the same way, whether living in Western or Eastern Europe.

On the one hand, individual choices of spatial practice in the context of everyday life were, in fact, the expression of a particular perception of urban space, specific to European cultural pattern. On the other hand, the aims of government policies were aimed at social and regional equalization, infrastructure, and industrial strategy. Conflict between governmental and individual goals often led to the constraint of expression of individual interests by governmental power. Different forms of coercion have not been able to fundamentally change values, aspirations and ambitions that underpinned these individual goals and interests, which could not be manufactured in accordance with official state principles and interests. This conflict led to the emergence and development of alternative manifestations of individual interests through informal mechanisms, in opposition to some of the imperatives on which the socialist urbanization project was based. There were informal responses from the population, seen as significant reactions to official policies. A relevant example is the rejection of the egalitarian aim of residence. Instead, the tendency has been to aim for increased social status by settling in areas that are well regarded. This example alone gives us an insight into the processes of mobility and the wider trend towards social differentiation by the very means provided within the framework defined by the broadly egalitarian aims of state policy. In cities where private housing market has not actually been removed, housing tenure patterns were, in a complex way, closely linked to the relative prestige of different residential areas.

While the egalitarian principle was applied with significant deviations in terms of residence choices, it was applied in the planning of urban housing and, in particular, in the planning of state housing. Two basic principles of socialist urbanization were "egalitarism and planned urbanization" (Enyedi, 1996: 109). The first principle concerns the equalization of living conditions both at work and in individual activities. This is the understanding of concept of equality in the socialist tradition, which is fundamentally different from the liberal understanding of equality. According to socialist understanding, people's talents and efforts are not considered as components of their identity, but as a changing part of the environment in which individuals live and are educated. Based on this premise, equality of opportunity (defining opportunity as a set of circumstances that favour an individual's destiny, both through the play of chance and through the individual's attitude and action) implies equality of outcome. People should share equally the benefits and resources of the society in which they live. Understanding equality in this way, it is not ethical, for example, for some people to be richer than others. Seen from this perspective, equality takes on another meaning, that of equity. In the theoretical socialist tradition, "equity as a value reflects an order of axiological relationships established according to the principle of combining personal and general interest in determining reciprocity and the proportion of rights and duties" (Miroş, 1977: 83). Such equality inevitably conflicts with freedom, as long as it has radically egalitarian implications in social distributions.

Egalitarianism became a slogan with great appeal in Central and Eastern European countries, where there were big differences in living conditions between cities and between regions. One of the most important areas in which egalitarian principles were applied was in the construction of housing, which was designed identically and had the same facilities. The planning of urban living space included very clear rules on types of use and spatial practices: everyone was entitled to the same amount of space, and the character of the population in state housing estates was socially mixed. Such a housing configuration aimed at an equal distribution of basic public services across different residential areas. General rules were applied concerning, for example, the number of kindergartens or the size of the appropriate shops for 10,000 inhabitants.

The egalitarian aims of socialist urbanization policies were more difficult to pursue in urban spaces representing the old parts of cities, where a certain type of urban culture persisted, albeit late, but rather close to the Western cultural model. There was a strong differentiation from one urban area to another, and therefore some obvious limits to the application of socialist urbanization practices. Egalitarian urbanism has had the best chance of success precisely in the newly-built, so-called socialist cities. The egalitarian urbanism instituted by the socialist system was based on the assumption that as socialism advanced, society would become increasingly homogeneous. The egalitarian use of urban space became an instrument of harmonization between the physical morphology of the city and the social structure. The consequence of this type of use was not, in fact, homogenisation, but, on the contrary, the intensification of intra-class differentiation:

> In reality, as its economy matured, the socialist city became more and more stratified. While East Central Europe societies became more egalitarian in the sense that the class of the very rich dissapeared and the share of those who were very poor diminished, the was much more differentiation within the working classes than hitherto. The size and importance of the white-collar professions grew remarkably. In consequence, the meaning of egalitarianims was repeatedly re-evaluated from the 1950s onwards.
> ENYEDI, 1996: 110

Stratification has become even more pronounced as government bodies have found it difficult to provide housing and public services on an equal basis. Lack of infrastructure became permanent as investment for such purposes was constantly delayed. The direct consequence of practising egalitarianism under crisis conditions was the creation of inequality. With virtually not everyone able to benefit from public services, a question arises: who will benefit from such services? The principle of differentiation becomes the functional principle: "Privileged classes, social gropus and individuals will have better access to scarce goods or services than those who are poorer, less powerful or less informed" (Enyedi, 1996: 110–111).

To the extent that the egalitarian principle became difficult to apply, it was combined with another, that of efficiency. Investment in infrastructure had to be directed only to certain areas. Enyedi identifies the combination of the two criteria, egalitarianism and efficiency, as an economy of scale applied to public services in a way that he considers unjustified: "economic efficiency is not a valid criterion to be applied to the location of the a non-economic institution such as school" (Enyedi, 1996: 111).

A specific element in the context of socialist urbanism in the countries of Central and Eastern Europe was the existence of rural settlements, to which urban planners could not apply the principles and tools of socialist urbanization. One of the main reasons was that these settlements were not included in projects for the construction of state housing. Beyond strict planning, there were many "spontaneous" elements in real urban development. Central planning was essentially a sectoral planning. Within this system, there was sufficient room for nuanced dynamics to manifest themselves, with the necessary dose of spontaneity. Individual elements in the urban development process (housing construction, education, public health, transport, communications) fell under the responsibility of different ministries. Municipalities were responsible for coordinating these components of modernization, but authorities at this level had no real decision-making power, and this explains why poorly coordinated sectoral decisions produced frequent bottlenecks in infrastructure development.

In summary, the most important features that have underpinned urbanization strategies concerning the development of urban settlements are the following:

1. Periodization of urban policy development in the socialist era: the 1950s, the period from the late 1950s to the early 1960s and the 1970s. In the 1950s there was no explicit urban policy, with sectoral planning dominating. Principles of socialist urbanization were applied rather sporadically, mainly in the area of state housing construction. In Central and Eastern European countries, the new cities served, on the one hand, to demonstrate the rapid success of communist governments and, on the other, as an experimental space for socialist urban planning. After almost four decades, most of these settlements remained strictly dependent on the industrial infrastructure rapidly developed by socialist economic policy or became industrial suburbs of larger cities. The late 1950s and early 1960s brought more consistent urban and regional strategies built on the principle of industrial decentralization. Modern industry was located in some provincial cities, contributing to the development of a modern urban system by reducing unemployment in different regions and decreasing inter-regional migration. Since the 1970s, focus has shifted from the strictly industrial component of cities to the wider integration of urban settlements, both at city and regional level, in terms of equalisation of living conditions and access to public services. Integration was not only aimed at urban settlements but also at rural ones.

2. Urban growth: the decentralization of industry, and later of tertiary and quaternary activities, was seen as beneficial in reducing inequalities

between regions, and regulations aimed to limit growth in large cities where infrastructure shortages were acute. Centralization and concentration were highly valued in the socialist political and decision-making system. Both at the political level and at the level of state enterprise management, the "big is beautiful" model was shared: big enterprises, big hospitals, big restaurants, etc. Between these two directions lay urbanization and regional strategies, with attempts at compromise solutions to resolve the conflict between equality and supposed efficiency. One such solution was "centralised decentralization", which involved locating industry in underdeveloped regions but in a few large centres, or keeping production units in the provinces under the strict control of the management of large companies.

3. The role of rural development in long-term strategies. Social differences between urban and rural areas have had a particular impact in the countries of Central and Eastern Europe, where poverty and rural deprivation affect large parts of the population. Sectoral strategies included plans to modernize the countryside by building roads, electrification, etc. The socialist theoretical tradition advocated a gradual blurring of the urban-rural divide: "The most important division of material and mental labour is the separation of town and country". The town "is in actual fact already the concentration of the population, of the instruments of production, of capital, of pleasures, of needs, while the country demonstrates just the opposite fact, isolation and separation" (Marx, Engels, 1976: 64). According to Lenin, towns "grow more rapidly than villages" and "are centres of the economic, political and spiritual life of the people and are the chief vehicles of the progress" (Lenin, 1963: 270).

The relationship between the ruling power and the countryside is described by Enyedi as one based on suspicion, since the peasants, overwhelmed by taxes, obligations to deliver food, and collectivization, showed a strong reluctance to support industrialization ideas and projects. But this is one explanatory perspective on the reality. Enyedi's problematization of the rural condition in the context of urbanization/industrialization has also an ideological dimension, not fully explaining the dynamics of rural reality in terms of social change. It is common knowledge that a large part of the rural population (in Romania, for example) preferred to move to the city because of the perceived superior quality of living and working conditions developed through industrialization (access to amenities, stable working hours, access to social services). Rural development has never been a real professional challenge for architects and other urban strategists, as rural space was by its nature not very attractive for spectacular projects, as urban interventions had to fulfill ideological imperative related to space so that political and symbolic goals could be achieved at the same time. Such a context explains the lack of viable strategies for the development of rural settlements until the 1970s, for strictly economic and efficiency reasons.

4. Urban development strategies took into account the development of a hierarchical urban system. In Central and Eastern Europe, the process of creating a modern urban system in a socialist context was a top-down process in two respects. First, urban development depended on decisions at the top of the governmental leadership through the allocation of development funds. Secondly, the priority was to modernize the top of the urban hierarchy, that is, the large regional centres and the capital, then to modernize the medium-sized towns and finally the small towns, which formed the base of the system. The settlement system was divided in two: modern towns and cities on the one hand, and traditional local centres on the other, with the added inability to link modern settlements to the surrounding rural areas. Gradually, this top-down urbanization has moved towards the integration of both rural and urban settlements. One of the ways of achieving this integration has been to provide non-agricultural occupations for the population of larger villages. Basic public services were also to become more accessible. But, explains Enyedi, as investment in infrastructure was increasingly scarce, the solution of concentrating rural settlements for efficient modernization was to demolish small villages, selecting these so-called non-viable villages arbitrarily.

5. A final feature is the concern for a steady increase in the urban proportion of the population. The very high proportion of rural population was seen as a symbol of backward past, so the gap in this respect between West and East also needed to be closed. One of the policies pursued to achieve this was the incorporation of many suburban areas into the administrative areas of cities.

Rural development in Central and Eastern Europe was a mixed story: on the one hand there were radical changes in the social structure, on the other hand there were still strong rural-urban dichotomies in living conditions. One indicator of social change was the high proportion of industrial workers among rural residents. Daily commuting became widespread practice in all countries in this part of Europe. Most of the commuters belonged to the white-collar category and lived in rural suburbs. Commuting was one of the specific social phenomena that accompanied the process of urbanization in socialist societies. Most of the commuters were generally in the first category of industrial workers, but they did not settle in the city, either because of the lack of housing or, more importantly, because of the significant economic advantages of combining work in the city with work in the country. This duality provided additional economic resources. The practice of this type of mobility became so widespread that, in some countries, the proportion of industrial workers in the rural population became higher than the proportion of the same category of workers in the urban population. Cities have become largely white-collar strongholds.

An important feature of urbanization in the context of cities was that a significant part of the urban population retained a number of rural attributes. An example of this is the strong and permanent link with rural areas of origin. Much of the urban population was made up of first generation rural immigrants. The number of peasants brought to the city was so large that what has been called the "ruralization" of cities, the transformation of the traditional pattern of urban life, occurred.

The relation between rural and urban areas had a strictly economic function, which was very important, so that the rural population helped their relatives in the city in a wide variety of ways: food supply, financial help to cover the costs of living in the city, etc. The specific characteristics and functions of this economic and social phenomenon based on the constant interaction between rural and urban areas led to the creation and development of a totally atypical model of urbanization: resources in rural areas make a major contribution to urban development. City dwellers used to go to the countryside during their holidays, helping with agricultural work and harvesting crops.

Rural influence has also had a large influence on suburbanization. Workers in the suburbs retained elements of the rural lifestyle, living, for example, in large, single-family houses with large gardens, orchards, vineyards and livestock, mostly built by themselves. Rural migrants transferred much of their rural ways of life, traditions and customs to the suburbs. Migrants from the same village often tried, once in the city, to live on the same streets or in the same neighbourhoods, thus building an extension of the ways that described the housing and daily life practices of the rural community of origin. The translation of specific types of sociability of rural communities into the urban living environment was an unplanned input with an overwhelming influence on life in the socialist city.

5   Elements of Urbanization in Romania

Urbanization as a complex process of development of urban and rural divisions, of amplification of the links between the city and the surrounding environment implies: 1. "a wide range of quantitative transformations of all categories of localities of a network on a given territory (population concentrations in large centres, territorial growth of settlements, building facilities, economic and social constructions, etc.)" and 2. the permanent and growing trend towards the assimilation of a new way of life, in line with modern society, referred to in everyday language as the urban way of life (Cucu, 1976: 177).

The model that underpinned urban development in Romania during the socialist period was planned urbanization. Urban development was based on the process of industrialization. The direct consequences of industrialization were: an increase in the number of employees in the non-agricultural sector, collectivization and mechanization of agriculture which led to a transfer of labour from the primary to the secondary and tertiary sectors.

Structural moments in the process of urbanization were the adoption of measures and policies that had consequences in reconfiguring the map of Romania in terms of urban population levels and socio-economic development. In the 1950s, the first stage of territorial reorganization took place, when the 58 counties were reduced to 18 and then to 16 administrative regions. The period from 1940 to 1960 was a period in which the foundations were laid for industrial infrastructure and agriculture as the economic basis for building a socialist society (Rönnäs, 1982: 146).

In 1968, the law on administrative reorganization is adopted, which requires the transition from the territorial organization in 16 regions to the division into 40 counties. This new territorial division became a powerful tool in the management of regional policies, as the counties were to become socio-economic entities, viable economic units with an average population of 450,000. The law adopted in 1968 provided for a lowering of the minimum population threshold for cities from 20,000 to 10,000 inhabitants. In this way, 52 rural settlements received the status of cities (Cucu, 1970: 40). 55 municipalities, 79 cities and 2679 communes were listed in the law adopted in 1968 (Mihăilescu, Nicolau, Ghiorghiu, Drinovan, 1993: 21).

In 1972, at the *National Conference of the Romanian Communist Party*, the systematization program was adopted. It aimed at structuring all urban and rural localities in a hierarchy in which each would occupy a predetermined position and function: "The development of a multilaterally developed socialist society and the gradual transition to communism involve gradually bringing the standard of living of villages closer to that of cities" (Ceaușescu, 1972: 50). The first article of the Law 58/1974 on the systematisation of territory and urban and rural settlements stipulated that "The purpose of the systematization is the judicious organization of the territory of the country, counties and communes, urban and rural localities, functional zoning in terms of land use, the establishment of the height regime, the density of buildings, as well as the density of inhabitants, planted and recreational areas, the equipping with socio-cultural facilities, technical-edilitary works, communication and transport routes, the preservation and improvement of the environment, the enhancement of historical and artistic monuments and historic sites, the improvement of the economic and social efficiency of investments and the continuous improvement of working, living and leisure conditions for the entire population".

The systematization policy was a "means of controlling and managing the rapid urban transition", with the aim of creating "a new demographic and economic map of Romania" (Rönnäs, 1982: 149). The systematization was structured along several major levels (Mihăilescu, Nicolau, Ghiorghiu, Drinovan, 1993). It was understood as:

1. A "general problem of modernization" (increasing the standard of living and the degree of comfort; systematization as a factor in the development of the degree of civilization of localities);
2. An "economic problem of land expansion" (by concentrating built-up areas);
3. A "problem of social organization" (by eliminating the differences between village and town, but also by generalizing the same living conditions in all regions of the country and for all social categories);
4. A "political problem of inter-ethnic equality" (ensuring the uniformity of the administrative organization of the country's population);
5. An "administrative problem" (not only land but also administrative concentration aimed at greater centralization of political power);
6. An "urban planning problem" (standardization of building types for all localities in line with "modern comfort standards"; architectural and functional standardization);
7. A "strategic problem of the formation of the new man" (the disappearance of the peasant, of an "old" ideal type, in the context of a provoked decline of the rural world).

Social homogenization and equity were major stakes and the basic principles of systematization. The 1975 *Programme of the Romanian Communist Party: for the building of the multilaterally developed socialist society and Romania's advance toward communism* advocated: "One of the essential guiding principles of the whole systematization drive will be to ensure equal living conditions for all citizens of the country, irrespective of nationality, in the spirit of the principles of socialist equity, the gradual erasure of the essential distinctions between town and village by raising the village to the level of development of the town. The number of new town centres to be created is 300–400" (*Programme of the Romanian Communist Party: for the building of the multilaterally developed socialist society and Romania's advance toward communism* 1975: 85–86).

In the context of communist systematization, urbanization would have occurred through "the gradual development of a further 300–350 new urban centres, in which industrial, educational, health and commercial establishments should be built as a priority. These new centres should be located in such a way that they are surrounded by approximately 3–4 communes, which, together with the existing towns, will ensure that all the problems of life of the inhabitants of the communes and villages concerned are adequately addressed" (Ceaușescu, 1972: 51).

One of the most important indicators of urbanization, the number of cities, increased significantly throughout the communist period: in 1948 there were 152 cities, in 1966 there were 183, in 1980 there were 236, and in 1989 there were 262 (Cucu, Iordan, 1984: 142–147).

The central objectives of the settlement programme were to produce urbanization without excessive population concentration and to eliminate the socio-economic differences between rural and urban areas. Systematization led to the transformation of a large number of rural settlements into towns, based on the criterion of economic potential. However, this criterion worked only partially because many rural settlements were transformed into cities not on the basis of the number of inhabitants or economic structure (the economic bases of many of them were poorly developed), but on the basis of their geographical location, so that some rural settlements were transformed into cities simply because they were located in regions where there were no other urban centres. The idea of a uniform expansion of urbanization across the country was therefore also at the root of urbanization.

A consequence of the urbanization process has been the generation of "intra-county variation" within urban population growth. In most counties (31 out of 39 counties, except Bucharest), the share of the urban population in county seats increased much more than in the other county towns: from 52.8% in 1966 to 58.9% in 1977. The concentration of urban population in the county seats was particularly marked in the poorer counties. Thus, in 10 out of 16 cities, the urban population increased between 1966 and 1977 by more than 75%, as they became municipalities of relatively poor counties (Rönnäs, 1982: 150).

Urban population growth during socialist urbanization was the result of two processes: implementation of administrative policies aimed at changing the status of certain localities, either by upgrading rural settlements to the status of towns or by incorporating them administratively into neighbouring towns; and massive rural-urban migration.

Within the framework of urbanization policy, the city (based on the principles adopted at the Plenary Session of the Central Committee of the Communist Party of Romania, 5–6 October 1967, regarding the improvement

TABLE 1   Distribution of Romania's *urban* population during socialism (1948–1985)

Year	Urban population (thousands)	Average population (thousands)
1948	3487,0	22,9
1956	4746,0	27,8
1966	6220,1	34,0
1977	9395,7	39,8
1985	11370,1	48,0

SOURCE: SANDU, 1987: 184

of the administrative-territorial organization of Romania and the systematization of rural localities) was defined according to the following characteristics: "a centre with a large population having political and administrative functions, a significant industrial, commercial, social and cultural potential, as well as multiple links with the surrounding area over which it exerts an economic and organizational influence" (Cucu, 1970:39). Population is one of the aspects, the basic element of urbanization. Urban population is understood as "the totality of people living in cities or certain localities declared urban by state regulations" (Cucu, 1976: 173). With regard to the criterion of "large population", during socialism, the urban population grew steadily (Sandu 1987)

In 1989, the urban population had reached 12.31 million people, with a share of 53.2 in Romania's total population, 8.82 million more than the urban population in 1948. For the period 1948–1977 alone, the urban population increased by a total of 5.90 million. Urban population increases as a result of administrative policies accounted for only one fifth of the total urban population increase. The largest contribution to urban population growth was made by rural-urban migration (Sandu 1987), as can be seen from the ranking of the shares of the different components of urban population growth.

Industrialization created the conditions for the development of significant geographic mobility, with the attraction of cities that offered work and housing opportunities resulting most in new industrial workers moving to the city. Radical changes occurred in the structure of the population, with "cities becoming centres of strong attraction for labour. The share of the urban population increased from 38.2% in 1966 to 47.5% in 1977; the number of towns increased by 53, and a significant number of cities expanded" (Measnicov, Hristache, Trebici, 1977: 6). The total number of cities increased from 152 cities in 1948 to 237 in 1985 (by 85 cities) and to 262 in 1989 (110 more than in 1948).

TABLE 2   Factors of *urban* population growth (1948–1982)

Years	Total Urban population growth	From which (%)		
		Natural growth	Migration growth	Reclassifications of localities
1948–1956	+1,761 125	17	70	13
1956–1966	+1,831 450	26	68	6
1966–1977	+2,933 631	35	49	16
1977–1982	+1,527 257	40	59,5	0,4

SOURCE: SANDU, 1987: 192

The demographic effects of industrial policies have started to be visible in the urban population structure, with geographical mobility playing a key role in urban population growth. According to the 1966 census, the proportion of the population who were born elsewhere than in the locality in which they were censused was 59% (in Bucharest it was 62.5%). More than half (57.6%) of the people in this category had settled between 1950 and 1966 (Measnicov, Hristache, Trebici, 1977: 47–48).

High-scale population redistributions by residential environment, achieved mainly through "strong rural-urban migration, of the "concentrated" type, in the context of a rapid pace of urbanization" took place between 1970–1976/1978 (Measnicov, Hristache, Trebici, 1977: 191). The intensification of industrialization between 1966 and 1977 led to a significant increase in migration balances at both county and provincial levels. In 1977, the largest increase in the positive migration balance was recorded for Bucharest (+35.5%). The highest level of negative balance is recorded for Moldova, which becomes a major source of migration for the period mentioned above. In 1977, Bucharest had a total population of 1,933,885. Of this, only 40% were born in Bucharest, the rest being distributed among the other provinces, the highest percentages being recorded for migrants from Muntenia (30% – 581,016 persons) and Moldova (10% – 198,693 persons) (Trebici, Hristache, 1986: 125). Bucharest is a very interesting case in terms of the mosaic character of the population by origin, attracting and integrating demographically different cultural and behavioural submodels. The pace of urbanization has homogenised all these different values and brought them together under the umbrella of economic attraction. Bucharest had the lowest birth rate in the country in 1977, although 200,000 Moldovans from the province with the highest birth rate lived in the capital. The economic factor proved much stronger than the cultural one in this respect.

As a result of urbanization in general and rural-urban migration in particular, there have been significant changes in the supply of housing in urban areas. Spontaneous migration of villagers in the sense that they were not forced by the state to migrate, but only provided the conditions for generating spatial mobility, led to a significant gap between housing needs and the flow of newcomers to the urban environment. The extent of rural-urban migration has led to an insufficient supply of housing in urban areas. Between 1951 and 1960, 125,070 apartments were put into use, while the number of migrants exceeded 1 million. The supply of housing gradually increased in the decade 1961–1970, when 529,319 apartments were put into use, and then increased significantly in the period 1971–1980, when the number of apartments reached over 1.2 million (Murgescu, 2010: 352).

The process of urbanization, with planned industrialization as its essential engine, has even generated perverse effects in the sense that it has produced a massive demand for housing in urban areas, a demand that could not be entirely satisfied by the funds allocated by the state, enterprises, cooperative and public organizations. Such a development required the application of administrative restrictions to control the spatial mobility of the population. Industrial workers who were the most favoured in this mobility process, moved to the city in stages: first they obtained a floating visa, were assigned to social housing (such as hostels), and then obtained flats and the full right to live in the city (obtaining a city identity card).

The attraction to the city was based on several factors. On the one hand, the increase in the quality of living conditions: access to the most important amenities such as running water, gas supply, central heating, plus the provision of various types of household appliances such as TVs, radios, washing machines, gas cooking appliances – all of these have fuelled not only the attraction to the urban, but also satisfaction with living in the urban. The main criticisms frequently raised about housing in typical housing estates brought into use during the communist period concerned excessive standardization, the relatively small size of living space, the low quality of some of the material and interior designs of houses. However, overall satisfaction was high as the majority of new arrivals and settlers in the newly built apartments came from rural areas where living conditions were poor in terms of access to modern amenities. Other key factors of urban attractiveness were the availability of material goods (increase in the number of state and cooperative commercial units) and access to cultural services. Cultural consumption was one of the specific vectors of urban development, with a significant increase in the supply of cultural goods and services during socialism (an illustrative example of this is the increase in the number of cinemas by almost 5,000 in 1970 compared to 1950).

While at the national level, the urbanization process has shown positive developments in terms of the levels reached by the quantitative indicators presented above, at the European level, Romania was below the European average in terms of the level of urbanization at the end of the communist period: 53.2% urban population in Romania compared to the European average of 69% (23rd out of 25 European countries at the end of the 1980s). The 1980s were a period of redefinition of urbanization policy in which the emphasis was put on the development of small towns, which led to a significant limitation of migration to large cities and, consequently, to an increase in the degree of dissatisfaction among population. Economic problems in the context of the 1980s led to reduced investment in urban infrastructure, an example being the reduction in the number of new housing given in use. From an average of 123,000 apartments per year in 1971–1980 to an average of over 140,000 apartments per year in 1981–1982, it fell to below 100,000 apartments in 1985 (Murgescu, 2010: 354–55).

A key dimension of socialist urbanization is the labour system. The imperatives of the socialist urbanization are also reflected in the dynamics of the labour force. From the point of view of social organization, urbanization has created the context for a number of specific differentiations in social categories. The imperative of eliminating the differences between country and town has also materialized in the changing structure of the employed population. The share of the population employed in agriculture halved between 1960 and 1989, from 6.2 million of the total employed population of 9.5 million in 1960 to 3.1 million of the total employed population of 10.9 million in 1989. The share of the population employed in industry increased significantly in the same period: from 1.9 million persons out of a total employed population of 9.5 million in 1960 to 4.9 million persons out of a total employed population of 10.9 million in 1989 (Murgescu, 2010: 340). One of the important changes in the structure of the employed population is the shift of a part of it from agricultural (rural) occupations to occupations based on wage-type employment relationships. This type of economic mechanism has been an important, albeit limited, source of economic growth. The agricultural labour force has been declining over the 4 decades: from 65.5% to 27.9%. Although this decrease is significant, equally significant is the increase of number of specialists in agriculture: from 11,200 specialists in 1960 to 65,600 specialists in 1989 (Murgescu, 2010: 363). This form of (technical) modernization of agriculture has not really met the needs and expectations of those working in agriculture, especially young people (limited earnings, limited opportunities for professional/personal fulfilment).

Urbanization and the construction of the "new man" as the main forms of socio-economic, administrative and political operationalization of communist systematization – one of the "miracles" proposed by the Ceaușescu regime (Mihăilescu, Nicolau, Ghiorghiu, Drinovan, 1993: 26) – are essential elements of the context in which the representations of work in socialist film will be analyzed. The question of urbanization was settled, on the one hand, at the level of official discourse and, on the other, at the level of the practices of materialization of this "miracle" intended to solve the problems of life of the future "new man" in terms of welfare and, above all, equality.

Egalitarianism as a principle of social order is based on an essential premise, namely that society "has the function of building socialism" (Casals/Câmpeanu, 2002: 114). The egalitarian class structure is "a fascinating historical achievement" but, under the pressure of underdevelopment, it is necessary to industrialize, which, "although a major historical undertaking, has nothing to do with building socialism" (Casals/Câmpeanu, 2002: 114). The process of urbanization in the context of industrialization generates structural differentiation between economic organization (with the functions of efficiency and effectiveness in industrialization) and social order (the imperative of the dominant value and normative orientations), between the "stage of development of the forces of production and their social character" (Casals/Câmpeanu, 2002: 112), a character expressed through forms of property and class structures. Operating with principles that are related to both the socialist order and the capitalist system generates what Câmpeanu calls "a syncretic mode of production" (Casals/Câmpeanu, 2002: 98), having incompatible functions, on the one hand industrialization, on the other hand the perpetuation of the absence of private property specific to capitalism. With these elements of the economic system, labour productivity, defined as the central goal of industrialization, is undermined by the double constraint imposed on the means of production and on labour: "an extra-economic one, imposed by the regime", which imposes on labour power a price lower than the historically determined value, and "an economic one, imposed by capitalist mechanisms" (Casals/Câmpeanu, 2002: 97). Labour productivity is achieved, but it is not competitive with that of the capitalist organization, as long as there is a significant gap between the real value of labour power and the value attributed to it. The specificity of syncretic or convergent mode of production is given by the proportion and nature of interference of three fundamental factors in the dynamics of development: economic organization, political regime, and social structure. While economic industrialization was possible, socialist organization of society was more of an artificial construct, legitimized mainly ideologically by a power structure which only faithfully reproduced incompatibilities between the economic and the social organization. Reversing the terms of the modernization equation in the socialist hypostasis generated, in a rather experimental formula, a type of unfinished construction, based on the premise that the socio-cultural order is determined by economic system, in terms of Marxist-type determinism. The relationship of determination is exactly the other way around: "what matters is the economic and financial infrastructure, and the other infrastructure, the social and cultural infrastructure, on which these two are based" (Pasti, 1995: 6).

Egalitarianism remains an ideological construct and a relatively useful tool in discursive political strategies, but it is not an assumed goal within practical social reality as it is politically used through the processes of industrialization and urbanization. Rather, we can speak of limited inequality, as resources were distributed according to political status.

Beyond the sphere of official discourse on major role of industrialization and working class (especially industrial) in increasing the degree of civilization of society, other discursive realities were constantly developed, conveying alternative ways of describing and evaluating social and economic changes claimed by the project of socialist modernization. One such alternative field was the filmic production. A form of discourse on modernization and its social contexts has also been developed in this field where convergences and divergences between discursive practice on modernization (urbanization) and concrete forms of subjective experience of modernization are examined. Factual and evaluative judgements incorporated in cinematic visions of what was declared and achieved in terms of modernization become elements of a reflection on alternative meanings attached to relationship between individual and political power, which integrate various manifestations of the social institution of work and decompose into individualizing layers numerous images of work and biographies of working people, and this not outside the system but within it.

6 Elements of Work System

Work refers to "a particular field of activity, namely professional and institutional" (Krasnaseschi, 1971: 6). It is defined as "a voluntary, conscious act whereby a quantity of capacity is brought together in an organized framework and with appropriate means, in order, in a systematic manner and under specialized direction, to produce certain goods and services for society" (Krasnaseschi,

1971: 6). The institutional nature of professional work can be analysed in the context of the notion of a system understood as a structure made up of several subordinate parts (subsystems or elements), which perform certain functions necessary to achieve the objectives pursued by the whole. The reliability of the system is a function of the reliability and coordination of the subsystems and elements. One of the specific characteristics of the system in the case of work is its dynamic, action-oriented character, in which the main internal elements are represented by: "the subject (man), the object (identifiable with the material or spiritual object of work), the means (which always have a character, but not an auxiliary role and are subordinate to), the purpose or telos ([...] which usually sums up a multiplicity of purposes)" (Krasnaseschi, 1971: 7) The subject is the one who "initiates the action of the system, executes a series of acts, directs, supervises, corrects, innovates, invents" (Krasnaseschi, 1971: 7) and is made up of "work groups and individuals". The group subject is a "social reality, which is part of the internal elements of the system". The individual subject of the work system "appears as the only element with a tiered structure, in contrast to the other elements, which are somewhat linear" (Krasnaseschi, 1971: 7–8). The object of work system brings together "raw materials, prefabricated materials, as well as the stock of information" (Krasnaseschi, 1971: 8) and is dynamic in character, changing according to the means of the system. Means of the system – "various technical, technological, constructive forms" (Krasnaseschi 1971: 8) – are those which determine the subject's modes of operation with the object, the time consumed to achieve the predetermined goals of work. The goal is the result of the balance between subject, means, and object.

The work system is generally "open". The specific element is the multiplicity of this openness. There are exchanges with elements of external reality and there is an internal openness made possible by the subject factor which "opens itself from within and directly to its own biopsychic and social realities" (Krasnaseschi, 1971: 13). The functionality of the work system is a function of its dynamics, a dynamics which is defined by a "simultaneous and one-way movement of all its elements and subsystems" (Krasnaseschi, 1971: 15). Any gap generates dysfunction and blocks the achievement of goals. The goal (outcome R) is a function of the functionality of: "the object (fO), the means (fM), the reciprocal relations between the components (S, O, M), the reciprocal relations between the system as a whole and society (Sys-Soc), the functionality of the subject, which is biological (B), psychological (P), social (G), and which depends at the same time on the concordance between one's own goals (TS) and those of society (TSoc)" (Krasnaseschi, 1971: 15).

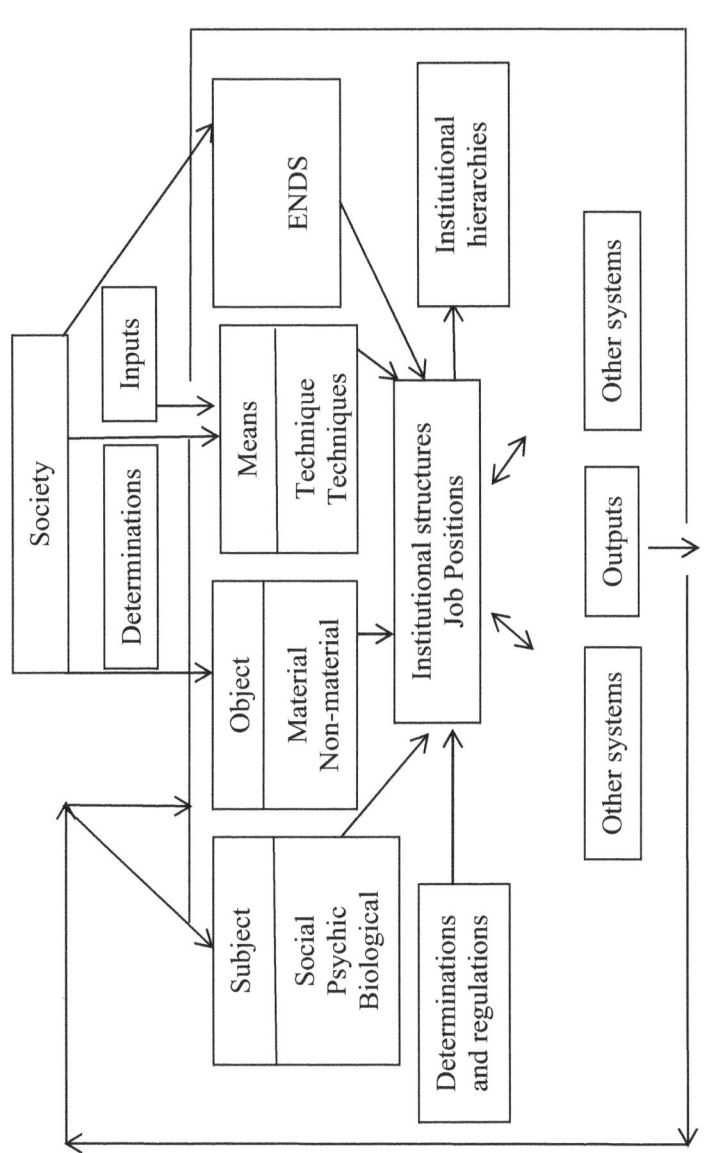

FIGURE 5 Work system/adaptation after Krasnaseschi, 1971:14

At level of existing reality, the work system exists through processes, processuality being its essential characteristic. The work process takes place in an organised manner, is divided into economic sectors and branches of activity (productive or extra-productive). Work processes are carried out in concrete units (enterprises, institutions) and involve two types of relations: administrative, that is "hierarchical relations, of instructions and reports, between enterprises, institutions and their supervisory bodies", and functional, that is"relations between enterprises and institutions which materialise through exchanges or collaborations directly concerning the object, means and effects of work processes" (Krasnaseschi, 1971: 22). Within the work system, the work station is "the place of concrete and direct realization of the work process, in all sectors, branches, enterprises and institutions, regardless of their hierarchical rank, aims, means and objects", "the point at which cooperation between subject, subjects, object, means is realized in order to achieve the aims" (Krasnaseschi, 1971: 23).

These defining elements of the work system (Fig. 5) will be followed and integrated in the analysis of cinematic representations of work, aiming to identify the discursive dynamics of films in relation to each of the morphological and subjective dimensions of this social system.

CHAPTER 4

Work and Socialist Realism

1   Social Value of Work: Preferable Modes and Desirable End-States

In 1982, Ceaușescu described an autochthonous vision of this social value: "We must always bear in mind the well-known truth that work is the decisive factor in the development of the forces of production, in the progress of any society. Work has played a determining role in the physical and intellectual development of man, man himself – it can be said – is the creation of work" (Ceaușescu, 1982: 26). The programmatic architecture of the socio-political order was built around the social value of work. At the basis of the formation of the new man was placed this value, which was to structure all the cultural-artistic products of society.

> work, useful social activity is the determining factor in the formation of socialist consciousness, in the moral and political education of the masses. [...] The society we are building is the society of those who work; it is based directly on the creative work of all its members. Every citizen must do useful work for society, must contribute actively to the general progress of the country. Free labour, free from exploitation, is the only source of increased national wealth, of the flourishing of the fatherland, of the prosperity of the people and of personal well-being; it must therefore be understood as a necessity, as an honourable duty of every citizen, and at the same time as the principal means of affirming the human personality, the creative force of every citizen. It must be clear to everyone that no one can live in our society without working in one sector or another of economic and social life.
> CEAUȘESCU, 1977: 64

The official view of the social value of work is formulated concretely in paragraph 10 from the document entitled *Code of Principles and Norms of Communist Work and Life, Socialist Ethics and Equity*, adopted as part of the project for the formation of the "new man" at the 11th Congress in 1974: "For every communist, for every citizen, work is a fundamental, honourable duty. Everyone must show a high professional conscience, competence, creative spirit, dedication and passion in his work; at the same time, he must show combativeness and intransigence against manifestations of indiscipline, superficiality and lack of responsibility in work" (*Code of Principles and Norms of Communist Work and Life, Socialist Ethics and Equity,* 1981: 13–14). Through this document, working people are ideologically assigned a series of political functions in the construction of socialism: The mastery of dialectical and historical materialism and the application of "Marxism-Leninism to the historical-material conditions of the country"; propaganda activity ("tireless propagandists of Party policy"); strict observance of Party discipline, "which is the same for all Party members, regardless of their position in society"; the "sacred, first-order" duty to defend the "monolithic unity of the Party"; the manifestation of concern and responsibility "for the continued development and defence of socialist, state and cooperative property"; to fight "against waste of any kind, negligence in the preservation and management of public property", "against theft of public property, embezzlement of socialist property, any theft of national property"; "to fight resolutely against the degradation of the environment"; "all communists are obliged to respect party and state secrecy, to give constant proof of high vigilance and revolutionary combativeness"; "the high duty to strive to strengthen the moral and political unity of the people, to cement brotherly friendship among all working people – Romanians, Hungarians, Germans and other nationalities – to fight against all manifestations of nationalism and chauvinism". Paragraphs 16 and 17 of the same document set out the system of values which was to guide the life of working people and social relations in socialist society: "the promotion in all social life of the principles of socialist ethics and equity, of relations of cooperation and mutual assistance, of solidarity, esteem, trust and mutual respect. [...] The communist must be honest, sincere, principled and correct, must not tolerate lies, falsehood, hypocrisy, and must combat attempts to mislead the higher organs, the comrades in labour, and evasion of responsibilities and duties". Point 18 stipulates the obligation to "combat any abuse of power, any influence peddling, any tendency to use for their own benefit and to the detriment of working people the positions and duties of responsibility entrusted to them by society". Communists must "resolutely combat subjectivism and arbitrariness in the assessment and promotion of executives, and take a firm stand against favouritism, nepotism, servility, and careerism". They must "resolutely fight against profiteering, parasitism, cheating, speculation and bribery, any form of obtaining illicit income, misappropriation by abuse or dishonesty of the fruits of the work of others". A political and moral duty is also "to fight against idealistic theories, mystical prejudices, superstitions, any manifestations of obscurantism". Another important responsibility established in code is that of basing family relations on principles of socialist morality, equality, respect, affection and mutual trust between spouses. Modesty is another core value: "Regardless of the position he occupies in society, the communist must show modesty; he must combat conceit, arrogance, contempt for his fellow men", and at the workplace, those in positions of responsibility "must acquire authority by exemplary moral and professional conduct in all respects". Communists had "to reject and condemn with the utmost firmness both national exclusivism and kowtowing to foreigners" (*Code of Principles and Norms of Communist Work and Life, Socialist Ethics and Equity,* 1981: 8–28).

2   Working People and the Role of Art in Socialism

Labour was an important thematic dimension of the leading political discourse in the context of socialist realism. Socialist realism, as a political strategy applied in the field of culture, was endowed at the normative level as a precise instrument of "education in the communist spirit", of knowledge of social life and its reflection as truthfully as possible in the work of art. The term "socialist realism" first appeared on 23 May 1932 in *Literaturnaja gazeta/ Literary gazette* and was used by Ivan Gronsky. Supported by Stalin and Maxim Gorky, among others, socialist realism became part of the official doctrine from the First Congress of Writers in 1934. According to socialist realism, art should not be a reflection of reality, but had to "depict reality in its revolutionary development" (Zhdanov, 1950: 12). This definition belongs to A. A. Zhdanov and was formulated at the First Congress of Soviet Writers in 1934.

The working class and the realities of socialist construction constituted the referential universe for all fields of artistic production: "The main source of inspiration for the man of art, whatever his nationality, must be the life and heroic work of our people, of the builders [...] of the new socialist order" (Ceaușescu, 1971: 14). In order to get to know closely the realities of life in socialism and of the working class, the idea of broadening contacts between artists and working people was put forward: "I believe that contacts with working people must be constantly broadened, going to factories, to villages, to institutions. On the one hand, this will help to broaden the cultural horizons of the masses, and on the other hand, the creators themselves will be able to learn from those who work, they will understand life better. Good things will come out of this close connection with working people, both for the workers and for the creators of art" (Ceaușescu, 1971: 20).

In *Statement on the current state of building socialism in our country, the theoretical and ideological problems and the political and educational activity of the people* (presented at the enlarged Plenary Session of the Central Committee of the Romanian Communist Party on June 1–2, 1982), Ceaușescu stated that "the working people, the popular masses in the towns and villages are the creators, the participants and the direct beneficiaries of mass cultural and artistic activity" (Ceaușescu, 1982: 66). Consequently, all theoretical, ideological, political and educational activities were intended to contribute "to raising the general level of knowledge of working people, to broadening their cultural horizons, to forming the consciousness of the new man of our society" (Ceaușescu, 1982: 54).

The basic premise of socialist realism was that art should reflect reality in a social-historical context, that is, reality through an ideological lens. The method of cinematic art was based on this premise. Reflecting in films the facts of life of working people, the social class most present in the official discourse on the relationship between film and the social, was a political imperative and a working definition that proved more or less effective.

Ideological elements taken from discourses on the role and function of socialist realism in the construction of socialism have important value in describing official practices of ideological control of cultural production and in drawing limits on the force they actually exerted on film professionals. As far as the affiliation to socialist realism defined by Zhdanov is concerned, it is very weak, the links between the Soviet realities of the interwar period (when socialist realism is defined and introduced in the Soviet space) are far different from the realities of socialism in Romania from the second half of the 1970s and continuing into the 1980s. Also, socialist realism could not have been strong in the context where the cultural influence of the West was much stronger in Romania than in the USSR at any time in the latter's history. Another important factor in explaining the weak influence is the nature of the relationship between political leaders and Romanian artistic elite (filmmakers, producers, actors), a relationship that was most often delicate to say the least, perhaps also because there was a certain distancing of this elite from the multiple realities of society: the reality of work, industry, urbanization, politics. At a time when acceptance of the domination of politics over cinematic art was problematic, there was no real formal aesthetic of socialist realism formulated and assumed in terms and in the name of this elite. Therefore, associations between politics, aesthetic theory and art in the context of socialism in Romania must be formulated with caution.

Speeches such as those from which the above excerpts were presented had the function of symbolically validating in fact an economic system that was multiply structured in a limited dynamic in terms of management of certain qualities of the working communities, that is, of a type of "accord between work and community" (Kracauer, 1998: 99), on the premise that works may be "good or bad, may harbour a social outlook or exclude one. [...] work does not serve the idea of community, but rather community serves the accumulation of power of un undefined work" (Kracauer, 1998: 99). Not all work is socially necessary, not all work produces means of production that meet a real, viable demand. According to Marx, any manifestation of work that does not have the character of social necessity is worthless. This way of thinking about work remains simple and unambiguous and is a dominant expression of the more general way in which the relationship between the theoretical social classes in the Marxist perspective, the bourgeoisie and the working class, was thought of. This dichotomous view may be functional theoretically, but materially and socially it is insufficient to actually discriminate between the social strata that make up the dynamic and complex fabric of a society. Historically, the working class brings together subclasses with varying degrees of social heterogeneity, from the urban poor to the impoverished artisans and from these to the lower classes of the peasantry. One of the functions of this heterogeneity is also reflected in the potential for articulating "social consciousness". The theoretical constructs of this consciousness, among which collectivist ideology of the Marxist type is dominant, do not faithfully capture the workings of this subclass distribution, which is reproduced in ways that bring together not only spontaneous ideas and reactions to economic developments, but also elements of historical memory and social myths. This awareness includes among others "the awareness of needs, aspirations of the future, the collective memory of dramatic historical events, [...], of political and labour union struggle [...], the consciousness of succesively suffered deceptions" (Gurvitch, 1964: 96–97). Hierarchies and struggles within the proletarian class seem to be more enlightening in realistically understanding and consistently explaining the failure of the socialist economic system. The sense of exploitation by state, the subjective meanings attributed to the movements of the technical bureaucracy developed within the working class and perceived as superior, the conflicts at the various hierarchical levels in the organizations are all sources and resources in the deconstruction of a class consciousness theoretically claimed to be univocal and the only revolutionary one, when in fact it turned out to be one "harassed, divided, ambivalent and torn by internal struggle", which "can withdraw within itself in an indifferent and prolonged apathy" (Gurvitch, 1964: 97). Work and work productivity, the social significance of work are functions of the mass sociability of workers, of passivity or activism at within economically differentiated class strata, of the degree of acceptance or rejection of the domination of a centralized and collectivist state, of political closeness or distance from other social classes. Work is also a function of structure of social time, of the temporal structure in which the forces of production and relations of production can be situated and measured, this being the case when it is possible for workers to participate actively in economic planning, an expression of democratic self-government and thus control over their own socio-historical time. For working class, time consciousness remains mostly "highly symbolic and does not include any quantification", taking the form of "fatigue, expectation, or hope" (Gurvitch, 1964: 99).

The socialist economic system itself produces a weakening of the substance of the value of labour from which it theoretically and philosophically claims. This undermining is caused by "the economically unproductive use of part of labour power", the material productivity of labour being "separated from its economic productivity" (Casals/Câmpeanu, 2002: 71).

Attempts at ideological grounding and especially at ensuring a strategy for managing a socio-economic order structured not necessarily on organic growth, but on the accumulation of power on the basis of materialistic thinking were constructed and delivered including through the mechanisms of cultural-artistic production. These attempts were necessary in the propaganda economy of the party, but not sufficient to legitimately fill a more general concept of work that often proved to be devoid of content, being no more than the expression of a machinery that only managed to survive through the massive resources of bureaucratization as an essential quality of the planned economy, and which had a perverse effect in that it did nothing really but brake and block the productivity of labour (at the material level) and provide an instrument not for managing (the working conditions of) people but for ruling them (at the political level).

CHAPTER 5

Image and Elements of Film Language

1　Image Concept and Cinematic Structure

Because film is defined by image, the dimension of sensoriality occupies an important place in its reception. This dimension allows the perception of the film image incorporating the representation of objects: "The image is an act which aims in its physicality an absent or non-existent object through a physical or psychic content which is not given in itself, but as "an analogical representative" of the object being targeted" (Sartre, 1986: 46). Image is anything tangible or intangible that allows us to see the world in perspective: "To see an object in space means to see it in context" (Arnheim, 1997: 54). Visual perception is always relational as we delineate the presence of elements based on relationships that exist between them and other elements in the visual field of reference. The appearance of an element in the visual field "was shown to depend on its place and function in the total structure and to be modified fundamentally by that influence" (Arnheim, 1997: 54). The meanings we attribute to objects are influenced by the physical contexts in which they are located: "If a visual item is extricated from its context it becomes a different object" (Arnheim, 1997: 54). The dimension of visual perception is processed in a visual logic involving a cognitive process. It is the space of manifestation of representations, images of forms or mental images understood as "faithful replicas of the physical objects they replace" (Arnheim, 1997: 102). Through representation to each image an idea is attributed and to each idea an image through the mechanism of memory (recognition of shapes and figures that in certain contexts designate certain objects and certain relationships between these objects). In visual practice, there is a distinction between two dimensions of visual perception and thinking: the denotative dimension of image (what is shown in an image) and the connotative dimension (the emotional and cultural associations associated with the elements depicted in the image): "Although all images may convey facts or information, they are rarely reducible to a single, straightforward meaning or message" (Geiger, Rutsky, 2005: 20).

Throughout history, the functions of image have been to establish a relationship with the world. Rudolf Arnheim, in *Visual Thinking* ([1969] 1997), identifies three functions of image: 1) image as sign: "an image serve as *sign* to the extent to which it stands for a particular content without reflecting its characteristics visually" (Arnheim, 1997: 136); between the visual signifier and its signified there is an entirely arbitrary relationship; insofar as images are signs, they serve only as an indirect means, functioning as mere references for the things they designate; 2) image as representation: "images are *pictures* to the extent to which they portray things located at a lower level of abstractness than they are themselves" (Arnheim, 1997: 137); 3) image as symbol: "an image acts as a symbol to the extent to which it portrays things which are at a higher level of abstractness than is the symbol itself" (Arnheim, 1997: 138); the symbolic value of image is defined *pragmatically*, by the social acceptability of the symbols represented.

Films, through images, offer visions of the world. What do we mean by worldview? Lucien Goldmann underlines the instrumental quality of this concept in the analysis of cultural production, which allows us to differentiate between the essential and the accidental in works of art, literary works, and philosophy. According to Goldmann, a world vision "is not an immediate, empirical fact, but a conceptual working hypothesis indispensable to an understanding of the way in which individuals actually express their ideas" (Goldmann, 2013: 15). The making of this world is possible based on two components: the first is given by the technical aggregate of which the film is made up, the second is given by the content that the filmmaker creates. Film images convey sensations and ideas. This double differentiation, morphological and functional, of the content of the film image generates a structure composed of image-sensation and image-idea. The sensation-image concerns the sensory-concrete dimension of the image in the sense that the sensations of the eye are nothing more than quick signs. The technical device that cinema uses only allows the recording and rendering in their space and duration of objects, people and of the relationships between them, while the meaning of these relationships constitutes the contribution of the filmmaker, his vision expressed in ideas technically translated into cinematic images. The transition from signs to the meanings of image is made based on the incorporation and cognitive filtering of the elements and relations between elements that make up a coherent visual body, thus resulting in the idea-image, which allows, through reception, the knowledge and understanding of what is represented.

Gilles Deleuze establishes a double delimitation of the regimes of image in film: the *movement-image* and the *time-image*. These concepts of image are structured on oppositional categories of Bergsonian origin that establish radical differentiations between: matter and memory processes, image and duration, sensory processes and spontaneous thought, the nervous system and different degrees of consciousness. According to Deleuze, *movement-image* corresponds to the sensory system and *time-image* corresponds to the memory and spontaneous thought. Film operates with two mutually dependent elements: the matter of the image (the physical constituents of image) and the image of matter (the expression of matter). The two visual systems theorized by Deleuze reflect tendencies of different natures in film: on the one hand, the tendency to describe the ways in which elements of the external world capture, organize, and structure memory and spontaneous thought through the sensory system, on the other hand, the tendency to discover ways in which the sensory system can be disturbed through pure memory and spontaneous thought. Film "does not give us an image to which movement is added, it immediately gives us a movement-image. It does give us a section, but a section which is mobile, not an immobile section + abstract movement" (Deleuze, 1997: 2). *Time-image*, according to Bergson, naturally extends into "a language-image, and a thought-image": "What the past is to time, sense is to language and idea to thought" (Deleuze, 1997: 99). The depht of field creates a certain type of direct *time-image* that can be defined "by memory, virtual regions of past, the aspects of each region" and this "would be less a function of reality than a function of remembering, of temporalization: not exaclty a reccolection but «an invitation to recollect»" (Deleuze, 1997: 109). The *time-image* quality of the image is structured on three dimensions of object dynamics in the kinematic field and which, according to Resnais, happen: "around the image, behind the image and even inside the image" (Deleuze, 1997: 125). The screen is "the cerebral membrane where immediate and direct confrontations take place between the past and the future the inside and the outside, at a distance impossible to determine, independent of any fixed point" (Deleuze, 1997: 125).

Of the constituent elements of film, the filmic image is the most important component of the cinematic language.

> It is the filmic raw material, but also a particularly complex reality. Its genesis is indeed marked by a profound ambivalence: the image as such is the product of the automatic activity of a technical apparatus capable of accurately and objectively reproducing the reality presented to it, while at the same time this activity is directed in the precise direction desired by the director. The image thus obtained is a datum whose existence is placed simultaneously at several levels of reality, by virtue of a number of fundamental characteristics.
> MARTIN, 1981: 25

The essential characteristics of the filmic image are defined primarily in terms of its relation to the real dimensioned in space and time. The reproduction of the real is ensured based on the qualities intrinsic to the cinema, linked to the nature of the technical aggregate it presupposes. A classic reference for the systematisation of these qualities is Marcel Martin's *The Cinematic Language* (1981):

1. The filmic image is *"realistic"*, that is "endowed with all (or almost all) appearances of reality", are "the ability to objectively reproduce reality". It "renders exactly, in its entirety, what is given to the camera, and the camera's recording of reality is, by definition, an *objective* perception: the authenticity value of the photographic or filmed document is, in principle, unquestionable". The reproduction of reality is made possible primarily by one of the fundamental qualities of film, which is movement and which gives "the specific and most important character of the film image". Another essential component of the image is the sound "by the dimension it adds by rendering the environment of beings and things, which we perceive in real life: our auditory field encompasses, at any moment, the totality of the surrounding space, while the eye cannot cover at the same time an angle greater than sixty degrees and even one of barely thirty degrees, in the case of a careful glance".
2. The filmic image is an *"univocal representation"*, "because of its instinctive realism, it captures only aspects of precise and determined reality, unique in space and time".
3. The filmic image is always at *"present tense"*:

> as a fragment of external reality, it is offered to the present of our perception and is inscribed in the present of our consciousness; the temporal gap is only made through the intervention of reason, the only one able to place events in the past in relation to us or to determine several temporal planes in the action of the film. [...] Every filmic image is in the present tense: the simple perfect, the imperfect, possibly the future are nothing but the product of our judgement when confronted with certain means of cinematic expression whose meaning we have learned to read.
>
> MARTIN, 1981: 28

The filmic image is characterized by concreteness and sensoriality, elements that give a strong *sense of reality*. The filmic artistic image constructs a specific vision of reality based on the fundamental components described above (movement, sound, perception of present time), which are intended to generate and reinforce the idea that what is seen on the screen exists objectively, to eliminate the distance between thing itself and its reflection or (re)presentation on the screen.

Image generates film's essential ability to construct virtual realities that may or may not be activated. Image is "anything, palpable or not, which enables us to get the world in perspective " (Sorlin, 2005: 5). Images are "models or derivations of reality" (Sorlin, 2005: 6). The notion of image helps to overcome the opposition between actuality and representation. Images are not reality, but they are our only access to reality. It is the image that mediates relations between people, between people and things. Some images are produced individually, but most – systems of images – are provided by the societies in which we live, and are therefore virtually common to all members of them.

Because the image is not reality, the fundamental mechanism by which it works is that of illusion – the illusion of reality. It is based on drawing the viewer into a sensory-concrete experience made possible by the technique of film, which complements and refines the human sensory aggregate. The principle of continuous flow (the forms of continuity of the flow of events in narrative or story) is defining for film understood as "the most perfect representation of the art of *moving dynamics*" (Eisenstein, 1987: 248). Addressing the relationship between the aesthetic and the technological in cinematic experience, Parker Tyler describes the socio-cultural nature of perceptual construction in context of cinematic experience:

> It seems to me, not that it [film] conveys more, necessarily, but that it is equipped to convey the most in terms of converting the experience of two things, *world* and *mind*, as respectively subject and object (or vice versa), with a maximum degree of the illusion of the total reality in term of audio-visual spectacle. This is so because film is situated at the source of the whole human apparatus of apprehension: it can affect and utilize the major senses, sight and hearing, into the most satisfying kinaesthetic spectacle of all the senses.
>
> TYLER, 1972: 57

The filmic lens is a mirror that psychologically and technically offers human images which oscillates between (aesthetic) approximations to nature (content) and idealizations of it in different looks (form): "among all the arts, the movies evoke the most urgent sense of comparison and contrast with life itself. Film is the art – and this is a pivotal definition – the finished "form" is the most easily soluble into raw "content" or ingredients of meaning" (Tyler, 1960: 141).

Another important component of filmic image is the relationship between image and word. The word "is a general and generic notion", while "the image has a precise and limited meaning": the film never shows us "the house" or "the tree", but "a certain house", "a certain tree", well specified, so that the language of images would be close to that of populations that have not reached a sufficient degree of rational abstraction in their thinking (Martin, 1981: 27). Martin takes up the example of the Eskimos – given by Jean Epstein in *Le cinéma du diable* ([1947: 56] 27) – who "use a whole dozen different words to designate snow, as melting, powder, frozen, etc.". The ability of film to express "general and abstract ideas" lies in the more or less symbolic character of any image: "a particular man can easily represent on the screen the whole of mankind" (Martin, 1981: 28).

In terms of the functions of the filmic image, an important role is played by the predominance of the expository character of the image, rather than a demonstrative one ("the image by itself *shows*, but does not *demonstrate*") (Martin, 1981: 32). The possibilities of constructing the image can provide beyond the simple representation of a fact "a precise *meaning*" (Martin, 1981: 32) through particular uses of the relationships between the different component elements of the image (characters, objects, places, etc.). The meaning of the image depends on the "filmic context created by the montage" – that is, the technique of joining images – and "the viewer's mental context, each reacting according to his or her tastes, knowledge, culture, moral, political and social opinions, ignorance and prejudices" (Martin, 1981: 33). The solution to the possibility of misinterpretation is "engaging in a critique of the filmic document from within – the film as a signifying totality can never be entirely equivocal", writes Martin – "and from the outside" (the influences that his personality and worldview may manifest in terms of pointing to a particular message of the film) (Martin, 1981: 34).

The filmic image is the result of a particular use of various specific elements of the cinematic language, such as shots, framing, camera movements, camera angles, to which are added a series of "non-specific filmic elements" (which "do not belong to the art of film as such, but are taken from other arts", such as *theatre* and *painting*) (Martin, 1981: 66): lighting, costumes, sets, colour, and acting. Main units of film structure are: shot, scene, and sequence. *The shot* is from the point of view of filming, "the fragment of film printed from the moment the camera motor starts until it stops", or from the viewer's point of view, it is "the fragment of film between two *splices*" (Martin, 1981: 165). *Scene* refers to the time and space in which the film's story takes place; it is therefore determined by "*the unity of place and time*" (Martin, 1981: 165). *The sequence*, a "specifically cinematographic notion", refers to a certain organization of filmed material; it is made up of a "*sequence of shots*" and is characterized by "*unity of action*" and "*organic unity*, that is its own structure, which is conferred on it by editing" (Martin, 1981: 165). A characteristic of this type of unity of film material is that of *unity*. The sequence represents "a series of edited plans characterised by an inherent unity of theme and purpose" (Geiger, Rutsky, 2005: 910). Unlike the sequence, which involves an editing operation, the shot is an unedited film fragment, "the basic signifying unit of film structure" (Geiger, Rutsky, 2005: 911).

The main element underlying the film's construction is the editing. It has the highest degree of specificity of all constituent elements of cinematic art. Editing *"is the organization of the shots of a film under certain conditions of order and duration"* (Martin, 1981: 156). The French theorist distinguishes between two types of montage, *narrative* and *expressive*:

> I call *narrative montage* the simplest and most direct aspect of montage, that which consists of assembling, according to a *logical* or *chronological* order – in order to tell a story – *the shots* that each bring a factual content and contribute to the progress of the action from a dramatic point of view (linking the elements of the action according to a causal relationship) and from a psychological point of view (the viewer's understanding of the plot). Secondly, there is the *expressive montage*, based on juxtapositions of shots, the aim of which is to produce a direct and precise effect by the shock of bringing two images together; in this case, *the montage* is intended to express a feeling or an idea in itself; it is no longer a means but an end; far from having the ideal aim of blurring in favour of continuity, making the simplest links from one shot to another as easy as possible, it tends, on the contrary, to produce the effect of breaks in the spectator's thinking, to make him stumble intellectually, in order to make more vivid in him the influences of the idea expressed by the director and translated by the confrontation of *shots*.
>
> MARTIN, 1981: 156–157

The first function of montage is "to provide images with additional meaning that their content alone would be insufficient to offer" (Gardies, 2007: 39). This is made possible by the montage points that represent "the precise moments where the shots are cut, that means where they begin or end, when they are joined" (Gardies, 2007: 50). Martin describes these moments in terms of their functions: "creating movement", "creating rhythm", and "creating the idea". With regard to first function, montage "is the creator of movement in the broad sense, that is of animation, of the appearance of life, and, if we believe the etymology, this is the primary role of film: each of the images in a film shows a static aspect of beings and things, and it is their sequence that re-creates movement and life" (Martin, 1981: 169). Unlike movement, which "means animation, displacement, the appearance of temporal or spatial continuity within the image", *rhythm* "is created by the succession of shots, according to their length ratios (which for the viewer give the impression of duration determined by the actual length of the shot and at the same time by its more or less captivating dramatic content) and size (which results in a psychological shock the closer the shot is)" (Martin, 1981: 170–171). The most important function of montage is the creation of the idea: when montage is not only descriptive but also expressive. A montage that fulfils such a role must "bring together various elements drawn from the mass of reality and to suggest, by confronting them, a new meaning" (Martin, 1981: 171). The function of creating the idea creates the space for the manifestation of social role of film. The shift from simply observing reality to constructing an idea about the observed reality is the specific difference on which the social importance of film is based. This idea was formulated by Vsevolod Pudovkin:

> To photograph any gesture or landscape from a single angle, as a single observer could record them, is to use film only to create an image of a strictly technical nature, because we must not be satisfied with the passive observation of reality. It is necessary to try to see many other things, which could not be perceived by anyone. We must not only look – but also examine; see – but also imagine; find out – but also understand. For these reasons, editing processes are an effective aid in film … Editing is therefore inseparable from the idea, which analyses, criticises, unites and generalizes … Editing is therefore a new method, discovered and cultivated by the seventh art, to specify and highlight all the connections, external or internal, that exist in the reality of various events.
> PUDOVKIN [*Cinéma d'aujourd'hui et de demain*, pp. 58–59] in MARTIN, 1981: 171–172

In the space of manifestation of the same function of idea creation, an important role is played by a non-specific filmic element, the dialogues (with their "attached forms: the *monologue* and the *commentary*"). The basic unit of dialogues is the word, which has the role of "element of reality and as a realistic factor" (Martin, 1981: 205), constituent factor of the image and whose importance lies in its significant role. Martin emphasises the "realist vocation" of the word, which is based on a certain quality and specific function of the word, namely that it constitutes a "*character identification element*": "there is thus a necessary match between what a character says, the way he says it – and his social and historical situation. [...] *the word represents a meaning, but also a human tonality*" (Martin, 1981: 206).

The specific modes of use (joining and combining) of the corresponding significant levels of verbal language (word) on the one hand, and of the factual content of the image on the other, generate a space of interference with the possibility of constructing new meanings (the function of creating the idea) in the conditions in which what is said in the film fulfils a function other than that of duplicating the content of the visual expression of the filmic image at the level of verbal expression. Two examples of such specific modes are those which operate on the principle of duality: the technique of counterpoint and that of contrast. Duality "between the word and the expression on the speaker's face", "the parallel linking of word and gesture" (Martin, 1981: 209) can generate such counterpoint or contrast effects.

The series of specific features described above configures a value matrix of the film articulated on three major dimensions, according to its relationship to reality: 1. an intrinsic value; 2. an instrumental value and 3. a constructive value.

The intrinsic value of film is given by its value as a cinematic work and derives from the nature of film's practical means of expression, which allows particular ways of thinking and feeling to be embodied in forms, a hypostasis defined predominantly aesthetically. The instrumental value is given by the hypostasis in which the film is an instrument of knowledge of the world based on the faithful rendering, (re)presentation and (re)production of external reality. It is about the level of a passive observation of reality and its unproblematic incorporation into the flow of images that establishes the moments of the cinematographic work.

From all the specific characteristics of the filmic image, the third quality and also an essential value of the cinematographic image emerges, namely the constructive one, in the sense that it does not only reflect, but establishes relationships between people and the outside world, using the outside reality as material. I have shown that the cinematic image creates a sense of reality, it is not reality. It not only indicates, but above all it represents, that is to say it also constructs. Such a quality explains the distinction and distance between reality and the sense of reality generated by this type of image. External reality is presented to us not through its symptoms, but through its images, in its absence, which presupposes the development of certain attitudes towards what is presented to us, presupposes thinking about, referring to the things that make it up. It follows from this that there is not necessarily a linear and intellectual relationship between external reality and its (cinematic) images, in the sense that when a thing acquires reality on the screen and possibly a name, this idea does not necessarily also have a real (existential) referent-thing. The correct definition of a thing on the screen – a projection surface – does not necessarily result in the existence of the corresponding thing. This is the space in which the constructive value (and function) of film is manifested in the imaginative sense.

2 Filmic Narrative: A *What* and a *Way*

The concept of "narrative" as applied to film theory is borrowed from literary and artistic theory. In order to understand the application of this concept to film, is useful to highlight some of the defining elements of narrative, starting from basic references in literary theory. An explanatory perspective belongs to theorist Tzvetan Todorov. Referring to literary theory, Todorov points out that it is not about describing literary works. The following passage, taken from Seymour Chatman's *Littérature et signification*, illustrates the specific methodological foundations of Todorov's literary theory:

> Because to describe is to attempt to obtain, on the basis of certain theoretical premises, a rationalised representation of the object of study, whereas to present a scientific work is to discuss and transform the theoretical premises themselves, after having experimented with the object described. Description is [...] a logically stated summary; it must be done in such a way that the main features of the object are not omitted, but indeed stand out even more strongly. The description is a paraphrase that exposes (rather than conceals) the logical principle of its own organization. Any work is, in this sense, the best possible description of itself: completely immanent and exhaustive. [...] But the description of a work can never lead us to alter its premises, but only to illustrate them. A literary theorist's approach [...] is quite different. If he analyses a poem, he does so not that in order to illustrate the premises from which he starts [...], but in order to draw from this analysis conclusions that supplement or modify the implicit premises; in other words, the object of literary theory is not the work, but literary discourse
>
> TODOROV [1967: 7] in CHATMAN, 1978: 17

Todorov refers to poetry, but the same principle can be applied to other literary genres (plays, novels), genres that are defined by two specific elements, plot and characters. The notion of narrative is defined based on two elements: a *"what"* and a *"way"*. "What" of a narrative corresponds to the story, while "way" corresponds to the discourse (Chatman, 1978: 9). In structuralist theory, narrative has two components: "a story (*histoire*), the content or chain of events (actions, happenings)", and what may be called "existents (characters, items of settings)"; "a discourse [*discours*], that is, an expression, the means by which the content is communicated" (Chatman, 1978: 19). In the tradition of Russian formalists (Vladimir Propp), the distinction is made between two notions: "the fable", or the basic story, "the sum total of events to be related in the narrative" and "the plot", "the story as actually told by linking the events together". The fable is "what has in effect happened", and the plot is "the way how the reader becomes aware of what happened", the "order of the appearance (of the events) in the work itself" (Chatman, 1978: 19–20). Discourses may vary (descriptive elements may take on different values from one fairy tale to another in terms of the economy of the characters), while actions follow a pattern, a fixed form, a structure that is reproduced regardless of forms of manifestation of existence. This is the methodological premise from which Vladimir Propp begins his analysis of Russian fairy tales, using the comparative principle. Propp identifies a series of stable functions of characters (the fixed element), beyond the diversity of images in which they are represented (the variable element):

> The functions of the characters can be precisely delineated. Fantasy tales record thirty-one functions. While not all fairy tales have all these functions, the absence of some of them does not affect the order in which the others follow. Their totality makes up a single composition and a single system, which we find extremely stable and extremely widespread.
> PROPP, 1983: 663

Regardless of the medium of transposition of story and of the modes of expression used, what demonstrates the element of structure resides in what French semiologist Claude Bremond (1964) calls "a layer of a autonomous significance", referring to the method used by Vladimir Propp in his analysis of the narrative messages of Russian fairy tales. What Propp studies in the Russian fairy tale is

> layer of a autonomous significance, endowed with a structure that can be isolated from the whole of the message: the story [*récit*]. So, any sort of narrative message (not only folk tales), regardless of the process of expression which it uses, manifests the same level in the same way. [...] the subject of a story may serve as argument for a ballet, that of a novel can be transposed tos tage or screen, one can recount in words a film to someone who has not seen. These are words we read, imeges we see, gestures we decipher, but through them, it is a story that we fallow; and this can be the same story. That which is narrated [*raconté*] has its own proper significant elements, its story-elements [*racontants*]: these are neither words, nor images, nor gestures, but the events, situations, and behaviors signified by the words, images, and gestures.
> BREMOND, 1964: 4

This ability to transpose the same story regardless of the modes of expression gives the narrative structure. The term "structure" comes from Latin, from noun "structura", meaning "construction" and verb "struere", meaning "to build". Structure is defined by the components of a whole, the relationships between them and the relationship of the parts to the whole: "mutual relationship of the constituent parts or elements of a whole, determining its nature, composition" (Nemoianu, 2013: 17). Linguistically, the structure represents the architectonics of language understood as "a group institution" whose "rules are imposed on individuals", "independent of the decisions of individuals", "a privileged domain of human reality", "source of structures which, on account on their age, generality, and power are of special significance" (Piaget, 1970: 74–75).

The overarching laws of linguistic "structure" are: synchronism, transformation, and self-regulation. Synchronism refers to the independent relationship between structure and history:

> the history of a word may give a seriously inadequate account of its meaning. In addition to its historical aspect language has a "systematic" aspect (Saussure did not use the term "structure"); it embodies laws of equilibrium which operate on its elements and which, at any given point in its history, yield a synchronic system. Since the basic relation in language ist hat between the sign and its meaning, and since meanings are relative to one another, the system i sone of oppositions and differences; while it is synchronic because the meaning-relations are independent.
> PIAGET, 1970: 76

The synchronic language systems are not static: "exclude or allow for novelty (acceptance or exclusion being a function of requirements determined by the system's laws of opposition or connection)" (Piaget, 1970: 11). Transformation is given by the creative aspect of language "which comes to light mainly in individual acts of speech" (Piaget, 1970: 81). The space of manifestation of the transformative function of language is that situated between language understood as social institution and discourse understood as individual performance, within a context which requires both adaptation and internalization of collective norms: "The speaker-hearer whose normal use of language is "creative" in this sense must have internalized a system of rules that determines the semantic interpretations of un unbounded set of sentences" (Chomsky in Piaget, 1970: 82). Self-regulation refers to the ability of structures to maintain internal order and balance:

> they are self-regulating, self-regulation entailing self-maintenance and closure. Let us start by considering the two derived properties: what they add up to is that the transformations inherent in a structure never lead beyond the system but always engender elements that belong to it and preserves its laws. Again, an exemple will help to clarify: In adding or subtracting any two whole numbers, another whole number is obtained, and one which satisfies the laws of the "additive group" of whole numbers. It is in this sense that a structure is "closed", a notion perfectly compatible with the structure's being considered a substructure of a larger one.
>
> PIAGET, 1970: 14

Applying the concept of structure to narrative, it is "a whole because it is constituted of elements – events and existents – that differ from what they constitute" or, in other words, the whole (the narrative) is more than the sum of its constituent elements. In a narrative, events "tend to be related or mutually entailing", they "manifest a discernable organization" (Chatman, 1978: 21). Self-regulation at the narrative level is expressed by coherence, that is, the absence of contradictions between the constituent parts.

From content to expression and from story to discourse, construction of meanings are developed, meanings of the message that film advances, based on the relationships between language and elements of content, that is based on the structure that determines the story understood as "the statement in its materiality, the narrative text that assumes the story to be told", "includes images, words, written references, noises and music" (Aumont, Bergala, Marie, Vernet, 2007: 82), elements that give a complex character to the filmic organization. The story provides the support, the architecture on which the relationships at the level of the signifying material are calibrated: "Film is not only a language, but a concrete universe of characters, things, situations, actions, all of which are realized according to certain meanings. Its elements are linked not only by formal relations, but also in terms of content, and these relations are especially significant" (Goldmann, 1971: 248). Dealing with aspects of film sociology, Pierre Sorlin refers to structure as to a "set of internal compositional laws that, in a film, regulate the organization and transformation of material" (Sorlin, 1977: 161). A representational structure used by Sorlin in film analysis is the so-called "«tree of truth» in which each situation makes possible a choice between yes and no" (Sorlin, 1977: 162).

Filmic narrative, "a history which begins, develops and ends" results from the sequence of images that make up a film and has as its main mechanisms "the heroes and their action" (Steriade, Câmpeanu, 1985: 49–51). "Coherent sequence of fictional events" is the core of the film narrative. The impression of reality of filmic actions is generated by the fact that these actions are essentially human in character, which further leads to the manifestation of processes of identification and projection, based on the reduction of narrative symbols to their signifiers, that is action, which increases the accessibility of film. The temporal ordering of significant relations of existents in the film is a defining feature of narrative. The film is other than a system of signs and symbols. It "comprises images, images of *something*", is "a system of images intended to describe, develop, narrate an event or a series of events [...] these images – according to the chosen narrative – become organized into a system of signs and symbols" (Mitry, 1997: 15).

The strategies for reading the cinematic image that emerge from such a structure are similar to those that Terence Wright describes for reading the visual image in the context of photography. In *The Photography Handbook* (1999), Wright presents three strategies of reading a photograph: 1. to look "*through*" the photograph (as if it were a window – realism) 2. to look "*at*" the photograph (as if it were an aesthetic object – formalism) and 3. to look "*behind*" the photograph (to consider what might have motivated it – expressionism). In a condensed formula for expressing these three strategies for reading the photographic image, the central concern is "recording the subject (realist) through photography (formalist) by a photographer (expressionist)" (Wright, 1999: 38). In a similar logic, in the context of the cinematic image, this involves the recording of a filmic story/narrative (or content) through film (form of artistic language) by a director (vision).

CHAPTER 6

Sociological Approaches to Film

1 Thinking the Film: Crystallised Images of the Real

With an accentuated tendency to cinematically see the world, mechanisms of a screen vision of society become a method of understanding and knowing social world through substantial microcosmoses composed not only of the image of things but also of the image of their duration, microcosmoses of whose meanings and significance are articulated not so much by the formal quality of the images but by their internal dynamics. An essential condition of the contemporary society is that "visual media and messages increasingly dominate mass communications" (Grady, 2001: 83).

A sociological look at the relationship between film and society is structured along two dimensions: the reflection of society in films and society's response to the influence of films. A sociological analysis of film "is always concerned with history – time and its passage and the changes it brings about. [...] Relating film to social and political history is a fascinating occupation, but one should recall that the generalizations offered, however plausible, cannot be proved" (Sobchack, Sobchack, 1987: 450). A sociology of film definitely requires an institutional perspective.

> Ultimately, sociological knowledge of film would surely mean a body of 'true' statementsabout the role of the institution in society, its effects, the irganisational context within which it operates, the nature, attitudes, and preferences of its audience, and the interrelations between these and endless other factors. In short, an exhaustive, intersubjectively verified, consistent, and generally applicable account of the many social worlds of the cinema.
>
> TUDOR, 1974: 15

A pioneer in the sociological research of film is Herber Blumer, professor at University of Chicago, who published in 1933 a study in the Payne Fund Series, "Youth and the Movies". The study was published following a survey of members of various social classes in several American cities (New York, North Carolina, Arkansas, and Illinois). The aim of the sociological research coordinated by Herbert Blumer was to highlight, based on the analysis of 1823 narratives in the form of "written life history or the motion-picture autobiography"

(Blumer, 1933: 3), the types of influence that fictional films exerted on the conduct of young people, insofar as these could be determined based on personal testimonies. Students, college students, high school students, civil servants and workers participated in the sociological research. The research findings highlighted the powerful influence that films had on viewers by conveying and internalizing behavioural patterns, stimulating the imagination, determining conceptions of life. Blumer's study traced the major lines of this type of cultural influence and its forms of manifestation, leaving room for a clearer identification of meanings of these influences according to various sociological parameters: how much and in what way does a particular genre of film influence a particular social class or a particular part of society? The answer to this question depends on a broader knowledge of the general context, social codes and level of social experience. For many people, film seems to be an authentic reflection of life and it does not even occur to them to question the values embedded in films. The need to find one's everyday reality or, conversely, the need to escape from the everyday are the two major functional facets of film.

Nineteen years before the publication of this study, in 1914, Emilie Altenloh published a dissertation entitled "A Sociology of the Cinema: The Audience", based on a survey of 2400 respondents (young people, workers, artisans, clerical workers, engineers, officers, students) in the industrial city of Mannheim and based on data collection on the frequency of visits to 4 cinema halls in the city. The research aimed to describe social representations of film and to establish connections between social grouping, entertainmnet and cultural interests, the nature of people's interest in the cinema. One of the findings of the survey was that the majority of respondents saw film as a source of escape and entertainment, rather than as a factor in education: "Cinema is the place where no intellectual effort is required, where the greatest sensations can be effortlessly experienced" (Altenloh, 1914 [2001]: 288), a cultural form that is generated, according to the author, by the need to counterbalance working time defined by the parameters of industrial society with another form of spending time, other than work time.

The relationship with reality is the strong criterion in defining the essential nature of film: "Most films are complex *crystallizations* of *social reality* and *social imaginary* (reality and imaginary being both objectified in the film and objectively susceptible to study)" (Morin, Friedmann, 1955: 122). Morin and Friedmann, at the Congress of Filmology in Paris, in 1955, set the basic premises for the sociological study of film, drawing attention to the nature of this art and, above all, to the method (content analysis) that would be appropriate for deconstructing film into categories relevant to sociological knowledge. The study of film elements, whether documentary or imaginary, makes sense if it uses parameters specific to sociological analysis: spectator categories, age categories, socio-economic conditions, etc. Systematic and objective analysis of film images contributes to the creation of new forms of sociological knowledge. Films provide useful essentialisations for "the knowledge of 1) feelings, 2) values, 3) ideas, 4) contents of a community" (Friedmann, 1955: 37). Elements of depth at the level of the socio-historical configuration of reality are revealed through an objective analysis of content, films allowing "the overcoming the dangers of subjectivism and relativism" (Friedmann, 1955: 37).

Beyond aspects related to film industry as system of production, distribution and consumption, of great significance "are the films and what their content reveals about the nature of a society's preoccupations and concerns" (Grady, 2001: 111), to what extent they can provide answers to questions explicitly "about political and social developments and their relation to movie representation" (Powers, Rothman, Rothman, 2018: 9)

Dealing with issues related to anthropological nature of cinema, Edgar Morin stresses the intimate link between reality and representation, between the real and the image: "the only reality we can be sure of is the representation, that is, the image, that is, non-reality, because the image refers to an unknown reality" (Morin, 1978: x); "the image can exhibit all the characteristics of real life, including objectivity" (Morin, 1956: 31). Through the elements of language specific to its form of representation, film has the capacity of "concentration of the reality" (Martin, 1981: 30). Hence the ideological concern to adapt the nature of the means of reproducing the reality to the nature of the discourse on the represented reality. As Michel Colin explains, the relationship between cinema and ideology is situated both at the level of the "basic technical apparatus" and at the level of the "content conveyed through the film" (Colin, 1985: 25). The ideological function of the film is structured on two levels: technical (the production process) and political (the production relations). This differentiation in ideological function corresponds to a theoretical differentiation between "empirical ideology" and "speculative ideology" – the double form of ideology – developed by Thomas Herbert. According to Herbert, "*the empirical ideology* is effectively fascinated by the problem of the reality to which the signifier must to adjust to: hence the inevitable "function of the real" attributed to man, as a producer-distributor of meanings on the surface of "reality" conceived as the *milieu* of the human animal" (Herbert, 1968: 79–80). Regarding the second form of ideology, "*the speculative ideology* refers to the connection between signifiers, but fails to recognize it: the difficulty arises in particular from the coexistence of two effects that need to be analyzed together, and whose conjunction ideological theory fails to discern: these are the "society effect", and the "language effect". What it cannot account for is the fact that the *function of recognizing* subjects among themselves necessarily takes place in the form of discourse" (Herbert, 1968: 80). The camera thus plays a dual ideological role: "insofar as it represents the whole of cinematographic technique (it is then put forward as the visible part for the whole of technique) and insofar as it is designed to reproduce reality according to certain historically (and therefore ideologically) determined iconographic codes" (Colin, 1985: 25).

Looking at films sociologically does not mean "to seek in films a more or less faithful reflection of society. [...] Film is part of social reality itself, both through its economic organization and through the mediation of the author, not to mention the reactions that occur, with temporal gaps, between film and reality" (Goldmann, 1976: 71–72). In addition to the advantage of popularity, film has the advantage of multiple possibilities to draw inspiration from major contemporary issues, becoming more and more an instrument of knowledge and expression, seeking to communicate in an appropriate manner a particular issue, based on the "close relationship that exists between film and everyday life" (Sobchack, Sobchack, 1987: 50). Genre films can be examined "as a response to social history and contemporary concerns" (Sobchack, Sobchack, 1987: 279), "not only can reveal the social and historical context in which a film was made, but also can reveal to the contemporary viewer the history of an attitude" (Sobchack, Sobchack, 1987: 452). The socio-aesthetic attitudes embodied in films and in the institutional contexts in which they manifest take forms that correspond to a greater or lesser extent to established value contents, which condition the continuity or, on the contrary, the rupture at the level of duration, history and therefore of the social imaginary with its symbolic forms.

> societies distil a time whose fabric is constituted by the accumulation of events or collective expectations going in the same direction and justifying a defined value system; this flow may or may not be conscious, i.e. explicitly historical and chronological, or not. At the very least, it remains internal to a given type of society and to the assumptions that constitute its living and virtual reality. When a rupture occurs and when, as a consequence, another type of society begins to define itself from within the old type [...], the values on which the world order and existence are based tend to disappear as desirable and substantive values, to harden into prescriptions, into demands that are all the stronger because they no longer correspond to the real human environment. At this point, the new values (not yet defined) are looking for themselves, mere tendencies or directions of mental life, aspirations, expectations of new emotions. These expectations constitute one of the fundamental elements of the overcoming of a society by another society in history, the most positive

elements of the anticipation of the lived over the as yet unlived, an anticipation whose forms are necessarily imaginary.
DUVIGNAUD, 1995: 96–97

Value dynamics within society structure the historical quality of films: "films are historical documents whose place is in the archives: how a play was acted in 19 ... by Mr. X, Miss Y". (Bresson, 1977: 3).

Gilles Lipovestky and Jean Serroy, in *The Global Screen* (2008), offer a view of film culture and its mutations in the context of hypermodern society (since the 1980s) in relation to past ages of film (early 20th century to the 1980s) and describe an explanatory perspective on the relationship film has with society and culture. Although the references of the two authors are aimed at a certain age of cinema (the hypermodern cinema), their approach is useful in that they develop a certain way of thinking about film, regardless of the temporal and spatial context in which it is placed, thus acquiring both theoretical and methodological relevance. The two sociologists propose an approach to film in *"its general economy"*, "an economy of film that is both cultural and socio-aesthetic, transpolitical and anthropological" (Lipovetsky, Serroy, 2008: 24). Regardless of the socio-spatial and temporal sequence in which it manifests itself, film becomes the observer of "the most diverse spheres of contemporary life" (Lipovetsky, Serroy, 2008: 25). Although the framework of analysis is set up for the analysis of cinema under hypermodernity, the principles underlying the thorough analysis of cinema are applicable to any cinematic spaces and epochs. From the overview of cinema of late 20th and early 21st century, the focus is made on a series of particular spheres of observation and analysis, centred on themes, issues, trends and territories specific to cinematic phenomenon. The following fragment sets out the basic methodological principles of such an approach:

> To think about hypercinematography does not mean looking for universal structures of film language or making a simple classification of images, but to highlight what this cinema says about the socio-human world, how it reorganizes it, but also how it acts on people's perceptions and reconfigures their expectations.
> LIPOVETSKY, SERROY, 2008: 24

Like the sociologist, but lacking the methodological tools specific to the sociologist, the filmmaker proposes through the cinematic images of social life both information about facts and social processes and the meanings associated to them. To consider film as a mirror of society can be an attackable premise if there is a distortion, an alteration of forms, of contours that include real components subject to an unavoidable cut-out. But what constitutes a value of film in terms of its proximity to reality is that, despite possible (and sometimes inevitable) alterations of contours, the meaning of things, of the facts presented is not altered. Film, as a work of art, "is not simply an imitation or selective duplication of reality but a translation of observed characteristics into the forms of a given medium" (Arnheim, 1997: 3).

Questioning the relationship between cinema and sociology in *Sociology through the Projector*, Bülent Diken and Carsten Bagge Laustsen argue that sociology has always been concerned with the question of representations, how representations can be related to social reality, and has related to it in terms of correspondence in the sense that if a representation corresponds to the represented reality more or less, then the most important goal becomes the construction of as accurate a representation of reality as possible.

> cinema is secondary pursuit that awaits sociological illumination. In this approach, the filmmaker and the sociologist are necessarily in competition because they both offer representations of the social world – and luckily, or so it seems, this is a game the sociologist easily wins. After all, filmmakers are not professional observers of the social world! Consequently, such a conventional approach reduces the study of cinema to a subfield within sociology, to a 'sociology of cinema' [...] To be sure, cinema is today one of the most important arenas for the distribution of lay knowledge regarding social distinctions. [...] Indeed, to the extent that films become popular introductions to social issues and they take poetic as well as visual liberties, social theory cannot avoid a critical engagement with cinema. Cinema has a distinct power to shape and fold the contemporary social (non)relations as well as the most intimate and the most public desires and fears of individuals. In a sense, cinema functions as a kind of social unconscious: it interprets, invents, displaces and distorts the object of sociological inquiry. What films offer is not just a reflection on society; they are a part and parcel of the society they portray. Cinema does not, however, only mirror/distort an external reality but alsp open up the social world to a vast domain of possibilities. Cinema is often an experiment with changing social forms.
> DIKEN, LAUSTSEN, 2007: 4–5

From a sociological perspective, film is a cultural artefact and at the same time a social document containing important social data that need to be deciphered through specific means of researching cinematic representations. Important distinction to be made in the sociological view of film is that between the aesthetic and the sociological, between the artistic level and the nature of the contexts in which one level or the other manifests itself. In the same type of society, in the same ideology, there can be various manifestations of artistic level understood as an aesthetic value measured in accordance with the principles and norms of the making of a work, regardless of its nature, validated and institutionally legitimized:

> Artistic value has no sociological equivalent and cannot simply be translated into a category of social attitude. The same social circumstances can serve to produce highly valuable and completely inconsequential products; that is, they can produce works which have nothing but a common social and political background, which ist o the art critic more or less a matter of indifference. The ideological components can be the same even if the artistic niveau is as different as can be, just as the artistic value can be equally high or equally low when seen from the most contradictory ideological, political, and moral viewpoints.
> HAUSER, 2011: 211–212

What sociology can do, including in the case of film considered as art, is to separate the elements that constitute a cultural product and then to study the relationships between them, their relationships with the ideological structures in which they emerged, the social status of the author and the audience. The sociological character of artistic works, including films, is independent of the psychological motives on which they are based.

Films convey and communicate more than a manifest message. This is where the area of analysis and interpretative work comes in, which deserves careful examination in order to identify, describe and explain the latent structures of meaning at the level of textual, narrative or iconic content. Films represent "meaningful documents with the potential to yield rich insights into the cultures and times in which they are made" (Geiger, Rutsky, 2005: 17). Their analysis allows the observation and revelation of a social world captured and framed in images constituted according to two types of orders of reality: objective and subjective (image as perceived through vision and image created by imagination).

> Essentially, analysis brings films and their narratives into the realm of the social, allowing us to put their effects into perspective, to compare them to other films and other kinds of cultural artifacts, and finally to begin relating the films we watch to the wider world around us.
> GEIGER, RUTSKY, 2005: 18–19

Relating films to the elements of historical epoch in which they are produced necessarily involves not only describing and explaining certain conditions of historical context, but also evaluating film content by its cinematic aspects, going beyond the level of expressing intentions and messages of authors (meaning of film) and extending knowledge to possible structures that favour the revelation of particular ways of understanding film (layers of significance of film) and articulate premises for new ways of (visual) thinking through which both sociological and philosophical ideas on contents of experience can be conveyed, "because the boundaries between film sociology and philosophical reflection have never been as firm as they might seem" (Ferencz-Flatz, 2018: 6).

The work of film analysing makes an important contribution to developing the ability to extend explanatory view of the social world into a wider historical context. According to Morin, fiction is a historically, socially and culturally conditioned product:

> In other words, affective needs and rational needs intertwine to construct complex fictions. These needs are variously determined according to ages of life and society, social classes, etc. ... At the same time, the dominant trends of fiction appear to us as cultural lines of force. We move without realising it from the anthropological to the historical and sociological level.
> MORIN, 1956: 168–169

Alongside the classical factors of socialization, we can attribute to cinema the role of agent in the process of internalization by individuals, groups and communities, of values, norms, practices and representations defining the cultural matrix of a society at a given time. Part of society in which they are made, films contribute to the transmission of the elements on which two essential components of any society are based, socialization and social control. The socializing function of film becomes possible if another essential function is fulfilled, namely that of forming orientations, that is internalized aspects of objects and relationships, which can be classified into: cognitive (degree of knowledge), affective (feelings) and evaluative (judgements and opinions). From functional perspective, film performs a socializing function, both in the classical dimension of the concept in the sense that we represent film as a complex of mechanisms that ensure the assimilation by individuals of the values, norms and rules of society, and as a mechanism that allows a reflexive orientation on the ways in which a society practices the transmission of cultural, social, political schemes. Rather, film develops the latter function in the sense that it becomes a vehicle not only for a passive accumulation of data, knowledge, representations, images about the past, present and future, but also an active factor in development of reaction patterns to elements of traditional culture and conservative character of socializing agents. In this approach, film can be thought of as a factor of social change, providing an institutional response to the fact that not all people are characterized by passivity, that their availability is not absolute.

The intimate connection of films with society generates a specific type of dependency resulting in their documentary value. Pierre Sorlin states that films "are not reality but they never totally get rid of the actual situation; like mirrors which frame, sets limits, sometimes distort, but eventually reflect what is in front of them, films exhibit aspects of the society which produces them" (Sorlin, 2005: 14).

The relation between film and sociology implies identifying in film consumption a mechanism for shaping a range of possibilities for understanding and re-evaluating social reality. Hence the growing importance of cinematic type of cultural socialization of individuals, becoming increasingly relevant, including for a sociological approach that exploits cinematic vision of society in which man becomes more and more a "homo cinematographicus" (Morin, 1956: 3).

The relationship between film and sociology is articulated not only when the former reveals, describes, allows the awareness of certain aspects of the reality in which individuals are situated, but also at a more fertile level for sociology, namely the production of data and sociological knowledge directly using visual methods, and not only analysing visual products. An essential dimension of the relationship between the two is a methodological one. Film, as cinematic reality, is established reality, on the other hand, it is a factor that, in turn, establishes reality, on the other. This underlines the meaning of using film in a view specific to public sociology. Film has a functional value for multiple categories of consumers, in the sense that it indisputably fulfils certain functions: recreational, knowledge, aesthetic. It is an agent of social memory and a factor of conjunctural crystallizations contributing to the definition of social situations and to the articulation of explanatory possibilities on the consensus or disparities that describe groups, communities, organizations or institutions. Like characters in drama, films display conventional deformations of reality, elaborating functional masks for a variety of real or fictional contexts, operating with multiple definitions of reality condensed in "frameworks" understood as social institutions: "a social establishment is any place surrounded by fixed barriers to perception in which a particular kind of activity regularly takes place" (Goffman, 1956: 152). Film also offers a type of setting, only of a different kind, a virtual setting, in which images of the characters or their "appearances" offer clues about the social status of the "performer" who may be a group, a community or a social class, and about the qualities of the structure of social interactions, in a perpetual disciplining of appearances in order to manage ("unleashed") impressions, a disciplining that takes form of a scenography elaborated with the help of socialization processes.

2   Sociology and Film: A Historical Perspective

In *Les Théories du Cinéma depuis 1945* (1999), Francesco Casetti writes a chapter about the relationship between sociology and film. From a historical perspective, the author states that for sociologists, film was for long time only a research object with the aim of highlighting recurrent elements of the social, structures of common knowledge rather than particular features of reality. For long time, sociology has been understood by film researchers as a useful but incomplete research tool:

> For a long time, for sociologists, cinema has been just another object of research: a phenomenon added to the list of others already under study and for which they have to highlight the common nature of social reality, rather than its characteristic features. Something that therefore fits into a wider panorama, but where it ends up getting lost: one of the multiple media: one of the multiple industrial structures: one of the multiple places where a culture is confessed. For the film scholar, by contrast, sociology has long been nothing more than a useful but also incomplete research tool: if it is true that it is important to understand how a film influences social orientations and behaviours, to what extent it reflects the aspirations and fears of a community, or which are the structures of production to which it refers, it is also true that we cannot help but wonder what it is that gives it an often more significant presence than others, from where it draws its depth, which are the horizons to which it is directed, what ensures its identity.
>
>   CASETTI, 1999: 123

Two of the most important theorists to claim important role of sociology in relation to film are Edgar Morin and George Friedmann. Relevant contributions by these authors have been published in *Revue Internationale de Filmologie* and *Bulletin de Psychologie*. In 1952, Morin and Friedmann argued that film is a human fact, in which unity, profound realities can only be understood and explained under the convergent focus of all disciplines that have man as their object. In the authors' second contribution (1955), the content and methods of sociological intervention are described: "any film, whether it's an art film or an escapist film, whether it's about dreams or magic, can be examined as a thing" (Friedmann, Morin, 1955: 121) The implication of this statement is that subjectivity can and should be studied objectively. Films are capable of revealing what the two scholars call "the shadowy areas of our societies that constitute what we can variously call: the representations, the imaginary, the dreamlike or the collective affectivity" (Friedmann, Morin, 1955: 121). Films convey and reflect "customs and habits, values, taboos, real practices and therefore they constitute documentaries, real sociological archives that can inform us about the life and functioning of a society" (Friedmann, Morin, 1955: 79).

Sociological approaches to film are structured around four main dimensions: 1. the *socio-economic aspects* of film; 2. the *institution* of film; 3. film in the context of the *cultural industry*; 4. exploration of the *representations of the social* in film (Casetti, 1999: 125). Theoretical and methodological delimitations that differentiate between film critics whose gaze is dominantly structured on the aesthetic component and sociologists who seek to identify elements of social structure in film practices are useful insofar as they generate effective discourses in terms of the potential for diversifying explanatory and evaluative perspectives on film across different audiences. An integrated view of film as a bearer and producer of multiple imaginaries hinges on the acceptance of the premise that the subjective experience specific to the aesthetic gaze can be subjected to deconstruction and then, through systematic measurement work, reconstructed into categories of socio-aesthetic knowledge. Film as a thing, not just a sensitive apparatus. It is a significant rapprochement between two different structures of visual thinking that can only work together by mutually accepting and validating the underlying premises of each other. This mutual acceptance is not common. However, it is worth noting when expressed in terms of a reflection with important methodological implications: "Films are also objects, not just experiences. In any of them there is a certain amount of thought and craft involved. The quality of that thinking and craft deserves to be assessed first and foremost – and not rhapsodised, as I thought at the time" (Gorzo, 2009: 24–25).

3   Film as Economic Production

Peter Bächlin, in his study *Der Film als Ware* (1945) – *Histoire Économique du Cinéma* (1947), written immediately after the First World War, stresses the importance of the economic dimension of film. This dimension becomes particularly relevant in the context of the capitalist economy in which, according to the German scholar, a film as an intellectual production has all the prerequisites for being a "work of art", but is also necessarily a "commodity" by virtue of the fact that specific industrial and commercial operations are necessary for its production and consumption. Bächlin refers to a relationship of cohabitation between the commercial and artistic dimensions of film.

Casetti describes this approach succinctly in his book, paying attention to the three dimensions in dealing with the economic character of film in Bächlin's perspective. Bächlin emphasises first of all the mass character of film, representing the direct consequence of the industrial structure of film which, in order to survive and live, needs large-scale production, distribution and consumption. Secondly, it examines the organization of the film enterprise: identifying and describing the main stages of the industrial process, the skills required, the corresponding financial implications, highlighting the major role that "risks" (classified into production risks, corresponding to the production stage of the film, and consumption risks, associated with the general market phenomenon) play in articulating the commodity status of film. It analyses the relationships between production, distribution and consumption. Mass character and standardization are the two essential elements common to the three economic stages (production, distribution and consumption). Casetti summarises the description of the essential elements on which this second characteristic is based and by virtue of which it manifests itself, referring to Bächlin's theoretical elements:

> His application involves both using "the most rational form of work possible" and seeking "the highest value of use" (Bächlin 1945). Hence the existence, in terms of production, of phenomena such as the division of roles, specialisation and coordination of skills, etc. (the studio seen as an assembly line where films are produced); or, in terms of consumption; the search for maximum exploitation of *universal appeal* (the film seen as a product that knows no frontiers). Let us add that standardisation "brings with it mediocrity, recipes and provokes continual artistic compromises" (Bächlin 1945); in a film, the signs are the appeal made "to the star system, (to) limiting subjects to certain well-defined categories, (to) propaganda" (Bächlin 1945). At the same time, it should also be pointed out that viewers go to the cinema by their own choice and for personal satisfaction, putting a limit to stereotype and repetition: "The use value of films prevents the extension of standardisation beyond certain limits:

that is why the difficulty producers face is to find a balance between an individual film form and a standard form" (Bächlin 1945).
CASETTI, 1999: 127

Although Bächlin conducted this study in a historical period when video cassettes did not yet exist, the basic principles of socio-economic analysis of film have remained central to all subsequent approaches in this field of study. Another essential dimension of film, the institutional dimension, derives from the extension of the value of large-scale use of films based on economic-industrial standardization processes.

4 Film as Social Institution

Film consumption has a potential in influencing consumers' attitudes, behaviours and social representations, in articulating mechanisms of understanding and criteria for evaluating issues and concerns that describe certain biographical sequences of contemporary society.

The notion of "cinematic institution" is introduced for the first time by Friedmann and Morin: "The cinematographic technique has produced an *institution*: cinema" (Friedmann, Morin, 1952: 95). Film "as *technique, institution, reflection* of a human universe, is a total fact of civilization. It is a kind of microcosm, through which we can find – certainly distorted, stylized, ordered – the imagination of a civilization, the one of which it is the product. By this, it is a matter of sociology" (Friedmann, Morin, 1952: 95). Film as an institution is a product of cinematic technique and is articulated on two dimensions: a dimension that we can describe as formal, related to the aspects of film understood as a cultural industry, and a substantial or constitutive dimension, related to the content of films. Production, consumption, practices and creativity, economic goods and social values, concrete behaviours and mental attitudes, all these are, in Morin's view, constitutive elements of the industrial structure of film. These distinct facets of the same phenomenon or, in other words, the different levels of reality of film are a function of a *"social organization"*, "a device that on the one hand encompasses, giving a sense of belonging, on the other hand dictates rules of conduct" (Casetti, 1999: 131).

As for the second dimension, Morin dwells on what he calls the need for film, that is, the need that leads crowds of people to devote part of their time to film consumption. Morin identifies and describes three characteristics associated with this need for film. The first of these concerns the *universality* of film consumption: beyond the differences that exist at the individual level between consumers of this type of cultural product, differences of taste, of expectations, there is a single body that recognises itself around common instances. One implication of the manifestation of this characteristic is that film has a structural function of mitigating heterogeneity at the individual level in the context of such a common instance and, consequently, of articulating homogeneity at the level of consumer ensembles. The second characteristic, on the contrary, concerns the tendency towards *stagnation*, meaning reaching a degree of cinematic saturation in the sense of film consumption, underlining the limits of universality.

Finally, the third characteristic refers to the emergence of *inequalities*, discontinuities in consumption, which explains the orientation towards researching "the autonomy and the dependence on the need for film in the historical-sociological conditions that envelop, overshadow or alter it" (Morin [1952a: 10] in Casetti, 1999: 131). Thinking and understanding film as a sociocultural phenomenon, as a complex mechanism that brings together diverse components and gives them rhythms and rules, legitimizes the idea of institution. One of the most spectacular institutional dimensions of film is the star. The star understood as a product of a social institution that brings together elements of representation of archaism and modernity in a multiple discourse that ultimately structures an anthropological view of this social phenomenon: "The star-goddess and the star-object, which are two faces of the same reality, send us, one, to fundamental anthropology, the other, to 20th century sociology" (Morin, 1977: 9). The *star-system* Morin writes about is an exclusive creation of American cinema and an expression of the controversial relationship between reality and fiction, character and actor:

> It was the cinema that invented and revealed the star. [...] The star seems to remain at the solar centre of the cinema ... Nothing in the technical and aesthetic nature of the cinema necessarily claims the star. On the contrary, the cinema can ignore the professional actor, his acting, his very presence, replacing him advantageously with amateurs, children, objects, cartoons. And yet, having the possibility of removing the actor, the cinema invents the star: it makes him a special person, even though he does not seem to participate in its essence. The star is typically cinematic and yet has nothing specific to cinema.
> MORIN, 1977: 13–14

The relationship between characters and actors-public personalities establishes the framework that structures a representation of the nature of film itself within social imagination. The performer's hypostases multiply in concrete reality and enhance the balance between the real and the unreal, destroying cinematic convention and transforming it into a plural reality that goes beyond the screen and reconfigures it into related social practices that become as important as going to the movies. The attractions, preferences, and consumption of stars on a large scale become the raw material for a distinct branch of film that produces affective connections between viewers and characters through "imaginary projections-identifications". These "characterize personality in the bourgeois stage, tend to bring fiction and reality closer together and try to feed them off each other" (Morin, 1977: 22–23). Stars are cultural constructs that have primarily a psychological value, satisfying the emotional needs of the masses, their needs being "stimulated and channeled through means of communication that the bourgeoisie owns" (Morin, 1977: 24). Affective life is both imaginary and practical and is regulated according to a fundamental claim, "the desire to live their life, that is, to live their dreams and dream their life" (Morin, 1977: 24).

Ian Jarvie, in *Towards a Sociology of Cinema* (1970) develops a similar approach to that of Morin in using the concept of cinematic institution. He thinks of film as of "a social phenomenon – one social institution among many" (Jarvie, 1970: xiv). Jarvie proposes a broader explanatory approach to what were considered *good* films. His interest focuses on identifying the broad mechanisms that explain the evaluative processes of films, mechanisms that exist at various levels of the cinematic phenomenon: from production and marketing, to representations and audience reflection, to the "appraisal and the sociological factors which may help explain why a film is good or bad" (Jarvie, 1970: xvi). Jarvie outlines two dimensions on which he structures his sociological approach to film: "the interplay between the cinema and the society – the social conditions – it serves/portrays/attacks; the structural impact of films as an institution among existing institutions, not as content among possible contents" (Jarvie, 1970: 7). This approach involves going beyond descriptive boundaries and developing explanatory frameworks based on a "critical sociological methods", an approach structured around answers to four essential questions about film: "Who makes films, and why?", "Who sees films, how and why?", "What is seen, how and why?", "How do films get evaluated, by whom and why?" (Jarvie, 1970: 14) The answers to these questions set the grammar on which major approaches to contemporary cinema operate, in an analytical structure bringing together: production, viewing, experience and evaluation. The production, distribution and consumption of films as basic forms of the cinematic cultural industry, on the one hand, the cinematic imaginary transposed into virtual realities which in turn are embedded in the present reality, on the other hand, become increasingly sociologically anchored, as the relationship with the social present, most often in terms of reflexivity and deconstruction, becomes a recurrent imperative for this component of the cultural industry.

5 Film as Cultural Industry

It was André Malraux who advanced the idea that film is fundamentally industrial. At the end of his essay entitled *Esquisse d'une psychologie du cinéma* (1940), he formulated the following postulate: "Besides, cinema is an industry". The industrial dimension of cinema is the result of "the scale of the technical, financial and human resources required" (in Martin, 1981: 17). The term "culture industry" was first used in the *Dialectic of Enlightenment* by Max Horkheimer and Theodor W. Adorno (chapter *The Culture Industry: Enlightenment as Mass Deception*). The sociological concept of the cultural industry is based in the approach of the two authors on a radically critical perspective on the structural characteristics in which the new industrial orders and new types of products were articulated. Aspects of culture become consequences of these changes in the social, economic and political order, of the phenomenon of mass consumption: "Culture today is infecting everything with sameness. Film, radio and magazines form a system. Each branch of culture is unanimous within itself and all are unanimous together" (Horkheimer, Adorno, 2002: 94). The cultural model in the context of expanding mass consumption is based on "the false identity of universal and particular" (Horkheimer, Adorno, 2002: 95). Standardization and mass production are essential elements of the cultural industry. Mass culture becomes the beneficial consequence of a system based on "standardized forms" and "technical rationality", in an economic system and its corresponding social context in which technology exerts an ever greater power over society, which eventually becomes alienated:

> All mass culture under monopoly is identical, and the contours of its skeleton, the conceptual armature fabricated by monopoly, are beginning to stand out. [...] Films and radio no longer need to present themselves as art. The truth that they are nothing but business is used as an ideology to legitimize the trash they intentionally produce. [...] The standardized forms, it is clamed, were originally derived from the needs of the consumers: that is why they are accepted with so little resistance. In reality, a cycle of manipulation and retroactive need is unyfing the system even more rightly. [...] For the present the the technology of the culture

industry confines itself to standardization and mass production and sacrifices what once distinguished the logic of the work from that of society.
HORKHEIMER, ADORNO, 2002: 95

Such a logic of configuration of the cultural industry explains the concept of consumer as an economic construct. In opposition to those who argue that the standardization of cultural consumption is a consequence of mass diffusion, Horkheimer and Adorno assert that the mass consumption aspect is not a cause but a consequence of a specific economic order: "The mentality of the public, which allegedly and actually favors the system of culture industry, is a part of the system, not an excuse for it" (Horkheimer, Adorno, 2002: 96). Masses are "the mesure but the ideology of culture industry" (Adorno, 2005: 99). A key feature of the cultural industry concerns the high degree of homogeneity of cultural products, a homogeneity which is a consequence of standardization and means the absence of real significant differences between different products. Two relevant examples of this are the difference between the Crysler and General Motors models or the difference between the Warner Brothers and Metro Goldwyn Mayer production companies. The different number of cylinders, the engine capacity may be differences, but only weak ones. The same goes for film, where differences can be, for example, given by the number of stars or the expense lavished on technology, labour and costumes. In fact, the major differences are only illusory. The only standard of value is the amount invested in producing the object, the end product. According to this understanding and way of relating to phenomenon of culture under industrialization, the result is a disintegration of the fundamental value of diversity at a time when the possibilities of classifying something in general are dramatically diminishing: "For the consumer there is nothing left to classify, since the classification has already been preempted by the schematism of production" (Horkheimer, Adorno, 2002: 98). Schematism as a mechanism for receiving, collecting, understanding and interpreting the content of cultural products specific to mass culture is another essential feature of the cultural industry.

> In a film, the outcome can invariably be predicted at the start – who will be rewarded, punished, forgotten – [...] The culture industry has developed in conjunction with the predominance of the effect, the tangible performance, the technical detail, over the work, which once carried the idea and was liquidated with it. [...] The so-called leading idea is a filing compartment which creates order, not connections. Lacking both contrast and relatedness, the whole and the detail look alike.
> HORKHEIMER, ADORNO, 2002: 98–99

Cinema is a structural mechanism with the capacity of crystallizing the fluid nature of perceptions of everyday life and of society. The boundaries between individual and social reality and the cinematic imaginary are blurred through a constant reproduction of this reality in a cinematic one. Due to the increasing sophistication of the specific technological means of cinema, on the one hand, and their efficient use, on the other, the boundaries between real life and cinematically fabricated life become uncertain, susceptible to substitution and mutual legitimization, so that it is no longer clear what constitutes an extension of reality in film and what of cinematically fabricated reality becomes an extension of real life. The idea of identifying film with reality and reality with film is formulated by Horkheimer and Adorno in the following passage:

> The whole world is passed through the filter of the culture industry. The familiar experience of the moviegoer, who percieve the street outside as a continuations of the film he has just left, because the film seeks strictly to reproduce the world of everyday perception, has become the guideline of production. The more densely and completly its techniques duplicate empirical objects, the more easily it creates the illusion that the worls outside is a seamless extension of the one which has been revealed in the cinema. [...] Far more strongly than the theatre of illusion, film denies its audience any dimension in which they might roam freely in imagination – contained by the film's framework but unsupervised by its precise actualities – without losing the thread; thus it trains those exposed to it to identify film directly with reality.
> HORKHEIMER, ADORNO, 2002: 99–100

The cultural industry is a "omnipresent phenomenon" (Adorno, 2005: 100). In the view of the two Frankfurt School scholars, the cultural industry is a particular hypostasis of an economic order, while the film institution becomes a hypostasis of the cultural industry. This approach is oriented towards the structural dimensions of the manifestation of the cinematic phenomenon in the post-war era. The two constitutive levels of this structure are: 1. general trends in the cinema, trends related to processes associated with production, distribution and consumption – standardization, homogenization, commercialization; 2. transformations in the relationship between art and industry, between the aesthetic and the social component, in the sense that the aesthetic declines as a standard of value in the constitution of the cultural product.

In the chapter *Cultural Industry Reconsidered* from *Cultural Industry*, Adorno returns with a nuance in the use of the term *industry*, arguing that it needs not to be taken too literally. He refers to "the standardization of the thing itself" and to "the rationalization of distribution techniques, but not strictly to the production process". Adorno gives as an example of cinema considered "the central sector of the culture industry", in which although "the production process resembles technical modes of operation in the extensive division of labour, the employment of machines and the separation of the labourers from the means of production – expressed in the perennial conflict between artists active in the culture industry and those who control it – individual forms of production are nethertheless maintained" (Adorno, 2005: 100–101).

In relation to this radical and critical approach to cultural industry, there are also more moderate positions, and others that are opposed to it. Sociologist Alberto Abruzzese (1973) offers different perspective on cultural industry. A first difference is methodological, because applying a sociological instrument to the sphere of culture in the context of the development of mass society implies placing the point of reference within it, and not outside it. Abruzzese describes the configuration of mass culture in terms of other parameters, identifying for the cultural industry a history, a rhythm, a dynamic sensitive to particular sequences of historical, social, economic and political development. There are phases of recovery of old social values, phases of projection of new social relations, there are more structured phases and phases of uncertainty, just as there are humanistic phases and technological phases. Abruzzese rejects the attribution of an exclusively static and uniform character to the cultural industry, considering that it does indeed have a compact, but not monolithic, character. Rather, cultural industry is situated on a certain continuum conditioned by social, historical and economic factors, with continuous folds and permanent gaps. Cultural industry becomes a fertile space in generating different dynamics and possibilities. Categories of themes, motifs and figures developed over time are constantly redefined, reformulated, reinvested with meaning and significance according to the context and time when the filmic construction is made. Recovery of myths and traditional discourses coexists with diverse facts and themes anchored in recent past. The passage below reproduces major dimensions of what might be called a dialectic of thematic categories in cinema, in Abruzzese's view:

> Always in cinema, one need only consider the stubbornness with which two traditionally very delicate frontiers are explored, that between culture and nature and that between the individual and society, to understand how filmic stereotypes are direct heirs of the deepest archetypes.
> in CASETTI, 1999: 139

Abruzzese argues that there is a richness of the cultural industry rather than poverty and simplicity. This richness, while seemingly offering us a diversity of possibilities to escape from reality, actually leads us, almost unconsciously, to a zone of reflection on the social we live in, which involves the direct participation of the consumer.

Reflection on this issue can be extended by reference to defining dimensions of culture itself. On the one hand, a material dimension that we can identify in the manifestation of technological phases specific to the industrial development of cinema, on the other hand, a non-material dimension relating to values, attitudes, beliefs, and norms that film produces and conveys.

6 Film and Representations of the Social

This subchapter brings together the main perspectives on the relationship between films content and the socio-historical contexts in which they are produced. This theme entails dealing primarily with the relationship between social reality and its representations. Starting from the premise that reality is a social construction, cinematic reality emerges as a particular type of social construction that has the function both to (re)construct and restitute (represent the past) and to project society in various aspects of its life. What is seen in films contributes to the articulation of a reality with the potential to activate itself through various forms of influence. Friedmann emphasizes the socio-historical character of cinematic representations as an indicator of the deeper tendencies of society:

> It is appropriate to analyze the content of films on a triple level: historical, social, anthropological. We can then grasp, on the basis of concrete examples, how the film reflects, in a more or less clear way, through its stereotypes, its "patterns" of conduct, its myths, both the time and the place from which it comes. We can also grasp the universal contents of films, which express tendencies and aspirations proper to man living in society.
> FRIEDMANN, 1952: 226

Filmic representation is a type of social representation, having the quality of producing elements in the social imaginary through cinematic representations/images that fundamentally define the concept of film.

In the following subchapters I will present three sociological approaches to cinema. Apart from differences between them concerning methodological aspects, the approaches differ in relation to the nature of the function they predominantly attribute to cinema, seen as an industrial product, a cultural artefact or a social document. These approaches focus on the instrumental function in the sense that they define the relationship between film and reality in terms of "reflection", "mirroring", "rendering" of social reality, even if different categories of analysis and meaning are used; there are approaches that legitimize constructive function in the sense that the same relationship is defined by the value of constructing the social, and not just rendering it more or less faithfully.

The three approaches centre around the relationship between film and reality, between work and image, present and virtual, society and cinematic image. These are the distinctions that make up the classical pattern used in social theory with reference to the social fact of cinema. While in its early days (the late 19th century) film's main function was to reflect images as realistically as possible, as phenomenon of cinema developed, it took on a function of a completely different kind, of constructing and questioning reality. The development of this function is exactly the result of those characteristics of cinematic language that generate a *sense of reality*. The *sense of reality* in turn produces a potential reality that is articulated in two steps: initially as virtual, with the possibility of its activation in the *present* reality. The approach according to which film reflects reality becomes unsatisfactory. It does not only fulfil an instrumental function, in the sense that it merely mirrors reality, but also produces it. The relationship between reality and its cinematic copy or image can only be a weak one. Cinema as a social fact not only reflects reality, but is part of reality which it can mirror more or less faithfully. It has the capacity to establish reality in that it allows the generation of a virtual, potential world (endowed with all the appearances of reality), even if it does not come to be activated, it allows those who consume film and participate in this cultural phenomenon to imagine the consequences of actions that have not yet occurred. This is cinema functioning as an indicator of virtual society. In this perspective, the classical relationship between film and reality changes radically in the sense that reality comes to mirror film, and not (only) the other way around.

6.1   *Siegfried Kracauer and the Discovery of the Non-visible Realities*

The function of *representing the social* is linked to the fact that films, including fiction films, always offer a portrait of the society in which they are made. In the theoretical tradition of European film, an important reference in this direction is Siegried Kracauer's study *From Caligari to Hitler* (1947). Kracauer offers an explanatory perspective on the cultural context that preceded the establishment of Nazism. Kracauer's hypothesis is that through an analysis of

German films it was possible to reveal the deep psychological tendencies prevalent in Germany between 1918 and 1933. The perspective of analysis that the German sociologist develops is based on several considerations:

> The films of a nation reflect its mentality in a more direct way than other artistic media for two reasons:
> First, films are never the product of an individual. [...]
> Second, films address themselves, and appeal, to the anonymous multitude. Popular films – or, to be more precise, popular screen motifs – can therefore be supposed to satisfy existing mass desires.
> KRACAUER, 2004: 5

It is true that Siegfried Kracauer proposes a psychological history of German film, but his approach is important in deciphering the values and functions that films are capable of. Why is Kracauer's study important? Because it succeeds, by analysing the latent content of films produced during the period known as *Weimar cinema*, in providing a carthography of aggregate psychological structures of German society as a whole, developing an explanatory perspective, retrospectively, for the social and political developments that marked German history in the years preceding the rise of Nazism. He establishes a model of analysis that has formed the basis of subsequent film studies, including sociological ones. The strong echo that the publication of his study generated had a strong influence on the school of criticism that had developed around the journal *Filmkritik*, yet in Germany the work was not published until 1958, long after it had been published in English.

In his essay *The Mass Ornament* ([1963] 1995), Kracauer formulates the fundamental premise for his critical theory of the culture industry, "from film to photography, from variety shows to Tiller Girls": "The position that an epoch occupies in the historical process can be determined more strinkingly from an analysis of its inconspicuous surface-level expressions than from that epoch's judjments about itself" (Kracauer, 1995: 75). In Kracauer's view, visible world is expressed by surfaces, and the interrogation of these surfaces leads to a "physiognomy" of the world. The foundations of this orientation can be found in Theodor W. Adorno from whom Kracauer borrows the term "physiognomy", while from Béla Balázs takes the idea of cinematic representation as "surface": "Film is a *surface art* and in it whatever is inside is outside", "it is a temporal art of movement and organic continuity, which in turn produce a convincing psychology or a false one, a clear or a confused meaning" (Balázs, 2010: 19). According to Kracauer, reality can be interpreted as a hieroglyph. Space is a social hieroglyph in which social structure and relations are inscribed. What is simultaneously manifested in it is the physical world, the materiality of things. The ability of film to capture and show "infinitesimal movements", "the multiplicity of transient actions" draws attention to a quality of reality that can be considered involuntary. Hence the existence of an underlying latent content that adds to the manifest content.

Kracauer's methodology moves away from the traditional methodological practices of ethnography (observation, interview and discourse analysis); he turns, in an obviously critical manner, to what he called the "unapparent surface manifestations" of everyday life, with the aim of re-examining the meanings that actually appear as obvious, rather than the hidden ones. Making present things visible is the principle on which his theory is based and which guides this type of empirical approach. Filmic reality is much richer than everyday perception. What distinguishes film as a form of aesthetic media is precisely its ability to make physical reality visible. Therein lies the essential quality of film. But it is not only the specific characteristics of language of cinema, but above all a certain perceptual capacity that must be present for this ability to be fully manifested. Kracauer highlights a technical dimension at the level of cinematic device and a personal dimension resulting from the sensory, cultural and psychological disposition of the perceptual apparatus.

> film is essentially an extention of photography and therefore shares with this medium a marked affinity for the visible world around us. Films come into their own when they record and reveal phisical reality. [...] [film is] a flow of random events involving both humans and inanimate objects.
> KRACAUER [1960: IX–X] in KOCH, 2000: 102

As Miriam Bratu Hansen points out in the introduction to Kracauer's *Theory of Film* (reprinted in 1997), visible worlds – physical realities – are different. She gives the example of a theatre performance and the example of a painting, both of which are real and can be perceived. But the reality that is the essential concern for film is "the existing phisical reality – the transitory world we live in". A common expression associated with this object of film – physical reality – is "camera-reality" (Kracauer, 1997: 28).

A description of the principles underlying not only Kracauer's critical method, but a certain philosophical position of his embedded in the very theory of film he developed is found in a letter to Theodor W. Adorno from February 1949, before the publication of his work entitled *Theory of Film* (text reffered to by Gertrud Koch (2000)). The removal of the cinematic lens from the general and its focus on the particular, the individual, the fragmentary are the elements that define his methodological thinking. Kracauer proposes a methodological approach based on the principle of individualization, in the sense that the focus shifts from the whole to the part, from the general to the individual, attributing to the part, the particular (the individual, the object) a revealing function for the knowledge and understanding of the whole (the group, society). The part is invested with the value of a signifier for the whole (signified) with the possibility of substitution. The whole becomes knowable through the analysis and interpretation of the individual part. From the perspective of classical methodological kit, Kracauer's method is placed in the tradition of methodological individualism, in opposition to the holistic tradition.

> In this book, again, film will only be an excuse. I wish to show what aesthetics laws and *affinities* to certain themes are developed by a medium which is fully the product of an age in which scientific interest in the links between the smallest elements is increasingly surpassing the dynamism of major ideas that embrace the whole human being, and 'transcending' our sensitivity to such ideas. [...] Or, to couch it in the language of film: the aesthetics of film can be assigned to an epoch in which the old 'long-shot' perspective, which belived that it in some way focused on the absolute, is replaced by a 'close-up' perspective, which instead sheds light on the meaning of individuated things, of the fragment.
> KRACAUER in KOCH, 2000: 95-96

The constitutive elements of film theory and method developed by Kracauer developsann understanding of films in terms of their function to reveal a reality that is present but at the same time almost unobservable, that is, to show things that are not ordinarily seen, phenomena beyond the level of consciousness, certain aspects of the external world that can be called "special modes of reality". The idea of such function is succinctly and suggestively expressed in a statement about film formulated by Luis Buñuel: "I ask that a film *discover* something for me" (in Kracauer, 1997: 46).

Kracauer's method is referential precisely because of the simplicity with which it relates filmic representations to reality. One important contribution of Kracauer to the development of a theoretical and methodological approach that goes beyond the limits of some aestheticizing perspectives, typical of specialized criticism, is developing a type of filmic analysis from a historical and, above all, a sociological angle, in the sense that film provides mirrors of society, having the necessary language skills to reflect some of the most secret aspects and subtle tensions existing within it.

6.2 Marc Ferro and Film as Witness: A Counter-Analysis of Society

Another approach to the relationship between film and society belongs to Marc Ferro, who is concerned with the relationship between film and history. Paraphrasing Marc Ferro, who in his book *Cinéma et Histoire* (1977) referred to the intimate link between history and cinema, we can say that the sociological reading of a film and the cinematographic reading of society are two axes to be followed in any approach that aims at investigating the relationship between film and society.

The article that presents Ferro's conception of the relationship between film and history, film and society, was first published in 1973 under the title *Le film, une contre-analyse de la société?* Ferro starts from the premise that film is to be observed as "a product", "an object-image" (Ferro, 1973: 114), whose significance is not exclusively cinematic. Film thus becomes a source and agent of history that is not dissociated from the culture that secretes it and its intended audience. Starting from the idea that "in the products of material civilization" of a society can be discovered "a unique documentary material" (Ferro, 1973: 110), Ferro proposes a new way of understanding films. Recognising the growing role of image in contemporary society, Ferro acknowledges the need to integrate film into practice of history, of knowing society. It is not a question of reading film from society, but, on the contrary, one of the possible readings of society from film, whatever its genre: actuality, documentary or fiction, political or propaganda. Film has the capacity to "confess" and, like any cultural creation, it is the bearer of ideological and political elements, of a social reality detached from the formal, ideologically manifest frameworks and representations of a society.

> Actuality or fiction, the reality of which the cinema offers the image appears terribly true; we realize that it does not necessarily correspond to the to the assertions of the leaders, to the schemes of the theorists, to the analysis of the opponents. [...] It [the film] destroys "the image of the double that each institution, each individual, had constituted before society" [...] It remains to study the film, to associate it with the world that produces it. The hypothesis? Whether or not the film is an image of reality, document or fiction, authentic plot or pure invention, is History. The postulate? That what did not happen (and why not, what did happen), the beliefs / intentions, the imaginary of the man, it is as much the History as the History.
>
> FERRO, 1973: 113–114

It is precisely this potential for detachment attributed to film that provides its essential quality of serving to develop what Marc Ferro calls "a counter-analysis of society" (Ferro, 1973: 113). Film has the ability to say more about what is not intended to be shown, it contains the essential possibility of revealing secrets, of exposing hidden aspects of a society, its shortcomings and problems. Film reveals aspects of the relationship with society, with the ideology, it allows to discover "the latent behind the apparent, the non-visible through the visible" (Ferro, 1973: 114), not claiming to create an orderly and rational whole, but rather contributing to evaluate it, "to refine it, or to destroy it" (Ferro, 1973: 114). Cinematic images "help to discover, define, delimit" (Ferro, 1973: 117). Based on the analysis of Soviet films (*Dura Lex* (1925, directed by Kulechov), *Se serrer/Uplotnenie* (1918, directed by Panteleev, the first Soviet propaganda film), *Jours de terreur à Kiev* (1918, author unknown, the first anti-Soviet propaganda film, shot in Kiev under the German authorities)), produced in the historical era of the birth of USSR, Ferro demonstrates how, starting from an apparent content, from the analysis of images, one can discovery the film's latent content and the "*zone of non-visible reality*" (Ferro, 1973: 117–118), making it an authentic testimony of a society bounded in space and time, with its tensions, uncertainties, dynamics, and reactions.

But what exactly did the French historian's cinematic research consist of? Ferro uses a comparative analysis of two propaganda films, a Soviet one (*Se serrer/Uplotnenie*) and an anti-Soviet one (*Jours de terreur à Kiev*). From a methodological point of view, Ferro made a presentation of scenarios and directing elements of films, developing a comparative analysis. The film *Se serrer/Uplotnenie* (1918) had as its author the Minister of Culture at the time, Anatole Lunačarskij. According to critics, the film "reflected the need for the fusion of the proletariat with the intellectual class" (Ferro, 1973: 118). The most important part of analysis begins with the presentation of other features of the film which, according to him, "were not retained at the time":

> The neighborhood delegate came to tell the worker the good news: he has in his pocket a requisition warrant for the teacher's apartment on the second floor. The worker feels embarrassed. He does not dare to soil the luxurious carpet of the hallway. The delegate pushes him: "You have the right to it". Once on the staircase, the worker hesitates again. The delegate rang his bell, rudely shoved him, and spat ostensibly in the stairwell. The warrant of requisition in the hand, the worker does not resign himself to penetrate in the apartment; the delegate bullies him, speaks in master. "You do not have to make manners, you are entitled to it". While at the sight of the requisition, his wife falls into syncope, the

professor welcomes the tenants with all his kindness. He offers them a form of cohabitation. "Not cohabitation, sharing", demands the delegate. Nevertheless, the worker and his daughter are gradually treated as boarders. But while the young girl, who was reserved, remained in her room, her father no longer confined himself to the room that had been allocated to him and where, on the first day, he ate his snack awkwardly. He takes his meals at the common table, and his daughter ends up joining him. Both of them witnessed the violent quarrels between the two sons about the revolution and Bolshevism. Obviously, neither the worker nor the daughter seems to understand anything. Following a fight, a policeman comes to arrest the elder son, who is hostile to the Bolsheviks and whom the detectives identify by his young officer's uniform; they do not even question him. The younger son falls in love with the girl, the old worker introduces the teacher to his club, the Karl Liebknecht Club. He is received as a friend, gives chemistry lessons that are like magic sessions for these uneducated workers. The workers do not know how to express their gratitude to the professor who becomes their advisor, their brother. But the civil war continues; it is necessary to fight. The professor and his young son are with the Reds; the eldest, recently freed, has gone over to the side of the Whites; he is killed in a fight.

FERRO, 1973: 119

The second film included in the analysis is an anti-Soviet film, *Jours de terreur à Kiev* (*Days of Terror in Kiev*). The subject of film is the anti-Bolshevik struggle, in which the national enemy is an ally, so the fighting continues on the Western front; French troops land not far from it, at Odessa. Through a more detailed foray into the film's latent content, Ferro uncovers a set of revealing elements that define the filmic discourse. Attention is focused on script elements and directing details that construct meanings and signifiers associated with a plane *not visible* at a first reading of the film. Characteristics associated with different categories of characters (social classes) provide a framework for the configuration of two structures of ideological oppositions between Bolsheviks and bourgeois.

> Among the Bolsheviks, promiscuity and turpitude reign: "and these are the people who rule". They throw a master driver to the ground, beat him up, take his belongings, rob him, take his car. At the police station, which is a real tobacco factory, alcohol flows freely; the inspectors are arrogant with the citizens, cowardly with their superiors; fear sweats from all sides. In the work camp, the person in charge is a bourgeois who has joined

> the army, and he is all the more intractable with the victims; this sadist "has no respect for white hairs nor for patriots". The other young rallied bourgeois is a traitor; he informs the Bolsheviks of what his friends are preparing. In contact with the Bolsheviks he is seen to deteriorate. In the bourgeoisie, on the contrary, order, honesty, uprightness. When the young thugs come to his house, sit at his table, finish his meal, the old man remains dignified. This drama tests his wife, who faints. After cursing his daughter, she embraces her when she wants to help her parents: until the end, she will show that she is a good mother.
> FERRO, 1973: 120

Based on the analysis of these two films made only a few months apart, Ferro shows that, although they are in opposition to each other in terms of the objectives assumed, these films actually have the same structure. Ferro's main points are as follows:

1. Both films deal with the relationship between winners of October 1917 and small bourgeoisie;
2. The objective is to demonstrate that fusion of classes is possible, respectively impossible;
3. The dramatic motive is given in both films by the situation of expulsion from or sharing of a bourgeois apartment. The mother is the most sensitive character in relation to other family members;
4. With the revolution, political disputes erupt within the family, dissolving it;
5. The final sequences are tragic, but, through two reverse omissions, we see neither the son hostile to the Bolsheviks dying nor the young bourgeois girl rallied to the Bolsheviks adapting to the new regime.

Other equivalences and similarities in the scripts of films are analysed: in both, the activists are not working people. In the first film, it is the district deputy who makes all the decisions, the worker just obeys. In the second film, the Bolsheviks are soldiers, a valet, a bourgeois, but never workers. Another similarity is that in both films, the closeness of the social classes is based on a love story. However, Ferro points out, there is an important difference: in *Jours de terreur*, the initiative comes from the young bourgeois girl who has left home, which was not "appropriate"; in the first film, *Se serrer*, it is the cadet son who falls in love; the worker keeps a very reserved attitude, indicating his good upbringing. Ferro states that the two films *"define good or evil from the same sign, the behavior of the girl"* (Ferro, 1973: 120).

Ferro actually performs a reconstruction of a historical, social and political experience and at the same time constructs a critical tool for reading film recovering a representation of social reality, revealing meanings associated with social and historical cinematic experiences omitted by the filter of the era in which they took place.

Ferro's theoretical and methodological model of the relationship between society and ideology in film is based on the relationship between film and manifest content, on the one hand, and area of social reality and latent content, on the other. But how are these structural elements integrated in an approach of reconstructing social experience of history? First of all, the film (fiction) offers us images of reality that are revealed at the manifest level, apparent content of filmic narrative, and that are easily accessible even at a first reading of the film. The identification of constructions of meaning deriving from script and directing elements becomes possible if applying a systematic method of identifying revelators, using specific research procedures and bringing into a visible plane non-visible elements associated with zones of reality. The two perspectives of reading allow the researcher to reconfigure the intimate relationships between fiction and reality.

It should be noted, however, that an extension of the visible does not also become a condition for a perfect mirroring of the reality of society: "the description and picture of a society that a film offers are always relative and mediated through a series of filters, screens, representative systems" (in Garçon, 1992: 26). Marc Ferro considers film a "privileged source allowing a novel approach"; is the assumption of this counter-analysis of society, according to which the film image is considered "more revealing of social repression than print sources" (in Garçon, 1992: 30). In Ferro's view, the fundamental purpose of any historical approach is the "re-enactment of a social experience", the resulting function being the "recomposition of the spectators' critical apparatus" (in Garçon, 1992: 17). This makes sense of a legitimizing vision of "reading of history or society through a filmic analysis that is therefore less concerned with the production of meaning than with the history of representations. Film becomes a cultural document, in the sociological or even anthropological sense of the term" (in Garçon, 1992: 30).

In this subchapter dedicated to Marc Ferro's theoretical and empirical development I have presented elements of a scientific approach that outlines a basic quality of film, that of revealing historical and social truths. In the following sub-chapter I will present an approach that emphasizes the function of cinematic image of knowing and influencing the way people perceive the world. Images themselves become more and more genuine agent of socialization, in the sense that they are the most effective and useful vehicles for internalizing dominant values and norms in society.

6.3 Pierre Sorlin and the Filmic Construction

Pierre Sorlin considers films not from the point of view of the work of art nor from the point of view of the type of cinematographic language, but "as images (made up of sounds, pictures and words) available in contemporary society" (Sorlin, 2005: 9). Films are made of "visual and verbal images, borrowed from the actual world and and artifically reproduced" (Sorlin, 2005: 11). Images are "our key to the world" and "shape our perception and knowledge" (Sorlin, 2005: 12).

> "Image" is defined here as anything, palpable or not, which enables us to get the world in perspective. We cannot think except in images which are models or derivations of reality. [...] The notion of "image" makes us get over the oppsotion between actuality and representation.Images are not reality but are they are our only access to reality. Our relationship with events and people is mediated by images; some we peoduce for ourselves but most are assigned to us by society we live in and are therefore common to virtually all members of the group.
> SORLIN, 2005: 5–6

Films are "global images" as their materials are combined to portray "situations, actions, individuals or groups" (Sorlin, 2005: 14). Contemporary art of masses, film performs an equalizing function, in that it moves from a panoramic view of society focused on and depicted by major themes to a foreground perspective focused on issues concerning life aspects of different social categories, in not so much historical as biographical hypostases. This shift in focus from the larger scene of history to the scene of individual biography is assumed by film:

> The impact of local problems, of particular situations, can be easilu detected in films; excellent works have already proved how much can be learnt about the history of pupulation by looking at the films it produces. As Arthur Marwick has pointed out, one of the most important reasons for studying film is that it directs historians' attention away from the traditional topics of high politics and macro-economics to matterswhich, affecting the ordinary mass of the people, are also of great significance: life style, moral values and culture in general.
> SORLIN, 2005: 4

The individual's relation to socio-historical situations in which he or she finds himself or herself is increasingly based on images of these situations, including cinematic ones. In defining the relationship between film and society, Sorlin starts from the premise that film does indeed, as Kracauer argues, reflects social reality, except that, by the nature of its means, film is obliged to resort to the fragmentation of reality with the help of specific cinematic operating tools such as cutting, montage, illustration, and recomposition. Film reflects what is considered to be representative of social reality rather than social reality as a whole. This is a filmic construction which Sorlin describes as "the process by which the cinema of a given epoch captures a fragment of the external world, reorganises it, gives it coherence and produces, starting from the continuum that is the sensible universe, a finite, perfect, discontinuous and transmissible object" (Sorlin, 1977: 270).

If Kracauer formulated the issue of questioning the non-visible at the level of the cinematic visible, therefore at the level of the finished cinematic product, Sorlin goes further and questions that layer of cinema linked to the stage of the actual constitution of the film. *The visible* at the level of the film is but a hypostasis of the visible within social reality. The difference between the two is given by the angle of placing the referent in the construction of *the visible*. *The visible* society existing in film depends on the choices of those who make the images that make up the film in relation to what is considered presentable, effective, and accepted by the audience. The selection criteria are found both at the level of filmmakers and viewers. Cutting out a fragment of the social reflects a set of representations, slices of imaginary, mental schemes, perceptual practices existing in society and which meets a high degree of acceptability, considered to deserve to become visible by the cinematic imaginary, to become admired or contested, however validated. This construction of cinematic visible draws in subtle forms and varying ways on recurrent thought structures, ideological anchors and elements of social imagery specific to an epoch. Not all aspects of a social reality have an equal chance of becoming capable of meeting the quality of a potential visibility that is represented cinematically. Not everything that exists and manifests itself in society deserves to become cinematically visible. Film does not operate outside the criteria that society use in determining what is representable, it fragments reality and makes it visible in its own way according to the structures of thought and imagination specific to a society.

Viewed as a "a vast and complex socio-cultural phenomenon", as a "total social fact", which includes important economic and financial elements (Metz, 1974: 9), film is seen as a production machine, as a fundamental institution of contemporary society or as a vehicle in reflecting value structures around which fixed points develop or which guide elements of movement along different socio-historical sequences. Film is "a part of history", "a discourse on the past" (Mazierska, 2011: 1), stores events, institutions, structures and people.

Referring to works of art, sociologist and art critic Pierre Francastel argued that they "are not pure symbols, but real objects necessary for the life of social groups. We have the right to search through them for evidence of the mental reflexes and structures of the past as well as the present" (Francastel [1951] in *Secolul 20* 1971: 148). Like works of art, films are also entitled to be seen as necessary objects of social life, all the more so as screen visions of individuals and groups, biographies and history have come to represent a challenging and effective mechanism of knowledge in the context of the post- and hypermodern visual:

> Each epoch ... brings with it the possibility of perceiving not a world given for all time, but of forming systems based on a certain, limited inventory of human actions and knowledge common at a given time to larger or smaller groups of individuals. Any space ... is both a structure and a provisional inventor of symbolic forms and relations.
> FRANCASTEL, 1970: 30

The attraction to visuality is an intimate constant of all ages and structures people's choices, preferences, interests and feelings, "the discovery of objects being more a function of their social and practical than mathematical significance" (Francastel, 1970: 72). The signs that make up a dominant visual system at any given time are reflections of these choices, preferences, interests and feelings.

CHAPTER 7

Theoretical Perspectives on Culture in Socialism

This chapter presents some of the significant theoretical elements underlying socialist thinking on culture. Presentation of some elements of dominant ideology at Marx is followed by the presentation of several developments of this theoretical perspective: Vladimir Ilyich Lenin's theory of reflection, Antonio Gramsci's theory of cultural hegemony and Louis Althusser's theory of interpellation.

1 Marxist Foundations of Culture in Socialism. The Dominant Ideology

The cultural Communist ideology has its theoretical foundations in the dialectical and historical materialism developed by Karl Marx. In order to understand the context in which a vision of culture was articulated in socialism, few considerations regarding the conceptual elements of materialism in a Marxist perspective are necessary.

The historical materialism developed by Marx is based on the premise that all history, "all *written* history" (Marx, Engels, 2008: 33) is explained by material conditions of existence, by mode of production that exists in a given space and at a given time, conditions and modes made by people under given circumstances. The individual is defined as an active, practical being, a producer of material objects and spiritual goods, who does not live in isolation, but is engaged in a historical and social existence, in a reality which is given by the totality of social relations, relations which are limited by the material bases of social life generated by the mode of production.

According to Marx, dominant ideas are consistent with the values, interests and goals of the dominant social classes in society, but are not necessarily produced and owned by them, and by no means by them alone. Their apparent sufficiency and independence results from a separation between intellectual activity and practical activity produced by the opposition between capital and labour and the division of work in capitalism. This ideology is the output of the social relations that isolate consciousness from existence, the individual from economic society and ideas from their material conditions, forgetting that it is existence that determines consciousness in its real contents, which generates alienation.

The materialist reference to economic foundations of society is based on the analysis of the mode of production which not only explains the mechanism but also describes the history: "The history of all hitherto existing society is the history of class struggle" (Marx, Engels, 2008: 33). Social relations are defined by the modes of production which establish relations of production between people.

> In the social production which men carry on they enter into definite relations that are indispensable and independent of their will; these relations of productions correspond to a definite stage of development of their material powers of production. The sum total of these relations of production constitutes the economic structure of society – the real foundation, on which rise legal and political superstructures and to which correspond definite forms of social consciousness.
> MARX, 1904: 11

In terms of relations of production, an example of this is the division of work inherent to the capital-labour separation, manifested in the institution of the wage-earner and, more generally, in the existence of social classes. Modes of production are determined by the level of development of forces of production, forces produced and inherited from the past (which include not only the totality of the material means of production, but also labour power, its level of development and the way it is used), which in turn generate a certain development of the productive forces.

In such a configuration of economic pattern, contradictions necessarily arise, not only when forces of production can be replaced by other forces of production (as the machine has replaced human labour power), but especially when the forces of production, in their development, oppose the mode of production which generated them in order to impose a new mode of production (from manufacturing to the factory, from manual labour to the machine, etc.). The analysis of the Marxist mode of production enables the understanding of how the concentration of capital is achieved, which ultimately leads to the emptying of the principle of private property; the development of the forces of production based on this capital takes place in such a way that the system of separating the ownership of the means of production from the possession of labour power, of dividing society into classes and of dividing work into specialised activities becomes obsolete: at this stage of capitalism, through revolutionary action, the domination of private property is abolished, the proletariat comes into possession of forces of production, the commodity-worker is replaced by man as a person.

> At a certain stage of their development, the material forces of production in society come in conflict with the existing relations of production, or – what is but a legal expression for the same thing – with the property relations within which they had been at work before. From forms of development of the forces of production these relations turn into their fetters. Then comes the period of social revolution. With the change of the economic foundation the entire immense superstructure is more or less rapidly transformed. In considering such transformation the distinction should always be made between the material transformation of the economic conditions of production which can be determined with the precision of natural science, and the legal, political, religious, aesthetic or philosophic – in short ideological forms in which men become conscious of this conflict and fight it out.
>
> MARX, 1904: 11

The mode of production of bourgeois society, capitalism, considered by Marx to be an obligatory stage in the development of communism, implies the separation of the ownership of the means of production from the possession of work power. In order for labour power to be used, it must be able to be sold and bought, which means alienated work that defines the condition of the wage-earner. Capital is "a social force" which in its formation, reproduction and development involves the appropriation of a part of production generated by performing work, wage labour. The formation and reproduction of capital therefore implies that not all that is produced by work power is fully embodied in wages. Thus, what is known as surplus value is realised through the work performed by the employee. The employer makes a profit from employee's unpaid work. Hence Marx's conclusion that capitalism means exploitation.

The way in which the mode of production is understood and defined also determines the understanding of man in that society: if the unit of economic exchange is work time and if work is a determining factor of production, production is not reduced to strictly economically defined work. Man is neither a solitary individual nor an element of humanity in general, but a historical and social being defined by belonging to a specific mode of production.

The Marxist conception investigates the material conditions of existence, the modes of production and, ultimately, the movement of forces of production, the determinants of action and the constitutive elements of the contents actually thought by consciousness. According to the materialist conception, consciousness is the product of existence, and the social world, the economic world, does not depend on the will, reflections or efforts of individuals whose individual reactions do not find place in society, but on the material elements of existence: "The mode of production in material life determines the general character of the social, political and spiritual processes of life. It is not the consciousness of men that determines their existence, but, on the contrary, their social existence determines their consciousness" (Marx, 1904: 11–12). The formation of ideas, of representations results from the "material behaviour" of people.

> Men are the producers of their conceptions, ideas, etc., that is, real, active men, as they are conditioned by a definite development of their productive forces and of the intercourse corresponding to these, up to its furthest forms. Consciousness [*das Bewusstsein*] can never be anything else than conscious being [*das bewusste Sein*], and the being of men is their actual life-process. If in all ideology men and their relations appear upside-down as in a *camera obscura*, this phenomenon arises just as much from their historical life-process as the inversion of objects on the retina does from their physical life-process. [...] That is to say, not of setting out from what men say, imagine, conceive, nor from men as narrated, thought of, imagined, conceived, in order to arrive at men in the flesh; but setting aut from real, active men, and on the basis of their real life-process demonstrating the development of the ideological reflexes and echoes of this life-process. [...] men, developing their material production and their material intercourse, alter, along with this their actual world, also their thinking and the products of their thinking. It is not consciousness that determines life, but life that determines consciousness.
> MARX, ENGELS, 1998: 42

A synthetic representation of Marxist materialism as a structure of binary oppositions that are part of a broader framework of materialist dialectics, as fallows:

The Marxist theoretical explanatory model is based on the idea of conflict between the two classes of capitalist society: the bourgeoisie and the proletarians. The dialectical relations between them manifest at two levels: on the one hand, at the level of the material conditions of social life (society's economic mode of production), and on the other, at the level of the content of society's ideas. These are the two constituent components of society: the economic "structure" of social life and the cultural "superstructure" of society, the latter being dependent on the former, a manifestation and reflection of it. The superstructure is the realm of ideas, of ideology. Cultural products in general and ideology in particular are used by the ruling class to establish the acceptance by the ruled of the system of values, principles and interests that

TABLE 3 Dialectic configuration of Marxist (socialist) materialism and philosophical materialism

Marxist (socialist) materialism	Old materialism (philosophical) Marxist critique
Socialized humanity: the individual as person, historical and social being	The individual as commodity
Belonging to a given society and mode of production	The individual isolated from the material conditions of society
The practical, active nature of the individual, producer of material objects	Passivity and reflection
The imperative of change/ revolutionary action (the only real, practical critical activity at Marx)	Passive critical activity
Consciousness reflects existence	Existence reflects consciousness
Transforming the world	Interpreting the world

define the ruling social class. The value of cultural production is instrumental, and its purpose is to legitimize the system of power and preserve its domination. Based on the idea that ideology is the expression of class interests, the fundamental dialectical relationship between the ideology of the dominant (bourgeois) class and that of the dominated (working) class emerges.

Theoretical developments on the role and method of culture in socialism developed by Marxists revolve around the relationship between structure and superstructure, between the economic basis of society and its culture and ideology.

2 Vladimir Ilici Lenin and the Theory of Reflection

One form of manifestation of the relationship between material structure of society and cultural superstructure is given by the relationship between existence and consciousness, whose conceptual development we find in one of the most prolific Marxist thinkers, Lenin. Around these ideas of Marxist thought were articulated some of the fundamental premises of theoretical and ideological developments applied to art and culture in socialism. Historically, it was

Lenin who first laid the foundations of materialist theory of culture as a form of manifestation of communist ideology. Lenin's materialist aesthetics is structured on the conceptual categories of Marxist ontology: "matter" (structure), "existence", "consciousness" (superstructure). The foundation that fuses these elements specific to dialectical and historical materialism into the vision of art is the theory of reflection. Reflection is a category of dialectical-materialist gnoseology that describes the nature of the relationship between subject and object, between consciousness and the external world.

> Our sensation, our consciousness is only an image of the external world, and it is obvious that an image cannot exist without the thing imaged, and that the latter exists independently of that which images it. Materialism deliberately makes the "naive" belief of mankind the foundation of its theory of knowledge.
> LENIN, 1972: 69

On the one hand, the relationship between what does reflect and what is being reflected is a logical and necessary one. On the other hand, this relationship is not one of identification, it merely allows an object to be expressed by a subject. The subject has an instrumental value in relation to the reflected object, in that it allows for a potential expression of the reflected object, a significant re-enactment of the object's content.

> "Social being" and "social consciousness" are not identical, just as being in general and consciousness in general are not identical. From the fact that in their intercourse men act as conscious beings, it *does not follow* that social consciousness is identical with social being. [...] Social consciousness *reflects* social being – that is Marx's teaching. A *reflection* may be an approximately true copy of the *reflected*, but to speak of identity is absurd. Consciousness in general *reflects* being – that is a general principle of *all* materialism. It is impossible not to see its direct and *inseparable* connection with the principle of historical materialism: social consciousness *reflects* social being.
> LENIN, 1972: 391

Reflection understood as a copy of reality, as a (mental) image projected through completely arbitrarily chosen signifiers, is rather a principle of order useful for structuring systems of representation and interpretation of reality and for legitimizing strategies to ensure social control. The relationship Lenin describes between consciousness and existence can be translated in a perspective close to hermeneutics, on the level of the relationship between the signified and the signifier. Consciousness is a significant equivalent of the signified, which belongs to another order of reality than the latter, a sign of recognition for something evoked on the basis of the relation between thought, support and the object of the signified (material existence, the external world). Consciousness is a means of expressing and interpreting existence and, through this, a form of its manifestation. If we accept that this consciousness is a form of manifestation of existence (activated mental images of existing reality), this implies a relation of partial identification. If we accept the existence of such a partial identification between existence (the external world) and consciousness (the contents of thought about the external world), it follows that existence is a reflection of consciousness to the same extent that consciousness is a reflection of existence, which would be in complete opposition to materialist thinking.

According to Lenin's (Marxist) conception, there is unity between creation and reflection in the act of knowledge. The underlying idea assumes that reflection is achieved through creation, the subject merely reflects the object. It follows from this that the act of creation is strictly identified with the act of reflection. However, the production of reflection, that is, the act of creation, does not include the circumstances of the production of this reflection, that is, it does not take into account extra-material relations in the realization of the act of reflection.

Reflection results in access to existence, to the outside world. The mechanism of reflection is conditioned by the use of signs, that is, by an operation of mediation, most often represented by designation. Access to existence, to the thing itself, through knowledge of the external world can only be mediated by signs which take on the function of representing the real. We have, on the one hand, an identification of the sign with the real, on the other hand, an identification of the real with meaning. In terms of action phenomenalization, we can reproduce this structure in the distinction between "to show" or "to reflect" and "to let it be perceived" or, in terms of verbal phenomenalization, between "to say" and "to imply". These categories become functional only to the extent that a socio-cultural context is defined, that is, a set of characteristics of the social structures in which these chains of identification manifest themselves. The condition for the functioning of these operations of identification between consciousness and existence, between the sign and the thing itself, is the existence of a consensus at the level of the representations of the signs that condition the reflection, because it is only consensus that establishes the value of truth, reality. And this consensus is in turn only a construction, a convention.

To accept, on the one hand, that reflection of external world is only possible through the instrumentality of signs that are created and conveyed in the same external world and that, on the other hand, signs, being conventionally created, are constantly being created, is to accept that images of reality are a function of changes in sign structures that contribute to the transformation of what is reflected, of what is (re)presented, of the signified, that is, to a dynamic of contents of thought about external reality. Reflection takes part in the construction of external reality. In such an explanatory pattern, the premise and the materialist claim of the fusion between what does reflect and what is being reflected becomes highly susceptible to ideological instrumentation.

3   Antonio Gramsci and the Hegemonic Ideology

One of the most important contributions to the development of the theory of culture in realtion to socialism belongs to Marxist thinker Antonio Gramsci, who marks a new stage in the materialist aesthetic research initiated by Marx and Engels. In one of his writings from the period of freedom, *Culture and Socialism* (dated 29 January 1916, in the socialist newspaper *Il Grido del Popolo*), before defining culture, Gramsci drew attention to how culture should not be conceived, namely: as a body of encyclopedic knowledge, properly, man should not be conceived as a receptacle of empirical data, of facts without any connection between them, which he should store in his mind, like the columns of a dictionary, so as to be able to respond on every occasion to the action of stimuli from the outside world. Gramsci states that such a form of culture is harmful "especially to the proletariat" (Gramsci, Bellamy, Cox, 1994: 9). In this form, the culture only creates people who think of themselves as superior to others simply because they hold in their memory a certain amount of data and facts that they externalize at every opportunity. In such a form he does not identify a culture, but what he calls "pedantry" or "intellectualism" (Gramsci, Bellamy, Cox, 1994: 9). In dealing with the nature of culture, Gramsci rejects the passive character of culture and emphasizes the idea that culture provides the individual with the means not so much to understand as to change the world.

> Culture is something quite different. It is organization, discipline of one's inner self, a coming to terms with one's own personality; it is the attainment of a higher awareness, with the aid of which one succeeds in understanding one's own historical value, one's own function in life, one's own rights and obligations. But none of this can come about through spontaneous evolution, through a series of actions and reactions which are

independent of one's own will -as is the case in the animal and vegetable kingdoms where every unit is selected and specifies its own organs unconsciously, through a fatalistic law of things. Above all, man is mind, i.e. he is a product of history, not nature. Otherwise how could one explain the fact, given that there have always been exploiters and exploited, creators of wealth and its selfish consumers, that socialism has not yet come into being? The fact is that only by degrees, one stage at a time, has humanity acquired consciousness of its own value and won for itself the right to throw off the patterns of organization imposed on it by minorities at a previous period in history. And this consciousness was formed not under the brutal goad of physiological necessity, but as a result of intelligent reflection, at first by just a few people and later by a whole class, on why certain conditions exist and how best to convert the facts of vassalage into the signals of rebellion and social reconstruction. This means that every revolution has been preceded by an intense labour of criticism, by the diffusion of culture and the spread of ideas amongst masses of men who are at first resistant, and think only of solving their own immediate economic and political problems for themselves, who have no ties of solidarity with others in the same condition.

GRAMSCI, FORGACS, 2000: 57–58

In Gramsci's view, the same is true of socialism. Only an intense critical activity of capitalist civilization allows the formation of a united consciousness of the proletariat. And a critique "is something cultural; it does not arise through spontaneous natural evolution" (Gramsci, Bellamy, Cox, 1994: 11). Criticism involves discovering the self as it measures itself in opposition to others, as it differentiates itself from others, and, once it has set itself a goal, it judges facts and events not only for what they signify in themselves, but according to the extent to which they enable the goal to be approached. "To know oneself", writes Gramsci, "means to be oneself, to be master of oneself, to asser one's own identity, to emerge from chaos and become an agent of order, but of one's own order" (Gramsci, Bellamy, Cox, 1994: 11). Such a development of consciousness is only possible by knowing others, by knowing their history, the evolution of efforts by which they got where they are, by which they created the civilization in which they live, in order to replace it with a new one. The ultimate goal in Gramscian conception of culture is "to know oneself better through learning about others, and to know others by learning about oneself" (Gramsci, Bellamy, Cox,1994: 12).

Culture is defined in terms of the capacity of self-knowledge, which has a fundamentally critical dimension since it is based on knowledge of the relationships with others, of rights and obligations in relation to others, of one's place and role in history. As far as art as a form of manifestation of culture is concerned, it is a matter of "the creative spirit of the people", and this creative spirit is a resource for the affirmation of the potential of critical cultural consciousness to create history. The value of culture derives in his view from its potential to act on reality.

In a writing from 1933 (an imaginary dialogue with the French philosopher and communist Paul Nizan) entitled "Literary Criticism", Gramsci expresses some ideas about the relationship between culture and the affirmation of socialism. He argues that a cultural change is necessary to start from below, from where people are actually in cultural relations, evolving towards the national scene to eventually become internationalists. Referring in particular to literature, he argued that it must "sink its roots into the humus of popular culture as it is, with its tastes and tendencies and with its moral and intellectual world, even if it is backward and conventional" (Gramsci,Forgacs, 2000: 392). According to Gramsci, literary criticism had to merge with social criticism, with the ideological struggle to form a new culture (a principle that can also be applied to other areas of culture): "When the politician put pressure on the art of his time to express a particular cultural world, his activity is one of politics, not of artistic criticism" (Gramsci, Forgacs, 2000: 392).

The process of forming a new culture consists more precisely in "theformation of specific cultural currents", which Gramsci sees "as entailing "rational" forms of conformism, in other words the voluntary acceptance and participation by artists in a progressive cultural tendency" (Gramsci, Forgacs2000: 392). What Gramsci rejects are coercive, external ways of generating artists' acceptance and participation in these trends. Acceptance of new cultural trends becomes the result of a process of understanding, so that when artists understand the historical necessity of a new culture, they will voluntarily accept its rationality and, moreover, produce works that will fit into the curve of the historical trend. This construction is based on the idea that it is not a new art that can be created, but a new culture in which new artists, and, consequently, new works of art, are formed, not created. Referring to Marx's observations on "the unequal relationship between the development of material and, for example, artistic production", Gramsci states (in the sub-chapter *Art and culture*):

> It seems evident that, to be precise, one should speak of a struggle for a "new culture" and not for a "new art" (in the immediate sense). To be precise, perhaps it cannot even be said that the struggle is for a new artistic content apart from form because content cannot be considered abstractly, in separation from form. To fight for a new art would mean to

> fight to create new individual artists, which is absurd since artists cannot be created artificially. One must speak of a struggle for a new culture, that is, for a new moral life that cannot but be intimately connected to a new intuition of life, until it becomes a new way of feeling and seeing reality and, therefore, a world intimately ingrained in "possible artists" and "possible works of art".
>
> GRAMSCI, FORGACS, 2000: 395

The acceptance by artists of a new way of "feeling" and "seeing" reality is possible as a result of the development of a critical consciousness, which in turn is possible as a result of social and economic developments in society.

The replacement of capitalist society by socialist society, of the bourgeois class by the working class, inevitably leads to the replacement of bourgeois culture by that of proletariat, culture (a form of manifestation of social consciousness) being, in classical Marxist tradition, a reflection of the economic structure of society. Development of economic and social forces will produce a new culture which will in turn form its own artists and artistic productions.

The relationship between art and politics is predominantly manifested with reference to the issue of the approximations, that is, the distances existing in society between "what is" and "what should be". The difference between artist and politician is given by the predominant orientation of the former towards the sphere of "what is" and the importance given by the latter to the component of "what should be". Finally, a dialectical movement between the two categories can be distinguished. This relationship, which can be considered a "divergent" one, is reflected by Gramsci in the following passage:

> For the politician, every "fixed" image is *a priori* reactionary: he considers the entire movement in its development. The artist, however, must have "fixed" images that are cast into their definite form. The politician imagines man as he is and, at the same time, how he should be in order to reach a specific goal. His task is precisely to stir men up, to get them to leave their present life behind in order to become collectively able to reach the proposed goal, that is, to get them to "conform" to the goal. The artist necessarily and realistically depicts "that which is", at a given moment (the personal, the non-conformist, etc.). From the political point of view, therefore, the politician will never be satisfied with the artist and will never be able to be: he will find him always behind the times, always anachronistic and overtaken by the real flow of events. If history is a continuous process of liberation and self-awareness, it is evident that

every stage (historical and in this case cultural) will be immediately surmounted and will no longer hold any interest.

GRAMSCI, FORGACS, 2000: 396

The idea of the voluntary acceptance by artists of new cultural currents generated as a result of social and economic transformations in capitalist society – to which I referred above – is also explained by the notion of "hegemonic attitude". But in order to see what the deeper workings of this linkage are, I will now turn to one of the central concepts advanced by Gramsci, namely the concept of "hegemony". Closely related to this theoretical-practical principle is that of "historical bloc". The two Marxist conceptual categories, structure and superstructure, form what Sorel called "historical bloc". According to Gramsci, "the complex, contradictory and discordant ensemble of the superstructures is the reflection of the ensemble of the social relations of production" (Gramsci, Forgacs, 2000: 192). The relationship between the two conceptual categories in Marx (structure or base and superstructure) in the perspective of the concept of "historical bloc" is explained as follows: if men become conscious of their social position and their tasks on the terrain of the superstructures, this means that between structure and superstructure a necessary and vital connection exists (Gramsci, Forgacs, 2000: 197). Material forces represent content and ideologies represent form (the distinction between form and content is purely indicative), since material forces would be historically inconceivable apart from form and ideologies would be merely individual fantasies apart from material forces. The idea of "historical bloc" and thus of the necessary relationship between the material conditions of existence and the realm of ideas or ideology is reinforced by one of Marx's statements that "a popular conviction often has the same energy as a material force or something of the kind" (Gramsci, Forgacs, 2000: 200).

Hegemony denotes a form of power or domination. The specific feature of this form of domination is that domination is based on consensus between the ruling class and the dominated class. The ruling class group exercises its power not by "direct domination" or "coercion", but through "consent and hegemony" (Gramsci, Forgacs, 2000: 420). Hegemony means "cultural, moral and ideological leadership" over allied or subordinated groups. In this sense, hegemony is identified with the formation of an ideological terrain, with political, moral and cultural leadership and with consent. Specific meaning of hegemonic leadership by the dominant class lies not in "to dominate" but in "to direct" the subordinate classes. This change of perspective that Gramsci develops in relation to the founders of Marxism lies in the emphasis on the importance of cultural direction, rather than political direction. Starting from the cultural-political relationship, Gramsci outlines a series of binary oppositions: "civil society" versus "political society", "consent" versus "coercion", "direction" versus "domination". However, the relationship between structure and superstructure conditions the double dimension of hegemony: "though hegemony is ethico-political, it must also be economic, must necessarily be based on the decisive function exercised by the leading group in the decisive nucleus of economic activity" (Gramsci, Forgacs, 2000: 423).

Gramsci considers the working class "a new social group that enters history with a hegemonic attitude" (Gramsci, Forgacs, 2000: 393). Proletarian hegemony is defined by Gramsci indirectly when he refers to the philosophy of practice: "It is not an instrument of government of dominant groups in order to gain consent of and exercise hegemony over subaltern classes; it is the expression of these subaltern classes who want to educate themselves in the art of government" (Gramsci, Forgacs, 2000: 424). According to Gramsci, hegemony, understood above all as a form of domination through culture, precedes the gaining of (political, economic) power.

In socialism, one of the most important manifestations of the tendency to create a new culture was establishment of a method of creation on the basis of which artists were supposed to produce those cultural and artistic goods that would serve the political, ideological, and symbolic aims of the ruling class (ruling class as the working class, because for Gramsci, the ruling class could be both the bourgeoisie and the proletariat). This method of creation was called socialist realism. Socialist realism is both a cultural trend and a method of creation, and implies a necessary relationship between culture and politics, between the artist and the ruling class group.

The institutionalization of this method of creation in the context of the affirmation of socialism has significant implications for the status of the creator of art, in that it generates what is called "a double belonging", namely: belonging to a world of art and belonging to a political world. The relationship between the two categories implies the interference of the former in the universe of creation and production of the latter. This relationship further leads to a problematization or polemic of the following kind: the aim of expressing a certain content (ideological, political) in an artistic way can lead to the failure of the work of art. If the artist is guided in his work by imperatives external to him and if what he produces is intended rather to translate into an artistic form a content of ideas expressing the ideological orientation of an era, he becomes a servant in the service of the ideas shared by the ruling class group. In such a situation we are faced with two categories of facts: on the one hand, the aesthetic fact, which has to do simply with art, and on the other, the cultural-political fact, which has to do with politics. The prevalence of the artist in t he personality of art creator (a situation in which the political world has no influence on him) and the prevalence of belonging to a particular cultural-political context and instrumentalizing artistically the relation to this context (a situation in which he consciously and voluntarily assumes an ideological option) are the two main sides of the dialectic of the relationship between art and politics. At the extreme, in the perspective of a political critique, this differentiation can be expressed in the form of two dialectical types: the artist and the artist as "political opportunist" (Gramsci, Forgacs 2000: 398). If we consider the premise that there is a weak relationship between artistic production and its placement in the context of a particular era, this dialectic is justified. If we accept the premise that there is (should be) a necessary and intimate relationship between the content of cultural-artistic production and the set of ideas, values and practices (politics and ideology) that characterize a particular epoch, then a political critique would only be justified if the relationship between the two domains is a top-down one in the sense that politics constrains art. On the contrary, the situation in which the choice to use reality in its social, cultural and political conditions as the working material for the creation of the work (regardless of the nature and type of the artwork) is one based on the artist's reasoning that does not suffer any kind of external interference – this situation is free from any kind of political criticism. This is also the space in which the relationship between culture/art and politics/ dominant ideology in socialism manifested itself, the main interface between them being the aesthetics of socialist realism.

4   Louis Althusser and the Theory of Interpellation

A relatively novel theory of ideology is that of Louis Althusser. Althusser starts from the dominant ideology at Marx, understanding it as the system of ideas, representations that dominates the spirit of an individual or a social group, but attributes to it a quality of a different nature. If Gramsci redefined the dominant character of ideology as hegemonic, situated at the level of the social category of intellectuals, Althusser goes further and configures a quality of ideology that he names *interpellation*.

Marx's dominant ideology is considered by Althusser to be an "imaginary assemblage (*bricolage*), a pure dream, empty and vain, constituted by the 'day's residues' from the only full and positive reality, that of the concrete material individuals materially producing their existence" (Althusser, 2020: 34). Althusser bases his view of the structure and functioning of ideology on two theses: 1. "Ideology represents the imaginary relationship of individuals to their real conditions of existence" and 2. "Ideology has a material existence" (Althusser, 2020: 36–39).

Althusser questions the nature of the imaginary on which ideology is structured and offers another explanatory perspective on this ideological existence. Althusser bases his explanations of ideology on Marx's ideas on the character of ideology formulated in *The Jewish Problem*. According to Marx, individuals construct alienated (that is, imaginary) representations of the conditions of their existence because these conditions of existence are themselves alienated, being dominated by the essence of alienated society, namely alienated work. What is reflected in the imaginary representation of the world in an ideology are the conditions of individuals' existence, their real world. Althusser changes the type of relation between the elements of reference of the explanatory model at Marx and argues that there are not the real conditions of existence that people represent to themselves in an ideology, but the relation of individuals to the conditions of existence that are represented to them by ideology. He places this relationship at the centre of the ideological, that is, imaginary, representation of the real world:

> It is in this relation that contains the "cause" which has to explain the imaginary distortion of the ideological representation of the real world. Or rather, to leave aside the language of causality it is necessary to advance the thesis that it is the *imaginary nature of this relation* which underlines all the imaginary distortion that we can observe (if we do not live in its truth) in all ideology.
> ALTHUSSER, 2020: 38

Any ideology represents, in its necessary imaginary deformation, not the existing relations of production (with other relations deriving from them), but the imaginary relation of individuals to these relations of production and those deriving from them. What is represented in ideology is not the actual system of relations governing the existence of individuals, but the imaginary relation of these individuals to the social relations in which they are actually engaged.

Althusser reformulates the question of the imaginary character of ideology in new terms, shifting attention to an external explanatory factor. Individuals do not construct the imaginary representations by which they relate to the social relations and conditions in which social relations manifest themselves, but these representations are given to them. His question concerns the imaginary nature of the relationship people have to the social relations that govern the conditions of existence and collective life. Why is the individual's representation of the individual's relation to the conditions of existence an imaginary one? And what is the nature of this imaginary? To answer the question of the nature of the imaginary, Althusser starts from the premise that ideas or representations do not have a spiritual existence. Ideology manifests itself through the use of mechanisms and instruments, and the most important device that brings them together is the state apparatus. The operationalization of ideology is made possible by such an apparatus, by the practices through which it becomes existent, material. Individuals live within an ideology, that is, a set of representations of the determined world. Imaginary deformation depends on their imaginary relation to relations of production and class. The imaginary relationship of individuals to the real relations that structure their reality is material in nature. Ideas conveyed in ideology and internalized by individuals are manifested in the acts they perform, acts that are aggregated into practices that are subject to an ordering principle through rituals, standardized forms through which conative reality is organised and regulated., "within the *material existence of a ideological apparatus*" (Althusser, 2020: 42). If for Marx, it is the social conditions expressed mainly in the relations of production that directly determine ideology (the dominant model) without any interface between them, for Althusser, ideology becomes existent to the extent that the ideas that are incorporated into it – through a process of reflection that may or may not have an imaginary character – manifest themselves in the form of individual acts, palpable in the concrete, material existence. The existence of the ideas on which the belief of the individual/subject is structured and made up is material in the sense that "*his ideas are his material actions inserted into material practices governed by material rituals which are themselves defined by the material ideological apparatus from which derive the ideas of that subject*". (Althusser, 2020: 43). Althusser's thesis on the material character of ideology implies accepting as true the premise that materiality is of different natures and that its forms of manifestation can be diverse.

Materiality is the medium through which ideology manifests itself and functions. Any ideology exists insofar as it functions in the material forms of existence. The function of ideology is to constitute concrete individuals into subjects. There is no ideology outside subjects. Any individual who lives within the ideology, within the "truth" of an ideology, is constituted a subject. The effectiveness of the ideological apparatus is so high that the reality established by it appears to us as true and self-evident. One example Althusser gives is that of ritual communication carried out on the basis of conventional greetings, the simplest example of the constitution of individuals into subjects by recognizing the other as different, unique. Similarly, the fact that we designate a certain thing by a certain word and that everyone possesses the same meaning of that thing, recognizes it unproblematically, is an ideological effect, an elementary one. In ideology, everything is presented as obvious. A peculiarity of ideology ist hat it imposes "obviousnesses as obviousnesses, which we cannot *fail to recognize*" (Althusser, 2020: 46). The operation by which individuals are transformed into subjects is called *interpellation*, the mechanism by which ideology works. Ideology exists by virtue of the negation of ideology. One of the effects of ideology is the very practical denial of the ideological character of ideology, through ideology. Individuals have an abstract character, while subjects have a concrete, material character: *"individuals are always-already subjects"* (Althusser, 2020: 50).

The explanatory configuration of the processuality of ideology that Althusser develops from the fundamental economic category at Marx, namely the mode of production in the context of dialectics more material than historical, is based on the use of the notion of structure (without being structuralist). At Marx, "the concept of working class as subject of consumption could be produced directly on the basis of the relations of productions" (Althusser, Balibar, Establet, Macherey, Rancière, 2016: 382). The definition of the capitalist class or of the proletarian class therefore "does not precede that of the social relations of production, but vice versa, the definition of the social relations of production implies a "bearer" function defined as a class" (Althusser, Balibar, Establet, Macherey, Rancière, 2016: 291). Althusser underlines the limits of a strictly economist interpretation of marxism. The political and the ideological, in Althusser's view, are not mere derivatives or economic or technological developments. There is a certain "overdetermination", that is, a relative autonomy of the political and the ideological in relation to the economic and the technological developments. Althusser locates ideology not (only) in principles, but in social institutions, with their practices and rituals. The state apparatus only makes sense in the context of class struggle, of the reproduction of relations of production. Only in this way can the effectiveness of superstructures be established. The ideological apparatus of the state does not result from the realisation of an ideology in general, but the ideology of the dominant class becomes dominant through the realization of these apparatuses, institutions. The establishment of these ideological apparatuses is a function of an uninterrupted class struggle: a struggle against the old ruling classes and their positions in the old and new ideological apparatuses, and then against the exploited class. Ideological apparatuses are "the form in which the ideology of the ruling class must necessarily be realized" (Althusser, 2020: 59–60), they are born at the level of social classes anchored in class struggle, in their conditions of existence, in their practices, in their experience of struggle.

CHAPTER 8

Ideology, Art, and Culture in Socialism

1 Socialist Realism: From Cultural Doctrine to Political Strategy

Socialist realism is a variation of the movement known as realism at the end of the 19th century and claims to be based on theoretical foundations of dialectical and historical materialism. Its specific difference from the terms of the classical aesthetics of this current is that it is given a strong class character. This current has imposed itself both as a communist doctrine in the field of culture and as a methodological principle valid for the creators of cultural-artistic products.

Socialist realism is a vision of the world and a method of constructing ideas and representations designed not only to increase the knowledge of the "main character" – the working class – and its living conditions, but also to legitimize communist ideas, to educate, and thus to socialize individuals politically through cultural consumption. This fundamental agent of ideologizing the relationship between art and reality – education – is represented as an essential factor of social change in Karl Marx's materialist theory, according to which people are the product of circumstances and education and therefore people who change because of new circumstances and new education forget that circumstances are also changed by people and that the educator himself must be educated. Circumstances, that is, those material conditions resulting from the production of means of existence, determine the material life of individuals. Social existence is the expression of material production, and social consciousness a derived form of social existence: "As individuals express their lives, so they are. What they are, therefore, coincides with their production, both with *what* they produce and with *how* they produce. Hence what individuals are depends on the material conditions of their production" (Marx, Engels, 1998: 37). According to the materialist principle that social consciousness is a reflection of social existence, the work of art as a form of social consciousness reflects social existence, that is, fundamentally reflects material conditions and connections in their socio-historical development.

> The production of ideas, of conceptions, of consciousness, is at first directly interwoven with the material activity and the material intercourse of men – the language of real life. Conceiving, thinking, the mintal intercourse of men at this stage still appear as the direct efflux of their

material behaviour. The same applies to mental production as expressed in the language of politics, laws, morality, religion, metaphysics, etc., of a people.
MARX, ENGELS, 1998: 42

What does "realism" mean in terms of a materialist approach to this Western cultural movement? The first thinker and theorist in the socialist tradition to develop a coherent view from the perspective of dialectical and historical materialism on the European realist movement is Friedrich Engels. He defines the notion of "realism" in a letter to the German writer Minna Kautsky (1885), author of *The Old Ones and the New* (*Die Alten und Die Neuen*), referring to "the sharp individualisation exhibited by the characters", Engels writes: "Each of them is a type but at the same time also a definite individual, a "This one" [Dieser], as old Hegel would say, and that i show it should be" (Marx, Engels, 1978: 87). In another letter to Margaret Harkness (1888), the author of the novel *City Girl*, Engels states: "Realism, to my mind, implies, besides truth of detail, the truthful reproduction of typical characters under typical circumstances" (Marx, Engels, 1978: 90). I come back to the category of "type" that needs to be defined and described. This is a category drawn from the theory of reflection developed by Lenin, a unity resulting from the relationship between the general and the particular. The fundamental function of this unit is to reflect the world in its essential characteristics. The typical represents the operationalization of the dialectic between appearance and substance, between the general and the particular. For Lenin, the typical means generalization. In his conception, the general and the particular are not in opposition, but are interdependent categories:

> the leaves of a tree are green; John is a man; Fido is a dog, etc. Here already we have *dialectics* [...]: the individual is the universal. [...] Consequently, the opposites (the individual is opposed to universal) are identical: the individual exists only in the connection that leads to the universal. The universal exists only in the individual and through the individual. Every individual is (in one way or another) a universal. Every universal is (a fragment, or an aspect, or the essence of) an individual. Every universal only approximately embraces all the individual objects. Every individual enters incompletely into the universal, etc., etc. Every individual is connected by thousands of transitions with other *kinds* of individuals (things, phenomena, processes) etc.
> LENIN, 1976: 359

The typical is the basic category in the production of a specific reflection, the last stage of the reflection process.

Starting from the diversity and particularities of experiences in reality, the typical is based on the selection of concrete experiences which are subjected to an operation of abstraction, by eliminating individual characteristics, obtaining a representative particular, an individualization of the material extracted from reality.

The function of concentrating reality, of rendering its essence, makes any typical image more powerful than the thing reflected. One of the elements in which the typical category is best reflected is the artistic image. It allows the integration of both the typical and the sensory, the general and the particular, the abstract and the concrete. In particular, the artistic image of filmic type, because of its specific characteristics, makes it possible to render things and phenomena extracted from reality in their concrete, sensory dimension, in their deindividualized form.

In the materialist view of the relationship between consciousness and the external world, we identify cultural products, works of art as manifestations of social consciousness, the latter operating with images of material existence. One category of images of material existence is given by images of artistic type. In realist art, they are endowed with a knowledge function through the ideologization of the creative process, while the aesthetic function, linked to the ways of instrumentalizing the means of artistic expression specific to art, becomes secondary. This dominance of the knowledge function is a consequence of the imperative of reflection, which becomes a methodological principle both in the conception and elaboration of artistic work and in its evaluation and assessment.

The ideologization of cultural-artistic creations, the redefinition of the ideological criteria underlying the conception and construction of the work of art, the political commitment of creators, the assumption of an ideological task, the work of art (cultural product) becoming an instrument of knowledge, through the process of reflection, of the material conditions of life and work of the socialist proletariat – these are the main influences of Leninist theorizing on culture. On the other hand, the function of knowledge based on the principle of reflection of reality has an instrumental value, in the sense that it is subordinated to another aim which is that of education (which in turn is defined as, on the one hand, final in relation to this hypostasis of the process of knowledge, and, on the other hand, as instrumental in relation to the assumed political aim of developing socialist consciousness). Marx's statement that "the educator must be educated" reinforces the idea of this division of the functions that cultural-artistic creations perform in the context of the affirmation of socialism. The idea of education was inforced with the affirmation of socialist realism, all the more as it was based on the premise that the main actor of social and political transformations, namely the working class, did not (yet) possess an awareness of its own position on the historical stage, and therefore this awareness had to be cultivated. Added to this was another important aspect of a practical reality, namely the level of education of those who were to be the driving force of revolutionary social change in socialism, the working class. Around 1900, illiteracy was a mass problem. In Russia, the data for that period indicate a total of 73% illiteracy in the population, of which 62.5% among men and 83.1% among women (% of the population over school age). For Romania in the same period, the data indicate a total percentage of 78.0%, of which 67.2% among men and 89.1% among women (Murgescu, 2010: 190–191).

It is not by chance that ideologues in the field of culture have turned their attention to the visual arts. And because the most important element of cinema is image, which is in itself persuasive, its use served the propaganda purposes of the ruling class, at a time when the majority of the population could neither read nor write. From this point of view, film played an essential role in promoting political ideas in the context of mass culture.

Compared to other established visual arts, such as painting and sculpture, film also gained its status as a visual art due to characteristics of the practical means of expression that define it: "movement in time" was a principle that was perfectly consistent with the idea of historical evolution in Marxist terms. History is seen as a story which has all the ingredients of a process of maturing man's external world and his inner drives. Film as story has the quality to distort, to organise, condense and select the subjective contents of the psyche and of the real environment in relation to temporal life-line providing a highly coherent picture integrating both: "as history develops, man's interplay with his changeful past is reflected in towns and temples and states and irrigation and finally in *stories* – in images of men's changing lives organised in time" – writes Christopher Caudwell in *Illusion and Reality. A study of the Sources of Poetry* (Caudwell 1946: 186). Cinema provides "a visual art moving in time" (Caudwell, 1946: 253). The quality of visual art is given by two categories: "Projective Laws of Structural Representation" and "Real Action imitated by Real People" (Caudwell, 1946: 260–261). In the present anlysis context, film is of interest not necessarily in terms of its quality as art, but in the sense of its belonging to a cultural system, on a historical level. This is where the problem of evaluating films comes in, not only from a strictly cinematographic (formalist) point of view, but from the point of view of their socio-cultural function.

Lenin was one of the first Russian intellectuals to take an interest in the cinema and in its cultural function. In what follows, I will focus on two statements made by Lenin who, on the one hand, establishes elements of materialist aesthetics, on the other hand, legitimize the position of cinema in history of culture, at a time when its uncertain character as an art was the subject of questioning film in general. In 1922, Lenin stated: "Some are of the opinion that if we give the people bread and entertainment, we will manage to overcome the hardships and dangers of the moment. Bread and entertainment are undoubtedly indispensable. But if bread is to be the food of the body, the art of the theatre and the cinema must become the food of the spirit. That is why the Russian people have the right to an art which finds its substance only and only in a constant search for truth and beauty". According to Lenin, "Of all the arts for us the cinema is most important" ([V.D. Bonci-Bruevici. *Lenin and cinema* in "Kinofront", Moskva, nn. 13–14, 1927] in Aristarco, 1965: 109). These statements highlight the fact that the value of film was not only given by the function of "searching" and "rendering" (reflection) of truth – of knowledge, therefore – but also by the artistic component of film. In 1919, three years before Lenin expressed these ideas, the Communist Party considered cinema "as a means of self-education and self-development of workers and peasants", being cited among "means of education alongside libraries, adult schools, houses of culture, universities, free courses" (on the occasion of the approval of the programme at the 8th Congress) (in Aristarco, 1965: 154).

The socio-cultural function of film defined from the positions of materialism has from the beginning exerted a strong attraction on the intellectuals, politicians and artists alike. Some intuited the immense potential of this art in educating and socializing the masses based on the ideology of socialism, others identified a knowledge function bringing together diverse expressions of cultural practices. One of the most important dynamics was manifested in the very nature of the function of cinema. Eisenstein draws a line between two essential functions: "Our cinema begins with the mass, elemental "protagonist"; the mass is the hero. Then, towards the end of the first fifteen years, the elemental, mass style of the first period grew more individualist on the screen, with a series of separate images, separate figures [...] A whole series of individual figures and characters appeared [...] shown in the whole diversity of their struggle, be it underground or revolutionary; their battles on the fronts during the Civil War and their work for the cause of building socialism" (Eisenstein, 1996: 17). As early as 1935, Eisenstein was already outlining the psycho-sociological premises of an educational function (in a political context) of cinema:

> The majority of people (and here I am talking about myself, but also broadening matters beyond my own personal experiences) approached

> cinema having, for the most part, passed their probation during the Civil War. It should also be noted that our participation in the Civil War and in the Revolution in many cases, indeed in the majority of cases, was more a technicality than a matter of long-term dedication. It could be said that we were in the same position that the "fellow-travellers" in literature were later to find themselves in. It was only with the end of the Civil War that, properly speaking, we saw for the first time the full scale of what we had been party to (perhaps without fully realising it) and this left a unique imprint on our attitude to the raw material of reality. I see the socio-psychological precondition for our perception of the phenomena and people of our revolutionary reality as "types", something inviolable, in the fact that when we returned from the Civil War we were encountering these phenomena for the first time.
>
> EISENSTEIN, 1996: 20

Only in the presence of an awareness of the sociopolitical context in which the film operates could the filmmaker's work ultimately become a sociologically effective activity.

2 Socialist Realism in Romania: Elements of Sociopolitical Context

The application of the socialist realism to cultural policies has known particularities generated by particular features of socialism in Romania. Marxist-Leninist doctrine, socio-cultural policy, collectivization and systematization were the main ideological foundations of socialism. But the ways in which the values, principles, norms and practices corresponding to these doctrinal components were put into practice were specific.

Before looking at the particularities of applyng the socialist realism, it is necessary to present the main elements describing the evolution of socialism in Romania. Some important moments for the articulation and development of the national idea in the Romanian socialism will be considered. These elements of broader historical context (the period 1950–1989) provide a not so much complete as significant image of the context that influenced certain developments of culture, including cinema, in Romania.

From 1953, after Stalin's death, what was called "de-Stalinization" took place, a form of reaction to Moscow's pressures and dominating tendencies on the socialist bloc. This period was also accompanied in Romania by loosening of ideological control over culture until 1956, when (amid the revolutionary movement in Hungary) Gheorghe Gheorghiu Dej reintroduced the drastic line of proletarianism, both to consolidate his position in relation to Moscow and to counteract the reactions of Romanian intellectuals to the consequences of this ideology on culture. In 1955, the Warsaw Pact was signed, when Romania objected to the presence of Soviet troops on Romanian territory. They were withdrawn in 1958, when NATO troops withdrew from Austria. In March 1965, Nicolae Ceaușescu is elected General Secretary of the Romanian Communist Party. At the 9th Congress of the Communist Party of Romania, in the same year, the "complete and definitive victory of socialism in Romania" was proclaimed. The period immediately following was characterised by a weakening of the Party's ideological control over culture. In 1965, the new Constitution was adopted. It provided for a new name for the party – the Romanian Communist Party, and Romania became a "socialist state" (until then it had been a "people's republic"). The Constitution established Romania as a "unitary state". In 1967, Ceaușescu was appointed President of the Council of State and became both the party leader and head of state. In 1967, during the crisis in the Middle East, Romania breaks away from Moscow's policy towards Israel and is the first state to resume diplomatic relations with Israel after the "six-day war". In March 1968, Communist leaders meet in Dresden, meeting occasioned by the situation in Czechoslovakia (where attempts were being made to establish an alternative model of socialism), which Romania's President did not attend. On 21 April 1968, Czechoslovakia was occupied by Warsaw Pact troops, and an attempt was made to establish a pro-Soviet government. On 21 August 1968, Ceaușescu publicly condemned the intervention of Warsaw Pact troops in Czechoslovakia. In 1968, as part of the administrative reform, counties were reintroduced instead of regions, thus a return to a "native" form of organization, rather than one inspired by the Soviet model. In 1969, President Nixon visits Romania, the first American president to visit a communist country. In 1971, Ceaușescu visits China and North Korea, where he becomes familiar with the techniques of promoting the cult of personality as practised by the leaders of the two communist states. In 1971, Ceaușescu condemns the Soviet intervention in Afghanistan and the Vietnamese intervention in Cambodia. In 1972, Romania joins the International Monetary Fund, the first Eastern European country to achieve this status.

The main elements of the political context for the time mentioned are: the tendency of the socialist regime in Romania to autonomise itself in relation to Soviet power and the accentuation of a national dimension which was reflected in most of the socialist policies. The national character of socialism or what has been called the "national-communism" stands out as one of the specific characteristics of this political system in Romania. The "recovery of national consciousness" and "non-interference in internal affairs" became the basic principles of Ceaușescu's political and cultural priorities at home, and in relations with other states, especially the Soviet state.

The idea of nationhood, closely linked to that of unity, was at the heart of Ceaușescu's political priorities and was supported programmatically. Three months after his election as General Secretary of the Romanian Communist Party, in the Report of the 9th Congress of the Communist Party of Romania (19 July 1965), Ceaușescu stated: "The disappearance of the exploiting classes has led to the strengthening of the nation, to the cementing of its unity. Only in socialism can the real community of economic interests, the common socialist culture of all citizens living in the same territory, be manifested in all their fullness, can the unity of the whole people be ensured in the work and struggle to achieve their aspirations for well-being and happiness" (Ceaușescu, 1968: 61, vol. 1).

Another important moment in terms of the clear affirmation of the role of the nation in the process of consolidating socialist society was in July 1972 when, in the Report presented to the *National Conference of the Communist Party of Romania*, Ceaușescu referred to the socialist dimension of the Romanian nation: "With regard to the question of the nation under socialism, it must be said that the victory of the new order has opened the way for the achievement of true national unity, for the strengthening and development of the nation on new bases. [...] The strong affirmation of the fundamental characteristics of the nation under the conditions of the forging of socialist society takes place in parallel with the change in the character of some of these characteristics and with the emergence of new characteristics which consolidate and strengthen – on a new basis – the socialist nation" (Ceaușescu, 1972: 554). In the Report presented to the 11th Congress of the Romanian Communist Party in 1974, Ceaușescu emphasized the role of the nation in the future of socialist society: "The future belongs to a society in which each nation will be master of its own destiny, in which the peoples will work together peacefully for the economic and social progress of each, for the development of universal civilization" (Ceaușescu, 1974: 104). The national dimension is also present in the formulation of the objectives of the political-educational activity which "must start from the knowledge of the past revolutionary struggle of our people, to be based on the traditions of its progressive culture, of the progressive and revolutionary world culture. It must not be forgotten that the people's way of living and thinking has been and always will be the foundation for the development of a truly advanced culture. We must therefore add to the creation of the present the creation of the past, giving due credit to the great achievements of our forefathers, to the advanced heritage of our revolutionary movement" (Ceaușescu, 1974: 93).

The national character of socialism in Romania has determined the specificity of this political regime, as well as the source of deviation from the Marxist development of socialism. On the one hand, Marxist theory has undergone diverse theoretical developments, on the other hand, in line with these developments, it experimented equally diverse modes of application. The particularity of the "national" in experimenting with socialism in Romania is one effect of the derivations made in practice of the Marxist contribution. We are dealing with a context of application producing a nuanced socialism, placed in contradiction with some of Marx's fundamental ideas. An illustration is the association between the idea of "communism" and the idea of "national", which is opposed to Marxist theory. In *The Communist Manifesto*, Marx and Engels write that "the working men have no country": "National differences and antagonisms between peoples are daily more and more vanishing, owing to the development of the bourgeoisie, to freedom of commerce, to the world market, to uniformity in the mode of production and in the conditions of life corresponding thereto. The supremacy of the proletariat will cause them to vanish still faster" (Marx, Engels, 2008: 61). On this one aspect alone (the national character), the distance between Marxist theory and its operationalization in the context of the various socialist regimes highlights the fact that socialism, in its practical reality, has looked quite different than its founding theorists intended. In the case of Romania, the national character of communism was articulated above all as a method of distancing itself from the USSR, with a main political instrumental value and only secondarily with a cultural one.

3   Directions for Action in Film-Making Work

Art was given an important role in building socialism, in developing socialist consciousness of the "new man". The class character defines the artistic production in intimate connection with the socialist consciousness: "The new hero of history – the working class, the people – who have acquired a socialist consciousness, becomes the hero of art, and communist ideas – its ideological foundation: art acquires a conscious historical significance and a vision of the historical perspective of development; the connection of art with other forms of social consciousness (with morality and especially with philosophy and politics) becomes deeper and more direct" (Borev, 1963: 522).

The theory of socialist realism used Lenin's ideological concept of culture and art and applied the theory of reflection in the field of artistic creation.

Socialist reality is the main source of inspiration for the artistic creators who were given the aim of producing realistic images of socialism. The way in which socialist realism was experimented in the Romania is inevitably linked to specific experiences of socialism in general, the most important of which is the national dimension, operationalized both at the level of ideological-political discourse and corresponding cultural policies. In the Soviet space, the one who formalized the theoretical foundations of Leninist ideology in the field of art and culture under the name of "socialist realism" was Andrei A. Zhdanov, the main cultural ideologist during Stalinism. In 1934, at the First Congress of Soviet Writers, Andrei A. Zhdanov promoted the ideological value of socialist realism method:

> knowing life so as to be able to depict truthfully in works of art, to depict it not in a dead, scholastic way, not simply as "objective reality", but to depict reality in its revolutionary development. [...] In addition to this, the truthfulness and historical concreteness of the artistic portrayl should be combined with the ideological remolding and education of the working people in the spirit of socialism. This method in literature and literary criticism is what we call the method of socialist realism.
> ZHDANOV, 1950: 12

In Romania, the one who promoted the ideology of socialist realism was Leonte Răutu, member of the Political Executive Committee of the Romanian Communist Party (1955–1981) and responsible for science, art, culture and propaganda. The idea of forming a new culture along with the establishment of a new society, the socialist society, and use it for building the "new man" is reflected in distorted way in the local version of socialist realism (according to Gramsci's theoretical developments within the Marxist theoretical tradition). In 1972, in the *Report on the economic and social development of Romania in the coming years and in the future, on the improvement of the planned management of society and the development of socialist democracy, on the increase of the leading role of the Party in the building of socialism and communism, on the international activity of the Party and the State*, presented to the *National Conference of the Communist Party of Romania* on 19 July 1972, Ceaușescu stated: "At the same time, under socialism we are witnessing the formation of a unique conception of the world and life, based on dialectical and historical materialism. A new science and culture is also being formed, a new, advanced ethic is crystallising, which contributes to the formation of a new man – the man of socialist and communist society" (Ceaușescu, vol. 7, 1972: 554).

The idea of the major role of art in the evolution of socialist society was expressed throughout the communist period, at top level official discourse. Ceaușescu's view of culture remained within the limits of the Leninist theory of reflection. In the following, I will present the main moments that structured the discursive ideological configuration of art and culture in the context of socialism in Romania, with focus on cinema.

In his speech at the meeting with the people of art and culture, in February 1971, Ceaușescu stated that the duty of artists is "to contribute to the creation of the new man, to the formation of socialist consciousness, to the development of socialist humanism, of those moral virtues that we wish to cultivate in every citizen and that the Romanian people have in their very mental structure" (Ceaușescu, 1971: 12). National art was to be "with a profound socialist content" (Ceaușescu, 1971: 16), with "a valuable content of ideas" (Ceaușescu, 1971: 17), to have a "profoundly realistic and dynamising character" (Ceaușescu, 1976: 59). A main element in the legitimization of art was the intimate relationship between it and "the profound and innovative transformations in our society", which constituted "a living source of inspiration for all those who wish to put their creative forces at the service of their homeland" (Ceaușescu, 1971: 7). The meaning of any artistic creation lies in the existence of a need that it serves. It was considered "an axiomatic truth that, in the end, art, like any social activity, must respond to a need", creative people must "respond better and better to the demands of the people, the makers of socialist society", Ceaușescu argued (1971: 11). Importance was given to the use of creative activities in the sense of transforming them into a vehicle for articulating the construction of an ideological identity, that is, of an imagined or invented man, a new man, therefore of a propagandistic mechanism. Resources for film production were theoretically allocated according to the needs of fulfilment of such tasks and directives related to film content (themes, typologies, discourses). In the same speech from February 1971, Ceaușescu stated: "We spend a lot on cinema and that is why we have high demands. These demands must not frighten anyone; we must organize our work in such a way that we can make films that meet the needs of our society. Of course we have good films [...] But unfortunately there are not many really good films and we should achieve a more radical improvement in this area" (Ceaușescu, 1971: 21).

A month after this speech, on March 5, 1971, cinema was again the subject of the President's criticism, this time the points of criticism were made in a much harsher manner, in his *Address to the Meeting of Filmmakers*: "It seems, however, that there are certain states of affairs which have caused, as our cinema has passed its youth, certain phenomena, so to speak, of "early sclerosis" to appear in the creation of cinema, in its direction and guidance, in its understanding of its purpose and mission. This is why I feel that we need to start by rejuvenating our cinema; naturally, I am thinking of rejuvenation not in the physical sense, in terms of the age of the people working in this sector, but in terms of conception, in an ideological and political sense" (Ceaușescu, 1971: 7).

According to the President, only a third of all films produced in Romania could be considered films "appropriate to the requirements of our time". The "appropriate" character was determined in relation to the definition of film's aim under socialism. The understanding of the cinema within the system of means of education, of training the "new man", had to start from the ethical and aesthetic principles of socialism. The role of cinema was "to understand the meaning of the work of the Romanian people, the future aspirations of our nation, and to convey them through the means of the cinematic art in the most attractive and diverse form, but with the richest and most original content of ideas. [...] With the material base, with the development of the productive forces of our society, comes the transformation of man, the raising of the general cultural level of the people. All this should, in one form or another, be reflected in Romanian cinematic art" (Ceaușescu, 1971: 13).

The blame for the unsatisfactory state of cinema, in President's view, was attributed both to film's governing institutions and filmmakers (directors, writers, actors). The President critically drew attention to the main problems he identified in the field, both quantitative and qualitative: 1. the low production of Romanian films, 2. the low diversity of Romanian film production in terms of film genres and 3. too few films addressed "with depth and courage contemporary issues".

The main lines of action in filmmaking work were: increasing the annual production of films to 25; making films "of all genres" ("historical, actuality, social-political, comedies, even as many good comedies as possible"); identifying sources of inspiration for filmmakers in the "present-day" concerns of the people, in "the tumultuous life of the builders of socialism"; cinema was to be "a mirror" in which the social concerns of working people could be expressed "synthetically, in artistic form"; films should have "a deep ideological content", should express "the Marxist-Leninist conception of life and the world", portray "the concerns, the life of the new man", "move the spectator, make him laugh or cry, rejoice or be sad, stir his conscience, his sensibility", and all this because "only such films can be understood and appreciated by the broad masses" (Ceaușescu, 1971: 16). The mass appeal was the main stake in the use of cinematic art for educational purposes: "no other art sector offers so many possibilities to create works that appeal to the broad masses, that can play such an important role in educating the masses, in shaping the new man. Cinematography is truly a mass educational medium" (Ceaușescu, 1971: 16).

By the mid-1970s, the national element became prominent in official discourse on the role of art. In the Report presented to the 11th Congress of the Romanian Communist Party in 1974, the reference to the past, the national "framing" of art is suggestive: "Throughout its existence, the Romanian people has created an art that expresses its way of life and work, its thinking and sensitivity, its thirst for freedom, its will to make a better living, its optimism, its confidence in its own strength, in the future" (Ceaușescu, 1974: 95). The past-future axis on which the official discourse is built is a relatively atypical element in relation to Marxist thought. In the *Communist Manifesto*, Marx and Engels stated: "In bourgeois society, therefore, the past dominates the present; in communist society, the present dominates the past" (2008: 55). The tendency to recover the past in the perspective of the present implies an important valorisation in the sense that the past takes on the function of legitimizing the present. This tendency is expressed in films of the time. Best example is *Mihai Viteazul (Michael the Brave)* (directed by Sergiu Nicolaescu, 1971), about which Ceaușescu said in his speech on 5 March 1971 (shortly after the premiere) that "it made a good impression on me" (Ceaușescu, 1971: 8). The idea of unity of Romanian nation at a time (the historical period referred to in film) when the idea of unity was not part of the political imaginary and therefore not part of the political vocabulary, served exclusively to satisfy the political and symbolic needs of the present.

Another dimension consistently assumed by artistic products was the need for realism. In the *Statement on the political-ideological and cultural-educational activity of forming the new man, conscious and devoted builder of the multilaterally developed socialist society and communism in Romania*, presented at the Congress of Political Education and Socialist Culture on June 2, 1976, Ceaușescu stated that artists had to "approach and portray reality in their works through the prism of the dialectical principle of the uninterrupted movement and transformation of society and man. Treating the facts of life and the acts of individuals divorced from the social-historical context in which they occur, without causality and purpose, as fatal, unknowable data, determined by a supernatural force, ultimately denotes a metaphysical outlook in the creative process, diametrically opposed to materialist-dialectical philosophy" (Ceaușescu, 1976: 59). In this address, Ceaușescu formulated clear objectives for artists in general and filmmakers in particular. The following excerpt from the speech expresses the local dimensions of socialist realism translated into rules that were to guide the cultural production:

It is understandable that, with the general development of our society, the demands of working people are also increasing in the field of cultural and artistic creation. The citizens of our homeland, the creators of socialist society, want as many literary, musical, plastic, cinematographic and theatrical works as possible to portray their achievements, concerns and dreams in the specific language of each art. Working people want to recognise their own moral physiognomy in literary and artistic works, not to find in novels, films or plays imaginary characters or heroes transplanted to our times from other historical stages or even from other planets. Some creators of art imagine that they can find interesting conflicts only in certain social environments, where some people unnecessarily complicate things and their very lives sometimes for lack of activity. Indeed, working people in factories and on the fields are much less complicated, they solve life and work problems much more simply and much more directly. But those who think that these wonderful creators of material and spiritual goods, the working people, cannot provide the most important sources of inspiration for artists are making a great mistake. It is precisely working people who are animated by the highest ideals and deepest convictions, who live their lives with passion and dedication, who are inspired by the spirit of justice and truth. They, the working people, express in the most striking way the true character of our people, its unique sensitivity and moral beauty. That is why creators must look for their heroes among the popular masses, among the people – the glorious builders of the new social order in Romania! It is to them, the working people, that we dedicate all that is best in our society, to them that we dedicate all our material wealth. It is therefore only natural that all that is created in literature, music, cinema, theatre and the plastic arts, in all the spiritual creation of our homeland, should belong to them. [...] The working people need a truly revolutionary art, one which portrays reality truthfully and objectively, which is permeated by a strong mobilising spirit, passionately striving for the betterment of society and man.

CEAUȘESCU, 1977: 81–83

The red thread of culture and art in socialism was the class character. In his *Statement on the current state of building socialism in our country, on the theoretical and ideological problems and the political and educational activity of the people* (presented at the enlarged Plenary Session of the Central Committee of the Romanian Communist Party on June 1–2, 1982), Ceaușescu stated that "the working people, the popular masses in the towns and villages are the creators, the participants and the direct beneficiaries of mass cultural and artistic activity" (Ceaușescu, 1982: 66). Consequently, all theoretical, ideological and political-educational activities had the role of contributing "to raising the general level of knowledge of working people, to broadening their cultural horizons, to forming the consciousness of the new man of our society" (Ceaușescu, 1982: 54). Together with radio, television, print media, literature and theatre, the cinema had a role "in the formation of socialist consciousness, in political and cultural education, in the formation of the new man", highlighting "reality", "life", "work, the achievements of our people in socialist construction, firmly combating the backward state of affairs" (Ceaușescu, 1982: 68). He also stated: "Cinema and theatre have important tasks. We have a number of positive results. But we must pay more attention to the content of films, plays, their educational message. Cinema and theatre are important means of educating the revolutionary consciousness of working people, of youth, and we must ensure that they play their role in our society in the best possible conditions" (Ceaușescu, 1982: 67). In 1982, in a speech delivered at the *Second Congress of Political Education and Socialist Culture* on 25 June, three weeks after the Plenary Session of 1–2 June, Ceaușescu reaffirmed the need to anchor everything produced in the arts in the facts of real life, since they should reflect "the life, work and aspirations of the people, contribute to the cultivation of noble sentiments of social and national justice, work and humanity, and to the formation of the new man with a high revolutionary consciousness" (Ceaușescu, 1982: 9).

In order to achieve the objectives of the political-ideological and cultural education of the population, the main source of inspiration for artists was "the soul of the new man, his conscience", opening to the artist "an unlimited horizon of investigation": "The research and the rendering of this exciting human universe this is what we ask of the creators of art. To glorify what is most valuable, most noble in our socialist society man" (Ceaușescu, 1971: 8–9). Working class and socialist realities were the main subjects for every field of artistic production: "The main source of inspiration for the man of art, whatever his nationality, must be the life and heroic work of our people, of the builders [...] of the new socialist order. This is the life-giving source that can ennoble any work, make the artist a creator of immortal value" (Ceaușescu, 1971: 14). In order to get to know closely the realities of socialist life and working people, the idea of broadening contacts between artists and working people was put forward: "I believe that contacts with working people must be constantly broadened, going to factories, to villages, to institutions. On the one hand, this will help to broaden the cultural horizons of the masses, and on the other hand, the creators themselves will be able to learn from those who work, they will understand life better. Good things will come out of this close connection with working people, both for the workers and for the creators of art" (Ceaușescu, 1971: 20).

Knowing the working-class living conditions directly was considered a basic source for the creation of artistic works. The affirmation of this creative principle is manifest not only in official discourse, but also in film discourse itself. Numerous filmic discourses expressed the relationship between art and communist ideology, identifying the artist's source of inspiration in the reality of working-class labour (especially industrial workers). In 1975, Sergiu Nicolaescu directed *Hot Days*, an actuality film that tells the story of the construction of the second Romanian ore carrier at the Constanța shipyard. The main character of the film, the director of the shipyard (Mihai Coman played by Sergiu Nicolaescu), during a visit he makes to one of the shipyard platforms to check the state of the ship's construction, as he passes by large industrial electric hammers operating at high intensity, addresses a young engineer who accompanies him with several lines that synthetically express the ideological consensus between art and work, artists and workers, in a symbolic view specific to the propagandistic tasks of the time: "I once read somewhere how a poet compared the beating of these hammers to the beating of the wings of a glass butterfly. What art that is! It would never have occurred to me".

4   Unfortunate Events and Social Consciousness. Mangalia Theses (August 1983)

A significant moment in the history of official ideological insights into film production was represented by the *Working Conference on the Problems of Organizational and Political-educational Work* held in Mangalia in the summer of 1983 (2–3 August), an episode that film historian Călin Căliman considers to have had "truly dramatic consequences for national film" (Căliman, 2000: 312). The aim of the cultural productions of the time, regardless of the artistic field, was to satisfy the ideological, revolutionary imperatives of the communist doctrine: "We need paintings and sculptures that reflect the realities of life, not just abstractions. We need truly revolutionary theatre and cinema!"

The August 1983 speech offered a radical ideological discourse, a vehement criticism of the factors and institutions responsible for communist propaganda. The harshest criticism was directed to fields of culture, art and education. Cultural and scientific activity and education were considered "factors of fundamental importance in the building of socialist society, in raising the level of civilization of the people" (Ceaușescu, 1984: 165). Criticism was aimed above all at the inadequacy of ideological activities which had to combat what the president called "backward concepts and mentalities":

> In society, in people's consciousness, some diseases of the past remain. That is why political and educational activity must firmly combat all bourgeois, mystical conceptions, the tendency to live without work, various backward mentalities in work and life.
> CEAUȘESCU, 1984: 181

The purpose of the political-educational activities based on "revolutionary, materialist-dialectical and historical theory" (Ceaușescu, 1984: 183) was to arm "the whole people with a new conception of life, of behaviour at work, in society, with a revolutionary conception in the work of raising our country to a new, higher stage of development!" (Ceaușescu, 1984: 182), to combat all forms of "nationalism, racism, anti-Semitism, of the enmity of working people, of peoples" (Ceaușescu, 1984: 182) and to contribute to the training of "the young generation for work, for struggle, to educate them in a revolutionary spirit" (Ceaușescu, 1984: 183).

Elements like importing music and dances from other countries become susceptible to "counter-revolutionary" interpretations. The speech from August 1983 is not only a return to the ideological foundations of socialist realism, but also a strongly nationalistic discourse. Referring to the mass cultural-artistic movement *Song of Romania*, - Ceaușescu said:

> Let's cultivate the feeling of love for the homeland, for the people. Let's develop music, Romanian dance, everything that is the creation of our people! We must not chase after some music or dance imported from elsewhere! Every people has its music, its creation – and we have a wonderful creation of our people and we must cultivate it, develop it, raise it to a new, higher level, put it on an even more solid basis, based on the revolutionary conception of the world.
> CEAUȘESCU, 1984: 184

While radio and television were considered "instruments of the Party for educating and training the new man, for spreading science, culture, based on the materialist-dialectical and historical revolutionary conception", and thus had to "improve their broadcasts" (Ceaușescu, 1984: 184), "important tasks" were set for the cinema. The ideology of socialist realism is enlightening for the part of discourse that focused on the role and tasks of national cinema in the context of communist propaganda. The following passage is a longer excerpt from the

August 1983 speech, in which cinema, in particular, represented by writers and directors, is strongly criticised for "misrepresenting the reality of our society":

> We need good, revolutionary films that show the great achievements of our people, that mobilize and portray heroes who are a model of work and life. Comrades, we have seen some films that not only do not present models of heroes in life and work, but on the contrary, they present elements that are perhaps still to be found somewhere on the periphery of society, but it is not these that our writers and directors or those who direct and organise film production should present. We must completely eliminate this state of affairs. Not long ago I saw a film showing a young worker on the Black Sea. But the hero of this film is nothing like today's young worker. What does the young worker in our homeland look like and represent? I meet, you know, millions of young people all the time. I talk to them, I know them. You see in them a love of work, a love of the Party and the homeland, a love of socialism; you see a determination to do everything to ensure that the tasks of great responsibility they have are fulfilled. Here, at the Danube-Black Sea Canal, soon to be put into operation, tens of thousands of young people have shown unparalleled heroism. And we find similar examples on hundreds and thousands of construction sites and economic and social units. But the writer and director who made the film and those who approved it clearly do not know the youth of our homeland.
>
> We cannot allow such films to be produced. Where is the Council of Culture, where is the Propaganda Section, where is the Ideological Commission of the Central Committee, which must see all these films? Why do we stage and market such films, which distort the reality of our society, the working people, the youth or other categories of working people in our country? We do not need such films and plays! We need an art, a cinema, a theatre that presents the essence, the model of the man that we must create! Even if we sometimes have to embellish a hero, it is good that he becomes a model, that young people know, that they understand that this is how it should be!
>
> In the past, we have seen films in which the main heroes were role models, who said: look, this is how revolutionaries should be! Now some say that it is not necessary to present such models, that we must avoid embellishing things. Of course, there is no need to embellish, because our society has achieved such great results that they need only be presented as they are. Let us render reality, but let us find not the weeds, not the rot in the forest, but let us find the young trees, let us find all that

is good and worthy in our society, in the work and life of the builders of socialism. It is the people – in whom the youth has a prominent role – the working people who have achieved all that we have achieved in the socialist development of our homeland. They are the heroes who must have their place in film, in theatre, in poetry, in art, in literature, in painting, in all fields of artistic creation! We must present them!

CEAUȘESCU, 1984: 184–186

Relating the time of this discourse to productions made from the second half of 1970s and early 1980s (until 1983), one can see that Romanian cinema abounded in films that subtly criticized the socialist system: from the issue of urban housing and job opportunities, to the scarcity of food resources and corrupt practices of socialist bureaucracy: *Filip cel bun/Filip the Kind* (Dan Pița, 1975), *Probă de microfon/Microphone Test* (Mircea Daneliuc, 1980), *Croaziera/ The Cruise* (Mircea Daneliuc, 1981), *Secvențe/Sequences* (Alexandru Tatos, 1982), *Buletin de București/Bucharest Identity Card* (Virgil Calotescu, 1983).

The speech in Mangalia influenced to a certain extent the choices of film productions during the 1980s in the sense that screen adaptations were predominant compared to the number of actuality films. During the 1980s, screen adaptations have been "a "vaulting arch" of national cinema and a "lifeline" for a film production increasingly burdened by ideological prejudices" (Căliman, 2000: 312). Mangalia speech remains significant for the official film criticism in terms of intensity and manifest character. A substantial part of Ceaușescu's critical discourse referred to film *Sand Cliffs* (1983), directed by Dan Pița. A detailed analysis of this film and the contextual elements that accompanied its production and reception will be presented in another chapter of the book.

CHAPTER 9

Actuality Film as a Matter of Realism

1   Here, Now, and the Future: Filmmakers as Historians

Of all thematic species of film, the most prolific in terms of ideologization potential is the actuality film, a rather rare species in Romania cinema. In this sub-chapter I will treat the "actuality film" in relation to reality and the "present", and the ways it uses to structure points of view on contemporary world.

What is an actuality film? What are the elements that define this genre? First of all, it should be pointed out that the "actuality film" is in fact "a very broad *thematic category*, present in various genres, from comedy to adventure film, from psychological drama to musical film" (Cantacuzino, 1976: 51). From a broader definition of this genre, actuality films are films "with a contemporary subject" (Căliman, 2000: 216). From the point of view of the method of construction of what we call actuality film, it involves "the "theft" from reality" or "direct contact with reality", it incorporates to the highest degree the meanings of cinematic realism, but not one understood as a mere "faithful copy of life, but the profound deciphering of its meanings and the discovery of the revealing detail" (Duma, 1983: 172–4). The relationship with realism is fundamental to the "actuality" of film, but realism understood "not merely as a copy, but as a superior extract, an essence of life, thus a transfigured reality that is nevertheless acceptable, plausible, credible enough to be followed by the fantasy of the art consumer" (Mănoiu, 1976: 147).

Mircea Constantinescu, in an issue of *Cinema* magazine (September 1988, No. 9), reffering to the concept of actuality film, advances a distinction between *film of actuality* and *film from actuality*:

> Any film is, in fact, of actuality: for the good and simple reason that it represents a view of today, of an artist of the image, on a story, problems, worlds, on a time and on people whose destinies are inscribed in this or that time, either today or a few decades or even hundreds of years ago. When film chooses the present as its source of inspiration, it is of the present. And, in fact, every film is an actuality because we make it today and, from time to time, it is of actuality because it is obsessed with the everyday that the filmmaker is trying to express.
>
> CONSTANTINESCU, in *Cinema* 1998: 3

Actuality film category can include other genres of films, as historical films, screen adaptations, whose filmic narratives, through filmic discourse and symbolic elements attached to the present, become sources of knowledge for the "present" time when the films are made.

Generally, the actuality film makes direct or indirect reference to the real context of society (the context of production), that express certain ideas and meanings about the present, about "here" and "now". A historical reconstruction, narratively set in a past time, displays a reading scheme of the present in which it is produced, through elements that may concern both content of ideas and expression. The film *Michael the Brave/Mihai Viteazul* (1971) offers a representation of the heroic deeds of the Romanian prince, but at the same time provides material for analysis and interpretation of the social reality in which its production is set. Nicolaescu's film displays the representation of historical moments marked by the emblematic figure of Michael the Brave, but it displays it through the eyes of 1970 Romania, when Romania was marked by pronounced tendencies towards national-communism. The film displays the historical figure as a hero of the struggle for unity, endowed with modern national sentiment, even though at the time of his historical deed, the concept of unity undestood as a political construction did not even exist, the idea of Romanian national unity appearing only in the 19th century, more than two centuries after the conquest of the prince. The way in which the narrative themes and the historical character are treated is a response to demands of a political context manifestly assuming the "recovery of historical consciousness" in accordance with the national dimension of communist political priorities. The actuality of film derives not only from the direct placement of the action in the temporal context of the film's production, but also from the vision embedded in displaying issues and subjects from the past.

Another criterion for defining the actuality of films is not simply reality, but its problems: "more precisely, the problems of a place and a time" (Ion Bucheru, *Cinema* magazine, No. 1/January 1988: 6). In socialist cinema, the criticism dimension was important, as ideas and subjects of actuality cinema were designed to reflect the continuous dialectical movement between: "what is" and "what should be". Actuality film, understood as a "chronicler in images of the present", the "backbone" of national film production (Căliman in *Cinema* magazine, No. 1/January 1989: 9) was a concept and at the same time an instrument with significant practical utility in terms of the advantage of satisfying political-ideological needs through a simple functional definition of this cinematic genre, invested with a reflection function, and also with a (positive) evaluative one of the most important social and economic developments of the communist project.

Cinema, in general, and actuality film, in particular, had "a heavy ideological and cultural responsibility" (Cantacuzino, Gheorghiu, 1976: 194). The actuality film was invested not only with a chronicling role, but especially with a historical one. The intervention of the filmmaker in the life of society – wrote Florian Potra in 1970 – is not reduced to an automatic recording of facts and events, but must assume a much deeper meaning, that of a history of contemporaneity: "This requires on the part of the filmmaker, a very attentive eye and a very sharp mind, capable of revealing the general through the particular, a special sense of the deep currents in existence, in the public and individual consciousness of people. The "portraitists" of their own era are called upon to be filmmakers, but at the same time "historians" of this era" (in *Lupta de clasă/ The Class Struggle*, No. 9/September 1970: 77).

The relationship between the political lines that guided cultural-artistic activities and the cultural products of these activities found a generous forms of manifestation in actuality films. Actuality films had to educate people by promoting human patterns, attitudinal and behavioural models that would fallow ideological imperatives. In the construction of characters, filmmakers should have had in mind "how people should be", and not just people as they are. It was believed that by exposing the population to such social patterns, the film would have made an important contribution to accelerating the eradication of shortcomings, negative elements that hindered the process of building the "new man". To put it simply, since there were significant gaps between the real man and the "new man", film had to play a major role in bridging these gaps. These roles of cinema articulate new way of seeing social reality, a way characterised by the need to move away from the "real people" as they are, and therefore to move away from realism, not towards it.

The construction of characters is only one facet of the film's ideologization. Another facet is the practice of thematic inserts that made direct reference to certain political themes, to aspects of real economic situation. Reality (economic, political) is systematically reflected in the film. With the growing affirmation of "socialist nation" which begins to compete with the "working class" (reference to the *Programme of the Romanian Communist Party: for the building of the multilaterally developed socialist society and Romania's advance toward communism,* adopted in 1974 at the 11th Congress, in which an important role was given to the nation in the building of communism), Romania's foreign economic policy evolves in line with the policy of autonomy from the Soviet power. One manifestation of this direction was the reduction of imports. The general context is marked by the economic crisis of 1973–1974 that affected all European countries, including the socialist ones, 1973 being considered "to mark the end of the period of accelerated growth and the beginning of a period of economic difficulties for most countries" (Murgescu, 2010: 321). Between 1970 and 1980, the level of imports into Romania decreases for most commodity groups (Murgescu 2010: 358–359). The theme of the economic situation is taken up and dealt with directly in film. In 1975, two years after the onset of the economic recession and just one year after the adoption of the political programme mentioned above, the film *Hot Days/Zile fierbinți* (directed by Sergiu Nicolaescu) was released. The film's script deals with the issue of imports, reflecting the views both of working people and of the party on the problem. In one of the film's sequences, we are shown a meeting of a committee of workers at the Constanța shipyard, where they are considering the possibility of giving up the supply of an imported propeller (necessary for the construction of an ore carrier) in favour of using one of Romanian production. The interventions of the participants are significant as the film puts real foreign policy issues on the cinematic agenda and displays a political position towards the more general national-international relationship expressed in the "us/them/others" formula. The following excerpt from the script shows an exchange between some of the employees and the site manager:

ASSEMBLY FOREMAN DUMITRU: The question of principle is whether we remain tributary to the foreigner or build with our own hands and heads the parts we need.
SITE MANAGER COMAN: To this principle we say yes and go all the way.
SITE WORKER: We are the internal reserves, comrade director, both at work and in politics. Make us share in the work, make us share in the decision. We are prepared to give up many imports. A matter of principle, interest and ambition.

Hot Days, SERGIU NICOLAESCU, 1975 (excerpt from the script)

In another scene, a discussion is held between the director of the construction site and the Prime Secretary of the Communist Party (played by Mircea Albulescu) in which the latter raises the issue of the foreign economic policy promoted by the party:

PRIME SECRETARY OF
THE COMMUNIST PARTY: We are not partisans of technical adventures, but mobilising the intelligence and

> manpower of a collective to reduce imports
> is a national cause and a Party task.
> *Hot Days,* SERGIU NICOLAESCU, 1975 (excerpt from the script)

2 The Political Nature of Actuality Film

A type of actuality film was the political film, a subject present in the debates of writers and directors, as it joined the issue gallery placed under the ideological imperatives of the time. The early 1970s was a pioneering period in which discussions on political film were more likely to be conducted around questions such as: What can or cannot be considered a political film? What should a political film look like? Do political films exist in Romanian cinema?

It was in February 1971 that *Cinema* magazine organised a round table on actuality and, in particular, political film, with the participation of the main categories of cinema specialists (writers, directors, producers, critics). From the producers' point of view, the definition of the "political" character of film transcended all distinctions of species or film genre. A political film could be a historical film, an actuality film, a drama or a comedy. Politics therefore had to be present in every film production, since there is no clear criterion for defining a political film. The political character of a historical film, for example, could derive from the significance the film had for the political actuality of the temporal context in which it was produced. Ion Brad, a representative of the "producers" (he was the first vice-president of the State Committee for Culture and Art), clearly expressed the position of the party during the round table on the difficulty of correctly framing and identifying the political actuality film:

> I think it's clear that political film is not a matter of genre: tragedy, drama, comedy. Nor is it a question of time: actuality or historical film. The other day I saw on the screens [...] the film "Michael the Brave". It's a historical film. One might say: it's an evasion into distant times. But it seems to me that a film like this is a political film. Let's think about what it means for our country, not to mention the international situation, the problem of the formation of a nation, of its affirmation in a very specific historical context, the problem of the struggle for non-attachment, against foreign invaders, the preservation and affirmation of national virtues. These are the problems of the day and will be, according to Leninist teaching, for a very long time to come.
> ION BRAD, in *Cinema* magazine, No. 3/1971: 11

The real problem lies elsewhere, in the lack of a tradition of actuality film. Ceaușescu's express demands in March 1971 not only for more films to be made, but also for films to be made that would portray the social and political issues of the "present" created a huge challenge for film-makers (writers and directors), but also for institutional leaders who had to organise the film production system in such a way as to achieve the results demanded from the top of the political hierarchy. One component of film production was the work of producing and selecting scripts. At the same debate in February 1971, the critic and editor-in-chief of *Cinema* magazine, Ecaterina Oproiu, drew attention to a structural problem of cinema from which the problematic question of political film derives: "The political film, which is an experience of the utmost acuity, cannot emerge in a leap, in a cinema that has not had sufficient practice in actuality film, has not yet the full lucidity of the analysis of social and human relations, has not yet succeeded in probing in – various genres – the multiple and specific aspects of our contemporary life" (in *Cinema* magazine No. 3/1971: 3).

The conclusion that emerges from the analysis of the discussions held at that time is that the cinema had major shortcomings in terms of actuality and especially political films, with some (very few) exceptions. The main problems were, on the one hand, the lack of scripts for such films, the absence of a structured actuality film as an institution/school and, on the other hand, issues related to the organization of cinema concerning the low degree of independence and responsibility given to the creative groups in the studios. The most important political films of the era are: *Desfășurarea/The Unfolding* (Paul Călinescu, 1954), *Valurile Dunării/The Waves of the Danube* (Liviu Ciulei, 1960), *Setea/The Thirst* (Mircea Drăgan, 1961), *Străinul/The Stranger* (Mihai Iacob, 1964), *Facerea lumii/The Making of the World* (Gheorghe Vitanidis, May 1971,), *Printre colinele verzi/Among the Green Hills* (Nicolae Breban, April 1971), *Puterea și adevărul/The Power and the Truth* (Manole Marcus, February 1972).

For the 1960s and 1970s, the main productions included in the actuality (and only secondarily political) category are: *Omul de lângă tine/The Man Next to You* (Horea Popescu, 1962), *Un zâmbet în plină vară/A Smile in the Middle of the Summer* (Geo Saizescu, 1964), *Un film cu o fată fermecătoare/A Film with a Charming Girl* (Lucian Bratu, 1967), *Meandre/Meanders* (Mircea Săucan, 1967), *Subteranul/The Underground* (Virgil Calotescu, 1967), *Diminețile unui băiat cuminte/The Mornings of a Good Boy* (Andrei Blaier, 1967), *Gioconda fără surâs/Gioconda without a Smile* (Malvina Urșianu, 1968), *Balul de sâmbătă seara/Saturday Night Ball* (Geo Saizescu, 1968), *Reconstituirea/The Reenactment* (Lucian Pintilie, 1968), *Răutăciosul adolescent/The Mischievous Teenager* (Gheorghe Vitanidis, 1969), *Așteptarea/The Waiting* (Șerban Creangă, 1971),

Șapte Zile/Seven Days (Mircea Veroiu, 1973), *Dragostea începe vineri/Love Begins on Friday* (Virgil Calotescu, 1973), *Proprietarii/The Owners* (Șerban Creangă, 1974), *Cursa/The Race* (Mircea Daneliuc, 1975), *Filip cel bun/Filip the Kind* (Dan Pița, 1975), *Mere roșii/Red Apples* (Alexandru Tatos, 1976), *Zile fierbinți/Hot Days* (Sergiu Nicolaescu, 1975), *Sunday Father* (Mihai Constantinescu, 1975), *Toamna bobocilor/Freshmen Autumn* (Mircea Moldovan, 1975), *Singurătatea florilor/ The Loneliness of flowers* (Mihai Constantinescu, 1976), *Serenadă pentru etajul XII/Serenade for the XIIth Floor* (Carol Corfanta, 1976), *Iarba verde de acasă/ The Green Grass of Home* (Stere Gulea, 1977), *Trepte spre cer/Steps to the Sky* (Andrei Blaier, 1978), *Din nou împreună/Together Again*, (George Cornea, 1978).

Actuality films produced during the 1980s are: *Probă de microfon/Microphone Test* (Mircea Daneliuc, 1980), *Croaziera/The Cruise* (Mircea Daneliuc, 1981), *Secvențe/Sequences* (Alexandru Tatos, 1982), *La capătul liniei/At the End of the Line* (Dinu Tănase, 1983), *Sfârșitul nopții/The End of the Night* (Mircea Veroiu, 1983), *Baloane de curcubeu/Rainbow Balloons* (Iosif Demian, 1983), *Buletin de București/Bucharest Identity Card* (Virgil Calotescu, 1983), followed two years later by a sequel, *Căsătorie cu repetiție/Marriage with Repetition* (Virgil Calotescu, 1985), *Un petic de cer/A Patch of Sky* (Francisc Munteanu, 1984), *Secretul lui Bachus/The Secret of Bachus* (Geo Saizescu, 1984), *Imposibila iubire/ Impossible Love* (Constantin Vaeni, 1984), *Pas în doi/Step in Two* (Dan Pița, 1985), *Anotimpul iubirii/The season of Love* (Iulian Mihu, 1986), *Orele unsprezece/ Eleven o'Clock* (Lucian Bratu, 1986), *Clipa de răgaz/Moment of Respite* (Șerban Creangă, 1986), *Punct și de la capăt/ Stop and from the Beginning* (Alexa Visarion, 1987).

The disscutions about actuality film in the context of national cinema is structured on two levels: the level of discursive construction of the role and method of actuality film, and the level of the actual production of films. The deviations between actuality film and the discourse on actuality film have been significant throughout the period mentioned. The distance between the representational identity of the film and the discursive identity becomes measurable through a comparative analysis of the elements of filmic construction: filmic narrative, cinematic image and character configuration. These two facets of film reflect the relationship between *the substance of objective content* and *the form of subjective expression* in film knowledge.

CHAPTER 10

Film Culture and Its Economy

Analysing and understanding film culture inevitably requires situating it in a society and a history. In this chapter I offer an insight into the socialist context in which Romanian cinema was organized and functioned between 1960 and 1989. Given the relevance of some historical elements in understanding the evolution of local cinema, references will go beyond the mentioned time frame in order to provide a consistent picture of the socio-political context in which film industry developed in Romania.

The structure of the chapter has three components: 1. the first is descriptive and provides an institutional view of Romanian cinema under its socialist development, offering detailed data about the film industry: production, distribution and consumption of films; 2. the second deals with the instrumentalization of the communist doctrine of socialist realism in official discourses; 3. the third provides description of actuality film as the main instrument of ideologization of Romanian film production under socialism.

1 The Institution of Film in Post-war Romania. Elements of Film Repertoire

In this subchapter I present some elements of the history of cinema institution under different aspects of its organization and functioning in the early period of socialism, with the aim of providing a broad image of historical and political context of film production. Another component will include data on film production, distribution and consumption in Romania during the 1960s, the 1970s and the 1980s.

What were the characteristics of the cinema phenomenon in Romania during the socialist period between the second half of the 1950s and the early 1980s, in terms of material and technical framework? Or, in other words, what were the material bases of Romanian cinematic life in a period that was undergoing major transformations in many aspects of socio-economic life? In order to answer this question, I propose in the first part a presentation of structural moments in the evolution of national cinema in the period immediately following the nationalization, pointing out the implications that certain political and administrative measures had for film production in Romania.

The socialist system of cinema organization was established with the adoption on 2 November 1948 of Decree No. 303 on the *Nationalization of the Film Industry and the Regulation of Trade in Film Products*. In 1948, 414 cinema halls were nationalized. Within the new social and political changes, the cinema infrastructure changed rapidly as many nationalized cinema halls were taken over by new cultural institutions in charge of ideological education and mass education activities. This change was operated by the Ministry of Arts. During the following years, only 258 of the 414 nationalized cinema halls remained active.

Another important moment is February 1949, when the state enterprise "Romfilm" is established as the institution responsible for "national film production, cinema network operations, import and distribution of films".

A more important moment in terms of the consequences it had on the possibilities of cinema network operating throughout the country was in January 1950, when a decision was taken to place the national cinema network under the provisional committees of the people's councils. This decision, which produced a type of decentralization of the cinema network from an administrative point of view, had damaging consequences for the physical situation of and cinema operations as they were placed in administrative areas without any competence in the field:

> The administrative dispersion of the cinemas, at that time, in the counties, did not, however, offer the possibility of their competent operation, lacking also a unitary guidance, all the more so as the provisional county committees had entrusted the responsibility of the cinemas to departments that had no connection with the film. In some counties, for example, the cinemas were managed by the "Green Spaces" sector or the population service sector!
> DUȚĂ, 1976: 38

Since the early years of nationalization, measures were taken to expand film culture in rural areas, which was a major task of cultural policy in developing a mass culture. Between 1949 and 1950, the first 1000 16 mm projection machines and 100 cinema trailers were imported.

In order to develop "modern cinematographic activity" (Duță, 1976: 38), the Committee for Cinematography under the Council of Ministers was established on 7 June 1950. A new structure that began to operate within this committee was the Directorate of the Cinematographic Network, and from 1953, the Directorate of Film Distribution was added. With the establishment of the Ministry of Culture in 1953, the General Directorate of Cinematography is set up to take over the tasks of the old organizational structure. In 1956, the two directorates, of the cinema network and film distribution, formed a single structure called the Directorate of the Cinema Network and Film Distribution (D.R.C.D.F.). In 1949 the first feature-length art film, *Răsună valea/ The Valley Resounds*, went into production. It premiered in 1950. Starting with the second half of the 1950s, there was an evolution of Romanian film repertoire. The cinema repertoire "comprises all the feature and short films running at a given time in the cinema network. [...] Thus, in a single year, the repertoire is made up of the premieres of that year, plus the hundreds of films still in circulation from previous years" (Duță, 1976: 41).

The structure of the film repertoire shows a continuous increase in the share of Romanian films. Changes in the share of Romanian films is an indicator of the cultural policy aimed at encouraging national film production. At the level of the official socialist cultural policy, such a policy was considered as an instrument of ideological-political education. The political vision of cinema expressed at the highest level emphasised the essential function of cinema to *mirror* the realities of socialist construction. The following fragment belongs to Ceaușescu and expresses the role of cinema. It does not only refer to the role of cinema, but also describes a method for its practice:

> We see cinema as an important means of educating and spiritually uplifting man, in the context of the many means of spiritual uplift and formation available to our society today, but for cinema to fulfil this important role in our socialist society it must come closer to the concerns of the people today, live the tumultuous life of the builders of socialism and render it in various forms in its true grandeur. The cinema must be for our people a true mirror in which the results of their creativity and efforts can be synthetically expressed in artistic form – and at the same time make our achievements in socialist construction known abroad.
>
> CEAUȘESCU in CANTACUZINO and GHEORGHIU, 1976: 1

The educational role of film in the sense of communist doctrine articulates only one facet of the cinematic phenomenon, and there are numerous examples of film productions situated at significant distance from official cultural objectives. The propagandistic dimension was often used only at manifest level of cinematic discourse, sometimes used with the purpose to affirm, on the contrary, principles and ideas which did not reflect the official imperatives.

Returning to the two components of film repertoire in Romania for the period 1956–1975, they recorded significant increases, with imported films remaining majoritary as in the early period (post-war period) there was no national film production, unlike the situation in other European countries. For example, national film production in Italy accounted for 50% of the total number of films broadcast annually. The Soviets imported films that accounted for 45% of the film repertoire, while the majority (55%) came from studio productions in the republics that made up the union. The situation was quite different in France, where domestic films accounted for only 28% of the repertoire and imports for 72%. A similar case was Hungary, where domestic films accounted for 13% and imports for 87%. (Duță, 1976: 42).

In Romania, most films were imported. Most films were imported from the USSR, and also from other socialist countries. These were mostly propaganda films, which affirmed the theses of socialist ideology and asserted the role of the new man as the builder of socialism. An overview of the most representative films imported in the 1950s and 1960s includes films from the USSR (*Brave Men, Ballad of Siberia, The 41st, The Cranes Fly, The Soldier's Ballad*), the German D.R. (*The Criminals Are Among Us*), the S.R. Czechoslovakia (comedies *The Baker's Emperor and The Emperor's Baker*), from the Hungarian P.R. (*Everyone in the Stadium, The Gags*), from the Bulgarian P.R. (*Favourite No. 13* and *Voices on the Island*), from the Polish P.R. (*The Last Stage, The Canal*) and from the F.S.R. Yugoslavia (*Kozara*).

By the mid-1970s there was a significant increase in film imports and at the same time a significant increase in the production of Romanian films. The majority of imported films came from the socialist bloc (between 80–85% of imported films). The annual number of films produced in socialist countries was around 350, while 65–70 films were imported from other, non-socialist countries. It should be noted that there was a significant difference between annual film production in socialist countries and that of other countries (the latter totalled about 2,500 films annually) (Duță, 1976: 43).

An important aspect regarding the extent of film imports in Romania is the selection process of imported films, so not every film had a chance to reach Romanian cinemas. The explanation for this selection was not based on cinematographic or aesthetic criteria, nor on commercial aspects, but on "a cultural-political act" (Duță, 1976: 42).

If in 1956, the year in which a unique institutional structure in the field of cinema was organized (Direction of the Cinematographic Network and Film Distribution), the number of Romanian premieres was 4, in 1975 it reached 26 films premiered in Romanian cinema halls.

From a production of 5 Romanian films in 1956 to a number of 26 films in 1975, there is a significant increase in film production and an indicator of the allocation of financial resources to film production. It is in this context that one of Ceaușescu's critical speeches to filmmakers took place, in which he

TABLE 4   Number of Romanian films within general film repertoire (1956–1975)

Year	Total number of films premiered	Of which Romanian films	Share of Romanian films %
1956	106	4	3,8
1959	132	5	3,8
1962	166	8	4,8
1965	160	15	9,3
1968	167	16	9,5
1971	173	17	9,8
1973	177	18	10,1
1975	187	26	13,9

SOURCE: MIHAI DUȚĂ, *FILM REPERTORY*, 1976: 42

drew attention to the fact that "there are not too many truly good films", given that "we spend a lot on cinema and that is why we have high expectations" (*Speech at the Meeting with People of Art and Culture* in February 1971).

A turning point in the evolution of local film production was 1963, when 12 films were produced, after a series of increases and decreases, because after that time, annual productions – with one exception, in 1968 – never fell below 10 titles. In 1971, the number of Romanian premieres was 18, after which it never dropped below 16. The number of local films for the 1960s was 121, and for the 1970s 238 (Steriade, Câmpeanu, 1985: 25). Significant increases of Romanian film production took place in the second half of the 1970s and early 1980s. Between 1976 and 1980, 129 feature films were made. The average production of films per year reached 25. Thus, in 1976 alone 22 films were produced, while in 1980 no less than 32 films were produced (Căliman, 2000: 283).

As far as cinema attendance in Romania is concerned, between 1970 and 1980, it is relatively constant, 50 times higher than theatre attendance, (this dimension of consumption in the cinema industry was determined based on a coefficient calculated by relating the total population of the country to the number of registered spectators in one year).

The data show that, on average, each inhabitant of the country went to the cinema 9.9 times in 1970 and 8.8 times in 1980. Attendance is much higher in urban areas, while the rural population goes to the cinema almost 3 times less than the urban population.

TABLE 5   Cinema attendance in Romania in 1970 and 1980

	Total (average)	Urban (average)	Rural (average)
1970	9,9	17,3	5,6
1980	8,8	13,9	4,9

SOURCE: STERIADE, CÂMPEANU, *PEOPLE AND FILMS*, 1985: 10–11

TABLE 6   Global cinema attendance (1977)

Romania	8,5	England	1,9
Bulgaria	12,9	France	3,3
Czechoslovakia	5,7	Italy	6,6
G.D.R	4,6	USA	7,2
Yugoslavia	3,5	Spain	5,8
Poland	4,0	Japan	1,5
Hungary	7,1	G.F.R	2,0
U.S.S.R	15,8		

SOURCE: STERIADE, CÂMPEANU, *PEOPLE AND FILMS*, 1985: 11

In the 1970s, Romania ranked higher than other countries in the world in terms of cinema attendance, demonstrating the activism of Romanian population in film consumption (ranking 3rd overall). For 1977, the international situation was as follows:

There was also a dynamic development with regard to film viewing by country of production. With the increase in the Romanian film production there is also a significant increase in the percentage of viewers who go to the cinema to watch Romanian films. For the period 1970–1980, the average number of spectators per film shown changed as follows:

The conclusion is that the flow of Romanian viewers to foreign films has decreased, while the attendance to Romanian films has increased significantly. In the period 1965–1980 there is a notable change in the relationship between socio-demographic evolution in Romania and cinema-going population. Thus,

TABLE 7   Number of viewers per film shown, by country of production (1970, 1980)

	Total	Romania	Other countries
1970	153.785[a]	158.697	354.473
1980	123.238	256.510	208.938

a   thousands of spectators
SOURCE: STERIADE, CÂMPEANU, *PEOPLE AND FILMS*, 1985: 11

TABLE 8   Total number of cinema-goers in Romania (1965–1980)

Total number of cinema-goers in Romania

1965	1970	1975	1980
204.739	198.739	185.658	193.607

according to the Statistical Yearbook of the R.S.R., the number of spectators (thousands) changed as follows:

During this period, the country's population increased by 1.5 million, while the cinema population decreased by 11 million. Romania's cinema population was over 190 million out of a total population of 22 million. 43.2% of the total population attended the cinema. The 200 million cinema attendance was based on an effective population of about 10 million out of the country's 22 million inhabitants. Regarding the frequency of going to the cinema in Romania: weekly – 9.8 (average) and two or three times a month – 20.1 (average). In terms of age characteristics, about two thirds of cinema-goers were under 30.

A total of 676 and 1707 films were shown in 1960 and, respectively in 1981, and the number of cinema-goers was 150 million and, respectively 206 million. For the same years, the situation regarding the share of Romanian films was as follows:

The number of Romanian films has increased faster than the number of viewers. However, the viewing of Romanian films has increased substantially. In 1981, on average, one in three cinema-goers watched a Romanian film – compared to one in ten 20 years earlier.

An interesting observation is that in 1981 the share of films imported from countries other than socialist countries increased significantly in the national

TABLE 9   Number/share of films by country of production within national film repertoire (1960, 1981)

	Total	Romania	Socialist countries	Other countries
1960	676	48 (7,1%)	466 (68,9%)	162 (24%)
1981	1707	304 (17,8%)	808 (47,3%)	595 (34,9%)

SOURCE: STERIADE, CÂMPEANU, *PEOPLE AND FILMS*, 1985: 25

repertoire, significantly more than films produced in socialist countries. It is true that the number of films imported from socialist countries remains consistently higher, but the level of increase for films from other foreign countries is higher than for the former, so that the gap between the shares of the two categories of foreign films increases visibly from 1960 to 1981.

In 1971–1973, at a time when the share of Romanian films in the national repertoire was around 11–12%, more than 20% of all cinema-goers chose to watch Romanian films. In 1975, 30% of cinema-goers went to see Romanian films.

In 1976, the Board of Directors of the Filmmakers' Association sent a telegram to Ceaușescu reporting the results of film production activity for the five-year period 1971–1975. Compared to 1971, the number of artistic feature films increased from 12 to 25, fulfilling the objective set by Ceaușescu in 1971 to increase film production to 25 films per year. Between 1971 and 1975, Romanian filmmakers made 108 feature-length art films, 379 short documentaries and popular science films, 146 animated films and over 1100 commissioned films requested by various institutions in the country. As regards the presence of Romanian cinema-goers during the period mentioned, 227,708,000 spectators watched Romanian films. According to the same report, Romanian films had been seen in 83 foreign countries (in *Cinema*, May, 1976: 3).

Increase in the number of films produced in Romania was generated primarily as a result of party and state control. In his *Speech at the meeting with film creators* on 5 March 1971, Ceaușescu drew the attention of the Romanian film management to the fact that only a small quantity of films was being produced, which meant that the material base of the cinema at that time was not being used satisfactorily. The solution advanced by the President was a precise "command" to those responsible for Romanian film production:

> Why do we release so few films? Why don't we make proper use of the material base we have been creating for almost 20 years? [...] With 9 films in a year, it is not possible, however much we would like, to create the conditions for each director to make film after film. Not to mention the fact that we also have to make historical films, social films, comedies, etc., and in this way the possibility of diversifying genres is very limited. [...] First of all, it is necessary to take steps to ensure that in a short period of time – I would set 1972 as the deadline – we can make full use of the production capacities we have and produce at least 25 films a year.
> CEAUȘESCU, 1971: 8–11

This explains why the number of Romanian films highly increased in the following years. The strong criterion in the evaluation of cinema production was the quantity, similar to most other fields of activity (industry, agriculture, construction). It is true that in the same speech, Ceaușescu stated that should not be lost sight of the qualitative plan, in other words "to consider what films we will produce" (Ceaușescu, 1971: 11).

In terms of "box-office success", between 1960–1979, the Romanian films that were watched by at least 4 million viewers (the average audience for Romanian films was 1.5–2 million viewers) were as fallows: 1. *Dacii/The Dacians* (1967), 2. *Nea Mărin miliardar/Uncle Mărin, the Billionaire* (1979), 3. *The Outlaws* (1966), 4. *Tudor/Tudor* (1963), 5. *Mihai Viteazul/Michael the Brave* (1971), 6. *Profetul, aurul și ardelenii/The Prophet, the Gold and the Transylvanians* (1978), 7. *Nemuritorii/The Immortals* (1974), 8. *Înțelegerea/The Arrangement* (1974), 9. *Baltagul/The Hatchet* (1969), 10. *Moara cu noroc/The Mill of Good Luck* (1957), 11. *Amintiri din copilărie/Memories of my Childhood* (1965), 12. *Cu mâinile curate/With Clean Hands* (1972), 13. *Răscoala/The Uprising* (1966), 14. *Secretul cifrului/The Secret of the Cipher* (1960), 15. *Dacă aș fi Harap-Alb/If I Were a Harap Alb* (1965), 16. *Alo? Ați greșit numărul/Hello, You've Got the Wrong Number* (1958), 17. *Alarmă în munți/Alarm in the Mountains* (1955). The first film attracted 11 million viewers, the second 8 million viewers (Steriade, Câmpeanu, 1985: 26).

In the 1960s and early 1970s, films made attracted a large number of Romanian viewers: historical films such as *Tudor/Tudor* (Lucian Bratu, 1962), *Neamul Șoimăreștilor/The Șoimărești Clan* (Mircea Drăgan, 1965), *Dacii/The Dacians* (Sergiu Nicolaescu, 1967), *Mihai Viteazul/Michael the Brave* (Sergiu Nicolaescu, 1971). Nicolaescu was one of the most watched directors of the late 1960s and early 1970s, both with the historical productions mentioned above and with other films: *Cu mâinile curate/With Clean Hands* (1972), *Atunci i-am condamnat pe toți la moarte/Then I Sentenced Everyone to Death* (1972),

Nemuritorii/The Immortals (1974). Sergiu Nicolaescu, the "most prolific filmmaker of the 1970s" (Căliman 2000: 230) made the most watched and one of the best selling films in socialism, the historical blockbuster *Mihai Viteazul/ Michael the Brave* (based on a script by Titus Popovici), which took almost a year to be shot. *Mihai Viteazul/Michael the Brave* (premiered in February 1971) was one of the films with the biggest budgets (approx. 51 million lei) and the most impressive cast of actors and extras. The sequel to this film, in the 1977 production *Buzduganul cu trei peceți/The Mace with Three Seals*, cost 19 million lei at a time when the average cost of feature films had been reduced by about 1.5 million lei. The film that made a "good impression" on Ceaușescu marked the establishment of "mass" character in Romanian film production. To illustrate the particular status of this film and the willingness of the state and the party to invest in cinema, I will give below some data that express the material and economic scale of the production of this film: 32 interior sets were designed and built, 10 battle camps, 37 filming locations set up; as for the set props: 30 cannons, 20 observation towers, battle chariots, 150 fences and battle baskets, more than 500 4 m spears, 2,000 horse harnesses, hundreds of flags were used; costumes: 1,000 uniforms for soldiers of the German army, 1,500 uniforms for the Transylvanian army, 3,000 uniforms for Turkish soldiers and officers, 2,000 costumes for the Moldovian army, 2,500 uniforms for the Wallachian army, 1,000 costumes for peasants, 15 costumes for the main character; 240 actors and 10 theatres from Bucharest and the country participated in the casting of the film; 365 members of the film crew, between 1,000–7,000 soldiers of the armed forces, 300–700 horses, 100–200 wagons, 1000 horse caretakers from state herds, thousands of kilograms of fodder, hundreds of trucks and cars. (Constantin Pivniceru, "Michael the Brave in facts and figures" in *Cinema* magazine No. 1/1971: 7) All these data on film production shows the potential of the "material base" of the Romanian film industry and also the immense resources that the state and the party, as the only producers in the country, were willing to allocate to satisfy the political-symbolic needs of the regime.

Summarizing based on data presented above, the evolution of Romanian cinema between 1960–1989 was structured as fallows: 1. constant increase in the production of local films; 2. increase in the share of productions from socialist countries in the national film repertoire; 3. constant increase in the number of viewers of Romanian films correlated with decrease in the number of viewers of films from countries other than the socialist countries; 4. historical films situated in the top of most watched Romanian films during communist.

These are relevant indicators of the cultural modernization, closely linked to urban development, cities being the main relays of cultural consumption. The quantity of services in this area increased significantly under socialism. Two indicators were the number of cinema halls and the number of cinema-goers. The exponential increase in the number of cinema halls was as follows: from 1,299 cinema halls in 1950 to 6,275 cinema halls in 1970. After 1970, the rate of growth stagnated and by the end of the 1980s, it turned negative, with the number of cinema halls falling to 5,453 in 1989. Film consumption has also shown significant increasing trend: whereas in 1950 the total number of cinema-goers was 52 million, in 1989 it reached 203.5 million (Murgescu, 2010: 354).

If we consider the top films with highest number of spectators and highest box office, a differentiation is visible between different categories of films according to cinema genre. For the 1970s, the majority of watched films is given by historical films (*Dacii/The Dacians, Mihai Viteazul/Michael the Brave, Nemuritorii/The Immortals*), followed by comedies and adventures (*Nea Mărin miliardar/Uncle Mărin, the Billionaire, Profetul, aurul și ardelenii/The Prophet, the Gold, and the Transylvanians, Înțelegerea/The Arrangement*). These factual data on both film production and film consumption need to be integrated into a broader frame given by the political context in which historical films were produced and watched. The propensity to exploit historical issues in cinema can be explained as national-communism was highly promoted in Romania after the 1960s, when "nation" and "people" were elements used both in official and cinematic discourse. Political interest in promoting in cinema historical themes in socialism, rather within a national framework than as an integral part of the Soviet bloc, has generated a high degree of attraction especially for filmmakers, an obvious explanation being the significant budgets allocated to production of historical films.

In terms of increasing the number of Romanian viewers of films distributed in Romanian cinemas (especially Romanian films), it should be noted that this was not a consequence of a free dynamic of film market (in the sense of the relationship between supply and demand), but was to a significant extent an effect of the systematic application of policies aimed at establishing certain cultural consumption practices at the mass level. Ideological interests aimed at promoting the values, norms and principles that defined the work ethic and life have always been at their basis, with the cinema providing an alternative institutional space for the promotion of necessary education in order to build the "new man" under socialism. An example was the practice of contracts between factories and cinemas that provided the framework for broad participation of the working class in film viewing. An excerpt from an interview with a worker from Bucharest (spinner and secretary of the U.T.C. committee of the combed wool spinning mill), reported in the magazine *Cinema* (No. 5/May 1983: 2–3) about the consumption of Romanian films, is relevant for this practice: "Our factory has a contract with the *Patria* cinema, so we have tickets for every film". It is true that the workers were practically not obliged to go to the cinema, but such a policy contributed essentially to an increase in the number of cinema-goers, especially in city cinemas.

2 Film Economy under the Spectrum of Profitability

Another context element that generated favorable conditions for increasing the number of spectators to Romanian films is given by the functioning of a cultural and artistic institution that had the aim of giving culture a mass character by attracting broad categories of people in the process of creation and production of artistic goods. This was the National Festival of Socialist Education and Culture "Song of Romania", established on the initiative of the President of Romania and whose first edition took place in October 1976 – June 1977 (in honour of the 100th anniversary of Romania's independence). Amateur artistic movements were created during this festival.

Amateur cinema was a product of this concept of a policy of making mass culture. This gave rise to what was called the cineamateur, the amateur filmmaker, and the *cineclubist*, a member of the cineclub, organization of amateur filmmakers, who were supposed to make a "specific contribution [...] to the cultural life of factories and localities". The film club was a specialized form of education and development of film culture, an "institution of film "literacy"" (Cantacuzino, Gheorghiu, 1976: 195) in which the following were organized: film screenings with collective participation, exhibitions and debates on films from the classic or contemporary repertoire, conferences to popularize themes related to the art of cinema. Discussions before and after the film screenings made a difference from the screenings in regular cinema. The two forms of manifestation of this institution were cultural film clubs and creative film clubs. The first creative film clubs were set up in large industrial centres: "Oțelul Roșu/Red Steelworks" and "C.F.R. Timișoara", main theme being linked to the professional activities carried out in them. The activities of the film clubs were endowed not only with educational and cultural functions, but also with some militant manifestos:

> Film clubs are a form of spending leisure time in an instructive and enjoyable way, stimulating the creative spirit of working people, who have the opportunity to acquire theoretical and practical knowledge about the art and technique of cinema. The films of the film-makers, born out of the love of working people for beauty and their desire to be active militants

in the field of the completion of the construction of socialism, aim to popularize the achievements of our order in the most diverse fields of activity, to generalize advanced methods of work in industry, agriculture, etc., to sing of the beauties of the fatherland, to pay homage to the constructive achievements of socialist man, while at the same time promptly combating any negative tendencies in the production process or in public life, in the ethics of working people.

GHEORGHIU, SAIZESCU IN CANTACUZINO, GHEORGHIU, 1976: 198

In 1986, there were 700 film clubs nationwide, with almost 7,000 participants, in addition to the pioneers', pupils' and students' film clubs ("Tractorul" film club in Brașov, "Siderurgistul" film club, C.F.R. film club, "Faur" film club of the "23 August" company in Bucharest are just a few examples). Between 800 and 900 films in 10 thematic and genre categories were shown at each edition of the festival (Velicu, in *Cinema* No. 3 (279) 1986: 2–14). Activities of film clubs took place in factories, plants, educational institutions, houses of culture. Workers, engineers, teachers, technicians, doctors and students participated in the cultural and artistic activities of the cinema.

The extent to which the amateur cinema phenomenon had become an institutional structure in its own right (debates, conferences and other forms of institutional manifestation were regularly organised), generated a series of conditions that favoured the increase in the attraction of this type of cultural practice, an attraction that manifested itself, on the one hand, in a direct manner, through the participation in the making of amateur films, on the other hand, in an indirect manner, through the increase in the consumption of films in general.

Another factor that had a direct effect on the increase in the number of spectators was the policy of creating and setting up screening rooms in the houses of cultures in villages, where at least one film a week was shown, which led to an increase in cinema consumption in rural areas. An important role in the expansion of cinema consumption in the villages had the cinema caravan, a "mobile" institution created and practised during communist with the aim of increasing the cultural level of rural inhabitants, using a didactic-propagandistic method.

Seen as a whole, film economy under Ceaușescu was a "profitable" one, says Horea Murgu – in an interview I have conducted as part of the research – filmmaker and professor at U.N.A.T.C., with massive experience in Romanian film production under socialism, having worked for over 30 years at Buftea film studios, participating in the making of hundreds of films. Why with benefit? Because the films were shown on more than 600 screens nationwide (including caravans and houses of culture where screenings were organised), while a ticket to the film was on average 2.50 lei, being a little more expensive in Bucharest, big cities and county seats, where the price of a ticket reached 4.25 lei. With a high number of viewers, the film industry was making a huge amount of money from the cinema, not paying copyrights. Ceaușescus view on the distribution and exploitation of films was that "if you have the film object, you can give it away, didn't you buy it?!" As a result, Romanian films began to be sold, especially during the period in which payment of foreign debts intensified: "films were taken from the archive, the credits were changed so that they would not be so conspicuous in front of some embassies" and they were sold abroad (especially *Anima* studio used to sell films abroad).

During socialism, the budget for a standard feature film (except for some films produced by Sergiu Nicolaescu whose budgets were much higher, including amounts paid directly in foreign currency) was between 3.5–4 million lei, that is approximately 350,000–400,000 dollars (taking into account that during communist the exchange value of the dollar varied between 6–10 lei). These sums covered important expenses because most of the films produced back then were made "on location", with massive trips, with teams of 40–50 people who would spend two to three months in the places where the films were shot.

Of course, the most important thing for a filmmaker was to get funding to make films, but the possibility of funding very often depended on a strictly economic aspect, namely the number of spectators who had seen the previous film. More precisely, if a film was watched during its screening (and Romanian films were usually shown within 2 weeks from the premiere) and had more than 1 million viewers, the director had a good chance of having the film shown again, and especially of obtaining financing for a new film. It was a common and sometimes ironic expression among filmmakers (especially directors) at the time: "Did you make the million?" This quantitative criterion generated a series of corrupt practices to satisfy it. Thus, "the big cheats were made on the number of viewers, because it wasn't a particularly hard fraud in the money sense, but they moved viewers from one cowboy and John Wayne movie to another, because they had the advantage from a million viewers onwards. If they made a million, they could still make money" (according to Horea Murgu). This is how the broadcasting of some films ended up registering millions of spectators, although "it was not a direct fraud, it was an administrative fraud". On the whole, "Ceaușescu did not cheat by making films and did not make more than he could afford. He didn't like cinema, he liked television" and this was because cinema was harder to control, even if at the macro level of propaganda it worked very well.

CHAPTER 11

Cinematic Representations of Work

1   Physical Frames of Work

In most of the films analysed there is a typical category of "characters" that make up the work infrastructure. These are objects of urban space attached to industrial changes: factories, shipyards, commercial warehouses, steelworks, chemical plants etc.

The construction site in Straja commune in *Dimineţile unui băiat cuminte/ The Mornings of a Good Boy* (Andrei Blaier, 1967), "Iron Gates 1" construction site in *Balul de sâmbătă seara/The Saturday Night Ball* (Geo Saizescu, 1968), "Meteor" commercial warehouse in Bucharest, Reşita Steelworks in *Filip cel bun/Filip the Kind* (Dan Piţa, 1975), "Romlux" factory in Târgovişte, binders and cement plant in Fieni in *Probă de microfon/ Microphone Test* (Mircea Daneliuc, 1980), "Oltchim" chemical plant in *Gioconda fără surâs/Gioconda without a Smile* (Malvina Urşianu, 1968), shipyard in Constanţa in *Zile fierbinţi/Hot Days* (Sergiu Nicolaescu, 1975), "Republica" factory in *Pas în doi/Step in Two* (Dan Piţa, 1985), construction site in Râmnicu Vâlcea in *Imposibila iubire/Impossible Love* (Constantin Vaeni, 1984), shipyards, factories and plants in *Iarba verde de acasă/The Green Grass of Home* (Stere Gulea, 1977), *Secvenţe/Sequences* (Alexandru Tatos, 1982), *La capătul liniei/At the End of the Line* (Dinu Tănase, 1983), *Cursa/The Race* (Mircea Daneliuc, 1975), *Dragostea începe vineri/Love Begins on Friday* (Virgil Calotescu, 1973) – all these cinematic spaces make up the advance of a country located mostly within industrial settings.

The dominant visual element is the *system* in the forms of manifestation significant for the type of socio-economic order that was the major thematic pillar in the film production of the time. Frames with factories, plants and enterprises in which different types of activities in the production process can be viewed provide visual expressions of structural changes in relation to which individual is situated on a continuum varying between degrees of acceptance/ adaptation/internalization of values, practices, and norms governing the labour system.

On the one hand, there is this vizualisation of the physical, morphological poses of work, on the other hand, there is a layer ot the revelators – signifiers of the relationship between the system and the individual that generates the discourse (the attribution of meaning to elements and relations between elements of this dominant vizual) and that is structured on precise choices regarding the use of cinematic language: types of shots, camera movements, camera angles and non-specific language elements. Critical commentary and the structure of deeper meaning result from this exploration of the interference between the two types of orders: the physical, present, objective existents and the visual forms in which they are embedded alongside elements of their subjective experience. Movement, sound, and image compose a whole which, in its particularity – the identified elements are articulated in relation to the class of objects to which they belong – establishes a general function of representation, that is, essentialization. Material and actional elements that emerge from such constructions give rise to a hierarchy of core values easily recognizable. Collectivism, sociability in the workplace, conformity, obedience are values around which the meanings and significances, the forms of deviations from these values are articulated in the cinematic discourse. It leaves room for questioning, for reflexive dialogues and lucid introspections that build the meanings of identity in individual and/or collective contexts. Through this kind of elaboration of system thinking, films of social critique offer the possibility for reflection with the potential to increase the social and political sophistication of individuals, that is, the capacity to capture, incorporate, filter and process information about social and political domains and elaborate inferences in relation to them, that is, to generate a process of knowledge that differentiates in terms of pluralistic value systems, as opposed to one-dimensional views based on strongly stereotypical and ideologically limited understandings.

Within such a view, a clearer nuance of the criticism of filmic discourses is necessary. The object of criticism does not dislocate the human presence from the frameworks of social processes, including work, but rather questions them from point of view of the understandings and practices of ideological schemes that can be taken up critically or not, that can generate new social situations that were not intended and that cannot be accepted as alternatives within a mode of social organization highly defined by the ideological function of the most important social institutions.

This type of reflection is built around a more general concept of space which is an important category in the analysis of representations of work. Physical space incorporates both morphological elements and those relating to the ways in which space is invested with subjective value within experiences and practices that make up various aspects of social life. The way in which space in film is given different values and functions is a discursive technique that can be critically or consensually oriented in relation to the dominant elements of a value system. Material objects, interpersonal or group interactions, the distribution of proximities and distances, roles performed in particular categories of space, activities and actions that are associated with one space or another, the degree of humanization of spaces by identifying the density of human presence within them, the quality of spaces by identifying its practical or symbolic characteristics and functions, the forms of vizualisation of space through by using particular elements of cinematic language (degree of brightness, camera angles, types of shots, camera movements), the dynamic or static character of space by identifying the presence or absence of forms of human/object movement within them, the gender dimension of space by identifying the characteristics of space in relation to the gender of the characters put to act, the ideological impulses of space by identifying the social and political values, value pluralities, power, authority and influence relationships, the endowment of spaces with intrapersonal, relational and collective content, differentiating between public and private, between exterior and interior, between ideological and sensitive, the degree of closure and openness of spaces, the potential for stimulating or attenuating tensions, conflicts, the dialectical potential of space, the social and ideological divisions of space, the sound, tactile and olfactory characteristics of space – these are some basic dimensions of the analysis of cinematic space, according to which multiple interpretative possibilities are advenaced, a dimensional matrix on which to structure new views on the relations between space and film, on the one hand, and between film and constructed reality (social representations), on the other. The evaluative orientations of representations of work are favoured and/or determined by the quality of the spaces in which it is practiced, visualized, thought. The visual organization of cinematic space operates with discursive angles which delivers various definitions and understandings of work situations, work objects, workers and of the relations between them, in a systematic order containing elements of subjective manifestations, resulting in a highly expressive resource for the social memory of work.

2   Apparent Indolents and Working Leaders: The Cinematic Division of Work

Marxist theory attributes an ontological function to work, understood as a fundamental social value. In 1876, Friedrich Engels stated that: work "is the first basic condition of all human life, and to such a degree that, in a certain sense, we must say that work has created man himself". In 1982, Ceaușescu proposed, rather colloquially, a local view of this value, considered the hard criterion of belonging to socialist society: "Every citizen must understand that in the Romanian socialist society everyone must work; there is no place here for lazy people, for those who violate the rules of social coexistence, for those who abuse, for those who steal the work of others".

In this subchapter I approach the subject of work as a sensitive red line of urban, modernizing life of the cinematic 1960s to the end of the 1980s. The thematic dimensions of analysis are as follow: 1. analysis of professional/occupational universe within the urban environment; 2. analysis of attitude towards work; 3. analysis of cinematic hypostases of the working man and woman in the discourse of cinematic actuality.

2.1   Images of Workers and Engineers: Producers of Means of Productions

This section offers an overview of professional and occupational landscape reflected in actuality cinema of the time, by identifying the categories of professions and occupations that describe the profile of the main characters in the selected films for analysis.

In order of the frequency of appearance of profession/occupation, most of the main characters are: construction workers, engineers (metallurgical engineers, agronomist engineer, construction engineers, petroleum engineers), plant and factory managers, workers in personal services, doctors and party officials. The professions/occupations with the lowest frequency of occurrence are in the fields of justice, press, and administrative bureaucracy.

If activities that describe the occupational statuses of main characters are considered, it can be seen that most of them belong to the specific fields of work in the production branches of economy, while a minority of the same category is employed in the consumer production branches. The view that emerges is that of an urban society that produces a lot and consumes very little. According to the cinematic representations, socialist Romania is predominantly populated by workers and engineers, together with technicians, followed by party activists and less by doctors and teachers/educators. The reality of work in socialism is based on several constant elements: 1. occupational diversity limited to the industrial branches; 2. predominance of the occupations attached to industrial branches of economy (urban characters work most often in the fields of industry producing means of production: metallurgy, mining, machine building, and less in consumer goods industries); 3. the interference of politics in work system (in the production process, in spheres of employees' private lives) in terms of subordination and control (through the presence of the activist or the intermediary figure of the specialist, placed in a higher hierarchical position in the bureaucratic system – director of an institution/economic unit, site manager, co-op president).

TABLE 10 Professional and occupational categories in Romanian films (1960–1989)

Main character category

	Film	Year of the premiere	Occupation/profession of main characters
	The 1960s		
1.	*Aproape de soare/Close to the sun* Directed by Savel Stiopul	1960	Steelworker, Crane Worker
2.	*Post-Restant/Post Restante* Directed by Gheroghe Vitanidis	1962	Engineer (2)
3.	*Cerul n-are gratii/ The Sky Has No Bars* Directed by Francisc Munteanu	1962	Painter, Monk
4.	*Doi băieți ca pâinea caldă/Two Lads with a Heart of Gold* Directed by Andrei Călărașu	1962	Baker (2)
5.	*Omul de lângă tine/The Man Next to You* Directed by Horea Popescu	1962	Construction Engineer, Lawyer
6.	*Puștiul/The Kid* Directed by Elisabeta Bostan	1962	Unemployed, Doctor
7.	*A fost prietenul meu/He Was My Friend* Directed by Andrei Blaier	1963	Sheet Metal Worker (retired), Clown, Surgeon
8.	*Partea ta de vină/Your Share of the Blame* Directed by Mircea Mureșan	1963	Unskilled Worker, Excavator Driver, Skilled Worker/Activist
9.	*Pisica de mare/Sea Cat* Directed by Gheorghe Turcu	1963	Design Engineer, Police Captain
10.	*Casa neterminată/ The Unfinished House* Directed by Andrei Blaier	1964	Architecture Student, Theatre Student
11.	*Un surâs în plină vară/A Smile in the Middle of Summer* Directed by Geo Saizescu	1964	C.A.P. Worker

TABLE 10 Professional and occupational categories in Romanian films (1960–1989) *(cont.)*

Main character category		
12. *Diminețile unui băiat cuminte/ Mornings of a Good Boy* Directed by Andrei Blaier	1967	Copyist, Clerk (in charge of labour protection), Accountant, Welder (2), Librarian (2), Rail-way Station Worker
13. *Șeful sectorului de suflete/Head of the Soul Sector* Directed by Gheorghe Vitanidis	1967	Chemical Engineer, Meteorologist
14. *Subteranul/The Underground* Directed by Virgil Calotescu	1967	Petroleum Engineer, Skilled Worker (Craftsman) (2)
15. *Un film cu o fată fermecătoare/A Film with a Charming Girl* Directed by Lucian Bratu	1967	Engineer, Director, Unemployed
16. *Meandre/Meanders* Directed by Mircea Săucan	1967	Architect
17. *Reconstituirea/ The Reenactment* Directed by Lucian Pintilie	1968	Prosecutor, Secretary of the Local Committee of the PCR, Camera Operator, Policeman, High School Graduate (2), Professor
18. *K.O./K.O.* Directed by Mircea Mureșan	1968	Engineer, Factory Director, Boxer, Actor
19. *Gioconda fără surâs/Gioconda without a Smile* Directed by Malvina Urșianu	1968	Chemical Engineer/Chief Engineer, Reporter/Poet, Hydrotechnical Engineer
20. *Balul de sâmbătă seara/Saturday Night Ball* Directed by Geo Saizescu	1968	Skilled Worker/Truck Driver, Amateur Singer, Dancer
21. *Apoi s-a născut legenda/Then the Legend Was Born* Directed by Andrei Blaier	1969	Railway Site Worker, Housewife
22. *Răutăciosul adolescent/The Mischievous Teenager* Directed by Gheorghe Vitanidis	1969	Doctor/Head of Department, Doctor, Nurse

TABLE 10 Professional and occupational categories in Romanian films (1960–1989) (cont.)

Main character category		
23. *Pantoful cenușăresei/ Cinderella's Shoe* Directed by Jean Georgescu	1969	Doctor, Theatre Cashier, Painter
The 1970s		
24. *Brigada Diverse intră în acțiune/ The Miscellaneous Brigade Gets into Action* Directed by Mircea Drăgan	1970	Police Captain, Platoon Officer, Major, Sergeant Major, Criminals/ Object/ Animal Thieves (3)
25. *Brigada Diverse în alertă/ The Miscellaneous Brigade on Alert* Directed by Mircea Drăgan	1971	Police Captain, Platoon Officer, Major, Sergeant Major, Criminals/ Money Counterfeiters (3)
26. *Brigada Diverse la munte și la mare/ The Miscellaneous Brigade to the Mountains and at the Seaside* Directed by Mircea Drăgan	1971	Police Captain, Platoon Officer, Major, Sergeant Major, Drug/Cult Objects Dealers (3)
27. *Așteptarea/The Waiting* Directed by Șerban Creangă	1971	Locomotive Engineer
28. *Puterea și adevărul/The Power and the Truth* Directed by Manole Marcus	1972	First Secretary PMR Organization, Deputy Prime Secretary, Engineer, Executive Secretary, Commander of the Regional Security Directorate
29. *100 de lei/100 lei* Directed by Mircea Săucan	1973	Actor, Unemployed
30. *Dragostea începe vineri/Love Begins on Friday* Directed by Virgil Calotescu	1973	Unskilled Worker, Factory worker, Skilled Worker
31. *Proprietarii/The Owners* Directed by Șerban Creangă	1974	Engineer, First Secretary of the County Party Committee, Economic Secretary

TABLE 10 Professional and occupational categories in Romanian films (1960–1989) (*cont.*)

Main character category		
32. *Trei scrisori secrete/Three Secret Letters* Directed by Virgil Calotescu	1974	Secretary of the RCP County Committee, Shipyard Engineer/ Deputy Director General, President of the Trade Union Committee, Party Committee Secretary
33. *Cursa/The Race* Directed by Mircea Daneliuc	1975	Heavy Machinery Trailer Driver (2), Unemployed
34. *Filip cel bun/Filip the Kind* Directed by Dan Pița	1975	High School Graduate, Director of Commercial Complex, Tailor, Commercial Manager, Skilled Worker (Retired), Street Shop Saleswoman
35. *Tată de duminică/Sunday Father* Directed by Mihai Constantinescu	1975	Mechanical Engineer, Attorney Economist, Model, Doctor
36. *Zile fierbinți/Hot Days* Directed by Sergiu Nicolaescu	1975	Shipyard Manager, Shipyard Engineer, First County Secretary, Actress, Graduate
37. *Toamna bobocilor/ Freshmen Autumn* Directed by Mircea Moldovan	1975	Professor, Doctor, Agricultural Engineer
38. *Orașul văzut de sus/The City Seen from Above* Directed by Lucian Bratu	1975	Teacher/Mayor, Engineer/Site Manager, Mayor/Ship Captain
39. *Muntele ascuns/The Hidden Mountain* Directed by Andrei C. Băleanu	1975	Site Manager, Miner, Mining Foreman
40. *Mere roșii/Red Apples* Directed by Alexandru Tatos	1976	Surgeon, Professor, Nurse
41. *Singurătatea florilor/The Loneliness of Flowers* Directed by Mihai Constantinescu	1976	Taxi Driver, Doctor

TABLE 10   Professional and occupational categories in Romanian films (1960–1989) *(cont.)*

Main character category		
42. *Serenadă pentru etajul XII/ Serenade for the XIIth Floor* Directed by Carol Corfanta	1976	Lathe Worker, Lathe Worker, Teacher
43. *Accident/Accident* Directed by Sergiu Nicolaescu	1976	Former Auto Mechanical Worker, Major Lieutenant, Colonel, Boxer, Car Shop Owner
44. *Iarba verde de acasă/The Green Grass of Home* Directed by Stere Gulea	1977	Professor, President C.A.P.
45. *Iarna bobocilor/Freshman Winter* Directed by Mircea Moldovan	1977	Agricultural Engineer, Teacher President C.A.P. (2), Technician/President of the PCR Youth Organization
46. *Trepte spre cer/Steps to the Sky* Directed by Andrei Blaier	1978	Cottage Manager, Designer, Line Workers Leader
47. *Din nou împreună/Together Again* Directed by George Cornea	1978	Agricultural Engineer (2), President C.A.P., Professor
48. *Gustul și culoarea fericirii/The Taste and Colour of Happiness* Directed by Felicia Cernăianu	1978	Construction Engineer, Chief Weaving Engineer, Weaving Technician, Master Weaver/Party Secretary
The 1980s		
49. *Probă de microfon/Microphone Test* Directed by Mircea Daneliuc	1980	TV Camera Operator, TV Reporter, Unskilled Worker
50. *Mijlocaș la deschidere/Midfielder at the opening* Directed by Dinu Tănase	1980	Lathe Worker /Rugby Player, Foreman Worker
51. *Croaziera/The Cruise* Directed by Mircea Daneliuc	1981	Hairdresser, Co-op Worker, Activist

TABLE 10 Professional and occupational categories in Romanian films (1960–1989) (*cont.*)

Main character category		
52. *Secvențe/Sequences* Directed by Alexandru Tatos	1982	Director, Operator, Actress, Commercial Unit Manager
53. *La capătul liniei/At the End of the Line* Directed by Dinu Tănase	1983	Lathe Worker, Planer Worker, Master Foundry Worker, Waitress
54. *Sfârșitul nopții/The End of the Night* Directed by Mircea Veroiu	1983	Prosecutor (2), Tram Driver
55. *Faleze de nisip/Sand cliffs* Directed by Dan Pița	1983	Medic, Nurse, Carpenter
56. *Buletin de București/Bucharest Identity Card* Directed by Virgil Calotescu	1983	Taxi Driver/Veterinary Doctor, Agricultural Engineer
57. *Un petic de cer/A Patch of Sky* Directed by Francisc Munteanu	1984	Hydropower Plant Manager, Inspector, Secretary
58. *Miezul fierbinte al pâinii/The Hot Crumb of Bread* Directed by Al. G. Croitoru	1984	Agricultural engineer (2), Director Agricultural Directorate
59. *Secretul lui Bachus/The Secret of Bachus* Directed by Geo Saizescu	1984	Journalist, Wine Warehouse Manager/ IAS, Factory Director, Inspector Financial Control, Driver
60. *Imposibila iubire/Impossible Love* Directed by Constantin Vaeni	1984	Line Worker, Construction Engineer, Laboratory Worker, Retired Actress, Driver
61. *O lumină la etajul zece/A Light on the Tenth Floor* Directed by Malvina Urșianu	1984	Metallurgical Engineer, Engineer, Lawyer, Masonry Worker, Theatre Director
62. *Pas în doi/Step in Two* Directed by Dan Pița	1985	Lathe Worker (2), Painter Worker, Pharmacy Student

TABLE 10   Professional and occupational categories in Romanian films (1960–1989) (cont.)

Main character category		
63. *Râdeți ca-n viață/Laugh as in Life* Directed by Andrei Blaier	1985	Chief Engineer, Site Foreman, Waitress
64. *Căsătorie cu repetiție/Marriage with repetition* Directed by Virgil Calotescu	1985	Veterinarian, Agricultural Engineer
65. *Promisiuni/Promisses* Directed by Elisabeta Bostan	1985	Seller, Worker, Mechanical Engineer
66. *Anotimpul iubirii/The season of love* Directed by Iulian Mihu	1986	Plant Manager, Chief Engineer, Trainee Engineer
67. *Clipa de răgaz/The Moment of respite* Directed by Șerban Creangă	1986	Steel Director / Engineer, Representative of the Ministry's Supervisory Directorate, Translator, Plant Secretary
68. *Vară sentimentală/ Sentimental Summer* Directed by Francisc Munteanu	1986	Agricultural Engineer, President C.A.P, Agricultural Technician, Secretary of the Communal Party Organization
69. *Declarație de dragoste/Declaration of Love* Directed by Nicolae Corjos	1985	High School Students (3), High School Teachers (2), Engineer, Doctor
70. *Liceenii/High School Students* Directed by Nicolae Corjos	1986	High School Students (4), Teachers (2)
71. *Secretul lui Nemesis/The Secret of Nemesis* Directed by Geo Saizescu	1986	Director of a Commercial Complex, Lawyer, Journalist
72. *Punct și de la capăt/Stop and from the Beginning* Directed by Alexa Visarion	1987	Mechanical Engineer, Plant Director, Worker
73. *Liliacul înflorește a doua oară/The Lilac Blooms a Second Time* Directed by Cristina Nichituș	1988	Teacher, Computer Engineer

TABLE 11   Distribution of professional and occupational categories by branch of economic activity

Socio-professional/ occupational category	Frequency of occurrence of profession/ occupation[a]	Field of activity
Workers (Skilled and Related, Unskilled)	49	Industrial Branches
Engineers (Metallurgical Engineers, Agronomist Engineer, Construction Engineers, Petroleum Engineers, etc.)	42	Industrial Branches
Heads of Institutions/ Administrative Officials (Heads of Industrial, Agricultural, Commercial, Medical Units/ Subunits)	24	Industrial Branches / Services
Doctors/Nurses	16	Health
Service workers (Hairdressers, Drivers, Waitresses, Bakers, Shop Assistants)	14	Personal Services
Party Officials/Political Bureaucracy	14	Political Bureaucracy
Artists	12	Cultural and Artistic Services
Teachers/Professors (Secondary, High School, University)	13	Education
Police Officers	9	Public Order and Safety
High School Students/ Graduates	9	Education
Lawyers/Attorneys/Prosecutors	7	Law/Justice
Reporters/Journalists/TV Operators	7	Press

TABLE 11 Distribution of professional and occupational categories by branch of economic activity (cont.)

Socio-professional/ occupational category	Frequency of occurrence of profession/ occupation[a]	Field of activity
Administrative Officials (Secretaries, Financial Inspectors, Ministry Representatives)	5	Public Administration
Sportsmen	3	Sport
University Students	3	Education
Economists, Accountants	2	Economic Services
Other Occupations	9	------------
Without Occupation	4	------------

a Occupations and professions were identified for the category of main characters in 73 films produced between 1960 and 1989

Engineers and leaders of economic/industrial institutions and structures form the industrial bureaucracy and have a significantly higher share of the cinematic representations than the social category of workers within the production flows. The same category of industrial bureaucracy outranks the category of administrative bureaucracy (civil servants), which does not play a significant role in power relations with the political, party bureaucracy. Out of the total of 38 characters holding positions of leadership and/or authority in economic and political structures, 24 belong to the industrial bureaucracy (directors, heads of industrial units) and 14 belong to the party bureaucracy structures (party secretaries, first secretaries of county party committees, chairmen of local committees, activists). These differentiations resulting from the quantification of relevant elements of presence for each of the categories mentioned provide a synthetic picture of the relations between main categories of actors at social, economic and political level in the context of socialist industrialization. The dynamics of the presence of these categories and of the relationships between them partly explains the distribution of the types of discourse used by directors – at different levels of intentionality – to describe aspects of socio-economic and political order, with different positioning of each of the categories depending on the critical dimension of director's view in relation to the ideological roles politically assigned to these categories, whether practical or symbolic. Workers occupy the most important position numerically, but their image is constantly articulated in a discursive relationship between this category and that of hierarchical superiors in the economic-industrial structures in which filmic narratives are set. Professional relations between workers (skilled, unskilled) and hierarchical superiors are often based on consensus and cooperation, even if not always consonant differences and attitudes are articulated in the reflection and illustration of the work process. If we were to represent the three categories of work system in socialism in the form of a pyramid, we would place the political bureaucracy at the top, the industrial bureaucracy in the middle and that of workers and technicians at the bottom. At levels 2 and 1, the layers involve multiple interferences and substitutions, in the sense that the industrial bureaucracy takes the place of party bureaucracy in terms of power relations on certain socio-cinematic segments. Industrial bureaucracy provides the interface between workers and politics and manages economic decisions passed through the filter of the party apparatus. Industrial bureaucrats are the central communication nodes in the work process, regulating the work process and work relations on the one hand, and processing political imperatives and incorporating them into concrete reality of work, on the other. Throughout the three decades, the 1960s, the 1970s, and the 1980s, the discursive relations between the three categories of characters are displayed as fallows: in the 1960s, the presence of political bureaucracy is to a very small extent represented at the level of main characters, while in the 1970s a significantly greater presence of characters belonging to political administration/members of party structures and their corresponding administrative-territorial substructures can be identified. Work and workers, however, take second place in the overall economy of practical ideology, while the industrial bureaucracy is far more important because of the power relations it has with the political bureaucracy. Work processes are located in a second general frame of the discursive economy, while it is the structure of work that is the main object of many discursive constructions, regardless of the degrees of individualization associated to them. In the 1980s, main characters belonged predominantly to the category of workers and leaders of economic-industrial institutions. However, there is a noticeable increase in the presence of a category that remains rather diffuse but constant throughout the 1970s, namely service workers: drivers, taxi drivers, waitresses, saleswomen, hairdressers, woman tailors. The character of the manager of economic unit (commercial complex and wharehouses) has a notable presence during the 1980s. The dominant images of worker in the 1980s are no longer those that present him or her in the frameworks of the flow of production, of top-down regulated labour relations, but in related hypostases that constantly question these frameworks and disintegrate them by focusing on reflexive dimensions of the worker's social identity. Skilled and unskilled workers are diluted as the bearers of socio-political possibilities that abounded in the construction of main characters of the 1970s, losing the scale of the hero type endowed with all forms of political fidelity and social competence to participate in the project of socialist construction. Rather, the number of administrative bureaucracy members begins highly to increase within the division of main characters, reproducing a real existing condition. *Filip the Kind, The Cruise, Microphone Test, Sequences, Impossible Love,* and *Step in Two* provide important discourses on this real dislocation of the category of (industrial) workers. They all contain discursive elements that criticize the work process in context of relationship between skilled and unskilled workers and structures of industrial bureaucracy. Ideological elements attached to the character profiles and social roles in films are contested in favour of the authority of those belonging to the industrial elite, passing through the passive filter of the civil servants. Members of industrial bureaucracy are also placed in diluted roles in terms of forms of manifestation of the socially and ideologically defined roles for the socio-professional category to which they belong. Elements of political subordination become parts of an impersonal mechanism that malfunctions and proves increasingly useless, accurately reflecting some developments of relations between politics and industrial technocracy. Processuality of work, working people in the concrete conditions of production, are situated in the background narrative, while the avant-garde is taken over by evaluative representations of processes of work and workers, indicating a move towards an increasingly reflexive, critical view of structure and process of work. Professional/occupational status gradually disintegrates throughout the 1980s, with characters' personal experiences taking on new fresh dimensions. Questioning human relationships beyond the professional ones becomes a dominance, industrial landscape being more a broad element of scenery for the manifestation of sensitive reflections on social and economic contexts in which social identities are articulated or fragmented.

2.2 *Main Characters and Gender Configurations*

Another dimension of cinematic analysis of socio-professional landscape is given by representations of female urban characters. I have followed particular types of characteristics of female characters in the selected actuality films with the aim of identifying identity aspects of urban female type in the key of cinematic realism and to configure a cinematic representation of urban woman under socialism. Films were selected based on the following two criteria: 1. the main characters are female and 2. the filmic narrative is situated from the point of view of the unity of space in the urban, either in the context of capital city or of the urban other than Bucharest. Using these two selection criteria, I made a significant (not necessarily representative) subsample on gender dimension: *Aproape de soare/Close to the Sun* (Savel Stiopul, 1960), *Casa neterminată/ The Unfinished House* (Andrei Blaier, 1964), *Un film cu o fată fermecătoare/A Film with a Charming Girl* (Lucian Bratu, 1967), *Meandre/Meanders* (Mircea Săucan, 1967), *Gioconda fără surâs/Gioconda without a Smile* (Malvina Urșianu, 1968), *Reconstituirea/The Reenactment* (Lucian Pintilie, 1968), *Balul de sâmbătă seara/Saturday Night Ball* (Geo Saizescu, 1968), *Apoi s-a născut legenda/Then the Legend Was Born* (Andrei Blaier, 1969), *Dragostea începe vineri/Love Begins on Friday* (Virgil Calotescu, 1972), *Cursa/The Race* (Mircea Daneliuc, 1975), *Tată de duminică/Sunday Father* (Mihai Constantinescu, 1975), *Zile fierbinți/Hot Days* (Sergiu Nicolaescu, 1975), *Toamna bobocilor/Freshmen Autumn* (Mircea Moldovan, 1975), *Filip cel bun/Filip the Kind* (Dan Pița, 1975), *Orașul văzut de sus/The City from Above* (Lucian Bratu, 1975), *Mere roșii/Red Apples* (Alexandru Tatos, 1976), *Iarna bobocilor/Freshmen Winter* (Mircea Moldovan, 1977), *Trepte spre cer/Steps to the Sky* (Andrei Blaier, 1978), *Gustul și culoarea fericirii/ The Taste and Colour of Happiness* (Felicia Cernăianu, 1978), *Din nou împreună/Together Again* (George Cornea, 1978), *Probă de microfon/Microphone Test* (Mircea Daneliuc, 1980), *Croaziera/The Cruise* (Mircea Daneliuc, 1981), *Secvențe/Sequences* (Alexandru Tatos, 1982), *La capătul liniei/At the End of the Line* (Dinu Tănase, 1983), *Buletin de București/Bucharest Identity Card* (Virgil Calotescu, 1983), *Faleze de nisip/Sand Cliffs* (Dan Pița, 1983), *Imposibila iubire/Impossible Love* (Constantin Vaeni, 1984), *Un petic de cer/A Patch of Sky* (Francisc Munteanu, 1984), *O lumină la etajul zece/A Light on the Tenth Floor* (Malvina Urșianu, 1984), *Pas în doi/Step in Two* (Dan Pița, 1985), *Declarație de dragoste/Declaration of Love* (Nicolae Corjos, 1985), *Promisiuni/Promises* (Elisabeta Bostan, 1985), *Căsătorie cu repetiție/Marriage with Repetition* (Virgil Calotescu, 1985), *Clipa de răgaz/The Moment of Respite* (Șerban Creangă, 1986), *Liceenii/The High School Students* (Nicolae Corjos, 1986), *Liliacul înflorește a doua oară/The Lilac Blooms a Second Time* (Cristina Nichituș, 1988).

The configuration of the female characters (main characters) has been established according to several socio-demographic characteristics. These are: socio-occupational status, relational status, and residential affiliation. Based on these characteristics, I looked for what could be a dominant female identity and a value matrix of the urban "socialist" type in its female role could be configured as follows:

Female characters most often work in education. The teaching profession is best represented. Next come the characters working as skilled and unskilled workers in various industrial sectors, engineers and cultural/artistic service

TABLE 12 Social characteristics of female characters in 36 films (1960–1989)

Film	Professional/ occupational status	Relationship status	Residence type
	Main character category		
1 *Aproape de soare* / *Close to the Sun*	Skilled Worker (Crane Operator)	Single	Urban 2[b]
2 *Casa neterminată* / *The Unfinished House*	Theatre Student	Single	Urban 1[a]
3 *Un film cu o fată fermecătoare* / *A Film with a Charming Girl*	High School Graduate Unemployed	Single	Urban 1
4 *Apoi s-a născut legenda* / *Then the Legend Was Born*	Unemployed	Single	Urban 2
5 *Gioconda fără surâs* / *Gioconda without a Smile*	Chemical Engineer	Single	Urban 2
6 *Meandre* / *Meanders*	Unemployed	Single	Urban 2
7 *Balul de sâmbătă seara* / *The Saturday Night Ball*	Dancer Amateur Singer	Single	Urban 2 Urban 2
8 *Dragostea începe vineri* / *Love Begins on Friday*	Unskilled Worker Skilled Worker	Single	Urban 1 Urban 1
9 *Cursa* / *The Race*	Unemployed	Single	Urban 2
10 *Tată de duminică* / *Sunday Father*	Economist Model	Single Married	Urban 1 Urban 1
11 *Zile fierbinți* / *Hot Days*	Actress College Graduate/ Unemployed	Single Single	Urban 2 Urban 2
12 *Toamna bobocilor* / *Freshmen Autumn*	Teacher Head of the Local PCR Women's Organization	Single Married	Urban 2 Urban 2

TABLE 12 Social characteristics of female characters in 36 films (1960–1989) (*cont.*)

Film	Professional/ occupational status	Relationship status	Residence type
13 *Orașul văzut de sus* / The City Seen from Above	Teacher	Single	Urban 2
14 *Mere roșii* / Red Apples	Teacher	Single	Urban 2
	Nurse	Single	Urban 2
15 *Reconstituirea* / The Reenactment	Without Occupation	Single	Urban 2
16 *Iarna bobocilor* / Freshmen Winter	Teacher	Single	Urban 2
	President C.A.P.	Married	Urban 2
17 *Trepte pe cer* / Steps in the Sky	Design Engineer	Single	Urban 2
18 *Din nou împreună* / Together Again	Teacher	Single	Urban 2
19 *Gustul și culoarea fericirii* / The Taste and Colour of Happiness	Chief Weaving Engineer	Single	Urban 2
20 *Probă de microfon* / Microphone Test	Unskilled Worker	Single	Urban 1/2
	TV Reporter	Single	Urban 1
21 *Croaziera* / The Cruise	Hairdresser	Single	Urban 1
22 *Secvențe* / Sequences	Actress	Single	Urban 1
23 *La capătul liniei* / At the End of the Line	Waitress	Single	Urban 1
24 *Faleze de nisip* / Sand Cliffs	Nurse	Single	Urban 1
25 *Buletin de București* / Bucharest Identity Card	Agricultural Engineer	Single	Urban ½
26 *Un petic de cer* / A Patch of Sky	Secretary	Single	Urban 2
27 *Căsătorie cu repetiție* / Marriage with Repetition	Agricultural Engineer	Married	Urban 2

TABLE 12 Social characteristics of female characters in 36 films (1960–1989) (cont.)

Film	Professional/ occupational status	Relationship status	Residence type
28 O lumină la etajul 10 / A Light on the Tenth Floor	Metallurgical Engineer	Single	Urban 1
29 Promisiuni / Promisses	Seller	Married	Urban 2
30 Filip cel bun / Filip the Kind	Seller / Tailor	Single / Married	Urban 1 / Urban 1
31 Pas în doi / Step in Two	Painter Worker / Student	Single / Single	Urban 1 / Urban 1
32 O iubire imposibilă / Impossible Love	Unskilled Worker / Retired Actress	Married / Married	Urban 2 / Urban 1
33 Clipa de răgaz / The Moment of Respite	Translator	Single	Urban 1
34 Declarație de dragoste / Declaration of Love	Teacher / High School Student	Married / Single	Urban 1 / Urban 1
35 Liceenii / The High School Students	High School Student / Teacher	Married / Single	Urban 1 / Urban 1
36 Liliacul înflorește a doua oară / The Lilac Blooms a Second Time	Teacher	Widow	Urban 1

a Bucharest
b Other Cities/Towns

workers (actresses, dancers, singers), followed by those in consumer services. A small number of characters occupy managing positions in institutional structures, whether industrial institutions or political organizations. Only one character of the sample holds a leading position in a party political organization.

In terms of relational status, 9 of the 36 female leading roles are married and one is a widower. Most of them occupy executive positions and are placed in

TABLE 13 Socio-professional configuration of main female characters in "socialist" city (1960–1989)

Socio-professional category	Frequency of occurrence of occupation[a]	Field of activity
Teachers/Intellectual Occupations	9	Education
Skilled/Unskilled Worker (Industry)	7	Industrial Branches
Engineers in Industry	6	Industrial Branches
Actresses/Models/Dancers/Singers	6	Art/Entertainment
Commercial and Related Personal Services Workers	5	Services/Consumer Goods
Without Occupation	6	_____
High School Students	4	Education/_____
Nurses	2	Health
TV Reporters	1	Press
Secretaries	1	Public Administration
Leaders of Political Organizations	1	Party Bureaucracy
Heads of Economic Units	1	Public Administration
Other (Economist)	1	_____

a Occupations and professions were selected for the category of female main characters from 36 films in the subsample and from the 41 female main characters (two female main characters for each of the films: *Saturday Night Ball, Love Begins on Friday, Sunday Father, Hot Days, Freshman Autumn, Microphone Test, Filip the Kind, Impossible Love*)

work collectives. There are 6 female characters with no occupation, bringing together different residential, social, and aspirational profiles: Ruxandra (*Un film cu o fată fermecătoare/A Film with a Charming Girl*), the whimsical character who wants to become an actress and spends her time in the bohemian circles of Bucharest, Neta (*Apoi s-a născut legenda/Then the Legend Was Born*), a disciplined woman well anchored in the community of a town where a railway is being built, Anda (*Meandre/Meanders*), charmingly interrogative and reflexive, Aura (*Reconstituirea/The Reenactment*), a playful and sensual character, or Maria (*Cursa/The Race*), labyrinthine and introspective. These characters diversify the female cinematic insight into atypical layers situated in static spaces (narratively well-defined spatial units, actions taking place in the same physical frameworks) or dynamic ones (transitory spaces and experiences: the road, the journey, or various geographies of social landscapes).

Regarding the distribution of characters in the films analysed, according to the type of residence defined above, close numbers are identified: 25 characters located in Bucharest, 24 in cities/towns other than Bucharest. Women working in the tertiary sector are more often married than women belonging to other occupational categories and are associated with the central space of the capital, while teachers are most often placed in cities other than Bucharest. Female workers, engineers and teachers are most often unmarried. The family institution is not a significant component in the identity structure of the female characters, nor is the maternal status. What a woman works and/or the ways in which she contests or accepts the work system is central to her identity structure, whether in films that adhere to the standard socialist realist character type or deviate from this type.

With regard to female identity in the context of work according to the degree of socio-professional integration in the work system, they are situated along several dimensions: characters who are already integrated in the field of industrial work (the dyer Maria in *Pas în doi/Step in Two*, the team leader Marieta in *Dragostea începe vineri/Love Begins on Friday*), characters who are initiated in the process of industrial work (the young Sanda Dobrescu in *Dragostea începe vineri/Love Begins on Friday*), characters who change fields of work, characters adapted to conditions of the work process, others not adapted or even in conflict with the work system (Ana Covete in *Probă de microfon/Microphone Test*), characters who occupy positions of authority and organise the work process (the chemical engineer Irina in *Gioconda fără surâs/Gioconda without a Smile*).

Compared to profiles of male characters, female characters also include occupationally undefined roles. There aren't many male main characters who don't have an occupation in the films analysed. We know in most cases what they do for a living, what their professions are, what positions and functions they occupy in various structures. As far as female characters are concerned, filmic discourse is more tolerant of non-working/non-occupying women than non-working men. Most of the women in leading roles accompany through their biographical constructions the biographies of the male characters that dominate the narrative and structure the relationships between other characters and different social realist hypostases. The female modal biography as its own life project is integrated into a framework with the male element at its centre, with its uncertainties, deviations, limitations, attempts, and expectations. A distinct note observable in a small number of films is the ambiguous identity of female character in social terms, lacking clear social status. This is the case of films, not many, of social criticism such as *100 de lei* and *Meandre/ Meanders* by Mircea Săucan, *Faleze de nisip/Sand Cliffs* by Dan Pița, typical of this identity construction. The characters Dora, Anda and Cristina appear as girlfriends/partners of the male characters, without being articulated in terms of their social identity. We don't know what they do for a living, where they live, what they consume, what is the wider relational configuration in which they are anchored. Their presence is dominated by introspection, interpersonal discussions on subjects related to intimacy, delicate biographical insights, prospecting a condition of a sensibility elaborated in distinct notes along a varied continuum of imagining women. The cinematic feminine configuration reveals rather in these cases expressions of a form of indifferent subordination (at the discursive level) of female characters in terms of the manifestation of their autonomy, their social competences, their location in institutional frameworks.

3 Work Attitudes and Evaluations: Two Ideological Hypostases of Work

The cinematic discourse on working life is structured on different layers: on the one hand, the discourse present in films that manifestly reflect the official ideology of work, on the other hand, filmic discourses that assume a latent criticism, centered on the conflict between ideological meanings and real practices of working life. To illustrate the two types of discourse, I propose an evaluative commentary based on a comparative analysis of two actuality films that enter these two categories: *Zile fierbinți/Hot Days* (Sergiu Nicolaescu, 1975) and *Probă de microfon/Microphone Test* (Mircea Daneliuc, 1980). In both films, the theme of work is present, only the perspectives on it are significantly different. .

The analysis of the two films follows these dimensions: the relationship between individual and work, the main characteristics of the characters placed in the context of work activities, elements of social status and family structure, aspects of consumption in relation to production activity, public-private relationship.

In *Zile fierbinți/Hot Days*, the evaluative perspective on work is highly ideological, in the propagandistic sense. The main character of the engineer and

TABLE 14　Ideological economy of characters in *Hot Days* and *Microphone Test*

Zile fierbinți/*Hot Days* (1975)	*Probă de microfon*/*Microphone Test* (1980)
Male (Main Character)	Female (Main Character)
Work Hero	Marginal Social Type
Production	Consumption
Work	Leisure
Producer of Means of Production	Producer of Consumer Goods
Institutional	Individual

shipyard manager (played by Sergiu Nicolaescu) is emblematic for the social type of the "working hero". The life of the individual is strongly identified with work. Outside it, the individual has no social value. The individual counts only as a producer of material goods. Most of the narrative places the character in the context of the action represented by the labour activities and the relations in the production process.

The most responsible position for an individual is to be placed in the context of action, and not of any kind of action, but of labour activity. Work is the major criterion in defining individual identity. Man does not count in any particular form of individuation, but as a man of work, through the function he performs in the concrete reality of labour process. Belonging to a labour community is most important in defining the social position of the individual. Respect of others and social prestige are effects of the professional or occupational status. A central idea of film is that of individual sacrifice for work. Work becomes a central character itself in that it integrates major aspects of individual's life: friendship, sociability, family, ethics.

In *Zile fierbinți*/*Hot Days*, we are dealing with a single facet of the world of work, in the sense that the relationship between the individual and work is one-dimensional, positively formulated in both content and expression. In *Probă de microfon*/*Microphone Test*, this facet is dispersed into trajectories and nuances resulting in a bazaar-like social (work) universe, in which attractions and rejections diversify, the relationship between individual and work is conflictual, depending on the degree of individual inertia to uniformising and constraining tendencies of a system generating inequality.

Although the two films deal with different aspects of work and of the relationship between individual and work, the cinematic discourse is based on the same sub-themes, as follows:

1. Both films present the reality of work in socialism under different aspects: on the one hand, work understood as a final value, on the other hand, work understood as an instrumental value, necessary to satisfy individual and social needs.
2. Both films deal with the relationship between individual and work by proposing an explanatory scheme for the integration or non-integration of work process in socialism; this scheme reflects the mirroring of the ideological model of work or the deviation from such a model.
3. Both films place the units of action in specific workplaces (shipyard, plant, factory), but the images of these spaces indicate significantly different modes of imagining the relationship between workers and the morphological work space.
4. Both films offer a view of working subject in work settings, the difference being that attitudes of main characters towards work are opposed: attitudes of rejection and attitudes of attraction to work are displayed.
5. Both films provide an evaluative perspective on working subject in the hypostases represented by the "hero of work" and the figure of the "marginal".

These elements of filmic construction indicate an interference between two discursive levels, which manifestly are opposed. The two oppositional types of biographies – a strongly standardized one, shaped according to ideological pre-definitions of the relationship between the individual and work in particular and the materialization of a social life project in general (*Zile fierbinți/ Hot Days*), and a strongly individualizing one, articulated outside of role stereotypes, of ideological internalizations as a process of social influence (*Probă de microfon/Microphone Test*) – offers a view of the structural limits of a way of thinking and organizing the relations between individual needs, choices, aspirations and imperatives, in accordance with a life project of his or her own and the objective conditions of a "historical" biography with its specific modes of attribution.

Able to condense characteristics that describe the two urban biographies, the films operationalize a mechanism of sociological imagination, clarifying the nature of the relationship between individual and historical context in which he or she is placed: on the one hand, there is the image/representation of the institutionalization of individual biography (in the case of Sergiu Nicolaescu's film), on the other hand, there is the image/representation of a multi-layered biography which delivers the imaginary (discourse) with a solid historical concreteness more close to a dialectical apprehension of the relationship between film form and internalization of social time understood as past, present, and future.

4   Working Subject and City Dweller between Hero and Marginal

The image of working man/woman is built on a polar axis that brings together two types of cinematic visions: a representation of working people whose social experiences are dominated by working life, and a representation of working people depicted in various hypostases of social life, engaged in different forms of sociability, outside work activities. There are two categories of working people according to the absence or presence of elements that describe their social life. What do working people do? What do they not do? In what hypostases are they portrayed? Around which experiences are configured the trajectories of their existence? What does their everyday life look like? What forms of sociability are practiced?

The universe of working people's lives is, on the one hand, reduced to productive activities in the case of ideologically manifest films, on the other hand, extends to a diverse range of extra-productive activities and concerns, resulting in a deconstruction of the myth of the "new man".

Depending on the degree of consensus between the filmic discourse on work and the ideological vision of work, I have divided actuality films in two categories: manifestly ideological films, in the sense that they propagate in a direct manner (at the level of filmic narrative, character construction, visual component) ideas and principles specific to the work ethic in socialism, and films with reflexive and/or critical accents, in the sense that they question the mechanisms and practices of ideological education on work. One indicator of this kind of differentiated view is the relationship between the individual and work: a relationship of identity in the sense that work is essential for social identity (individual = work or individual = [productive] activity) and a conflictual relationship in the sense that the individual challenges and rejects a certain established order according to which the work system operates (in terms of work opportunities, work relations and work practices). People at work are differentiated by the presence or absence of certain aspects of social life: types of activities, daily routines, concerns, interests, and preferences. Male characters with reflexive overtones in *Diminețile unui băiat cuminte/ The Mornings of a Good Boy, Filip cel bun/Filip the Kind* or *Pas în doi/Step for Two* are projected in complex and nuanced social configurations, manifest different forms of sociability (sociability in the workplace, sociability in the group of friends), cultural consumption activities, leisure practices, recreation, elements of personal care and hygiene, aspects of private life, relational life, introspections and intrapersonal dialogues. At the level of the category of ideological manifest films, these configurations are very limited in terms of the social characteristics and practices mentioned. The main character in *Zile fierbinți/Hot Days*, an engineer and shipyard manager, is visible in a limited number of activities and social situations, unlike the worker characters in the films mentioned above. Dimensions of social life such as work, housing, sociability, cultural consumption, socio-professional mobility are expressed in the biographies of the reflexive characters through the following activities: going to the cinema, going to the restaurant with friends/girlfriends, buying flowers, walking down the street, going to the restaurant with co-workers, participating in the artistic activities of the site's theatre group, eating together with colleagues (*Diminețile unui băiat cuminte/Mornings of a Good Boy*), going to the restaurant with girlfriend, going to the restaurant with father, playing billiards, travelling by bus, drinking alcoholic drinks, changing jobs, having dinner with family, attending a friend's birthday party (*Filip cel bun/Filip the Kind*), going to the disco, pillow fights, sports (boxing, fencing), playing musical instruments, having sex, walking in the park, listening to music, telling jokes and playing pranks on colleagues (*Pas în doi/Step in Two*). The character of the site manager in *Zile fierbinți/Hot Days* is predominantly situated in the institutional workspace. Most of the situations in which the character is placed are those defined within the frameworks of the production process on the one hand, and of the relations with the political bureaucracy on the other. Other activities: birthday celebrations with a few friends/relatives, taking meals alone at home and on the construction site, helping an elderly employee get a refrigerator.

One of the themes related to work is the intergenerational conflict: conflict between parents and children, especially the father-son relationship. Intergenerational conflict is articulated in terms of attitudes towards work structured on two basic mechanisms or principles: *consensus* with the socialist imperative of work as an absolute value (the "old" generation) versus *conflict* with certain mechanisms and practices of integrating the individual into the social reality of work (the younger generation). Given that in the socialist Romania of the 1960s and 1970s, the generally low number of places at university generated a high number of rejected candidates, the option for work was the best solution at hand. This is a common profile for main characters category in: *Diminețile unui băiat cuminte/Mornings of a Good Boy* (1967), *Dragostea începe vineri/Love Begins on Friday* (1973), *Filip cel bun/Filip the Kind* (1975), *Singurătatea florilor/The Loneliness of Flowers* (1976). This option is structured along two dimensions: on the one hand, a vision lacking an individual projection of one's own social path (hypostatised in its professional/occupational dimension), and on the other hand, an individualizing vision in which the option for work is structured not only according to the nature of a professional or occupational practice, to the employment opportunities that society provides, but according to a certain individual understanding of all these structural elements, as a result of passing them through the filter of individual reflection. The choice of (a particular) profession/job is the consequence of the manifestation of values and aspirations shared by individuals and not an end in itself.

Attitudes towards work in the two situations reflect the quality of the relationship between individual and society. In the first case, we are dealing with a relationship in which the individual is a mere spectator, the passive recipient of rules, practices and norms internalized through socializing mechanisms. Influence is a one-dimensional one, from society to the individual. In the second hypothesis, we are dealing with the social type that problematizes the relationship with society, questioning the relationship between certain aspects of its social condition and certain characteristics of society. The individual is placed in the position of an "actor", and not just of a "spectator", endowed with the capacity to become aware of the distance between the condition of individual existence and the external historical scene. It is not only society that influences the individual, but the individual can also intervene and contribute through the choices and actions that make up his or her biography to the redefinition of the meanings associated with the more general condition of society. It is not the choice for a particular type of work that is the strong criterion in the design of the individual's social path, but a much more important choice linked to the existence of one's own life project: "It is not enough to know what kind of work you want to do, you must know what kind of life you want to live" (*Filip cel bun/Filip the Kind*). The controversy between the two visions of work actually unveils two different thinking mechanisms, two visions of life. Characters like Vive (played by Dan Nuțu) in *Diminețile unui băiat cuminte/The Mornings of a Good Boy*, Filip (played by Mircea Diaconu) in *Filip cel bun/Filip the Kind*, Petre (played by Dan Nuțu) in *100 lei/100 de lei*, Gelu (played by Dan Nuțu) in *Meandre/Meanders* or Andrei (played by Valeriu Săndulescu) in *Casa neterminată/The Unfinished House* belong to the category of young people who are not adapted to work under socialism, are representative of the rebel type, characters who refuse social conventions, who do not question the system but question existence itself. This reflexive construction of the characters stood in opposition to the model of the work hero character. The characters listed above openly deconstruct the hypostasis of what was intended to be the "new man". The focus is therefore not on the figure of the "new man", the communist, but on the figure of an equally old man and, by extension, on a society in which there is also theft, violence, nonconformism, lack of education, people who do not work and do not want to work, a society in which there is also maladaptation, uncertainty, atypical definitions of institutions and social situations.

As an anti-hero, the character Petre in *100 de lei* has a biographical path "atypical" for the characters of the time: an individual who is not accepted to college, who has no job and has no desire to look for one, he is the socially deviant type who steals a can of sardines from a general store, throws a bottle of milk into a garbage bin on the street in full view of passers-by after drinking a small quantity of it, gets into physical altercations with unknown individuals, chases a young woman down the street, drives a Buick. With such a character, the film positions itself against the accommodating tendencies of cinema to bend to varying degrees to political imperatives regarding character construction. The film is realistic, the temptation for the real is major, but not in the ideologizing sense of the official doctrine of socialist realism.

The imperative of reflection is not enough, more important is the choice of what (must be) reflected. It is not by chance that Mircea Săucan's film was subject to draconian censorship. Moreover, it went so far that the negative of the film was burned for political reasons, keeping only two copies. Another Mircea Săucan film, *Meanders*, went through the same censorship process. *Meanders* and *100 de lei* configure an existentialist dimension of the relationship between individual and society, between characters and the wider sociopolitical context, between different ways of perceiving reality, with a content almost postmodern.

Alongside *100 lei* and *Meanders*, other films subject to censorship were *Dimineţile unui băiat cuminte/The Mornings of a Good Boy* and *Casa neterminată/The Unfinished House*. What these films have in common is the type of central character who doesn't integrate into the "new man" type. In these films we are not dealing with positive heroes, as was required in the days, positive heroes in the propagandistic sense. The characters integrate into a different category of "positivity" in the sense that they are positive heroes in that they are characters who differentiate themselves along their own existential paths. This category includes characters like those in *Cursa/The Race* (Mircea Daneliuc, 1975) and *La capătul liniei/At the End of the Line* (Dinu Tănase, 1983), representing social types that are not necessarily also landmarks type characters. The protagonists of *La capătul liniei/At the End of the Line* and *Cursa/The Race* are not so much heroic characters as complex characters: Crişan (played by Mircea Albulescu) is a master turner, a former prisoner following his involvement in a work accident, the lathe worker Cicea (played by Dan Condurache) is an ambiguous guy, on the verge of delinquency, sensitive and vulnerable, who's clinging to his friend whom he believes can lead him on a better way, the driver Anghel (played by Mircea Albulescu) in *Cursa/The Race* is a character who has difficulty in communicating with others, with the outside world, but who demonstrates deep forms of human sociability and availability.

The architecture of characters in these films of the 1970s and 1980s reveals a construction mechanism structured on multiplicity: the characters have composite facets, their actions are susceptible to plural meanings, their relationships are recomposed in ways that are not permanently consonant, highlighting a system of value pluralism. Desirable elements are combined with undesirable ones. Through a contrast mechanism, the characters become more exciting and more striking as social types, increasing the element of authenticity – the authenticity of characters, of life events, of actions describing the narrative trajectories. Being a hero in the sense of being a landmark as a social type is no longer dominant in the landscape of "actuality" characters. Some characters are landmarks, others to a lesser extent. An example of the first category is the character of Doctor Mitică Irod (played by Mircea Diaconu) in *Mere Roșii/Red Apples* (Alexandru Tatos, 1976), set in a provincial urban setting and characterised by professionalism, moral principles, and confronted with the shortcomings of a system that tolerates corrupt practices, underground mechanisms of social upbringing and false careerism. The character is not impressive; on the contrary, he belongs to that category of "exemplary" heroes in terms of ordinary character and absence of spectacular expressions.

To sum up, the actuality films produced between 1960 and 1989 show an important dynamic in the construction of (main) characters. In the 1960s, most characters are defined directly in relation to society. Some of them have reflexive overtones, advance existentialist nuances, but all of these elements are situated alongside the striking visualisation of a system, generating the effect of emptiness, of distance between the character and the type of reality presented, which changes significantly in the context of films made in the 1970s. In the 1970s and early 1980s, when most of the life situations atatched to characters and in which they are put to act are taken from the system, without there necessarily being a pronounced image of the system as such on a secondary dramatic level. The attraction for the real in films is expressed through conventional lines and dialogue, through authenticity in the character's reaction, through the kind of hero who is natural, ordinary, troubled. The presence of work in the form of work activities, the material frameworks of work, only serves to provide a context for the formulation of some reflections regarding the articulation of personal biographies not through institutional springs, but through fragments of subjective experience in which the attention is focused on interpersonal relationships, sliding between uncertainties, limits, and contestations.

5 Work and Social Space: An Ideological Pattern of Job Distribution

A specific cinematic frame of the worker is that of the commuter worker, a specific category of worker created and developed in the context of socialist urbanzation, of managing the urban-rural divide. One of the major aims of urbanization was to eliminate the essential differences between village and town, to raise the village to a degree of civilisation specific to the urban world. Apart from planned interventions in the field of administrative organization, an important role in the emancipation of the rural way of life was assigned to certain urban social categories who were sent, through the mechanism of distribution, to work, populate and civilise the rural world. Political attempts to eliminate class distinctions and to homogenise society provided prolific themes related to the mechanisms of developing the social identity of workers assigned to the countryside and of the socio-ideological relations with members of the host communities.

At a time when there was a strong inertia among recent university graduates towards the practice of being assigned to rural localities located at a long distance from urban areas, some actuality films developed a corrective function understood as an ideological counterpoint to a factual social situation. This was done under the modernizing imperative that asserted the elimination of the differences between village and town through emancipatory incursions, in the "style" of a supposed urban culture, into the traditional, peasant environment. Films legitimized a type of option regarding a social, professional, family path, which was established "from the centre" and which limited the possibilities of affirming individual choices regarding the trajectory of one's own biography.

The lack of attraction to the countryside among young intellectuals, specialists and other professionals was correctively counterbalanced in films. The conflict existing in reality was diluted by the consensus in the film. A consensus that was mostly induced. The choice to live and work in a village was given in a positive evaluation, with various nuances, which nevertheless reflected the differences and disagreements between the cultural model and lifestyle in the countryside and those in the city, but precisely in order to reinforce in a peremptory and "realistic" way the idea of the success of a project with far-reaching social, cultural and economic stakes. We are dealing with a counter-analysis of society, in the sense that in a reverse reading and interpretation we are in fact identifying aspects of the reality of a social and demographic mobility before 1989.

What we see in the film is at least a dissonant form of what existed in reality, if not the opposite of system and mechanisms of working life in socialism. This model of constructing a value model to be followed in terms of attitudes towards work and acceptability of social ways and mechanisms of organising it, with the specific means of art, established a method of attempting to affirm and legitimize practices and options related to work at the level of form, that is, (cinematic) discourse. At the manifest level, the actuality film played a constructive role in this sense, but in relation to other contextual elements (the film set in relation to the real circumstances of the issue it deals with), it takes on an inverse function, of deconstructing an ideological pattern that was overtaken by the real practices of working life, shaped in turn by the spontaneous reactions of individuals engaged in their own life trajectories. Not only through the difference, but through the opposition that the film develops in relation to reality (the situation of work in the context of the urban-rural relationship, for example), through a certain discourse and therefore through a certain evaluation, it places ideology and its references at the level of artistic expression under the spectre of failure. Attempts to use film to reframe ways of thinking about the acceptability of a certain way of life and a certain style of work have also had a perverse effect, actually increasing the degree to which (artistic) perception deviates from the official view.

This is the case of many films that deal with the subject of work in the context of the demographic mobility in socialism and that bring together in an ideological vision the rural-urban interference within the social experience of work. *Toamna bobocilor/Freshmen Autumn* (Mircea Moldovan, 1975), *Iarna bobocilor/Freshmen Winter* (Mircea Moldovan, 1977), *Din nou împreună/ Together Again* (George Cornea, 1978), *Căsătorie cu repetiție/Marriage with Repetition* (Virgil Calotescu, 1985), *O vară sentimentală/Sentimental Summer* (Franscisc Munteanu, 1986), *Punct și de la capăt/Stop and from the Beginning* (Visarion Alexa, 1987).

In equal conditions in terms of educational level, the characters who end up working in rural communities are included into two major categories: 1. graduates with a background in technical professions (construction engineer, agronomist, doctor, veterinarian); 2. graduates in exact and social sciences (teachers).

Based on this classification of characters, we distinguish two categories within the same class: the intellectual and the specialist. The differences between characters with the same professional/occupational status and belonging to different residential backgrounds (urban/rural) are ideologically structured as follows: positive valorization of the main character (the urban specialist or the intellectual) in relation to the supporting character (the rural specialist or the intellectual). Positive valorization is expressed along two main dimensions: on the one hand, the level of superiority in practicing profession (professional ascendancy both in terms of professional formation and studies and professional competence in practice), on the other hand, moral and political ascendancy and legitimacy to deconstruct existing social conventions in the rural community and to establish other values, practices and norms in this new space of belonging.

The biographical trajectories of many urban characters highlight a general tendency in actuality cinema to invest these characters (in the urban-rural context) with the function of emancipation as a manifestation of modernization in the host rural communities.

The effects of this function are equivalent to some forms of social changes, at least in terms of three dimensions: 1. cultural, 2. structural and 3. demographic.

1. People who migrate from town to village bring with them a cultural background based on specific values, attitudes and practices concerning: housing, work ethic, sociability, relating to difference, aspects of adaptation and integration into the rural or small town community;
2. One of the mechanisms of integration and construction of belonging to the rural community is the institution of marriage; this mechanism has two types of manifestation: on the one hand, marriage between an urban character and a local character (placed in the rural environment), on the other hand, marriage between characters, both from the urban environment (both with the same level of education, usually higher education) assigned from the centre (or, in other cases, being a personal choice independent of system of distribution of jobs) to rural localities in the country. This narrative dimension allows the representation of an established way of organising the workforce on the one hand, and of producing change in the socio-demographic structure of the rural community, on the other hand;
3. Placing a small part of urban population (intellectuals/specialists) in the countryside produces changes in the sociodemographic configuration of this category of social space, demonstratively shown cinematically through the process of officially and centrally managed occupational mobility, but also through others such as mixed marriage in terms of residential environment of belonging, the latter being a particular effect of such a planned process of social mobility.

Synthesizing the representations of relationship between urban and rural hypostatized in the relationship between modernizing urban character, expression of the "new man", and traditional rural community, of the "old man" type, a pattern of interaction unveils that is structured on several elements. The interaction often involves two asymmetrical categories of actors: an individual in relation to a community. The individual is most often represented by the figure of the specialist or of the intellectual, the emancipatory hero initially situated in conflict with the conservative rural dweller, whose inertia and suspicion of the idea of change will eventually be annihilated by the ideologically structured intervention of the urban figure. As a rule, the urban character initially punishes the rural community for various problematic aspects of its organization and functioning (corrupt practices, "backward" mentalities, inertia to change, rejection of the new), before the community finally rewards him by integrating him. The interaction between the individual character (the specialist or the intellectual) and the collective character (the rural community) provides the framework for the manifestation of a process of initiation for both. Influence is not always one-dimensional (only from urban to rural); rather, there are mutual assimilations and internalizations, more or less transitory, whose dynamic results not in the elimination but in the fluidization of the boundaries between the two worlds representing two ways of life, two cultural patterns. The "new man" thus becomes susceptible to multiple deviations from the official model of the working man, whatever his field of activity.

If the symbolic tools of the social imaginary are used, a matrix that brings together all the elements of a symbolic form of the myth can be easily identified. The civilisation of the rural man through the appropriation of working and living conditions in the villages to those in the towns remains a myth deconstructed cinematically by dislocating the ideological vision attached to these relationships. The meanings and significances conveyed in terms of urban-rural relations give us the image of various forms of cohabitation, sometimes conflictual, and not necessarily of substitution.

In this explanatory perspective, the urban social type of the intellectual or specialist is the one that establishes new criteria for ordering the facts and social relations, the actions that make up social experience, the biography of the community. It re-establishes a principle of order, justice, cohesion and solidarity within community, whether it is the community as a whole or the social space in which professional activities are carried out. It is often in the professional sphere that conflicts are generated which, in order to be resolved, lead to the essential relations between the two sides, and which most often end in a transition from conflict and suspicion to consensus and trust.

The cinematic vision reproduces an ideological view of the relationship between urban and rural, emphasising in terms of superiority the civilising role of the urban factor in its "human" aspect. It is the urban character who has arrived in the village and who challenges and manages the delicate process of supposed elimination of the differences between village and town. In reality, we are dealing not with an elimination of differences between the two environments, but with exposure to a certain type of experience of difference and differentiation, which generates "local" reactions and responses. A general observation for all films of the period dealing directly with this subject is that instead of the so-called "elimination" of differences between village and town, we are rather dealing with a process of identity "relocation" in the case of urban characters who usually end up being integrated into the rural community or, in a more expressive formulation, being "tamed". This operation is usually carried out in three steps:

1. t1 moment when the premises of the conflictual relationship between the urban character and the community are laid out, most often based on attitudes and behaviours of rejection of the urban (modernizing) pattern, which is embodied in the ways of being and doing of the urban character send to live and work in the rural, the conflict being most often structured at the level of professional and interpersonal/group social relationships;
2. t2 moment when the conflict is explicitly actualized;
3. t3 moment when consensus is established at the level of relations between the urban character and the community character, on the one hand, based on the community's partial acceptance of elements of social change, on the other hand, based on the urban character's accommodation to the experiences of everyday life in the countryside.

The conflict is in fact a conflict between two "golden ages", in the symbolic terms of the political imaginary: between the past – the "golden age" present in the social imaginary of the rural community – and the present/future – the "golden age" of the urban individual ("hero-saviour") invested with a modernizing role. What emerges from their confrontation at discoursive level is not necessarily any elimination of differences between the two worlds, but the emergence of a space of interference that accommodates both golden ages, both cultural patterns, both ways of life.

The urban character of the "hero-saviour" is often the one who reacts to the social and moral conventions of social life in the host community. The urban character (or the urban character originally from the countryside) is the one who tries to subject the community to a reforming, emancipatory principle, both at the institutional level and at the intra- and inter-individual level, especially concerning aspects of social life such as work, family, sociability.

The manifestation of work experiences becomes an essential link in the contestation of a social order (persisting in the rural world) and contributes to the decantation of elements that make it possible to reach a common denominator at the level of two apparently opposed value systems susceptible to multiple rationalizations. The quality and political meanings of work experiences in the context of distribution mechanisms derive from the instrumentation of the double relation between rural and urban: 1. centripetal relations (attraction to the urban in the context of the central urban); 2. centrifugal relations (attraction to the rural). At the level of each dimension two forms of manifestation of the same type of relationship are identified, as follows: 1. the attraction of rural inhabitants to the city; 2. the attraction of inhabitants located in small or large urban periphery to the city/large urban; 3. the attraction of urban inhabitants to the rural.

CHAPTER 12

Domination, Hegemony, and Interpellation. Film and the Impossibility of Getting Out of Ideology

How can we theorize around cinematic reality as part of a larger social reality in the context of socialism? What is the relationship between the apparatus of state ideology and the cultural institution of cinema as a system of production, distribution and consumption? What is the relationship between cinema and ideology in the context of the critical manifestations of some Romanian filmmakers? How is the dominant character of ideology (Marx) distinguished from the hegemonic one (Gramsci) and both from the interpellation character (Althusser) in different stages of cinema under socialism? These are some questions through which I intend to identify a series of meanings at the level of the depth structure of film institution in relation to internal (film content) and external (political, economic, social) conditions under which it manifested, that is, within ideology. How far did film emerge from socialist ideology? How much from other ideologies did it borrow through its concrete forms of manifestation (films) in the construction of social representations conveyed in films? What degrees of freedom can be identified in the manifestation of official socialist ideology in concrete cultural practices (film production)? These questions compose an interrogative matrix based on which I advance a series of inferences regarding the relationships and interdependencies between ideology and film, the "exits" from socialist ideology by the filmic discourse and the use of the ideological state apparatus in order to deconstruct it, the forms of coexistence between the cultural structure and the concrete practices of its contestation within the same structure.

In Marxist perspective, the dominating quality of ideology implies accepting as true the premise that the ideological state apparatus (institutions of the press, art) has a direct influence on individuals, and is exercised without any real significant possibility of challenging the value and symbolic order conveyed by cultural products. In the Gramscian conception, the ideological apparatus acquires a purely hegemonic quality and is confined to the social class of intellectuals who define the dominant value orientations and regulate the ins and outs of the cultural system (which functions by defining certain ends for the attainment of which certain categories of means are used which are considered to be the most appropriate in accordance with the ideology which must be reproduced in order to ensure further reproduction of the relations of production in society). According to Althusser, the hegemonic function becomes weaker, under the form of interpellation, in the sense that the nature of the relation between subject and real conditions of its existence is imaginary, mediated by the ideological state apparatus. Althusser develops the ideological equation from an equation in two variables (v. 1 individuals – v. 2 real conditions of existence) to an equation in three variables (v. 1 individuals – v. 2 real conditions of existence – v. 3 individuals' imaginary relation to the relation between themselves and the real conditions of existence). This imaginary relationship is made possible through intercession of ideological apparatuses of the state, institutions that introduce and convey ideas and representations that become concrete through practices and rituals.

Within cultural practice, the three ideological qualities are not exclusive. Rather, we are dealing with a broadening of imaginative perspective (both theoretical and ideological) on their potential for manifestation and their limits within what Bourdieu called "field of power" understood not just as "the history of the struggle for a monopoly of the imposition of legitimate categories of perception and appreciation" (Bourdieu, 1995: 157).

> The field of power is the space of relations of force between agents or between institutions having in common the possession of the capital necessary to occupy the dominant positions in different fields (notably economic or cultural). It is the site of struggle between holders of different powers (or kinds of capital) which, like the symbolic struggles between artists and the 'burgeois' in the nineteenth century, have at stake the transformation or conservation of the relative value of different kinds of capital, which itself determines, at any moment, the forces liable to be engaged in these struggles.
>
> BOURDIEU, 1995: 279

The three levels mutually reinforce each other, giving the image of a continuum of (existing) ideological reality, taking different values from one socio-historical sequence to another. This continuum becomes functional in an approach to analyse the depth structure of ideology (ideological practice), that is to identify the revelators, only through differentiation and recognition of differentiation between the three forms of ideology manifestation by those who act according to or against ideology being within ideology, developing mechanisms of negotiating the legitimacy of meanings and significances conveyed through cultural products. This is also the case of several filmmakers during socialism who created films understood as a critique of the political system and of the social order, films produced within the socialist production system and in the context of the cultural ideology of socialist realism. How are the three qualities of ideology (domination, hegemony, and interpellation) distributed in such a configuration?

1 Film and Ideology: Two Constructions

One expressive perspective within the representations of work in film under socialism is a visual one, which alone can be object of a significant discursive introspection. Materialization of work, work in the form of objects that satisfy practical and symbolic needs of the socialist system are useful dimensions in the critical discussion regarding the aesthetic and social developments of value and practice of work in film.

1.1 Cave (Illusion): A Projection on Work and the City. The Mental Image of Work in the Context of the Visual Image of the City

In *Filip cel bun/Filip the Kind* (Dan Pița, 1975), the idea of living in the "socialist" built space only manifests itself as a projection. The presence and actions of main character, a young high school graduate who failed the university entrance exam, in search of a job, is a pretext for describing the future condition of living in a socialist city, incorporating work resources ordered and distributed inclusively for the fulfillment of symbolic imperatives of a dominant ideology. On a visual level structured by elements of cinematic technique, general and panoramic shots, used to capture the landscape of housing blocks under construction or almost finished, give us the image of a city populated by apartment blocks which, in turn, are not populated by people and, above all, by those who built them. None of the film's characters, whether main or supporting, live in a "socialist" apartment block. This directorial choice leaves room for critical commentary – in visual terms – on the thought structure of a new urban order made possible by the management of multiple resources of labour force, but in a context that does not indicate the distribution of these goods to those who would officially be the main beneficiaries, namely the working people.

What we identify in the content and expression of the scenes filmed in the exterior and interior of the apartment block under construction is the image of an ideological thought passed through the critical filter of the one who takes the sign of this thought from the acctual (present) reality and recomposes it with the means of cinematic art in the form of a "new" product intended to be consumed by the imagination and that generates a different subjective experience of the work and the city. From the point of view of the relation to the real, what the film delivers is a transformation into an image of an individual reaction to social life, based on its materialization in the field of representation. The cinematic positioning of the physical morphology of socialist urban dwelling outside the experience for which it is strategically designed, conceptualized and turned into the concrete forms of material existence is equivalent to a virtual annihilation of a present reality. The annihilation of this particular form of expression of the material condition of existence further suggests the idea that the determination of consciousness based on material embodiment of ideology, according to the Marxist conception, is unlikely to become an actual, viable reality.

In analysing this film which is highly significant for the urban actuality of the 1970s, I have paid particular attention to certain elements of visual representation of work in the context of the city which I have found useful in identifying latent structures of meaning associated with the presence of work and working people. In this regard, I describe a particular construction of the cinematic image of work in the finite hypostasis of an urban construction (apartment block) and which incorporates in the form of a symbolic expression an ideational construction susceptible to reflexive considerations. The image in the film to which I refer displays an apartment block, under construction, filmed in low-angle shot from its open interior space. The frame includes the outer walls of a block – seen from the open interior space of the building – which are exposed like the walls of a tunnel, oriented vertically, at the end of which the only visible element is the sky associated with the figure of light. The position of the camera generates an image in which the morphological elements of the block object appear as asymmetrical, without a balanced relationship between them, suggesting the idea of faulty thinking underlying the construction or the limitations of a mind to see the necessary relationships between these elements so as to truly serve human and social needs, in an intelligent, honest, and integrated political vision. The visual structure of this cinematic frame reveals all the elements necessary and sufficient to identify a representation of the symbolic structure of Plato's allegory of the cave. What emerges from the way in which elements that make up the visual whole of frame are ordered and arranged is a relationship of identity between the cave and the "socialist" built space (in the expression of an apartment block generically and practically incorporating the idea and the practice of work). The issue of spatial determinations generated by the ideological vision on urbanization at the time is transferred into a sphere of symbolic analogy between the mythical spatial figure dominated by "shadows" and the spatial figure that is the product of an ideology. The new urban physical morphology is assimilated to an archetypal spatial form identified in the figure of the cave. This visually configured vision has implications both ontologically and epistemologically. The cave brings together both a condition of existence and a condition of knowledge. It is a symbol of the absence of knowledge, of ignorance, of a constrained ontological condition by placing it outside "truth" and "intelligence", "right" and "beautiful", that is, according to the Platonic conception, outside of "light". This kind of condition is susceptible to misidentification between the hidden nature of an ideological purpose and the practical and human utility of the actual constructed objects. Similar to the condition of the prisoner in Plato's cave: "on some occasion, some individual prisoner might use the term "ox" with the mistaken impression that it refers to the shadow of a model of a horse" (Harte, 2007:201).

By analogy, identifiable in the cinematic visual construction, the socialist living space incorporates all these elements described above, it is therefore a space of "illusions" (or errors) created by the real work of the real working people. The image functions as a critique of the political vision of the relationship between individual and political power captured in the particular hypostasis of the relationship between individual and space "conceived" by political ideology of the time, a critique articulated on both ethical and aesthetic dimension. The significance associated with the condition of material existence, the urban setting and, by extension, with the socio-economic structure in the context of socialist politics is that of a practical and at the same time symbolic return, of a degradation of the idea (or reality) of city, building, and space. The symbolic effect is the invalidation of a present system, of an actual time, a "material time", by means of a critical commentary on the designed space of the city associated with a certain quality of thought and, through this, with a certain willingness to confer reality, meaning and value to the objects and facts attached to it..

The use of the low-angle shot angle and of the subjective point of view ("the look" of the camera becomes the "look" of the viewer) contributes to the construction of an accurate evaluation of the ontological condition of man in socialist habitat – a "primitive" condition, as anyone looking at this setting can easily identify himself or herself, in a symbolic sense, with the "prisoner" man from the Platonic cave. The image has a critical significance all the more striking as the camera angle reproduces the character's angle of view – the cinematic gaze becomes the gaze of the character who perceives, filters the visual information of the object of work, of the built space, and we, along with him, perceive and filter the same information based on which we can develop an evaluation of the relationship between individual and concrete conditions of work, between individual and ideology.

Theorizing around the nature of ideology, one conclusion is that through such (institutional/filmic) practice, a hegemonic quality of ideology can be identified in the sense that it is the filmmaker (the artist/the intellectual) who make use of the cinematic institution invested with the role of building cultural education of the masses by (theoretically/officially) conveying the socialist value system in order to formulate a critique of this system and of its ideology. Moreover, through the discourse on ideology – the invalidation of ideological premises of the socialist project – ideology also acquires the quality of interpellation since what the director proposes – a critical view of the system that includes and conveys elements of ideology – is an intellectual, and therefore, imaginary construction. On the one hand, there is a meaning of the image (a potential intentionality of the director in film construction), on the other hand, there is a significance or there are several significances that belong to the viewer/viewers, those who see the film and can operate, based on individual, cultural, social factors, with these significances in an ideological context of which they are part. The frames in which working people are displayed provide some indicators of values not consonant with socialist value system: religion, individualism, reflexivity. Visual frames with working people deliver multiple meanings: a saleswoman in a street shop lives in an apartment that bears the signs of a different social class, structured on values suggested by concrete objects: a cross on the wall (religion), Baroque-style single bed, other old decorative elements visually suggesting a dominant social class still present only through some material elements of its existence, objects that come into the possession of the new class-emblem, the working people. Elements associated with life in film are placed not in the space of socialist project, but in spaces of a "bourgeois" class that in visually manifest dispalys remains present within the ideology that contests it.

1.2 The Ideological State Apparatus and the Counter-Analysis of Socialist Education: Work and the Process of Socialization in a Ciné-Verité *Style*

The practice of socialist education in an urban environment dominated by factories and plants is an important theme developed in *Probă de microfon/ Microphone Test* (Mircea Daneliuc, 1980). The reportage as a type of investigation provides the narrative framework for cinematically discussing the issue of education in terms of critical commentary. The film renders these practices on a secondary thematic level, concerning the process and actions of forming the "new man". The factories are the main figures in the series of institutional factors entrusted with educational tasks among working people, tasks designed to establish a new, communist culture of (institutional) belonging. Work is not only a value, but also a means by which the individual can be educated. This educational purpose of work is deconstructed in the film through the antagonism between the utopian nature of educating individuals at work, in an attempt to transform them into multilateral, harmonious individuals, perfectly integrated into the society they belong to, and the significant discrepancies and conflicts encountered in (their) real life.

The value of elements of propagandistic educational discourse practised in factories of newly built industrial cities is challenged and invalidated in film by the manner of cinematic representation of the theme. Characters (workers, employees in various hierarchical positions in enterprises or factories, citizens interviewed on the street) who express ideas and values of socialist ethics in a propagandistic manner and are subject of interviews conducted by reporter (Luiza) and camera operator (Nelu) are displayed through a television screen. They represent an expressive interface of the socialist value system. This choice in the elaboration of visual frameworks implies a critical delimitation between propagandistic nature of verbal communication and visual elements accompanying the narrative path. Standardized TV frames function as labels that structure a discursive differentiation between propaganda and critical thinking, form and content, idea and concrete existence.

It should be noted that during socialism, in the context of actions aimed to train the "new man" and propagate socialist culture, what was called "educational modelling through the press and television" was practised, with newsrooms being given clear educational roles. Through these elements of image content, the film displays a disjunction between what the camera records at the level of real life, the *pulse of reality*, and what is propagated for the purpose of creating utopian standards for the profile of an ideal man with precisely defined values, attitudes and behaviour – ideology. Film discourse on the mechanisms of constructing propaganda about the "new man" and the use of television as a propaganda tool develops a powerful critique of both.

The precarious internalization of values and principles of socialist education among working class members is suggested in film in an expressive manner by the verbal system component within film narrative. Investigating social reality in the context of industrial uban, through reportage, provides an opportunity to reveal how workers understood, practised and related to values and principles of socialist ethics and, in particular, to work ethics. In a discrete manner, marked by fine accents of humour and irony, these cuts reflect a dramatic distance between what official propaganda stated (officially translated into what was called the *Code of Principles and Norms of Communist Work and Life, Socialist Ethics and Equity*), the so-called new social ethics expressed in film through the voices and filter of those to whom it was officially addressed, and what people actually lived, that is, the concrete ways of life.

The claim to a society in which people have exemplary attitudes and behaviour is devoid of real means and ironically deconstructed in film. The discrepancy between the fact of a rape, reported at the beginning of the film by a woman in Luiza and Nelu's reportage, to which are added other facts reported by other interviewees pointing to various forms of social deviance, and the projection of a society in which every individual must become at least "exemplary in all respects" through a process of education and/or re-education is edifying in this respect.

The film includes sequences that are significant for the idea of putting into practice those values and principles concerning the formation of the "new man". The value of work, the discipline in the workplace, the control of the individual's life both in the workplace and in the sphere of personal life, the organization of leisure time and education of the individual both in terms of disciplining him in the workplace and in terms of cultivating and developing cultural and artistic skills are some of the issues developed in film. Excerpts from the script presenting interviews conducted by the protagonists are significant in this respect:

On adapting to the workplace

WORKING WOMAN: We welcomed them into the team, we helped them, we followed their every move and every step both in the company ... and outside.

On cultural education activities

WORKING WOMAN: We mentor young girls, we bring doctors into the club (Femina) to guide them ... poetry evenings, we even have some female poets...

On shared values

REPORTER:	Tell me, how do you choose your girlfriends?
WORKING WOMAN:	Cheerful and hardworking.
WORKING WOMAN:	I like cultural work, life, fun.
WORKING WOMAN:	Patience because you have to work with the man...

On "social problems"

FACTORY REPRESENTATIVE:	When the steelworks is finished, the whole social situation will balance out.
REPORTER:	I mean, in what sense?
FACTORY REPRESENTATIVE:	I mean in the sense that men will come to our town, more men ... About 80% women,

young girls ... and that creates a social problem. Of course they want to get married, make a home ... Of course we've created all the conditions for them to feel like one big family ... Here we have the home for non-family members.

On the principles and norms of work and socialist ethics

REPORTER: How do you think he should be morally, at work, at work, how he should be, conscientious, what time he should come, that is, to do ... to perform...

RESPONDENT: Constantly at work, as early in the morning as late at night...

REPORTER: What do you think a salesperson's model should be towards the customer?

RESPONDENT: It has to be an example ... in every way. First of all, serving, talking, serving ... the highest level must be him, right? Especially in this period, which is now.

On education for work

TEACHER: Let our students, future graduates, become good citizens with a work-for-work education.

On re-education

JUDGE: So, sanctions have been applied that lead to their re-education among the collective of which they are part or if they were not part...

REPORTER: Do you consider that we, we who educate youth, also have our own moral problems, which could also be addressed?

JUDGE: Yes, of course, every one of us .... and as much as we try to say we're perfect ... of course...

On shortages

RESPONDENT: We can't find a bottle of mineral water in the whole city and I don't drink any other kind of water, because it's toxic for me and it's good for me.

What provides a high degree of realism to the film (facts, opinions, views expressed throughout the narrative) is the presence of a significant number of real-life characters. Most of sequences that are cuts from the social reportages undertaken by the reporter and the camera operator are shot in a *cinema-verité* or *live-action style*. The people who appear in the investigative reportages (at the door of an apartment in block of flats, in a hostel, in a factory, on the street, at the railway station, at the police station, on the train) are not professional actors, hence the added realism and actuality, which increase the very credibility of critical discourse practised throughout the film.

Communication competences of those being interviewed have attached difficulties of expression, grammatical errors, logical hesitations, frequent incoherence in speech. This poor quality of speech of most subjects interviewed (characters who in the interviews express the values and principles of socialist ethics regarding work, family, sociability) is developed through highly ironic discourses, in the sense of a negative evaluation of the way ideology was practiced, of the socialization of individuals in order to acquire the values of socialist ethics. Those who promote the belief in the edification of the "new man" as an ideal type are people who are deficient in verbal communication skills as they speak incorrectly in Romanian, people that the spectators can easily laugh at. Ideological elements are integrated into the real value system at the level of acceptance, not internalization, hence the gap between discursive appearance conveyed including at the level of different social categories displayed in film and the real definition of social situations, practices, and meanings attached to them, that is, social institutions.

In the fabric of such a vision of working life, the camera acquires a double function: a view of institutionalized and ideologized regularities of the social order concerning work and a view of internal dynamics of individual biographies in the context of this order: on the one hand, the value criteria of a social order presented in public discourse, on the other hand, a factual reality situated at a significant distance from predefined rules of the discursive order.

Two different worlds are being represented and are partially dialectically articulated: on the one hand, a world of urban life defined in normative and ideal terms, in which all elements converge towards a perfect social equilibrium, whose main construction mechanisms are the programmatic socialization of individuals and exercise of social control that ensures the regulation of their attitudes and behaviours. On the other hand, a real-life world in which there are forms of deviation from the utopian social equilibrium, proffered from the ideological platform. This latter world includes a greater diversity of evaluative criteria that individuals practice in everyday life, hence a certain fluidity in the sense of certain degree of freedom associated with experiences of working life in the context of the everyday urban, in relation to the rigidity and utopian character of set of values, principles, roles and their associated interpretations imposed through socialization by institutions and authorities that determine what is desirable, a rigid and static set whose operationalization places individuals in limited situations in terms of possibilities of developing socio-political competences and critique.

The film sets a clean lens on both worlds, leaving it up to the viewer to make an evaluative judgement. From the quasi-utopian world reproduced in a wooden language by representatives of various socio-professional categories, a world with claim of an obligatory exemplarity, to an everyday world with problems, limitations, inequalities, and uncertainties, formulated by the main characters in film, the camera, both that of Daneliuc the director, and of Daneliuc the actor (in the role of the film operator), exposes and cinematically discusses not only a conflict between the two worlds, but also a parallelism between them, and, through this, develops a frame for critical reflection on mechanisms of individual biography, on the one hand, and of social history, on the other. There is an ideological structure that regulates social and economic relations between individuals and groups, there are instances of ideological socialization that influence subjective representations and experiences of individuals, but there is also a more or less tolerated imaginary of freedom in which people *go about their lives*, appropriating in subjective ways the structural elements that define the order in which they are set and live.

Daneliuc's film is recognized in Romanian history of cinema as a film of important social critique. It is a film produced in the context of socialist cinema system, a system whose ideological goals were to build a cultural reality that reflected the reality of building the communism. The film is therefore a product of socialist film system. What the director succeeds in doing is using resources and tools of film production system – that is, using the material, concrete conditions of the dominant ideology – the socialist realism – to deconstruct from the position of the filmmaker (a member of an artistic elite) the practices and rituals of a dominant ideology choosing hypostases through which depicts mechanisms of that ideology (institutional apparatuses) and concrete conditions of existence in which they function – the relationship with subjects – real characters who unproblematically (passively) subscribe to an ideology they do not recognize (understand) as ideology. Reportage as a journalistic genre was a tool of ideological intervention through which the "weeds", the "rot in the forest" were brought to the surface, with the aim of establishing for the masses attitudinal and behavioural patterns to be followed and practiced and to show how an individual should not be, should do, should exist. On the principle of differentiation, the journalistic practice of investigating, by the reflexive nature of communication act, established what was desirable and what was not desirable from the point of view of the social defined by state ideology. This is a first level of analysis of filmic discourse. On a second level, the critique penetrates this institutional matrix of ideology, describing and explaining the nature of relationships between ideology (institutional mechanisms) and unproblematic subjects of ideology, and, finally, developing a (negative) evaluation of nature of the dominant ideology itself and of the practical strategies by which it actually manages to fail, indicating the limits and types of errors on which individual and institutional realities were socially constructed and objectified.

CHAPTER 13

Evaluative Structures of Work in Seven Romanian Films

1   *Diminețile unui băiat cuminte/The Mornings of a Good Boy* (Andrei Blaier, 1967)

Diminețile unui băiat cuminte/The Mornings of a Good Boy is a film made in 1966 and premiered in January 1967, directed by Andrei Blaier, based on a screenplay written by Constantin Stoiciu. The film presents an insight into the biography of a young high school graduate who tries to find a job after failing the university entrance exam. The film narrative is structured around the actions and events that accompany the main character Vive (played by Dan Nuțu), situated in social contexts that bring together situations, people belonging to different socio-professional categories, coming from different residential area, each with their own value schemes and social experiences, with their own expectations and life projects. Workers and intellectuals are the two categories portrayed in the film. The systems of binary oppositions between them gradually dissolve into seemingly fluid trajectories that give consistency to the discourse on relations between the two social classes in an ideological context that affirms the need to equalize the social conditions of workers and intellectuals.

Librarians, welders, waiters, accountants, clerks are brought together in interaction and communication situations that highlight the value profiles and the nature of the means each chooses to achieve its own life's goals. Among these core values, the one that constantly shapes the architectonics of all the characters' identity is work, whose ideological division takes on nuances edifying for extended meanings of equality as social and political value overbid at the era, capturing fertile mental and visual images in the social imaginary of the categories represented in the film.

1.1   *Workers and Intellectuals. Meanings and Significances of Ideological Constructions*

Work attitudes are distributed along different values, depending on age and work experience. On the intergenerational axis, a distinction is made between: on the one hand, an uncritical attitude in the sense that work is seen as the most important reason for social existence by the "old" generation

TABLE 15   Professions and occupations of characters

Main and supporting characters	Socio-professional category	Area of activity
Vive	Welder Copyist Administrative Clerk	Industrial Branch
Romache	Librarian	Education
Fane	Welder	Industrial Branch
Vive's Father	Railway Worker	Transportation Services
Vive's Mother	Housewife	--------------------
Vive's Girlfriend	High School Graduate	--------------------
Emilian Cioba	Accountant	Industrial Branch
Ștefan	Engineer	Industrial Branch
Mariana	Librarian	Education
Stela	Canteen Waitress	Services/Industrial Branch

(*THE MORNINGS OF A GOOD BOY*, ANDREI BLAIER, 1967)

(represented by parents) or the category of workers with larger work experience, and on the other hand, a reflexive attitude for the category of young people, without this meaning a rejection of the idea of work, but thinking and projecting the life of work not in terms of assigning a final value to work, but in terms of a continuous individual life project. Relationships are usually disputed between father and son, while the mother character performs a mediating function, most often manifested in favour of the position advocated by the younger generation/son. The discourses on work are significantly nuanced. Work is an essential identity factor, yet it is not enough to work because not all work is given high social prestige, not all work has an important social value. The main character's occupational status as a copyst is an unsatisfactory one for his father, a former railway station worker.

Office work, copying work is not serious work. The only work that matters is the work in production process, work on the construction site. Laziness, sleepiness, tiredness, difficulty in getting up in the morning are elements that describe the daily practices and routines of young people in urban Bucharest, who do not show, apparently, determination, enthusiasm, maturity, responsibility, values and attitudes discursively attributed to the parents' generation.

	Dialogues between family members (father and son)
VIVE'S FATHER:	You've become a bohemian, sir, it's hard to get up in the morning! How's it going with you? How's it going? Work, work ... Service is far away! You know I heard the buses aren't running today!
VIVE:	I'll walk.
VIVE'S FATHER:	You? On foot? Have you young people disabused yourselves of walking on your feet. Long live the bus! [....]
VIVE'S FATHER:	Tired, tired! Job is away! I hear the buses aren't running today either. [...] Yesterday you got up at six, ran to the office, came home and went to bed. You went to town, came home and went to bed again. Two days ago you did the same thing. Same thing today. Doesn't it surprise you that I know your life from the outside? You don't like listening to me.
VIVE:	Exactly.
VIVE'S FATHER:	You're doing wrong! [...] What do you young people really want? You have everything, everything! Maybe you have too much of everything!
VIVE:	Forget it, Dad, to each his own! Try to understand.
VIVE'S FATHER:	Get the fuck out of here ... Fuck knows, you don't want to grow up, you don't want to grow up, you're still the same as you were two years ago! What are you gonna do with your life, mister? Hm? You're still the same old fool you are now. [...] Go to Straja, they're building something there, maybe there's something for you too!

Diminețile unui băiat cuminte/Mornings of a Good Boy,
ANDREI BLAIER, 1967 (excerpt from the script)

Physical work is endowed with a more important social integration function than intellectual work. The librarian Romache (played by Ion Caramitru), Vive's friend, is an uncertain character who only appears sequentially in discussions during meetings with his high school friends. His intermittent appearance suggests a precarious social identity, poorly articulated in terms of professional status. He is the type who comes from the city, "lazy", and who lacks the everyday verve, the forms of sociability that characterise, in counterpoint, the collective of welders on the site where Vive works. The librarian Mariana (played by Irina Petrescu), the wife of the engineer Ștefan (played by Octavian Cotescu) is the type of a dull character, with vague social traits, dominated by desires and goals for the fulfillment of which they seek the means in a provincial, industrial city.

Romache and Mariana are characters who are dissatisfied with the work they do, in search of new lines of identity redefinition and fleeing the urban space of the capital. The urban centre/city is associated with the social category of intellectuals, it is seen as a source of powerlessness, inaction, identity uncertainty, social failure and futility. Mariana, having left Bucharest and accompanied the engineer Ștefan, gives up her job as librarian on construction site and enrols in a qualification course. The librarian's occupation is by its nature associated with a some sort of intellectual reflection, a possibility of critical thinking and nuanced evaluations, elements that are not quite incorporated into a pragmatic and utilitarian vision specific to the more (perceived) practical and physical univers of the working class. The ideological delimitations between the two social classes are clearly outlined in the film. The workers in film – ironworkers, welders, waitresses, other workers on the construction site – are displayed in dynamic perspectives, presented as bearers of the principles necessary and useful for the consistent and coherent formation of the individual's social identity. They are those who do not question their social conditions very much in terms of the relationship between them and possible life projects; they are those who show a high degree of job satisfaction in the social institutions in which they carry out their work activities and who have certain criteria for assessing the quality and value of the work of others in terms of ethical ideas and principles that take on a prescriptive function, imposing themselves as rules worthy of being followed by those belonging to other professional categories or other social classes. They are people who have confidence in the work system and who do not even think of questioning or challenging in any way the principles underlying the organization of this system and the ways in which it functions. What is important is that the individual develops the technical skills in order to be able to perform the predefined work tasks to an optimal level of productivity. The worker type in film is one with a high degree of obedience; he is the one who easily identifies with most of the members of the working group to which he belongs. There are no significant differentiations between members of the occupational group. With regard to workers, there are not many moments when they express their own opinions and attitudes towards the wider social scene in reflexive terms, outside the social sphere by which they define themselves ideologically. Evaluation of the purposes of work, the significance of work in the economy of personal biography are often expressed in a trenchant way, leaving no room for interpretation, changes of perspective.

Dialogue between Vive (in charge of labour protection) and Fane (welder) on the construction site in Straja:

VIVE: And what will you do in life, Fane?
FANE: Well, what am I gonna do? Well, what I've been doing. I'm going to weld a mountain of spherical tanks. That's what I'm gonna do. That's exactly what I'm gonna do.
VIVE: And do you like it?
FANE: What if I like it? That's what I learned, that's what I do.

Diminețile unui băiat cuminte/Mornings of a Good Boy,
ANDREI BLAIER, 1967 (excerpt from the script)

1.2 Discourse on (Social) Other

The filmic discourse on work developed along Vive's attempts to define his own identity can be analysed on two levels, each with a distinct value in relation to the interference and/or delimitation between the two social categories represented in film.

At first level, we are delivered a descriptive and evaluative grid that establishes a socially and morally superior position of workers: they are the ones who manifest the social values of trust, affirmation of equality, forms of sociability through which they validate the collective identity of the social class of belonging, they are the ones who literally build a material and social order through using their labour force in a system that regulates through work other aspects of social life of individuals. The basic elements of this productive and effective profile for the purposes of the activities carried out in industrial sectors of the economy are related to the level of professional qualification, a necessary indicator for social validation within the belonging group. It is the workers who populate the intellectual's frame of reflection and provide keys to resolving the latter's existential dilemmas and uncertainties. Physical labour in industrial production is a beneficial resource for alleviating anxieties, for mitigating the effects of a degradation of social institutions present in film, as family, marriage, sociability in the workplace, education. Intellectuals seem to be the victims of their own social conditions, unable to redefine their identity and needing the help of *another*, who is member of the working class. One of the mechanisms of this redefinition or clarification of identity is the integration in the field of industrial labour, in the production flow. The character Romache gives up his job as a librarian in Bucharest to work on the construction site. The librarian Mariana also attends a qualification course.

At a second level of film analysis, there is a discourse that subtly addresses this one-dimensional view of the relationship between intellectuals and workers, offering another evaluative grid on the succession of situations and options that compose film narrative. There is a latent layer of signification, revelers of a form of contestation of what appears as obvious in the manifest discoursive layer.

What young people choose, their options in terms of work and the conditions under which work is carried out, what and how they think about work, how they deal with personal problems in the context of work – all these seem to be constantly evaluated in the film by the eye of the older generation, that of parents, of those who have unproblematically accepted work and whose criteria for determining what is a model of success in life seem to be the only legitimate ones to follow. The reaction of Vive's father when he returns from the construction site is significant in this respect. The father almost mockingly disapproves of his son's return home, suspecting him of the inability to adapt to the working conditions on the site. In his perception, someone who gives up work is weak, socially handicapped, not worthy of the respect of others. He cannot conceive of anyone rejecting work, the social order that derives from the unconditional practice of work. The son's ironic lines to his father when he asks him about the reasons for returning at home ("I don't know why I left. I missed you") arouses the father's anger, who addresses Vive with insulting words ("you moron") and violently corrects him by slapping his face. For Vive's father, giving up work on the construction site is equivalent to a failure to grow up, by which he means the integration into the industrial labour field, integration into an order that conforms to social practices that have been learned and reproduced uncritically. The individual choice to give up work is unthinkable for a generation that defines itself primarily through work. Outside of work, the individual's social identity is shaky and the chances of social recognition and community prestige are significantly reduced. The child's biographical background is considered an indicator of prestige within the social group to which he or she belongs ("What do I tell people? My son came, slapped his ass and left. He got scared"). Those who follow the parents' generation's model of success in life deserve the respect and admiration of others; those who do not are subject to intolerance and social exclusion. Vive's evasive answers to his father's repeated questions contain elements that indicate ambiguity, the possibility of inarticulate attitudes, leave room for interpretation, raise difficulties of understanding for those who cannot decode other possible meanings of a choice, of an option. Vive's father's violent verbal and physical reactions when he replies to him in nuanced terms (using words which by their denotative meaning signify uncertainty, confusion, doubt, possibility – "I don't know", "maybe", "try") indicate certain limits of knowledge, of social tolerance in the sense of understanding and accepting the differences, of accepting the other who may understand his work, his family, his social success differently. A certain quality of verbal expression is suggestively used in the construction of father character, a quality which is precarious and signifies the limits of a communicative competence, a fundamental indicator of one's level of intellectual development. Physical and verbal violence, intolerance, and poor verbal communication skills make up a profile of the experienced worker and of a parent who sets himself up as a moral authority and who claims legitimacy of imposing desirable moral conduct on the younger generation.

> Dialogue between Vive (back from the construction site) and his father:
>
> VIVE'S FATHER: What is it, sir? They kicked you out?
> VIVE: No, I left alone. [...]
> VIVE'S FATHER: Did you really leave? Come on, say it straight, before I take your pants off and burn some belts! Hurry up, you'll be late!
> VIVE: I don't know, Dad. I don't know why I left. I missed you. [Vive is slapped by his father].
> VIVE: Wait, Dad! I'm home. [...]
> VIVE'S FATHER: Why did you come home, sir? So your mother can pull you up in the morning when you get up?
> VIVE'S FATHER: Aren't you sick of me, you asshole? What do I tell people? My son came, slapped his ass and left. He got scared. Why are you scared, Vive, Daddy dear?
> VIVE: I don't know if I was scared. Maybe I came to say goodbye to someone.
>
> *Diminețile unui băiat cuminte/Mornings of a Good Boy,*
> ANDREI BLAIER, 1967 (excerpt from the script)

Vive eventually opts to return to the construction site, joining a group of welders, thus achieving the optimal standards legitimized by his father's generation regarding the social institution of work. But this choice is followed by a novel element, the accident that occurs during the course of work activity.

A few weeks after joining the welding team, while trying to make an electrode mark on a pool, Vive slips and falls. The work accident is the narrative element that points to an essential meaning of filmic discourse, which may or may not be intended by the author. Vive's final choice to take a job as welder ends with a failure and has harmful consequences for him, putting his life in danger. Accepting the values and norms conveyed by his parents' generation can only be an accident, an exception, not the rule. There is no real reconciliation between those who think and practise work within the framework of a dominant ideology and those who have resources to challenge and contest the ideological ready-made pattern of work without necessarily invalidating the idea of work.

2 Filip cel bun/Filip the Kind (Dan Pița, 1975)

In 1976 (exactly 100 years after Engels's famous idea about work, namely that work created man himself), the 11th issue of *Cinema* magazine included an article entitled *"Filip cel bun/Filip the Kind or a Young Man in Search of his Human Identity. As a Man of Work"* (p. 2). Even if the film was considered theistic in terms of ideological discourse, on a closer view, there is a more nuanced and realistic discourse on the perceptions and practices of work in socialism.

A red thread that structure both the development of filmic and visual narrative is given by a critical view that implies a filtration and an interpretation of various aspects of life in socialism – with emphasis on work – offering images and hypostases of social reality situated at great distance from the political vision of general relations between individual and society, a vision which is concretely formulated in the principles, norms and ideals of socialist society, embodied in official documents as the *Code of Principles and Norms of Communist Work and Life, Socialist Ethics and Equity* (adopted as part of the project for the formation of the new man at the 11th Congress in 1974). The cinematic vision of the social world of work provides a deconstruction of a (false) myth, that of the "new man".

The professional division of the characters offers a fragmented, uneven landscape, hence the realistic and ambiguous nature of a reality that fails to articulate itself coherently in desirable meanings. Work and its meanings beyond the role of integrating the individual into a functional structure are treated in a diffuse manner. Personal tensions, everyday problems, social expectations and moral questions are interwoven. The overall picture of the social structure is present, but this is not the purpose of the commentaries within the discourse, but what goes beyond the structure, the dynamic element, the intermediary movement between elements of thought about reality through which the very nature of the structure and of its implications, that is, the social institutions on which it is based, are questioned.

2.1 It's Very Important to Get to Know the People at Work

The film offers multiple images of the urban working culture of the time and exposes structural difficulties in social life: difficulties in finding a job, corrupt

TABLE 16   Professions and occupations of characters

Main and supporting characters	Socio-professional category	Area of activity
Filip	High School Graduate	-
Angela	Saleswoman at a Street Shop	Services
Atanasiu	Director of Commercial Complex	Industry Branch
Alexandru	Former Worker/Retired	Industry Branch
Lupu	Former Worker/Retired	Industry Branch
Filip's Mother	Dressmaker / Housewife	-
Lucian	Foreign Trade Worker	Services
Marin Pătrașcu	Master Steelmaker	Industry Branch
	Storeroom Manager	Industry Branch
Simona	Housewife	-
Stănescu	Veterinary Doctor	Health
-	Teacher	Education
Istrate	Construction Worker	Industry Branch
Gică Ionescu	Master Steelworker	Industry Branch
Filip's Colleague	Student	Education

(*FILIP THE KIND*, DAN PIȚA, 1975)

practices developed in factories and plants, social inequality, corrupt social upbringing and limited access to material and relational resources. The system that allows access to job and promotion opportunities is based on corrupt practices that have nothing to do with the egalitarian principle affirmed by politicians. The film provides a critique of the official rhetoric embodied in the discussion between a superior from a commercial warehouse in Bucharest and a young man looking for a job, a sequence that provides an opportunity for the blatant exposure of real deviations from what the official work ethic, norms and principles of communist life represented at the doctrinal level.

The commercial warehouse in the capital where the main character of the film, Filip (played by Mircea Diaconu), is temporarily employed, becomes a metaphor for the ways in which the socialist system exists and functions, for the perverse effects of what was intended by the socialist doctrine of the "new man". If we consider the group of characters built around one of the central figures of industrialization – a commercial warehouse in Bucharest where there were goods "worth tens of millions" – and who held positions in the upper hierarchy of bureaucratic system, human and social types are described and characterized by: corruption, immorality, greed, monopoly on access to resources (material, labour, influence), authority and power, deviance, precarious intellectual level. In a distinct key of interpretation, the warehouse is not only a space for the accumulation and "storage" of "goods", of material goods, is also a space where fragments of social history accumulate, a "repository" of values, practices and norms specific to a corrupt bureaucratic system, characterised by degradation, alteration and at the same time having all the resources and mechanisms necessary to survive and reproduce itself successfully.

During Filip's visit to commercial warehouse where he had been sent for employment following an intervention, the warehouse manager (played by Draga Olteanu-Matei) describes to him the actual practices within the economic unit regarding the criteria for evaluating human resources and the rules for organising the material ones. Industrial life and labour market, as the film reveals, are deeply unequal and corrupt. Distribution of goods, resources and power is not based on work and capabilities, but on the use of positions of power and authority that allows a minority the monopoly on management of material and political resources and, consequently, on opportunities of increasing social status. Satisfying consumer demands is the priority only for a minority, and not for the "whole people".

> **Dialogue between Filip and the manager of Meteor commercial warehouse in Bucharest**
> We're going around the warehouse now to get acquainted with the people, with the goods, comrade, you know it's very important to get to know the people at work ... Here you'll have enough work. Comrade Atanasiu phoned for you, it's been arranged. I know your father, he's a good man, honest, hard-working, he's done his job. I've been working here for 20 years and I've had the opportunity to meet ... Comrade Commercial Director also started like you. Hey! He went to high school, college. Other comrades were promoted to other jobs. We take care of the youth. That's how it is with us ... Here, you know, if you see your work, you have all the chances! We, comrades, encourage comrades who want to learn, to promote, we create all the conditions for them to feel good, at ease. The warehouse is big, comrades! You'll see there goods worth tens of millions. Of course, there's still stealing and underhand dealings. Money is tempting. Now, it's up to you to stay honest or go the wrong way. [...] We help comrades who want to learn, to promote, we create all the conditions for them, you didn't want to. Many of our comrades have made complaints

against you, even comrade Atanasiu who recommended you! Comrade Filip, some people here have put their cheeks on for you, you should be ashamed of yourself! When everyone is working in this country, all comrades want to learn, to promote, what are we doing here?! You're putting us to shame, comrade! Shut up! Now I'm talking! You listen to me all the way! You've learned to answer in one voice! Comrade Atanasiu complains about you, that you're arrogant, that you're impertinent – look, and now you're laughing at me! – that you're doing business underhand, I want to know, when are you going to straighten up?

    Filip cel bun/Filip the Kind, (DAN PIȚA, 1975) (excerpt from the script)

2.2   *Housing, Administrative Bureaucracy, and Social Inequality*

An element of the critique of socialist bureaucratic elite is the distribution of housing types according to the social category of those who live in them. There is significant association between type of housing and socio-moral description of the characters using these spaces. The "bourgeois" house represents such a material character and is visually identifiable by the dimensions and the aspects of the material living space: the height of the walls, the distance between the facade of the building and the street, the "landscape" of the interior space described by the abundance and excess of furniture, decoration and art objects. The bourgeois house or frame is presented as interior universe that incorporates corruption, immorality, opportunism, cowardice, lack of education and poor intellectual uprbringing (reflected by expressing themselves incorrectly in Romanian), corruption based social upbringing as main form of imposture, trickery as method of success – elements that describe the main and supporting characters occupying this type of housing in the film.

  The material element of the bourgeois house is given the value of critical commentary addressing the communist nomenclature and certain practices of the administrative and party bureaucracy. The home of a former factory director and party activist (the character Atanasiu played by Lazăr Vrabie) visually provides the setting for a sentence to be passed on all those who, in the name of working class, obtained their own advantages and resources of economic power and social influence, turning the work of state employees into a "personal affair". This character's home offers the image of a vast space populated by people belonging to the communist bureaucratic system. The party organised on the occasion of his son's birthday becomes the pretext for revealing in spectacular cinematic expressions the structural flaws of a system that validates corrupt mechanisms of social success and, by extension, of a society in which the sense of values such as work, truth, competence, justice, is severely atrophied, in which socialist ideals have proved to be nothing more than a pretext and a screen for favouring and satisfying personal and group interests.

A former factory manager, campaigning for workers' rights, becomes the director of a commercial warehouse and rises up within the hierarchy of the state bureaucracy, ending up living in an impressively "bourgeois" house, where luxury, opulence, and an impressionistic aesthetic atmosphere dominates, the perfect visual setting for identifying a fracture between the nature of the means used and that of the ends pursued, the hypocritical formulas of social upbringing. Comrade Atanasiu shares a personal view of work and despises those who think differently, those who, part of younger generations, are not obedient, cannot be ideologically disciplined and for whom work is not necessarily the only important social value.

> Dialogue between two former "beneficiaries" of working class labour, Lupu and Atanasiu, about the young generation
> LUPU: The day before yesterday we were like them.
> ATANASIU: We weren't like them, Wolf, listen to me! They have something else in their heads: music, buzzing, chewing gum, playback, I see them on the street and I feel my laughter swell. What are you guys? Girls? Boys? What do you want? Money? Go to work!
>
> *Filip cel bun/Filip the Kind* (DAN PIȚA, 1975) (excerpt from the script)

The "bourgeois" house of comrade Atanasiu, once a militant and false defender of interests of working class, a character in the category of the "insatiable", who have "everyone at their hand" and who "have done a lot of harm", brings together various categories of characters, a sign of the resources of manipulation and control, influence and clientelistic practices, being the most visible material indicator of success. The image of housing is suggestive of the idea of bureaucratization of human relationships (family, friendship, collegial), which is a form of alienation.

Characters belonging to administrative and party bureaucracy are seen in caricatural and grotesque views. Significant in this respect is the sequence in which the worker in charge of the commercial warehouse (played by Draga Olteanu Matei) and former worker and fellow factory colleague Lupu (played by Gheorghe Dinică) dine at a party. The images are those of a small "big feast" suggesting atrophy of social conscience, reduction of individual aspirations to the satisfaction of basic needs, wearing the moral clothes of the parvenus, the brutal manner in which the membership of an elite group is developed, whose members tacitly validate themselves through corrupt practices, replace education with personal experience and ability to cheat and who casually imitate the forms of consumption of an older elite in whose name they seek to satisfy personal interests and desire for power. The scenes in which food is consumed in absence of certain manners of eating, using close-ups with the faces of main characters, configure a symbolic structure which integrates excessive pleasure, instinctive class sensibility, dialectical relationship with a hypothetical elite atmosphere, the ascendancy of primary needs over conscious feelings. The scenes provide at the same time a parable of administrative and party bureaucracy.

The descriptive elements presented above compose the image of a typical fake "bourgeois" way of life, regardless of the fact that characters who populate the monumental interior space belong mainly to working class and to political bureaucracy. In "typical circumstances" (in Engels's terms), that is, in private settings that suggest a "bourgeois" atmosphere, characters reproduce typical behaviour. The physiognomy of the bourgeois home is at the same time the support of moral and intellectual physiognomies of the social categories or types embodied by the characters who animate this space and give it a form of life. Facial features and faces of things come together in predictable material and human profiles revealing motivational and intellectual structures of the characters. Visual appearances of characters compose a structure of meaning that reveals a human society as a whole. The significant association at the level of narrative and visual construction between the fact of placing certain units of action and characteristics attached to them (exposure of certain parts of the body, types of behaviour, attitudes, reactions, gestures, consumption, use of space, management of proximities and of power relations with others) in typical space identified for "bourgeois" home reveal details of a discursive mechanism which in symbolic perspective attaches to "bourgeois" home the expression of a bourgeois society seen as decadent, corrupt, and deviant. There is in film an ideological division of the living spaces, with the function of witnessing hypocritical practices of a system that operates on exactly the opposite basis to that officialy expressed. The blue and white collars are integrated in the very physical and social space of the world that the ideology in whose name they act, work and earn a wage and resources of power seeks to deconstruct, to eliminate.

3   *Iarba verde de acasă/The Green Grass of Home* (Stere Gulea, 1977)

Graduate of the Faculty of Mathematics, Ștefan Corici (played by Florin Zamfirescu) decides to return to his home village after turning down the opportunity to pursue an academic career in Bucharest, based on what he considered to be a compromise. Corici takes up a post as mathematics professor in a village school and prevents the removal from office of the school director by the young teacher Victor (played by Ion Caramitru), apparently reinstating an institutional order based on meritocracy, competence, and justice.

The film develops an inventory of moral and social meanings attributed to professions and occupations in the context of a process of social change under socialism. Industrialization, physical displacement in the context of the need to provide work in different industrial areas, new experiences of urban work for social categories coming from the countryside and vice versa are main elements around which experience of socialist everyday is articulated with its modes of understanding, evaluations, and redefinitions. The main work activity described in film is educational, indicating the importance of education in the process of social change and in the elaboration of a culture promoted by the socialist project, within the morphological forms and contents of this change. Any social change occurs first and foremost within the value system, which is the one that changes most slowly in any society. Education is one of the most important socialization factors and the quality of education, that is, the quality of its institutions, of those working in this field, depends on the quality of processes of social change, of influence that can ensure efficient and effective social control. Education is set against the process of propaganda, an instrument of political power through which a different education is delivered, one oriented towards an unproblematic acceptance or compliance (rather than internalization) of ideologically defined rules and norms, which are the basis for what is intended in terms of long-term political objectives (elimination of class differences, equalization of social conditions in rural and urban areas through changes in administrative system and modernization, and the equalization of economic and social opportunities).

3.1   *A Critical Commentary on Socialist Modernization*

The reversal of value relations in the film across social and generational categories provides a counter-analysis of the unintended effects of this process of modernization that has generated elements of social dislocation in the absence of an education in terms of change, adaptation to an economic and social order based on a value orientation development, and not only on their material forms of expression.

The narrative structure has a composition of themes and sub-themes associated with two referentials – the urban world (central urban, Bucharest) and the rural, traditional world, (Mioveni). The discursive relations between the two environments is based on the idea of a representational continuum

TABLE 17   Professions and occupations of characters

Main and supporting characters	Socio-professional category	Area of activity
Ștefan Corici	Mathematics Teacher (Rural Middle School)	Education
The University Professor	University Professor (Bucharest)	Education
Irina, the University Professor's Daughter		–
Serafim	Worker on a Construction Site	Industry Branch
Dumitru, Ștefan's Brother	Store Manager (Mioveni)	Services
Vasile	President of the Communal People's Council	Administration/ Party Bureaucracy
Poldi	Pensioner	–
Ghimboașă	School Inspector	Education
Viorel Meteș	Professor (Son-in-Law of SPC President)	Education
Ștefan's Colleague	Teacher	Education
Mrs Chiriacescu	Teacher	Education
Viorel Meteș's Wife	Daughter of the SPC President	–
Burcea	Party Instructor	Administration/ Party Bureaucracy
Eugen Vârtaciu	Professor	Education
Florin Frânculescu	Sport Professor	Education
Costică	Mioveni Railway Station Manager	Services/ Transport
Mitrică	Worker on a Construction Site	Industry Branch
Luci	Singer	Art and Culture

(*THE GREEN GRASS OF HOME*, STERE GULEA, 1977)

between the two worlds in which elements of social identity alternately and sequentially substitute one to each other in a view that relativizes the labelling and sterile delimitations between social categories, value systems, and social practices. The social category that plays a leading role in film is that of the intellectuals, variously described in films under socialism. Although the narrative paths of the characters and actions seemingly indicate a polar view of existential and social journeys of the protagonists, the film includes a layer of reflexive interrogation of how, in present reality, approaches and characteristics of professional categories were articulated in the ideological context assuming the elimination of the differences between intellectuals and workers, urban and rural residents.

The film includes elements of representation in terms of apparent binary oppositions with regard to the two social frameworks: city and state, modernization and traditionalism. The discursive fabric extends to the level of several dimensions significant for the experience of adaptation to the "other" identified in the *other* residential space, the *other* value system, the *other* educational category, the *other* occupational category, the *other* social condition. Urban and rural are also linked with different moral values and different work ethics. The intimate mechanisms of valuing work in the two spatial contexts highlight different perceptual orientations, structured on individual (not necessarily) versus collective values. One of the discursive techniques is the mechanism of counterpoint, visually and narratively structured at the level of what is represented: social situations, characters, contexts of interactions, aspects of different social institutions, ways of developing sociability, the nature of expectations and concerns according to the social status of the characters.

The process of modernization brought with it elements of attraction to the countryside which manifested themselves in the development of practices imitating some of the forms of the new, the essential expression of the modern. Types of construction specific to urban areas, the experience of "height" (housing building) indicate a sense of belonging to a more or less legitimate local elite, of a social condition with a modernizing face.

The countryside in the film is not an idyllic one, inward-looking, closed universe, but strongly anchored and influenced by the changes brought about by socialist modernization. The imprint of modernity on the village is expressed through elements related, for example, to aspects of housing. Teacher Corici returns to his native village where "the road remains the same", but where, at the same time, "these new houses have sprung up like mushrooms after the rain" because "that's the fashion now", that is, "houses with a storey, with a balcony". This material expression of modernization is at the same time related to the development of a new type of local elite based on socio-economic mobility facilitated by urban-rural mix in the context of rural-urban migration. The character of the musician who appears in one of the opening scenes to greet the teacher whom he mistakes for a county official gives a significant framework-image for social change in the countryside.

THE LOCAL MUSICIAN: even Mr. Busuioc, the one who sold sesame when we were kids, wouldn't stop until he made his own ... In the summer his daughter comes from the city with the children, sits on the balcony, crochets and scolds her brats.

Iarba verde de acasă/The Green Grass of Home, STERE GULEA, 1977 (excerpt from the script)

Forms of adaptation to the economic conditions of industrialization, occupational mobility, changes in value orientations of people, forms of disintegration of social institutions as sociability, housing, work provide a discursive structure of the influences of socialist modernization. Corici returns to his native village to find his father working on a construction site. An elderly peasant on a building site offers a relevant image for the idea of redefining occupational identity in the context of modernization and, by extension, of one mechanism of urban influence on rural. The father-son relationship is developed in a counterpoint narrative strategy, in the sense that the young university graduate refuses the city life and a university career, while the father from the country gives up land-related concerns and work and goes to work on a construction site. The reversal of the relationship between the two characters in terms of their work choices provides an expression of the reversal of the relationship between two cultural patterns: from rural to urban and vice versa, and, more than that, an expression of the readiness to adapt to elements of change that does not depend essentially only on external factors, but also on individual vitality and social necessity that manifest themselves regardless of the political regime, economic system, and/or social order.

If we make a brief profile of the two characters, a binary structure in terms of attraction to urban and rural can be identified at a first reading: the character in the film who chooses to live (return) to the village belongs to the category of intellectuals, is young, with a higher education degree, with recognized competence in his professional field, while the older character, belonging to the category of peasants, gives up working the land to work in construction industry. Apparently, filmic discourse defines the attraction/rejection relationship between village/city in favour of the return to the village. The urban experience of both son and father remains definitively under the spectre of failure. The narrative resolution of conflicts and dissonances that the characters face points to a solution: the option for the rural, when one of the stakes of socialist project of urban development was precisely to eliminate the ways of being and doing specific to the rural life, in favour of the supposed civilisation of the village, which would ultimately lead to the elimination of the differences between village and town/city. The solution advanced in film is exactly the opposite.

Another dimension in representing the conflict relationship at intra-community (rural) level, is given by the moral typology of characters. The main character, Ștefan Corici, a mathematics teacher, is a rural native who studies in Bucharest and finds himself having to decide on his professional future in a context perceived as being dominated by coercion, opportunism, and compromise. The exchange below highlights a comment on the social value of work, contextualized in the scenario through the theme of socio-professional success.

ȘTEFAN CORICI: I don't remember me asking you to help me and you had to tell me that my university future depended on that tutoring.
PROFESSOR: Oh, we have our egos. I'd like to give you some advice. While you're still a nobody, it's best to hide your egos. If you want to be somebody in life. Otherwise...
ȘTEFAN CORICI: But I don't want to owe anyone for my future.
PROFESSOR: Hm, my dear, it's naive to think you can make it on your own. Take it from me.
ȘTEFAN CORICI: You might be right. But I want to try. Maybe it'll work.

Iarba verde de acasă/The Green Grass of Home, STERE GULEA, 1977 (excerpt from the script)

The ansewers describe a social success model based on money, exchange relationship, opportunism, influence resources, favouritism, compromise. Agreements and negotiations settled in informal settings, in private spaces, arrangements based on the manipulation of power resources and their distribution based on corrupt authority, mutual validation of incompetence and reproduction of corrupt practices of increasing social prestige are mechanisms of social construction of reality, present both in urban and rural areas. The forms of expression differ, the mechanisms are the same. There is no such thing as a better or worse rural or urban, only elements of social and political context that are perceived to function differently, even though they are based on the same functional mechanisms. The moral demarcations between the two environments are rather affective, subjective in nature and actually highlight a continuum of individual perceptions and definitions of situations in social and political settings that actually operate according to the same principles and practices.

A character developed in opposition to that of teacher Corici is also an educational worker, Victor (played by Ion Caramitru), who works at the countryside. He uses different instruments in order to ensure his chances for social success, not ones based on work, merit, but on corrupt practices, shabby arrangements, unscrupulousness. The opposition between these two characters is a mirror representation of a type of similarity between urban and rural worlds in terms of evaluating work: similar tools and means for achieving ultimate goals in the form of professional and social success are found in the village and the city alike.

3.2   Institutions and the People They Are Made Of

This descriptions of characters and of actions attached to them is useful because it allows the development of a social critique of ways in which social and institutional relations functioned, in which biographies were developed. The unmasking of the shabby arrangement that "a little teacher from the country" orchestrates to remove from his post the director of the school in the village in order to take his place and thus create the necessary conditions for him to move up in the social hierarchy is equivalent to invalidating and deconstructing a model of social upbringing positively valued by some social categories not only in urban but also in rural areas.

The images of teacher Corici are significantly different from those of his colleague. While the former is portrayed in hypostases describing aspects of a social and professional life based on values such as work, friendship, competence, respect for the past, honesty and truth, the latter is portrayed in hypostases describing the conditions and stages of a social status project based on use of influential resources to achieve positions of power and authority which, by their nature, provide social prestige. The marriage to the daughter of the county president, the plot to replace the school director by bribing a school inspector are mechanisms of such social upbringing strategy. The values describing Ștefan Corici are work, seriousness, honesty, modesty, helpfulness, sociability, competence, responsibility, combativity, while character Victor is described, contrary, by opportunism, unscrupulousness, selfishness, and arrogance. Ștefan Corici is presented in professional, institutional settings – teaching in a classroom full with pupils. Victor is shown in private life settings, in poses that reflect the predominance of psychological needs, of satisfying the need of self-esteem, rather than values as professional competence, social responsibility, altruism, sociability, trust, communication.

Another divergent construction is associated to the relationship between the university professor from Bucharest and teacher and school principal in the village of Mioveni. The character of the professor and head of the department who offers Ştefan Corici the position of assistant professor at the Department of Mathematics at the University of Bucharest (at the intervention of his daughter, who is in a sentimental relationship with the young professor, in exchange for a favour related to tutoring) is represented as an exponent of a value model that emphasizes the importance of individual and importance of having access to power resources in order to develop a succesfull biographical itinerary.

A suggestive description of the two characters is provided by a visual construction that expressively outlines this divergent relationship between them. On the one hand, the profile of the university professor presented in a close-up, perfectly framed by the frames of a painting depicting a prominent personality of Romanian culture. The overlapping of the two social types is illustrative for the dialectic of representation of two educational patterns.

The pragmatism, individualism, and arrogance of the university professor in the city are in opposition to the modesty, humanism, and honesty of the teacher and school director in the village. The university professor is the social type who holds a position of authority and decision in the education system and who uses his resources of influence and power to decide career paths and trajectories of young scholars in a relationship of exchange. Such a career model highlights the structural shortcomings of the career development system, based on favouritism and nepotism. In one of the opening scenes, in which the young university graduate reproaches his girlfriend, the university professor's daughter, for intervening on his behalf, the answer he receives is suggestive for the way of thinking about the nature of the adequacy of means to the ends of socio-professional success, a certain type of institutional practice of professional promotion and, implicitly, of a broader dominant value system.

ŞTEFAN CORICI: You shouldn't have told him to intervene on my behalf.
PROFESSOR'S DAUGHTER: But there's nothing wrong with that, he's just my dad.

Iarba verde de acasă/The Green Grass of Home, STERE GULEA, 1977 (excerpt from the script)

The young professor is aware of his level of professional competence, but the fact of intervention, if he had accepted the position within the department, would have remained an element of suspicion regarding his professional career development. The young man rejects any kind of scenario that could in any way alter his own view of his biographical path. He is an agent of a deconstruction of a core value system regarding aspects of social life as work, family, sociability, on the one hand, in close relation with socio-demographic characteristics such as age, residence, occupational status, on the other. A matrix of such a process includes a few dimensions: 1. the deconstruction of an intergenerational conflict; 2. the deconstruction of a pattern of fake professional success; 3. the deconstruction of a corrupt bureaucratic system.

Teacher Corici questions the community in terms of institutional practices that dominate it, revealing altered forms of their manifestation, the atrophy of important social values such as work, honesty, respect, interpersonal trust, respect for history, competence, and education.

A synthetic view of the gallery of characters set in the countryside reflects its division into two broad categories of social types according to their value manifestations in terms of work, family, social success, sociability, and social communication. The country teacher, the county president, the school inspector, the head of the railway station, the manager of a general store, the peasants are included in this gallery. On the one hand, there is the old elite: the county president, the director of the general school, who are rural characters associated with strong orientation towards work, household care, community relations based on respect and reciprocity. On the other hand, there is an elite in formation: the young teacher and son-in-law of the county president, the school inspector, the manager of the village general store, associated with a value system based on pragmatism, self-interest, group interest, increasing social status by corrupt means.

Ștefan Corici leaves Bucharest and takes the opportunity for a career advancement, returning to his home village, where identifies the same practices and mechanics previously invalidated. The image of these two worlds indicates a fluidization of the boundaries, of the differences between the two physical spaces (urban and rural) which are imbued with the same social practices. The shift from land work to industrial work outlines the framework in which these practices become meaningful. Geographical, socio-occupational displacement are effects of the socialist modernization. The attachment to the land, the work of the land, taking care of the household, the relationships of mutual support, the neighbourhood relations, the intra-community sociability forms – all these, according to filmic discourse, have been diluted in the context of industrialization, generating a delicate diversification of biographical projects, making values more fluid and susceptible to multiple substitutions, phenomena that are not always accompanied by processes of acceptance and internalization as mechanisms of adaptation to the novel elements of social and economic reality.

Elements in Corici's character development such as tension, similarities and interferences perceived and lived in the city and the countryside have an important psychological value, in the sense that, beyond some lines of obvious opposition that increase the expressiveness of filmic discourse, they develop a broader reflection on the availability to incorporate, process and filter the new elements brought by socialist modernization, but also the limits of this process in creating the necessary premises for mitigating the limits of this availability. Individualization through the redefinition of social identity is present throughout the narrative, with the two environments being both a ruin and a setting in which social change can occur. It's a delicate balance between the two worlds, a balance that the director doesn't necessarily resolve by the solution of returning to the village. It is merely a premise for the construction of a commentary that invites viewers to consider the meanings and significance of processes of social change in multiple tonalities, with new possibilities of social construction and understanding of reality, which may prove more or less realistic and functional.

4   *Probă de microfon/Microphone Test* (Mircea Daneliuc, 1980)

Probă de microfon/Microphone Test is a film about (young) workers and their social condition under socialism. The film is made in a society at a time when work was compulsory, when everyone had to have a job. Apart from this social quality, the individual could only be a "parasite". Daneliuc deconstructs this ideological imperative by showing that institutions designed to ensure this condition of socialist modernization were malfunctioning and that the reality of everyday life was one dominated by mechanisms of survival and escape creating an alternative reality to the one defined by means of propaganda used by important social institutions (working environment, television, party structures, branches of cultural production).

The narrative context in which the director places his criticism of the political system is shaped by the story of a film operator, Nelu (played by Mircea Daneliuc), who together with TV reporter Luiza (played by Gina Patrichi) makes a series of investigative reportages on various themes and issues of social life. The interviewed subjects come from different social and professional categories, from factory workers, hierarchical superiors in industrial units, to bureaucratic officials, pensioners, teachers and judges, people who practice mild forms of deviance. Narrative is built around the relationship developing between the camera operator Nelu and Ana Covete (played by Tora Vasilescu), a young unemployed woman caught travelling by train without a ticket, whom he meets while filming during one of these investigation reportages. She exploits the relationship to achieve specific material and financial ends, trying by any means possible to get a job in Bucharest and secure a modest living, despite restrictions and official rules limiting the access of people without permanent residence in Bucharest to job opportunities the capital had to offer. Eventually, after her attempts to find a job and settle in Bucharest fail, the young woman takes a job at the Fieni factory, where she marries, while the camera operator leaves to complete his military service.

4.1 Looking for a Job

The professional configuration of the characters offers information especially about the main characters. By the nature of their professions, they have the role of investigating reality, concrete life situations, inconsistencies, what goes beyond the festive framework of communist morality, the double discourse of the reporter who in the name of the moral lesson brings out the human

TABLE 18 Professions and occupations of characters

Main and supporting characters	Socio-professional category	Area of activity
Nelu Stroe	TV Operator	Press
Luiza	TV Reporter	Press
Ana Covete	Worker/Unemployed	Industry Branch
Lică	Unemployed	–
Nelu's Father	Pensioner	–
Nelu's Mother	Pensioner	–
Biță	TV Operator	
Magda	Owner of the House where Ana lives	–
Magda's Daughter	Child	
–	Labour Officer	–
–	Electrician	–
Sile Pricop	Dolphin Trainer	Other Branches
Gabi	Laboratory Worker at a Steel Plant	Industry Branch
Sile's Mother	Pensioner	-

SOURCE: *MICROPHONE TEST*, MIRCEA DANELIUC, 1980

element with all its deformities, with its lack of knowledge, with its deviations from what was considered to be desirable, with its manifestations susceptible to being included in narrow, incomplete and discriminatory categories. A camera operator and a working woman provide the main framework of interaction in which practices and institutions with their constitutive limits, options, expectations and reflections that escape the filter of the ideological lens, using the tools that the ideological state apparatus puts at their disposal, are displayed.

Supportingcharacters have an interesting role in terms of critical discourse. Most of them are retired, without us knowing what their previous professions/occupations were (the operator Nelu's parents, Sile's mother), unemployed (Ana – sequentially, Ana's brother), for others no information is given about their professional status (Ana's roommate). The structure of differentiation between main and supporting characters reproduces that of the political commentary that the film formulates at a latent level on how ideological division of social prestige of professions is propagandistically articulated. Not all professions are desirable in terms of a standard of prestige that satisfies the symbolic needs of political communication at the time. The lines exchange between the TV reporter Luiza and the dolphin trainer Sile at the Dolphinarium in Constanța is significant in this respect:

SILE (DOLPHIN TRAINER):	Comrade, you are from television, each to his own job.
TV REPORTER:	Well, what is your job? ... Is that what you call your job? What would the man on the tractor or the lathe say?
SILE (DOLPHIN TRAINER):	Each to his own trade. If you can do what I do ... whatever!
TV REPORTER:	Eh, what are you getting upset about?

Probă de microfon/Microphone Test, MIRCEA DANELIUC, 1980 (excerpt from the script)

4.2 Figures of Work and Themes of Urban Centrality

The representations of work and working people are closely linked to social perimeter of the urban, sliding between the spaces of Bucharest and those of several industrial cities. Constanța, Fieni, Târgoviște, together with the capital, form the physical landscape in which interpersonal conflicts, institutional deficiencies, spontaneous attractions, social inequalities developed in the context of an egalitarian ideology, atypical survival mechanisms as formulas of response to limits of a pattern of social existence derived from ideological scheme that does not take into account the human element are incorporated. The images displayed in film offer a counterpoint to the clichéd visuals of socialist education and portray the real tensions between these two layers: the authority of the state and the real life of individuals with its multiple differentiation processes.

The problems encountered during the protagonis's attempts to find a job in Bucharest provide the pretext for describing the relationship between the capital city and the provincial industrial city. The representation of the central urban space is structured on two dimensions: on the one hand, the attraction for work, on the other hand, the attraction for consumer goods and services. Bucharest is represented as a figure of urban centrality, a pole of attraction for people from outside the city (in terms of residential status) by virtue of its varied social functions. Housing conditions, employment opportunities, diversity of consumption patterns and access to them are main resources for increasing social status.

Elements describing aspects of the social situation of the characters (type of housing and living conditions) mark a perspective with important valorising accents on Bucharest as a central space. The main male character, the camera operator, lives in a house building other than a typical socialist apartment block, together with his parents. The filmmaker filming workers, citizens living in socialist apartment blocks does not live in such an apartment. Likewise, the main female character lives in a rented apartment owned by an acquaintance. These elements are relevant for the social situation of the characters (residence, spatial and occupational mobility) and discover certain difficulties related to obtaining a job and housing in Bucharest during the 1970s and the early 1980s. That was a time the most prolific in terms of state investment in urban infrastructure and especially in housing construction.

The protagonist's housing situation (renting an individual apartment during her stay in Bucharest) gives us an insight into the ways and practices of circumventing the established forms of control over the housing situation of individuals under socialism. The possibility of finding a job highly depended on housing situation (registered residence). Having a Bucharest identity card was a prerequisite for getting a job in the capital city. The difficulty that the protagonist encountered in obtaining a job in Bucharest, generated by not having a Bucharest identity card, creates the image of a capital city which is not opened to the outsiders (outside a registered residence in Bucharest) as they do not have access to resources such as job opportunities. On the one hand, Bucharest is described by specific attractions: diversity of consumption, anonymity, job opportunities, better housing conditions, varied forms of leisure and cultural consumption. On the other hand, a certain inaccessibility to this social space is evident. The centripetal sense of relation to the central urban and the inaccessibility/rejection of this type of space creates the image of a high inequality, of an asymmetrical allocation of social opportunities.

The discrepancy between the reality of everyday urban life (the life situations of the characters) and what constitutes the content of the images and script elements depicting the fragments (on issues related to urban deviance, work ethic, socialist values) that the two TV reporters film during their professional activities suggests the idea of a disjunction between the communist ideology regarding the individual behaviour at work, in society, the cultural values and practices, and the real needs, interests and expectations of individuals with their own life strategies, and which manifest a parallel dynamic to what was the code of values, norms and principles that defined and regulated social life in socialism. The fragments filmed for the reportages display ideas, attitudes and opinions that are ideologically positively valued: themes related to the behaviour and moral attitudes of the individual, examples of good practice in work activities, belonging to a dominant value model.

Images of working people in film differ according to the categories of space in which they are situated. In the provincial urban areas, working people are mostly shown in outdoor or institutional spaces, with domestic/intimate spaces being insignificant. In the central space of the capital we identify most of the frames and scenes in private, domestic, interior spaces. The house of the camera operator Nelu, the house of the reporter Luiza, Ana Covete's rented house are the main private spaces presented in the film. The province is more associated with public urban space, while the capital displays elements of private housing. In none of the sequences filmed in any of the three towns (Constanța, Târgoviște, Fieni) there are working people filmed in private interior spaces. The sequences show us cut-outs of public (or semi-public) spaces as: the interior space of the Romlux factory in Târgoviște, the nursing home in the same town (in which the hall is the predominant space), the courtyard of same factory in Târgoviște, a museum, a restaurant, the interior space of the Dolphinarium in Constanța and the exterior public spaces around the factory (the street, the space around the entrance/exit of the factory). Pictures of private interior spaces are found exclusively in Bucharest. Categories of such (private) space include private family interior space (the interior space of the central male character's home represented by the living room, the kitchen, the bathroom, the hallway) and private individual interior space (the personal room).

FACTORY REPRESENTATIVE: When the steel plant is finished, the whole social situation will be balanced.
REPORTER: In what sense?
FACTORY REPRESENTATIVE: I mean in the sense that more men will come to our town, more men ... About 80% women, young girls ... and that creates a social problem. Of course they want to get married, to start a home ... Of course we create all the conditions for them to feel like a big family ... Here we have the home for non-family members...

Probă de microfon/Microphone Test, MIRCEA DANELIUC, 1980 (excerpt from the script)

Elements of cinematic language make an important contribution to the articulation of the image of work and workers in the provincial setting. The types of shots used (general shots, panoramic shots) and the types of camera angles are the most relevant in this respect, providing an aesthetic orchestration of reality. The significance and importance of the use of these elements of cinematic language derives from a series of functions associated with such elements. The overall shot has not only a descriptive role but also a certain ideological and psychological significance. People as silhouettes barely perceptible in the visual field give the impression of a reintegration of the individual into a predefined order, into a structure that escapes introspection. The general shot makes the human presence a subject of ideology, it objectifies it, placing it in an uncertain moral environment with rather negative valences. Loneliness, powerlessness are expressively suggested by the use of general shots on physical spaces, incorporating practical andsymbolic elements of the economic system and of the political regime. Other elements of cinematic language such as the high-angle shot express hopelessness, failure, the idea of defeat, fragility, vulnerability, and collapse. The general shots on the provincial town (Fieni, Dâmbovița county) and the numerous frames in which the high-angle shot is used (views of the factory, of people leaving the factory building after work, of elements that indicate a certain quality of the physical urban space in which people live and work) suggest a representation of the relationship between the individual and the context of carrying out work activities, on the one hand, and between the individual and the political power, on the other. The general shots and high-angle shot views are suggestive, on the one hand, of the idea of the relentless manifestation of social forces on individual biography. On the other hand, the same images offer an expressive representation of the failure of the political structure to accommodate the social order to economic organization. The orderly lines of workers coming out of the factory gates suggest economic structure, the management of labour power, the lack of awareness of the working class's own strength, the illusion of a unitary social identity. As they move away from the factory gate and into the space of the industrial city, their routes divide. Women and men become uncertain figures on a map of a loosely articulated social fabric, individuals who do not want to fight for any prefabricated ideal, who do not necessarily have any consciousness of their class unity, but possibly, at most, a sense of belonging to the same space and work practices, and who do not seem likely to mobilize against any real or imagined ruling class. The same images in succession provide a commentary on the project of building socialism, revealing a social dispersion of workers versus their economic organization. The images of workers diluted in the integrative landscape of a politically legitimized economy are suggestive of the structure of a collective social identity aggregated to the rank of a working class that disintegrates before coagulating into a coherent form and consistent content, oscillating in dissonant lines between the real, the ideal, and the normative, a class constrainedly and discontinuously disciplined on ideological rather than theoretical grounds within a value system that is not pluralistic but incongruent in social, economic, and political rationality.

The strict regulation of the occupational status of citizens by the state through restrictive rules and associated practices is illustrated in the denouement of the film narrative: Ana Covete, after unsuccessful attempts to find a job in Bucharest, ends up being employed at the Binders and Cement Plant in Fieni. The attempts of the two protagonists to circumvent the rules and practices that defined the system of state control in the field of labour opportunities and housing are a form of opposition to and contestation of the system of rules and norms that regulated the life of the individual in its essential dimensions (work, housing, family).

The ideological game played discursively between the woman who is an unskilled worker and the man with a liberal profession outlines a dialectical mechanism underlying representations of the two categories of the urban (the capital and the provincial city) and configures different ways of being and doing for each of them.

The socio-spatial mobility illustrated by Ana Covete's departure from Bucharest and establishment of her place of work and residence in an industrial city is reflected in visible changes in aspects of individual expression: the character's appearance, details of her clothing, specific attitudes and gestures, a specific use of the space in which the character is situated, symbolic behaviours, uses of material objects, elements of impression management in public

Bucharest/Capital City	An Industrial Town
Male, liberal profession, career, individual home, diversity, single relationship status, consumption, sunglasses, diverse clothes, colours, make-up, sexuality, cigarettes, shop window, market, taxi, dynamic, occupational mobility, escape, individual, Leonard Cohen, time, work time, individuality, close-up shot	Female, skilled worker, socialist housing for workers, marriage, monotonous clothes, community, work programme, static, industrial work, conformity, Song of Romania, space, extra work time, collectivity, general shot

FIGURE 6   Ideological displays: Bucharest and an industrial town

and private spaces. These differences are expressively displayed in film at both narartive and visual image levels. A representational dynamics of the characters' images in the film is intimately linked to their professional/occupational status and the category of urban space in which they live and act (clothing, scenery, gestures, attitudes, chromatics, types of frame, postures, elements of expressiveness). Elements of dress aesthetics, make-up, smoking, opposing conventions, management of sensuality and sexuality, will and expressiveness, all these make up Ana Covete's character when situated in Bucharest, while work uniform, lack of make-up, monotony, obedience, uniformity, and conformity make up Ana Covete's character when situated in industrial cities. The differences between the two discursive layers (fixed in distinct units of space) are perceived both at the level of content (appearance of characters, settings, situations) and at the level of expression (lights, colours, make-up, costumes, types of shots, acting). In terms of general characteristics, the working man or woman in the capital city is located in a space dominated by movement, diversity, consumption, attractiveness, while the working man or woman in a provincial city is located in different visual settings, of an urban poor in environmental elements, decorative objects, street furniture, a space mostly filled with factory interiors or with exteriors dominated by silhouettes of the same industrial units. Working people in their collective frames (images of groups of workers in the production process or coming out of the factory gates at the end of working hours) are discursively associated to a greater extent with the province than with Bucharest.

The compositional elements of images of the two urban frames of workers are grouped into indicators of different patterns of everyday life, proposing a structure of differentiation based on social distances which are both visually and narratively present. Differences in consumption practices, different levels of acces to urban commercial services (shops) provide an indicator of the degree of diversity associated with working people's consumption according to the type of urban in which they are situated and put to act. The image of a mannequin in the window of a shop in Bucharest (symbolizing individualism, the principle of differentiation, consumption, standardization, and feminine aesthetics) and the image of a group of working women from Fieni leaving the factory, depicted in front of the window of a Gostat shop (symbolizing the collective character, the class uniformity, the banal other, and the principle of identification), are significant for the idea of social distance and discrepancies between two urban worlds that are physically (geographically) not far from each other. Attraction to consumerism (buying clothes and makeup) is expressed through the image of the mannequin, reducing capitalism to aestheticism, but neither does socialism seem to offer a more effective order in the sense of a dynamic and efficient social organism. The women walking home after a day of work, carrying bags with food in both hands, do not appear to be intangible, spectacular, do not visibly differentiate themselves from one another, but neither do they suggest the success of a social system that does not seem susceptible to egalitarian manifestations. On the contrary.

4.3   Elements of the Social Condition of the Marginal

A specific theme developed in film is the labour condition under socialism. The impossibility of getting a job in Bucharest for those who did not have a permanent residence in the capital is an aspect of this theme. The film illustrates the implications and consequences of labour planning policy that generated discrimination and exclusion as forms of marginality. Ana Covete is a striking figure of the marginal, that conceptual figure specific to urbanity in general. This marginality is expressed precisely through a series of characteristics (including sociodemographic ones): violation of (so-called) moral rules in institutional frameworks of work, occupational and residential mobility, absence of precise layers of social meaning, lack of social attachments, utilitarian character of interpersonal relationships.

The perspective of the permanence of open options, of a life strategy susceptible to frequent changes and conjunctural redefinitions, the transitory character of the way of understanding and relating to work, interpersonal relations, the definition of needs and expectations, the means used to obtain various type of social resources – all these describe a social type whose path critically draws attention to the way in which mechanisms of accessing work and housing opportunities were thought out and structured in socialism.

In relation to values and norms that system promoted in its efforts to build "socialist consciousness" and form the "new man" (socialist attitudes towards work, values promoted through cultural education of working people, values of social coexistence), the protagonist is placed in an atypical situation of significant deviation from such an ideological view in terms of values, attitudes and behaviour. Ana Covete has no job, she was fired from her last job (Romlux factory in Târgoviște) because of her bad reputation (compromising the family of the chief engineer in the factory, who was transferred to the plant, thus leaving "a slap on the cheek of the factory"), has a poor financial situation, breaks the rules and practices minor forms of deviance (travels by train without ticket), lies, exploits resources of female attraction in order to obtain material or financial advantages or resources of influence to solve personal problems. The forms of attachment cultivated are fugitive and transitory, she does not trust institutions, she seeks survival formulas that reveal process of generating social inequalities. The protagonist's material interests, personal preferences and life strategy are portrayed in counterpoint to values of socialist ethics. The character belongs to social type of the marginal. It is defined by a series of precise characteristics corresponding to the following dimensions:

The marginal status is temporary, as the narrative of the film reveals. The resolution of certain aspects of the heroine's situation makes the marginal character eventually integrated into society according to the socialist value standards (not having a job was considered illegal). The narrative provides an explanatory model: socio-spatial mobility becomes the mechanism by which individual develops opportunities for access to increased social status. By increasing social status I understand moving from certain values or characteristics (occupational status, relations status, residential status) to values or characteristics situated higher up the scale of values considered highly desirable, within the value orientations having the character of norms. The final sequences present Ana Covete as a member of the workers' collective at Fieni plant, integrated into the working and living community, married, in a new

TABLE 19 Urban profiles. The figure of the marginal

Socio-demographic dimensions	Characteristics/values
Gender	Female
Relationship Status	Single
Occupational Status	Unemployed/Occupational Mobility
Residence	Urban/Mobility
Age	Young
Education	Medium Level

social condition that calls for new roles to be performed. On a factual level, increase in social status was achieved. On a subjective level, the film leaves rooms for multiple reflections.

At the level of the individual's subjective perception on his or her own life situation, of his or her own well-being, film proposes another key in reading and interpreting the elements describing the factual situation. Although Ana Covete has a job, got married (a wish expressed throughout the film) and has a home by virtue of having got a job, her own perception on these elements of the new social condition is not necessarily positive in terms of evaluative discourse.

The heroine's self-perception of her new condition is problematic, unsatisfactory. The film uses the logic of counterpoint to construct such a meaning. The final sequences show the heroine leaving the factory after work, together with other members of the workin collective group, and shortly afterwards meeting the man who had become her husband near the Gostat shop. The film operator, who had meanwhile left in order to satisfy his military service, came to visit her, not knowing that she had married. The images give us all the information in order to see the changes occured in the protagonist's social status. At the level of the significant dimension, the cinematic representations follow a counterpoint strategy, advancing a different evaluation. This construction of

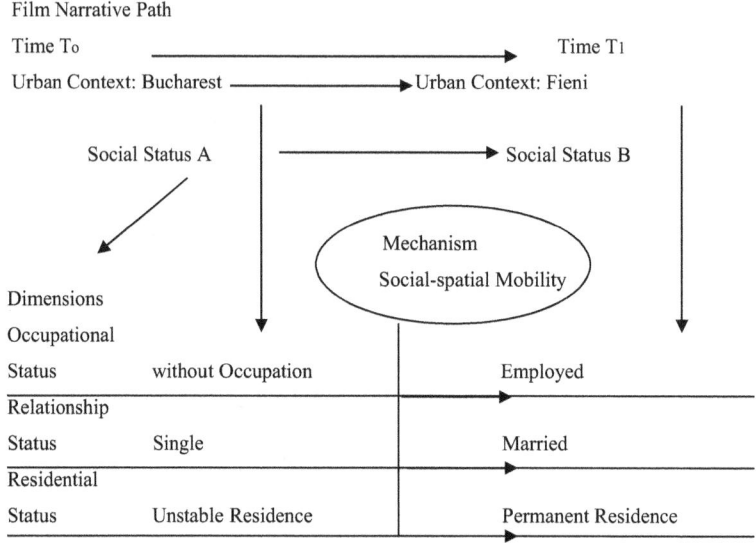

FIGURE 7   Elements of socio-spatial mobility under urbanization

meaning is made possible by use of a visual tool that brings together elements on three main levels:
1. Characters. This involves, on the one hand, the acting component (paralanguage elements: mimicry, gestures, postures; facial expressions like surprise, sadness, anger), on the other hand, non-specific filmic elements (costumes of the characters, decorative elements of the set);
2. Characteristics of the unit of place, that is, of the physical urban space in which characters are situated. The final sequences showing the moment of reunion between the Ana and Nelu depict a marginal urban area near a railway station, on the outskirts of the town, giving us the image of an industrial town whose public space lacks elements of urban planning and cleaning that produce a perceptive view on a certain type of urban comfort and attractiveness. On the contrary, the aspects illustrated in images depicting elements of the local urban landscape (the street) in the final cut suggest the degradation and precarious sense of social condition of the worker diffusely integrated in the physical and social frameworks of an ideology. Elements of the physical space in which Ana Covete is situated alongside other workers take on an evaluative function for the condition of an entire social category of passive subjects of the dominant ideology. Unpaved street, mud, potholes, to which are aded the high-angle shot of the street and of some spaces in its proximity where abandoned industrial tubes can be seen in the space for pedestrian traffic, areas left uncovered at the end of some industrial works – these descriptive elements give the image of a hostile city, of poor quality of public space in the context of the industrial urban where people are brought to work and live;
3. Image definition. Lighting – the visual tonality of the images generated by the weather features during filming (obviously a directorial choice) contributes to the construction of the image of the environment in which the industrial worker and the narrative discourse on the relationships between the characters are placed. The dull landscape, without precise contours, populated here and there by silhouettes lost in a prefabricated environment, ordered in a disciplined way in movements and directions of social existence, suggests the dilution of human relationships through their institutionalization, provides an analogy to the structure and meaning of their social identity.

To these elements are added the use of certain specific cinematic elements in order to articulate a counterpoint reading of the film's end. These are the use of wide shots, high-angle shots, slightly tilted frames, elements that suggest the idea of defeat, of the power that social forces exert over the individual.

The social condition in which the protagonists are situated at the end of the film presents them as *institutionalized* individuals. The army and the cement plant are contextually two agents of this institutionalization. The final sequence cinematically renders the (power) relationship between biography and history, between individual and society.

Alternating representations of work reproduce a multi-layered structure of meaning, as revealing dissonances between ideology and unchanged reality. On the one hand, a formal substructure of labour process is displayed, which is represented by images of the production process, organization and distribution of labour forces in physical frames, formal definitions of work situations. The elements of this structure are given by material objects of work contexts and by the human presences that populate these contexts. Description of production activities, elements of communication specific to positions of authority in institutions of work, modes of transmission of values and norms governing work relations and communication in predefined settings, performance of work tasks and responsibilities and communicative roles based on principles defining work ethics, interactions between people at work, physical and social relations in the context of work activities, occupational socialization, ideology of belonging to the the work community, the dominance of work in the structure of social identity, the visual and textual forms of formal socialization at work (clothes, vocabulary, physical hypostases of work, proximity, standardization of gestures, the use of work objects) – all these are situated in the narrative corpus, giving the image of a system of work in which uniformity, standardization, routine, obedience, social control, productivity, planning are constitutive, fixed elements around which there is a much more fluid, nuanced, contradictory, plural and real, subjective experience. Tensions generated by the difficulty of getting a job, informal socialization in work contexts, social prejudices regarding the occupational identity, the limit of tolerance to the violation of predefined norms and principles in social and work relations, the instability of housing and limited resources in achieving terminal values, disjointed interactions, renunciation, compromise, lack of communication, life situations not settled in time or atypically defined, weak sense of belonging to work community, ambivalent identity of work (role distance), spontaneity and violation of social conventions, uncertainty – all these give the image of a dynamic of social identity with an irregular pulse, of an informal structure of the social in which work has an instrumental value. Even if at cinematic level these two structures are situated on different narrative and visual layers, meaning is developed at the confluence between them. What results is a social organism with artificially activated (supra-ideological) components and a morphology of humanity that is not always reproduced in precise contours and that dilutes the predefined forms in which it is put to manifest, making transience a way of life and a form of knowledge.

5   *La capătul liniei/At the End of the Line* (Dinu Tănase, 1983)

La capătul liniei/At the End of the Line presents the story of two workers, Nea Crişan (played by Mircea Albulescu), a former master foundryman, who was convicted following a work accident. After his release from prison, he tries to reintegrate into society by finding a job at a steel mill. The stages of this reintegration are the red thread along which the film narrative is developed. The other main character is Cicea (played by Dan Condurache), a lathe worker, who also falls into the category of socially deviant characters, having been convicted of driving without a licence. The two are joined by the main female character Ani (played by Ioana Crăciuneacu), a waitress at a restaurant in a provincial town.

The definition of the social situations of the three main characters sets the area for reflection from the outset to be developed throughout the film. The representations of work in Dinu Tănase's film are structured along several dimensions articulated at both narrative and visual level: 1. elements of representation of work activities (work in the industrial sector of steel industry, work in the field of commercial/food services); 2. elements of representation of the relationships between characters belonging to the social category of workers; 3. elements of representation of the labour system, meaning the institutional framework in which the characters are put to act, make decisions, carry out work activities, express positions in relation to the object of work, etc.; 4. elements of representation of the relationship between ideology of work and the subjective experiences of working people.

The occupations and professions represented in film belong to industrial and service sectors: lathe worker, master foundryman, planer (steel industry), waitress (food services), receptionist (hotel services), policeman (public safety services), barber (personal hygiene services), train conductor (transport services), singers (artistic services). Correspondingly, the economic units that appear in the film are: steelworks, *Minerva* restaurant, a railway station, a hotel, a police station, a canteen, a barber shop. The physical frames of work bring together images of the industrial and economic units in which the characters work or in which they are put to act at different points along the narrative.

TABLE 20   Professions and occupations of characters

Main and supporting characters	Profession/occupation	Area of activity
Crişan	Master Foundry Worker	Industrial Branch
Cicea	Lathe Worker	Industrial Branch
Ana	Waitress	Services
Matilda Iliescu	Unemployed	----------------------
Puşcaşu	Chief of the Staff Department (Steel Plant)	Industrial Branch
--------------------	Chief Engineer	Industrial Branch
--------------------	Receptionist	Services
Matilda's Mother-in-Law	Housewife	----------------------
Ana's Mother	Housewife	----------------------

SOURCE: *AT THE END OF THE LINE*, DINU TĂNASE, 1983

5.1   *Towards a Personal Definition of Work Ethics*

A constant element in the discursive construction of relationship between characters and socio-economic frameworks associated to them is the dominance of interpersonal quality of institutional and working relationships. The image of economic/industrial system is used as a background for elements of construction in terms of the characters' subjective experiences, personal problems, uncertainties and social constraints. Focus is put on introspective reflections, intimate views on life situations that are put together in a single frame, giving the image of multiple surfaces, of mirrors in which the characters question elements of their social identity and of the society in which they live. The responsibility, the feeling of guilt carried for a serious work accident make of Nea Crişan a complex character, who dilutes the ideological composition of the meanings of work, which he transforms into sources of permanent questioning, both in relation to himself and in relation to those who have institutional authority in terms of distribution and management of labour resources. Crişan has certain limits in communicating with the others, his interventions dose a certain intra- and interpersonal tension, which is articulated both on the relationship of friendship with Cicea and on the relationship of love with Ani. Crişan and Cicea are two different characters in terms of personality characteristics; what unites them is their status as workers, their belonging to a common social class. Cicea is expansive, uninhibited and daring, often involved in deviant behaviour, trying to attract the attention of others, easily getting into physical altercations or capturing attention through elements of humour and personal attractiveness. Crișan is solitary, the mature social type with a personality configuration based on values such as work, responsibility and friendship. Cicea shows massive resources of sociability, is a dynamic presence, even if often with bad consequences, in any type of situation. Relationships between the two are often based on confrontations, including physically. What binds them throughout their attempts to reintegrate into society is the fundamental social value of friendship. The social prestige of work, the collective recognition of work performance are very important for Crișan, while for Cicea they have more of a demonstrative value on the basis of which the need to belong to a social group is structured. Significant in this respect are the scenes inside the factory where Crișan and Cicea are made to execute some pieces on the lathe under the watchful observation of factory superiors. The spectacular element that Cicea uses in the action of executing a simple piece has the function of invalidating the technical performance of Crișan, a character who constantly expresses throughout the film an edifying tension for the kinds of problems related to the social identity of work that cannot be resolved by simple individual introspection.

He is an individual who has lost the prestige of his work as a result of the accident for which he was blamed and for which he served his sentence, but who miss – with the participation of his friend Cicea – the chance to recover his identity. The resources of credibility and trust are exhaustible, the reality of work – by its efficient and effective standards – does not accept people who have been wrong at some point, even if they have taken the blame for that mistake.

5.2   *Human Element and Mechanical Sensitivity*
The film interrogates in an extremely fine way the fluid springs that underlie a society's willingness – through the way its institutions are developed – to tolerate deviation from the norm. Moreover, it gives us an unfolding of its formal and especially informal mechanisms by which it regulates these deviations and manages their meanings in real the institutional contexts of work.

The processuality of industrial work is present in the film in the sequences filmed in the steelworks of the Republica factory in Bucharest. The images are of an almost metallic finesse, incorporating the tense relationship between the human element and the industrial machine in unprecedented views. The fact of working captured in the hypostasis of executing a piece on a lathe does not have a final value in itself in the sense of identifying work with an object of an ontological nature (to be = to work). Work has an instrumental value for clarifying social and moral issues concerning rather attitudes towards work in terms of responsibility, competence, recognition and social trust. The scenes in which we see Crișan and Cicea working indicate the social nature of the construction of the prestige of work and the precarious attention paid to the individual human element in the formal process of work. Cicea is visualized in this sequence in the same setting as other working people who feel drawn to the character manifesting spontaneously, spectacularly, attracting through gestures, expressions, elements of verbal communication the attention and appreciation of those around him. Crișan is seen alone in the frame, expressing a state of tension, of discomfort, which he feels in the situation generated by his friend. The execution of the pieces is merely an opportunity to highlight the interpersonal conflicts between the two protagonists and the value and attitudinal structures on which these conflicts develop. What is contested in the work scenes is not the professional competence, but the validation of the other as a person with needs, problems, expectations, hopes, desires, fluctuating on an often uncertain, intangible and fleeting continuum.

The elements of fine detail in the visual representation of the mechanical pieces and of the machinery used in the execution of work activities stand out in contrast to human intervention – the variable element susceptible to high precision, but equally susceptible to failure. Professional competence is expressed by the degree of precision with which machines are handled, by the efficient management of production time in relation to the final objective of the work activity, that is, by the productivity of the work. The component elements of the lathe machinery in the sequence of piece execution tests follow one another in images dominated by the human element, moving, to the same extent transient and susceptible to error, while the metallic accents of the stationary machine seem to visually suggest the presence of a precise order that reveals itself in its material manifestations, embodying the mass of fluid expressions of human presence in the context of the machine.

It is interesting how the levels of social identity of individuals are discursively delineated according to social contexts in which they are made to act. The characters reflect rather pluralistic value systems, in the sense that some elements of attitude and behaviour are not necessarily consonant with each other, indicating significant value distances at the hard core of their personality configuration. Cicea is a deviant type who drives without a license, rides the train without a ticket, but at the same time proves to be a successful worker with professional skills that are valued as such. He displays a nonchalance that sometimes takes on insolent overtones, but he is also a better communicator than his friend Crișan and has a significantly greater capacity for social adaptation. Crișan is a very good worker, but has lost confidence that he can still be productive at an optimal level, often hesitates and fails to assert his positions firmly in various situations. He is more attentive and sensitive to the values and social norms that are considered desirable in society, he respects them faithfully and is aware of their importance for his reintegration into work and thus into society.

The social types represented by the two protagonists are complex and deconstruct the unitary, coherent vision of the socialist hero as a worker. Their social situation is neither clear-cut nor easy to fit into one category or another. They are both situated in an intermediate sphere, in a zone of almost constant questioning about the social roles they have to perform, the management of needs and expectations that define a life that they both want to be clearer, more permissive, more accessible. The major conflict they both feel, each in a different way, is that between the typical condition of the worker and the condition of the deviant person in society, even if the springs underlying this common characteristic – deviation from the norms of society – are radically different for them. Between these two poles of opposition we identify them through a series of experiences through which the characters reveal themselves to us in social, intrapersonal, emotional, professional, relational aspects. The social identities of the two are as fluid and uncertain as the physical spaces in which they are situated throughout the film. The units of place chosen for the actions of the two friends are by their nature intermediate, transient, fluid spaces: the street, the train station, the hotel, the restaurant, the halls of institutions, the police station, temporary living spaces. Both fluctuate between different destinations, between different living spaces, between urban and rural, between insecure places of work. The common element in these scenes of socio-professional uncertainty is that they are always together, an indicator of the core value of friendship.

La capătul liniei/At the End of the Line provides a representation of the worker that seems sliced up in terms of a binary opposition, but is not exclusive in defining the broader social subtypes developed. Even as deviant, Cicea is also a type of hero who deconstructs the uniform and standardized patterns of the worker. He resembles a star, he is the skilled worker who captures the attention of others, who transforms the execution of a piece on the lathe in front of his peers into a performance followed by applause, who imposes himself not by resemblance to others, but by differentiation, by the spectacular nature of his presence, by the aesthetic manipulations of objects that populate the physical spaces in which he acts. Cicea's appearances are permanently polished, like a perfectly executed piece. He delineates himself from collective identity, even if he can only assert himself within its limits. The hard-working character, Crișan, is a type who follows the rules, who doesn't want to stand out, who is aware of his professional competence, but who doesn't make a fuss about it, doesn't practice it demonstratively, as Cicea does, doesn't aim for either real or imaginary self-assertion. The tensions between the two, the tensions between them and others, reflect the fault lines of a social order shaped in ideological expressions that fail to consistently validate the very core value on which it is founded, namely equality. The competition between the two is not about being recognized as working people, for one qualification or another, but about being validated and accepted as they are, in *their* social and, above all, human condition, which is a challenge that is as imaginary cinematically as it is theoretically real.

6   *Faleze de nisip/Sand Cliffs* (Dan Pița, 1983)

Faleze de nisip/Sand Cliffs is a screenplay of novel *Sand Days* by Bujor Nedelcovici. The film is a document of the time, focusing on social issues, a constant preoccupation in Dan Pița's filmography. The film premiered on 31 January 1983 and was the subject of harshest official criticism at the highest political level.

Doctor Theodor Hristea (played by Victor Rebengiuc) is at the seaside with his girlfriend Cristina (played by Carmen Galin) and a good friend, Ștefan (played by Marin Moraru). The doctor, the victim of a theft (a video camera, a tape recorder, a photo camera, a bracelet, a golden cross), becomes an investigator himself, accusing a young carpenter, Vasile Mihăilescu, known as the Kid (played by Gheorghe Visu) of the theft. The film follows the doctor's insistent attempts to get the accused to admit to the authorities a theft he did not commit, based on an impression rather than real evidence. The physical resemblance that the doctor perceives between the young worker on the beach and the offender is the only evidence he brings against him. The local investigating bodies prove powerless to solve the case. The character of the young man accused of theft loses his job as a result of prolonged detention for investigation. The end of the film does not propose a solution to the case, the investigation does not reach a conclusion, the ending is an open one, inviting to reflection on the evolution of the relationship between characters, which can be read as an x-ray of social mechanisms of construction of relationships between different social categories in terms of influence, power, control and social prestige.

6.1 "Young Trees" and the "Forest Rot"

In the realist-socialist view, the film hero could only be a working man, moreover, a working man whose attitudes and behaviour are based on heroism and sacrifice. In opposition there is the anti-hero, who challenges the ideological use of work as a form of social control. The rendering of reality in the local practices of the method of socialist realism involved an operation of differentiation, selection and presentation only of the categories of positive (working) heroes who embodied the "young trees", "all that is best and most worthy in our society", far removed from the characters unsuited to socialist order, the awkward characters who in Ceaușescu's mind represented "the weeds" or "the rot in the forest", as he said in the speech in Mangalia, in August 1983.

Part of Ceaușescu's critical speech referred to the film *Faleze de nisip/Sand Cliffs*. The young "the worker from the Black Sea" was one of the main characters in the film. Vehement criticism of the film was followed by its withdrawal from cinemas. *Faleze de nisip/Sand Cliffs* was the only film to which critical commentaries were made overtly in a speech at the highest state level in the history of Romanian cinema. In issue No. 8 of *Cinema* magazine in 1983 (the same month as Ceaușescu's speech in Mangalia), on page 3 of the magazine, the part of the speech containing the critical references to cinema in general and to Pița's film in particular was reproduced in full. The text was accompanied by an image of the presidential couple (one of the magazine's constant practices of visual ideologization during the 1980s). The harsh criticism had been appropriated by the film community. Thematic subtitles accompanied Ceaușescu's speech on the second page of the magazine: "Exemplary hero, not idealised" or "New content and a new form for youth films". The critical themes of the speech were taken up and developed in articles in the first pages of the magazine. An excerpt from one such article:

> Fundamental flaws of our films are frankly addressed, both in terms of the selection of significant characters and phenomena from reality, and in terms of the spirit, the message of the film inspired by actuality. Noting that lately it has become fashionable to "recruit" marginal characters from the outskirts of society, to the detriment of presenting characters who define – by their majority existence and their superior conception of history and life – our socialist reality, the party's general secretary clearly demanded that Romanian films be more firmly oriented, unequivocally towards conflicts in which characters representative of the social times in which we live are involved, and to bring to the fore heroes who constitute a model, because only in this way, respecting the essential truths of our

life, can film become a moving artistic document, can it strive to capture the essential facets of reality from its infinite facets.
NICOLAE DRAGOȘ, *Cinema* magazine, No. 8, 1983: 2

The strong ideological counter-offensive came in the next issue of *Cinema* magazine (No. 9/September 1983), on page 2: "Revolutionary romanticism and model characters on the spot, on the Danube-Black Sea site". On page 3, a quotation from Ceaușescu re-established the ideological order in the social reality of work: "Here, at the Danube-Black Sea Canal, soon to be put into operation, tens of thousands of young people have shown unparalleled heroism. And we find similar examples on hundreds and thousands of construction sites and economic and social units". The change of perspective could not be accepted. The character of the young worker in Pița's film did not fall into this category, he remained a "marginal character", he did not show heroism, he was just a worker "on the periphery of society".

What elements of content are likely to have had attracted criticism from officials and censorship of the film? In what ways does the film deviate from the ideological imperatives of socialist realism in its construction of typical characters and its reflection of social-historical reality? In what follows I propose an analysis that attempts to answer these questions.

6.2   *The Kid – A Young Worker at the Black Sea*

The characters in the film represent different social and professional categories. The table below shows the distribution of characters in terms of social status in their professional and/or occupational dimension and the corresponding fields of activity:

This configuration reflects a division of the areas of activity according to the category of characters, thai is main and supporting characters. Most of the main characters (the doctor, the photojournalist, the nurse) are self-employed, working in the service sector (health, press). The Kid is the only one of the main characters who belongs to the social category of workers. Also interesting is the gender division of the characters, on the one hand, according to the category of characters (main or supporting) and, on the other hand, according to their situation in the context of work activities. The majority of the main characters are male (doctor, photojournalist, worker), while the majority of the female characters are in the category of supporting characters. As for the characters who are shown in the film carrying out work in institutional settings, these are: the doctor, the policemen, the fishermen and the professor. The landscape of the work process is predominantly male. This is contrasted by the lack of work activities in the case of the female characters, or the placement

TABLE 21 Professions and occupations of characters

Main and supporting characters	Socio-professional category	Area of activity
The Kid (Vasile Mihăilescu)	Worker (Carpenter)	Industrial Branch
Theodor Hristea	Doctor (Surgeon) Hospital Director	Health Administration/Party Bureaucracy
Ștefan Albini, the Doctor's Friend	Photojournalist	Press
Cristina, the Doctor's Lover	Nurse	Health
Raicu, the Head of Investigation	Major	Justice
Comrade Popa	Lieutenant	Justice
Supporting Character	Professor	Education
The Workshop Colleague	Worker (Lathe Worker)	Industrial Brunch
The Workshop Craftsman	Worker	Industrial Brunch
Maria, the Kid's Cousin	Hairdresser	Personal Services Branch
Boris, the Kid's Uncle	Fisherman	Industrial Brunch
Secondary Characters at the Fish Collection Station	Fishermen	Industrial Brunch
Anica	Saleswoman on the Beach	Street Commerce
the Kid's Father	Pensioner	-
the Kid's Aunt	Pensioner	-
Amira, the Kid's Girlfriend	Unemployed	-

SOURCE: *SAND CLIFFS*, DAN PIȚA, 1983

of their work activities exclusively in the domestic sphere and especially in the supporting characters.

Based on these sociological clarifications regarding the distribution of certain social characteristics at the level of the characters, I will refer in the following to the representation developed on the relationships between socio-professional categories presented in the film. At the level of the main characters (the doctor and the carpenter worker), the filmic construction reflects a conflictual relationship. The following excerpt from the script is significant in this respect, highlighting the social distance between the victim (the carpenter worker) and the accuser (the doctor and hospital manager):

THE KID:	I don't fight. I can even fight you, who are friend with everyone here.
DOCTOR HRISTEA:	Eh...
THE KID:	Yes, yes, yes, I saw, I'm not from the countryside.
DOCTOR HRISTEA:	I'm a simple citizen like you.
THE KID:	That's not true. You're a big boss and I'm a poor carpenter. Then how?

Faleze de nisip/Sand Cliffs, DAN PIȚA, 1983 (excerpt from the script)

Social relations in socialism are not based "on equality and social justice, on the common goal of making all the people well and happy" (*Code of Principles and Norms of Communist Work and Life, Socialist Ethics and Equity* 1981: 6), but on strong class inequalities. In the case of the young carpenter, the reference is the individual and his autonomy; in the case of the doctor, the reference is the power credited through membership of the party system and social control as a direct effect of this status condition. If between the two social categories represented by Doctor Hristea and the Kid the relations are conflictual, as for the relations between doctor and police officials and investigators, they are consensual, based on subordination and obedience: the institution of *miliția* (the name given to communist police) is subordinated to the imperatives of the representative of bureaucratic and party system (the doctor). The police officials try to satisfy the doctor's need for justice, regardless of whether this is based on appearance rather than truth. The strong criterion in managing the theft case is not the truth, but the personal will of the representative of the system of authority, based on social, material, relational resources, specific to having a superior position in the bureaucratic system. The doctor practises influence peddling, abuse of power, the tendency to use for one's own benefit and to the detriment of the working people positions and tasks of responsibility entrusted to him by society (*Code of Principles and Norms of Communist Work and Life, Socialist Ethics and Equity* 1981: 18–19) – these are precisely those manifestations that should have been prevented and combated according to the socialist value system. It is worth noting that the doctor is not defined primarily by his professional status (he practices sporadically as a surgeon), but on the basis of his position in the bureaucratic system (he is a hospital manager with positions in numerous committees and commissions). His position in the bureaucratic party system gives him access to material resources, power and influence. The doctor is perceived by the representatives of local investigating bodies as belonging to a professional and political elite and, by virtue of this membership, is entitled to influence the development of the investigation. The scene in which a policeman brings Pepsi soft drink and cakes and put them on the table in front of the doctor and his friends, who are at the local police station to take part in the investigation, is significant in this respect. The doctor from the "capital" is given preferential treatment, the hospitality of the local authorities, who are posing as members of an institution that enforces order. By portraying such practices, the film reflects certain rituals of subordination and the reproduction of social inequalities that actually existed in society. The social profile of the doctor is briefly described in the film: " awarded at school, leading sportsman, renowned surgeon, director", "ordinary careerist who takes advantage of his father's origin, his qualities", "always on top of his sins", he has everything he wants. These biographical elements, as expressed in the discussion between the doctor and his friend, Ștefan, provide data for a genuine intellectual physiognomy of the social type represented by the character. What are the elements that describe the model of success? "Power, travel abroad, ascension to a university position, access to the circle of", "a few hundred extra lei, the power to command nurses, doctors" – these are the types of resources and benefits that define the doctor's success in life, listed by Ștefan, the chronicler of the doctor's biography and the critic of his friend. The social mechanisms of construction of this privileged status are: the "political base", a "giant slalom among giants", manipulation and opportunism as methods of increasing social status, of success. The political base, an expression of belonging to the party system and discipline, is the hard core, the engine of social success. "When you live among wolves, you learn to howl like them", the doctor suggestively describes the practical mechanism for the acquisition of the Party's philosophical conception of the world and life. The character's political ascension – his appointment as hospital director, celebrated with champagne and black roe (typical ingredients of the culinary aesthetics of well-being) – is equivalent to his professional failure. The relationship between the political power acquired by moving up in the hospital's administrative hierarchy and the doctor's professional competence is expressed in the criticism voiced by Ștefan Albeni:

ȘTEFAN ALBENI: How many hours wasted trying to make yourself accepted, how much energy wasted with people you hate and despise. Why? For what? For a few hundred extra dollars, for the power to command nurses, doctors? It's not worth it, the stakes are too low. You're supposed to be a doctor, not a director, a doctor. You have golden hands. When a doctor has the talent of a surgeon, he has no right to work in a stone mine, even if that is his hobby.

Faleze de nisip/Sand Cliffs, DAN PIȚA, 1983 (excerpt from the script)

The doctor is representative of a system that validates corrupt mechanisms of social success and, by extension, of a society in which the sense of values such as work, truth and justice is severely atrophied. What is the cultural model of success in life? The answer is suggestively formulated in a reply of the doctor to his friend: "Build yourself a character, give yourself importance! Only in this way you can rise above others who trample you underfoot and laugh at you". The doctor's character lacks nuance, perceives reality in a polar way, does not tolerate points of view different from his own, is not capable of empathy, is not able to change perspective ("I don't allow anyone to force me to do anything but what I want" – says the doctor), sees things only in black and white, when "between black and white there are theoretically an infinity of shades"- his friend points out.

The filmic narrative does not propose an approach to solving the case, but a pretext for highlighting various forms of manifestation of the doctor's will in order to impose his idea of the truth of what happened, placing himself outside the truth. Replacing reality with the idea of reality, with the image of reality, is the prerogative of the narrative development. The mistake the doctor makes is to establish an identity between appearance and reality, when "likeness is not reality". It is an indicator of the loss of a sense of reality that his good friend reproaches him for: "You modify reality in the hope that it will conform to your ideas, you mutilate it, you've lost your sense of reality, that's your illness".

The power relationship around which the narrative is built develops between the doctor and the young worker. What are the representations of the working class and, in particular, of the young worker in the film? What are the forms of invalidation of the socialist realist imperatives of the film's portrayal of working life that might have drawn criticism and the film's unfortunate course?

According to the communist ideology of the "new man", the most responsible position for an individual is to place him or her in the context of action, and not of any action, but of work activity. The biographies of the main characters in the ideological manifesto films are highly standardized, modelled according to normative pre-definitions of the relationship between individual and work: the working man is portrayed as the "type" who has the best qualities and traits: he is accomplished, healthy, hair-cut, fair, honest, hard-working, with a spirit of sacrifice for work. The man does not count as a person in his particular individuality, but only as a man of work, that is, by the function he performs in the work process. The identity that matters is that which is articulated in the concrete reality of this process. Belonging to the work community is the strong criterion in defining social position. Respect from others, social prestige are effects of professional or occupational status.

The profile of the worker (the carpenter) in film deviates dramatically from this model. The Kid's character is a young man who works in a carpentry workshop in the harbour of Constanța. He is 22 years old, has completed his military service, is unmarried, does not drink, does not smoke, does not live with either of his parents (separated: his mother, a canteen manager, his father, retired, collects bottles from the beach), dresses in jeans, wears a tank top and flip-flops, believes in himself, claims he has never stolen anything and does not lie, and loves the sea. A master worker from the carpentry workshop describes him as "a good boy, hard-working, in his place", "punctual, nice", who "eats lunch alone", then goes home because "he doesn't like the collective". In his spare time he builds a sailboat, "stays after hours and works". The pie vendor on the beach describes the kid in the presence of the Major: "He comes, asks for a pie, pays for it, takes a few steps, sits there on the sand [...] and stares at my daughter". We learn what the carpenter feeds on, food being an important indicator of social status. A significant aspect of the construction of the two central characters in the film (Hristea and the Kid) in terms of class differentiation also concerns the social division of wealth in terms of food consumption. Class differences are also expressed through the contrast between the exotic nature of the food consumed by the doctor and the popular nature of the food consumed by the worker: the doctor and hospital director eats crabs, black roe, melon, drinks champagne, while the young worker eats cheese pie bought from the beach. The sound/music consumption of the two characters is another telling detail. The Kid likes to listen to the sea, the doctor listens to opera music with his girlfriend, reflecting the binary opposition between "nature" and "culture". Such cinematic representations subtly reproduce certain social stereotypes and also constitute a form of ritualization of social inequality.

The young worker in the film is not depicted in a work-related role, does not display the typical zeal and enthusiasm, does not exhibit the "social consciousness" of the "real" hero in the theistic films of the time. On the contrary, he is a solitary, apparently socially unadapted type, with vague, unarticulated social and institutional ties, susceptible to reprehensible deeds. The character lacks the demonstrative character of the working-class hero. The significant deviation of the hero from the value, attitudinal and behavioural model that guided the construction of characters anchored in actuality dramatically reduced the possibilities of including the character in an ideologically valid category of heroes. The Kid is not a "typical" character in the sense of the conception of socialist realism, primarily because he is not a "positive" type, in the sense that he is supposed to bring together the best qualities and feelings of the expected "new man", qualities and feelings cultivated in the context of socialist society (ideal positivity as basic idea of Soviet revolutionary romanticism). The deviation that the character of the Kid proposes is given by a degree of inertia to the uniformizing and constraining tendencies of a system that generates inequality, a degree of contestation of the structural limits of a way of thinking and organising the relationships between individual needs, choices and imperatives, in accordance with one's own life project and in the objective conditions of a "historical" biography, with its specific modes of attribution and control. The relationship between the individual and work is not a positive, typical one, but one susceptible to multiple contestations, which is a critical commentary on the principles that ideologically define work culture. The fact that the character is not very communicative with his colleagues in the workshop, not integrated into the work collective, does not mean a rejection of the idea of work, but thinking and projecting the life of work not according to the attribution of a predefined value, but according to his own life project. The Kid is described in positive terms by the workshop craftsman – punctuality, kindness, reliability, good manners – attributes defining an optimal quality of work activities carried out by the young carpenter. The component of social relations and sociability at work is uncertain, susceptible to negative evaluations in the narrative, making the character atypical in the social realist gallery. It is an individualizing perspective in which the choice of work, the ways of practising work relations are structured not only according to nature of professional practice, but according to a certain value orientation of the individual. In such a perspective, it is not the option for a particular type of work, that is, the most important criterion in the design of social biography, but a much more important option linked to the existence of a life project of one's own. It is true that the Kid, following the investigation, leaves the construction site where he was only "mocked by the workers from the workshop", becomes an "unskilled worker with vocational school", works in the local mill. His social losses are significant: he loses his job at the workshop, leaves his aunt's home, becomes undesirable to the parents of the girl he was planning to marry. His social status is destroyed. The doctor's insistence on trying to truncate reality according to his perception, returning to search for the Kid after a few months in prison, is ironically counterpointed by the character of the young man's cousin: "Or maybe you've come to do social research? To see if the ex-convict has integrated into our society, if he's been employed in the same job and is now a leader?" The irony is discursively equivalent to deconstruction of a fixed form of representation of the working class in the ideological imaginary, of attempts to transform individuals into multilateral, harmonious persons, perfectly integrated into society – a model outdated by real practices of working life, shaped by spontaneous reactions of individuals engaged in their own biographical trajectories, conflicts and uncertainties. The Kid does not fall into the category of typical (in the ideological sense) characters of the working hero. He is not a model worker, a leader in production, with a spirit of friendship and collaboration, he is not an "advanced example for all those in whose midst he lives and works". He is the social type who "didn't want to howl like the wolves, who rebelled and defeated you" – beyond the significant social losses – Ștefan describes him succinctly, addressing himself to the doctor. The Kid's biography is cinematically reflexive, is not a "given" but a "construction" resulting from a process of permanent dialogue, negotiation, and compromise, that is, from a process of continuous differentiation.

6.3   A Counter-Analysis of the Official Critique of the Film

The criticism voiced in the August 1983 speech was clearly aimed at the unrealistic treatment or "distorted presentation" of the social condition of young workers. Thus, a problem of reflection of an important aspect of socialist "reality" – the condition of the working class. This discursive episode is one of the explanations for the film's censorship and withdrawal from cinemas. It is an external perspective based on the de facto content of Ceaușescu's speech (even though the title of the film was never mentioned in the speech, it is common knowledge that the critical commentaries referred to Pița's film). But what about the internal perspective? What was it that actually led to the censorship measures and, ultimately, to the banning of the film from release? By internal perspective I understand the set of perceptions, ways of understanding, explanatory visions of those who participated in the making of the film or were part of the cinematic context of the time, direct or indirect witnesses of this episode of censorship.

In order to illustrate this internal perspective, I will refer below to the views on the history of this censorship case expressed by the film's protagonist, actor Victor Rebengiuc, in an interview I conducted as part of the research. The reasons for the high-level criticism would have been found elsewhere, says the actor who played Dr. Theodor Hristea. According to him, the real reasons that led to the banning of the film were not related to the portrayal of the young worker in the film, but to the central character of the film, the doctor and hospital director Hristea. "The problem was not with the young man, but with the doctor, who in his desire for success uses his party membership", says Victor Rebengiuc. The fact that "a young man walks on the beach, steals or doesn't steal, goes to prison rightly or wrongly, that had no relevance whatsoever", explains the actor. The character of the doctor is a guy who wants power, and being a party member and a holder of a position in the bureaucratic state apparatus gives him that power. Being a party member and holding a position of leadership provided the resources to manipulate people, institutions (the police (*miliția*), the medical system). The presence of the party in the film through the membership of the main character would have actually attracted the attention and criticism of those in charge of ideological control. The image of a party represented as a resource and an effective means of social parvenitism, of a party above the law, above the police (*miliția*), even above the state, could not be accepted by the ideologists of the party themselves. In the same interview, the actor claims that there was a certain arrangement ("complicity") between the director and the actor in order to construct the character of the doctor in such a way as to make present a subtle criticism of the party bureaucracy, the character of the doctor being a typical representative of it.

According to opinions expressed in other interviews conducted during the research, the banning of the film was not based on a very careful and rigorous analysis of Pița's directorial proposal, particularly in relation to the construction of the main characters (the worker and the hospital director). It would have just been a case of bad timing. Filmmaker Horea Murgu describes the episode as an "unfortunate accident", caused by a simple negative impression formed after watching the film to which Ceaușescu had been invited after a volleyball match on the Romanian beach. It is ironic that the beach, where much of the film's actions take place, is also the place where film's unhappy history began.

Although *Faleze de nisip/Sand Cliffs* was shown at the *Scala* cinema in Bucharest for only three days (the law stipulated that each film that had a premiere had to run for two weeks), during this time changes were made to the content of the film (in the absence of filmmakers) and it was eventually banned. Although it was banned shortly after the premiere, statistics from the late 1980s show 39,428 viewers who would have gone to see the film (Căliman, 2000: 407). The film was withdrawn from director Dan Pița's filmography for the rest of the socialist period.

6.4   One Film. Multiple Discourses

Each of the two perspectives of analysis (external and internal) of the film contains its share of subjectivity. What is important is the reflection on the mechanisms of construction of the official criticism of cinema that constitute defence mechanisms of an atrophied and altered system and invalidation of social reality itself. "Fear of the real", to use an edifying line from the film. The withdrawal of the film was equivalent to an outright rejection of self-criticism at the level of the official system. It is true that this criticism was voiced by a filmmaker, and not by a representative of the party system or any social category, but in the eyes of the audience this distinction remains one of nuance and possibly unobservable. The content of the film was perceived as a critique of the bureaucratic state system primarily at the level of the political elite, that is, a small group. If the film had not been censored, this criticism, once formulated and manifestly represented, would have lost real subversive capacity, functioning as a valve to regulate conflicts between ideological imperatives and the expectations of different social categories in the sense that, in principle, the idea and the fact of recognizing certain limits, weaknesses, are in themselves positively valued. The effect has been exactly the opposite, in that the banning of the film has made it historically more visible and important to both those who have seen it and to those who have not.

Whatever the director's intentionality, whatever the particular circumstances that contributed to the production of this film, what is important is how we can identify the mechanism that made this cultural good atypical. The presence of the film in the filmography of the 1980s period is structured on several elements that are significant for the social value of this document, in general, and for understanding and knowing of the mechanisms of construction and reception of representations of work in the context of socialist realism, in particular:

1. at the official level, criticism, censorship and banning of the film were motivated by its problematic, "distorted" representation of the condition of the working class and, in particular, of young workers;
2. the film invalidates the ideological model of the working man (reflected through values and norms in official documents such as the *Code of Principles and Norms of Communist Work and Life, Socialist Ethics and Equity*); the character referred to in Ceaușescu's critical speech belongs to the working class. The condition of the working man in the film does not reflect the "model hero" as a typical reference in the construction of characters in the key of socialist realism as a creative method;
3. the "cinematic" operationalization of the institution of work invalidates the doctrinal toolkit of socialist realism on the reflection of work life: the social character of work, sociability at work, integration at work, the spirit of sacrifice, the heroic character of working people in institutionalized settings are missing;

4. the young working class, represented by the character of the carpenter, is defined along two critical levels: on the one hand, the atypical character in terms of the ideological pre-definitions of working life – the hypostasis of the anti-hero of work, on the other hand, the potential for challenging the political system and deconstructing social conventions based on stereotypes;
5. there are alternative explanations for the reasons behind the criticism followed by the censorship of the film; one explanation concerns the criticism of the bureaucratic party system, represented by the character of the doctor/hospital director; membership of the party structure – the party as a social and political institution – is represented as a mechanism for illegitimate use of power resources and the increase of social status;
6. in the film, strong social polarizations can be identified, based on the social division of work; the socio-professional status of individuals unequally structures access to different types of social and political resources (material, influence, power, social prestige, etc.);
7. the broadcasting and its official criticism had important effects in the Romanian public space. Social institutions took over the official criticism and amplified it in the public space for the purpose of rapid ideological fall back of the cinematic imaginary of work. An example of this is given by the debates and investigations organized by *Cinema* magazine, in whose pages were published, shortly after the critique of Mangalia, interviews with "model" workers from the Danube-Black Sea Canal, with the aim of rehabilitating the heroic condition of young workers, builders with a "vision of the future", spectacular characters from the life of the construction site, situated at a great ideological distance from the "marginal" character of the Kid in Pița's film;
8. the central characters of the film (the young carpenter and the doctor/hospital director) are typical, but in a different perspective from the manifestly ideological one. They are typical and significant because their traits, the situations in which they are made to act, the social conflicts they try to resolve throughout the film reveal certain tensions between individual biography and the institutional frameworks that regulate it.

The effectiveness of film results from the fact that representations of certain socio-professional classes and messages conveyed through cinematic, cultural, and political codes can be received and understood by the audience based on a cultural and political background shared by both the author of film and the audience. Through the whole narrative development and accompanying filmic expression, the film recomposes forms and experiences of a social world (mechanisms of a social order, the functioning of institutions, social relations, reality of work, social practices, social inequalities), attaching to them new possibilities of reflection and analysis for a better understanding and common knowledge of the relationship between individual and ideology or political power under socialism and not only.

In the 8th issue of *Cinema* magazine in 1988, an interview with director Dan Pița was published under the title "Refusal of enclosure is part of my structure". In this interview he stated: "I am interested in the social. The relationship between the individual and society is a problem that concerns me to the point of obsession. To what extent man is prepared and educated and helped to carry human existence further, better, higher". Dan Pița's "obsession", put into narrative and cinematic images, is a form of sociological imagination, one of the most effective.

The elements of factual and interpretative situating of the represented realities in film at the level of the categories of social actors mentioned above (directors, actors, filmmakers) lead to a question that I consider useful in order to formulate a critique of the methodology used, and not necessarily of the methods used: why are there several versions of a fact that took place at a given time, regarding the definition of the situation of the making, content and distribution of a film? The very fact of asking this question in the context of an investigation of social representations of film opens a line of reflection on the existence of a significant limit to the interpretative methodology that underlies the identification of the relationships between politics, ideology, aesthetic theory and film practice. How a film is received over time, how these representations change over time, how the social memory of cultural products is constructed and reconstructed are elements that question the very ways in which the object of research is constituted and defined. Perhaps one of the *possible* explanations lies in the intimate nature of the relationship between social science and ideology in general, an explanation which involves arguments that are more a matter of methodological theory and which need to be identified and developed.

7   *Imposibila iubire/Impossible Love* (Constantin Vaeni, 1984)

An expressive character in the gallery of working heroes is Călin Surupăceanu (played by Șerban Ionescu) in *O iubire imposibilă/Impossible Love* (based on the novel *Intrusul/The Intruder* by Marin Preda), directed by Constantin Vaeni (1984). It is one of most expressive cinematic deconstructions of the myth of working hero in socialism. The film questions the type of hero at the time – namely the false hero. The filmic narrative is built around the biography of a young builder who lays the foundations of an industrial construction, of a new town.

With him, a whole series of characters and their actions located predominantly in the industrial occupational field build the (social) structure in which the main character is situated and whose journey only acquires significance in relation to dynamics of other elements of the structure.

7.1 The Project of a Town with No Name

Surupăceanu drives the first stake into the ground of a construction site, he represents the human emblem in the place where a plant was to be built. Years later, he suffers an work accident that considerably reduces his physical working capacity, and he becomes a bicycle guard. The idea emerging from the character's biographical construction is that, in socialism, there is only need for heroes who are healthy, beautiful and fulfilled, and when faced with a dramatic moment they are abandoned by society, their social status destroyed. Society values the individual only as a man of work, in the highest of his physical capacities, which enable him to carry out the most important action of the "new man", namely work, and not just any kind of work, but productive one. The accident suffered by Surupăceanu leads to the downfall of the hero, he is a forgotten hero, few people remember that he was an enthusiast, the man who started a construction and, with this construction, a new world, the construction of the plant leading to the construction of a new town.

The film raises the issue of work condition in socialism. The character's dramatic path provides a key to understanding a latent structure of meaning that includes the relationship between man and work on the one hand, and the relationship between individual and the institutional order in which he is situated, on the other. The newly built town, the material framework of socialist urbanization, is placed in a controversial relationship with the human element. The individual, and not in any case, but the individual through his work, has only an instrumental value for the construction of the material conditions of socialist modernization. According to the Marxist conceptual relationship between "material conditions of existence" and "social consciousness", the film's ideological display provides an inversion of this relationship in the sense that individual's consciousness (concretely transposed in enthusiasm, confidence, social responsibility) generates the physical morphology or material condition which is in turn translated into a new construction, a new town. The new/industrial town, as an emblem of socialist modernization and as a symbol of the "material conditions of existence", annihilates individuality, the human element itself that created it.

TABLE 22 Professions and occupations of characters

Main and supporting characters	Profession/occupation	Area of activity
Călin Surupăceanu	Line Worker	Industrial Branch
Dan Mihăilescu	Construction Engineer	Industrial Branch
Maria Petre	Laboratory Worker	Industrial Branch
Costică	Driver	Industrial Branch
Mrs Sorana	Actress/Retired	Cultural Branch
Ambrozie Cazaciuc	Night Watchman (at the Coop.)	Industrial Branch
Miss Nuți	Worker	Industrial Branch
–	Painter	
Iulica	Waitress	Personal Services
Antim	UTM Secretary / Worker	Industrial Branch
Vasile	Topographical Engineer	Industrial Branch
Ioana Surupăceanu	Pensioner	–
Mărin Surupăceanu	Craftsman (Sieve Maker)	Craftsmanship
Vasilică	School of Qualification	
Dămăceanu	Professor	Education
Geta Polihroniade	Chemical Engineer	Industrial Branch

SOURCE: *IMPOSSIBLE LOVE*, CONSTANTIN VAENI, 1984

The function of main character is to deliver through the strategy of antithesis the image of a hostile material (town) setting, understanding by the "new" town a material and symbolic form of ideology, of the socialist (urban) project. The relationship of the individual with the urban world that it (literally) created is presented in a first phase – the initial situation – as a "normal and good" state, defined by the typicality of the situations in relation to a pre-existing model in the cinematic situational instrumentation of the actuality and by the positive character of the relationship of the individual to the social context in which he is placed and made to act, while the final stage of biographical construction provides a state of identity degradation (identifiable by the low level of social recognition and prestige), generated by the redefinition of the individual's socio-occupational status.

The nature of the relationship between the subject (the hero) and the object (the town as the built urban world) is one of decline, in the sense that a transition to an earlier stage of the relationship with the object is made, the urban world of the new town, to whose building the character has essentially contributed. The subject passes from the position of actor (active display) to the position of spectator (passive display), as a result of an external determination, of a pre-existing mode of social valorization of roles that individual holds on the social scene. Hero is defined not by his social status but by his sphere of action, that is, by the functions he performs within predefined frameworks of the way of life.

The value of the individual is a function of the category of performed work activity. Placement in the sphere of productive work activities is associated with the positive path, in the sense of the identity construction of the working hero, while the displacement of the character from the sphere of active (productive) work leads to the social decline of the individual and the placement of his biography not within the social system of which he is a part, but at its margins or even outside it. The price of labour power is secondary in shaping labour and power relations between members of same working collective. The social prestige of work is much more important in the informal hierarchies that are generated within the same social class. Intra-group differentiation develops based on the practice of a particular type of work, productive work, and, moreover, any deviation, even in the form of an work accident, is more an expression of a limit of human potential to fulfil the standards of work performance evaluation than an effect of unforeseeable circumstances that cannot be controlled.

7.2   *The Work Hero and the Cancellation of Reality*

How does this particular character stand out in the actuality filmography of the era? Through an atypical character, and this time atypical not because he is not "positive", but because he fulfils a novel function: that of offering through his own biography a counter-analysis of society. The novelty is determined not in relation to reality, but in relation to a pre-existing model of certain categories of characters – the "typical" character of the "positive" working hero, on the one hand, but who is also in a "positive" relationship with the society to which he belongs, on the other. This is the generally accepted pattern, which is abandoned in favour of a new one, based on which the individual's relationship with work is reflected but also problematized the relationship with the system that ideologically validates a certain life of work.

The difference lies in the fact that, unlike the generally accepted function of this category of characters (the man of work), that of positivising the individual-work, individual-society relations, the redefinition of the link between the elements of these relations operates in terms of disjunction, in a critical evaluative perspective, that is, challenging the "typical" both in terms of subject class (the hero) and circumstance class (the life situations/social context in which the hero is placed). This disjunction operated at the level of the two classes gives us by extension the image of the relationship between subject (hero/individual) and object (work/the town/"socialist construction") as a failed one. The valorization of urban individual in the context of work can be expresssed as a "dramatized" dynamics, structured according to the following elements shown in the figure below:

By the development of a "novel" biography of the character, the film deconstructs a model, that is, a fixed form of representation in the cinematic imagination of the relationship between individual and work, in particular, and between individual and a specific type of (socialist) society, in general, a form that expresses a common opinion, in the sense of an opinion validated in ideological vision. The biographical path of the protagonist is identified in the "biographical" path of the socialist urbanization project itself. The film's character eventually becomes an individual without identity, in the sense that he "died" for the world he created, just as the town he built remains a place of uncertain identity, being suggestive in this sense the fact that the newly built town has no name.

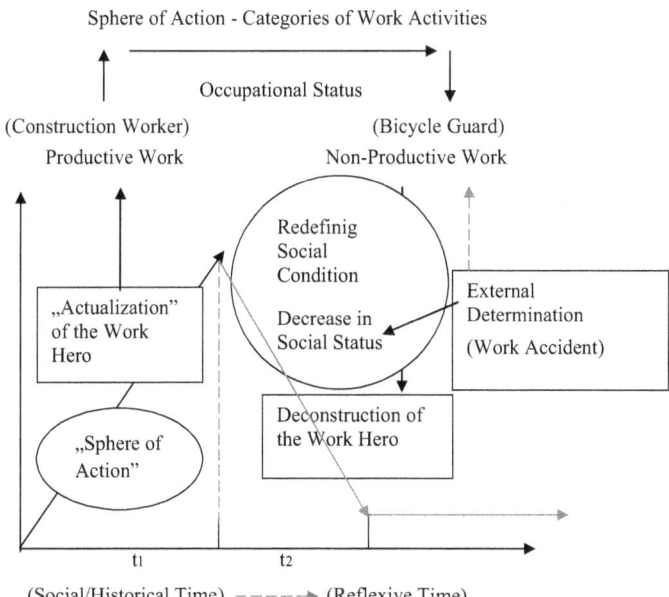

FIGURE 8   Dramatization of the biography of work hero in *Impossible Love* (1984)

The construction of *this* working man raises significant reflection on the ways and mechanisms of the work system's response to atypical situations, by breaking a predictable, controllable pattern. But perhaps it is precisely through the type of response to such situations that the system's potential not to transform an individual difference into a social inequality that can manifest itself not only through the management of formal employment, but also through the psychological pressure generated by the perceptions and attitudes of others in atypical work contexts is truly assessed. Călin Surupăceanu is a product of the work system who, through the succession of situations in which he acts as a working man, comes to question the limits of the ideology on which this system is structured and to invalidate its basic principles. The character creates the premises for validating a new perspective of questioning the meanings and significance attributed to the value and social valorization of work, and does so from the position of one who has shown a high degree of trust in the institutions that formed him as a man of work. There is no clear separation between the actual work activities and other aspects of the character's social life: intimacy, leisure, friendships and other forms of everyday sociability. He does not see work and personal life as exclusive. His life does not begin after he finishes his work. Elements of work life and elements of (intra)individual life mix, interfere in a complex, dense fabric that can only be broken up into opposite categories in theory. For Călin Surupăceanu, work is, contrary to the Marxist view, "a manifestation of life". Work is not in opposition to sitting "at the table, at the tavern seat, in bed" (Marx, 2006: 19). Life does not begin where work activity ceases, rather, it takes place along a continuum which integrates all manifestations of the individual, even if ideologically they are not always consonant.

Referring to the hero of the film he made, director Constantin Vaeni, in an interview for *Flacăra* magazine from 1982 (No. 45, 12 November), described him as "an impeccably beautiful and complex hero", coming "into conflict with the world he builds and for which he does not hesitate to sacrifice himself ... which is more of today's time than the very world he builds, it is actual without being conjunctural. He refuses at all times falsehood, mystification, and betrayal".

CHAPTER 14

Conclusions / Open Ending

The possibility of recovering the meanings of certain forms and modes of working life as an important component of the social through a sociologically disciplined look at films produced under socialism was the premise undelying this book. The scientific usefulness of such an attempt becomes meaningful only if it develops an analytical mechanics of film with potential to function independently of the socio-political contexts in which it manifests, to generate clearer understandings of the distinctions that exist between work theories, work ideologies and work policy strategies.

For today's younger generations, films (about work) made during socialism are probably little known or given little importance simply because they are part of a different historical actuality, insufficiently explored and to a small extent tangible. Anchoring into the present, an ordering principle of mass communication society, ideologically slices resources of interest in past and future according to two factors: the time and the perceived usefulness of the objects of knowledge attached to it. All the more so as labels, elements of polar thinking, cognitive schemes and subjective experiences accumulated in contexts of dominant value systems structure evaluative and knowledge positions in relation to the three conventional dimensions of time. For a teenager or a young person today, a film made during the 1970s or the 1980s has rather a psychological value or utility, in the sense that it helps to clarify or confirm already constructed representations and sedimented schemes attached to the present and to the imagined social reality of an epoch. "Socialist" actuality is just a methodological hypostasis, a contextual, variable element. Such a hypostasis can reach different values, can designate social universes that are delimited by practices, values, norms and negotiations between them. The aim of the sociological research at the heart of this book was to provide a contextual and indicative architecture of a theoretical and methodological apparatus based on which, in the mass of films produced in a society, ideological resources feeding social representations of a nuanced reality can be identified and analysed, in one hypostasis of the social, namely work. To the extent to which the analytical intervention in film productions of the socialist epoch goes beyond their actuality character and is based on a principle of knowledge with social precise functions, contents and expressions analysed are a valid resource for social knowledge and have the quality of surviving actuality, articulating an image of reccurences, of types, that is, of elements that can reveal structures of multiple (social) realities without being reduced to them.

Representations of work reproduce a multi-layered structure of meaning, acting as revelators of dissonances between ideology and reality as it is. On the one hand, a formal substructure of work process is highlighted, and which is represented by images of the production process, of the organization and distribution of work forces in physical spaces, within formal definitions of work situations. Elements of this structure are material objects of work contexts and human presences making these contexts dynamic. Cinematic description of production activities, of communication elements specific to various positions of institutional authority, of modes of transmission of values and norms governing work relations in formal frameworks, of work task performance and fulfilling of responsibilities and communicative roles based on work ethics, of interactions between people at work, of physical and social relations at work – all these are images of a system of work in which uniformity, obedience, social control, productivity, and planning are fixed elements around which there are also experiences, the subjective ones, that are much more fluid, nuanced, contradictory, and diverse. Tensions generated by the difficulty of getting a job, social prejudices about certain social conditions, limits of tolerance for social rule-breaking, instability of housing and limited resources in achieving final goals, disjointed interactions, renunciation, compromise, lack of communication, unclear life situations or atypically defined, spontaneity, violation of social conventions, irregular pulse of identity and unpredictable dynamics of its components, uncertainty – all these give *the image* of a fragile structure of the social in which work (as institutional work) is only one form of its manifestations, having an instrumental value for other goals, the final goals, and, most of all, this image creates possibilities for developing premises for a perpetual negotiation of the necessity and functions of work both at the ideological, symbolic level and at the level of the lived experience of work. Even if cinematically, these two structures are situated on different narrative and visual layers, significance is built on the lines of confluence and influence between them. What results is a social organism with artificially activated (supra-ideological) components and a (possible) morphology of humanity that is not always reproduced in precise contours and dilutes the predefined forms in which it manifests, making from transience a way of life and a form of knowledge.

The ideological conditions of work, the discipline and rhetoric attached to the culture of work in various economic and social sectors, the bureaucratic practices of industrial and party elite, the forms of ideological control of work and cultural production, underground socio-cultural mechanisms of its circumvention are part of a historical context, but beyond the context, filmic discourses are made up from the fabric of universal themes: the relationship between the individual and the social system, between the individual and the political power, the functions and dysfunctions of economic system and political regime, synthetic expressions of a society's potential for contestation or, conversely, of resources of obedience and conformity, critical evaluation of social institutions, processes and mechanisms of socialization through which value orientations, symbolic forms, descriptive and normative restrictions are shared. Films embody, at different levels of intentionality, sometimes unobservable dynamics of these institutions whose significant and not necessarily representative revelators can be identified through a process of systematic and objective analysis.

Like works exhibited in a museum, films reconstruct elements of thought structures, creatively recompose their institutional forms and expressions. They slide between dispersed, intolerant, written history and provocative, dominant, visual social memory, differentiating between them according to their capacity to incorporate into the social imaginary possibilities of a political sensibility.

References

Abel, Richard (ed.). 2005. *Encyclopedy of Early Cinema*. London and New York: Routledge.
Adorno, Theodor W. 2005. *The Culture Industry. Selected Essays on Mass Culture* (edited and with an introduction by J. M. Berstein). London & New York: Routledge.
Altenloh, Emilie. 2001. "A sociology of the Cinema: the Audience". Pp. 249–293, in *Screen* 42:3.
Althusser, Louis. 2020. *On ideology*. London, New York: Verso.
Althusser, Louis, Balibar, Étienne, Establet, Roger, Macherey, Pierre, Rancière, Jacques. 2016. *Reading Capital. The Complete Edition*. London and New York: Verso.
Arendt, Hannah. 1998. *The Human Condition*. The University of Chicago Press.
Arendt, Hannah. 2002. "Karl Marx and the Tradition of Western Political Thought", in *Social Research*, Vol. 69, No. 2.
Arnheim, Rudolf. 1997. *Film as Art*. University of California Press.
Arnheim, Rudolf. 1997. *Visual Thinking*. University of California Press.
Aristarco, Guido. 1965. *Cinematografia ca artă. Istoria teoriilor filmului* (*Cinema as Art. History of Film Theories*). Bucharest: Meridiane Publishing House.
Aumont, Jacques, Marie, Michel. 2007. *L'Analyse des Films*. 2e édition. Paris: Nathan.
Aumont, Jacques, Bergala, Alain, Michel, Marie, Vernet, Marc. 2007. *Estetica filmului* (*Film Aesthetics*). Third edition – Revised and added. Cluj: Editura Ideea Design and Print.
Balázs, Béla. 2010. *Early Film Theory. Visible Man and the Spirit of Film*. Edited by Erica Carter. New York: Berghahn Books.
Banks, Marcus. 2001. *Visual Methods in Social Research*. London, Thousand Oaks, New Delhi: SAGE Publications.
Bazin, André. 2014. *Ce este cinematograful?* (*What Is Cinema?*) Vol. 1. Bucharest: UNATC Press.
Berger, Peter L., Luckman, Thomas. 1991. *The Social Construction of Reality. A Treatise in the Sociology of Knowledge*. London: Penguin Books.
Berki, Robert Nandor. 1979. "On the Nature and Origins of Marx's Concept of Labor", in *Political Theory*, Vol. 7, No. 1.
Borev, I.B. 1963. *Sistemul categoriilor estetice* (*The System of Aesthetic Categories*). Bucharest: Scientific Publishing House.
Bourdieu, Pierre. 1995. *The Rules of Art. Genesis and Structure of the Literary Field*. Stanford California: Stanford University Press.
Blumer, Herbert. 1933. *Movies and Conduct*. New York: Macmillan.
Bremond, Claude. 1964. "Le message narratif". *Communication*, 4. *Recherches sémiologiques*: 4–32. https://www.persee.fr/doc/comm_0588-8018_1964_num_4_1_1025.
Bresson, Robert. 1977. *Notes on Cinematography*. New York: Urizen Books.

Brooker, Peter. 2002. *Modernity and Metropolis: Writing, Film and Urban Formations*. Palgrave Macmillan.

Cantacuzino, Ioan. 1976. "Peisajul filmului românesc de azi" ("The Romanian Film Landscape Today") in Ioan Cantacuzino and Manuela Gheorghiu (eds.). Pp. 47–57, in *Cinematograful românesc contemporan (1949–1975) (Contemporary Romanian Cinema (1949–1975))*. Bucharest: Meridiane Publishing House.

Cantacuzino, Ioan, Gheorghiu, Manuela. 1976. *Cinematograful românesc contemporan (1949–1975) (Contemporary Romanian Cinema (1949–1975))*. Bucharest: Meridiane Publishing House.

Casals, Felipe Garcia (Pavel Câmpeanu). 2002. *Societatea sincretică (The Syncretic Society)*. Bucharest: Polirom Publishing House.

Casetti, Francesco. 1999. *Les Théories du Cinéma depuis 1945*. Paris: Éditions Nathan.

Caudwell, Christopher. 1946. *Illusion and Reality. A Study of the Sources of Poetry*. London: Lawrence & Wishart.

Căliman, Călin. 2000. *Istoria filmului românesc (The History of Romanian Film)*. Bucharest: Romanian Cultural Foundation Publishing House.

Ceaușescu, Nicolae. 1968. *România pe drumul desăvârșirii construcției socialiste. Rapoarte, cuvântări, articole. Iulie 1965-septembrie 1966 (Romania on the Way of Completing the Socialist Construction. Reports, Speeches, Articles. July 1965-September 1966)*. Vol. 1. Bucharest: Political Publishing House.

Ceaușescu, Nicolae. 1971. *Cuvântare la întâlnirea cu creatorii din domeniul cinematografiei (5 martie 1971) (Speech at the Meeting with Filmmakers (5 March 1971))*. Bucharest: Political Publishing House.

Ceaușescu, Nicolae. 1971. *Cuvântare la întâlnirea cu oamenii de artă și cultură, 10 februarie 1971 (Speech at the Meeting with People of Art and Culture, 10 February 1971)*. Bucharest: Political Publishing House.

Ceaușescu, Nicolae. 1972. *Raport la Conferința Națională a PCR (Report to the RCP National Conference)*. Bucharest: Political Publishing House.

Ceaușescu, Nicolae. 1972. *România pe drumul construirii societății socialiste multilateral dezvoltate (Romania on the Way to Building a Multilaterally Developed Socialist Society)*. Vol. 7. Bucharest: Political Publishing House.

Ceaușescu, Nicolae. 1974. *Raport la cel de-al XI-lea Congres al Partidului Comunist Român (Report to the 11th Congress of the Romanian Communist Party)*. Bucharest: Political Publishing House.

Ceaușescu, Nicolae. 1976. *Expunere cu privire la activitatea politico-ideologică și cultural-educativă de formare a omului nou, constructor conștient și devotat al societății socialiste multilateral dezvoltate și al comunismului în România (prezentată la Congresul educației politice și al culturii socialiste, 2 iunie 1976) (Presentation on the Political-ideological and Cultural-educational Activity of Forming the New Man, Conscious and Devoted Builder of the Multilaterally Developed Socialist Society and Communism in*

Romania (presented at the Congress of Political Education and Socialist Culture, June 2, 1976)). Bucharest: Political Publishing House.

Ceaușescu, Nicolae. 1977. *România pe drumul construirii societății socialiste multilateral dezvoltate. Rapoarte, cuvântări, interviuri, articole. Mai 1976 – decembrie 1976* (*Romania on the Way to Building a Multilaterally Developed Socialist Society. Reports, Speeches, Interviews, Articles. May 1976 – December 1976*). Vol. 13. Bucharest: Political Publishing House.

Ceaușescu, Nicolae. 1982. *Expunere cu privire la stadiul actual al edificării socialismului în țara noastră, la problemele teoretice, ideologice și activitatea politică, educativă a poporului (prezentată la plenara lărgită a Comitetului Central al Partidului Comunist Român, 1–2 iunie 1982)* (*Presentation on the Current State of Building Socialism in Our Country, the Theoretical and Ideological Problems and the Political and Educational Activity of the People (presented at the enlarged Plenary Session of the Central Committee of the Romanian Communist Party, 1–2 June 1982)*). Bucharest: Political Publishing House.

Ceaușescu, Nicolae. 1984. *Cuvântare la Consfătuirea de lucru pe problemele muncii organizatorice și politico-educative din 2–3 august 1983, în România pe drumul construirii societății socialiste multilateral dezvoltate* (*Speech at the Working Conference on the Problems of Organizational and Political-Educational Work, 2–3 August 1983, in Romania on the Way to Building a Multilaterally Developed Socialist Society*). Vol. 26. Bucharest: Political Publishing House.

Chatman, Seymour. 1978. *Story and Discourse. Narrative Structure in Fiction and Film.* Ithaca and London: Cornell University Press.

Codul principiilor și normelor muncii și vieții comuniștilor, ale eticii și societății socialiste (*Code of Principles and Norms of Communist Work and Life, Socialist Ethics and Equity*). 1981. Bucharest: Political Publishing House.

Colin, Michel. 1985. *Film, Langue, Discours. Prolégomènes à une sémiologie generative du film* (*Film, Language, Discourse. Prolegomena to a Generative Semiology of Film*). Paris: Klincksieck.

Cucu, Vasile. 1970. *Orașele României* (*The Cities of Romania*). Bucharest: Scientific Publishing House.

Cucu, Vasile. 1976. *Geografie și urbanizare* (*Geography and Urbanization*). Iași: Junimea Publishing House.

Cucu, Vasile, Iordan, Ion. 1984. *Geografia României II. Geografia umană și economică* (*Geography of Romania II. Human and Economic Geography*). București: Editura Academiei Române.

Dahrendorf, Ralph. 1959. *Class and Class Conflict in Industrial Society.* Standford, California: Standford University Press.

Deleuze, Gilles. 1997. *Cinema 1. The Movement-Image.* Minneapolis: University of Minnesota Press.

Deleuze, Gilles. 1997. *Cinema 2. The Time-Image*. Minneapolis: University of Minnesota Press.

Deleuze, Gilles. 2004. *Desert Islands and Other Texts 1953–1974*. Edited by David Lapoujade. Translated by Michael Taormina. Cambridge Mass and London: The MIT Press.

Diken, Bülent, Laustsen, Carsten Bagge. 2007. *Sociology through the Projector*. London & New York: Routledge.

Duma, Dana. 1983. *Autoportretele filmului (Self-portraits of the Film)*. Bucharest: Meridiane Publishing House.

Duță, Mihai. 1976. "Aspecte ale spectacolului și repertoriului cinematografic" ("Aspects of performance and cinema repertoire"). Pp. 37–46, in Ioan Cantacuzino and Manuela Gheorghiu (eds.), *Cinematograful românesc contemporan (1949–1975) (Contemporary Romanian Cinema (1949–1975))*. Bucharest: Meridiane Publishing House.

Duvignaud, Jean. 1995. *Sociologia artei (Sociology of Art)*. Bucharest: Meridiane Publishing House.

Eisenstein, Sergei. 1987. *Nonindifferent Nature. Film and the Structure of Things*. Cambridge: Cambridge University Press.

Eisenstein, Sergei. 1996. *Selected Works. Volume III. Writings, 1934–37*, edited by Richard Taylor. London: British Film Institute.

Elsaesser, Thomas. 2000. *Metropolis*. London: British Film Institute

Engels, Friedrich, Henderson, W. O., Chaloner, W. H. 1968. *The Condition of the Working Class in England*. Standford: Standford University Press.

Enyedi, Georgy. 1996. "Urbanization under socialism". Pp. 100–118, in *Cities after Socialism. Urban and Regional Change and Conflict in Post-Socialist Societies*, edited by Gregory Andrusz, Michael Harloe and Iván Szelényi. Oxford: Blackwell Publishers.

Faure, Élie. 1971. *Funcția cinematografului (The Function of Cinema)*. Bucharest: Meridiane Publishing House.

Ferencz-Flatz, Christian. 2018. *Filmul ca situație socială (Film as Social Situation)*. Cluj-Napoca: Tact Publishing House.

Ferro, Marc. 1973. "Le film, une contre-analyse de la société?". Pp. 109–124, in *Annales. Économies, Sociétés, Civilisations (Annales. Economies, Societies, Civilizations)*. 28(1). http://www.persee.fr/web/revues/home/prescript/article/ahess_03952649_1973_num_28_1_293333.

Francastel, Pierre. 1970. *Pictură și societate (Painting and Society)*. Bucharest: Meridiane Publishing House.

Francastel, Pierre. 1971. "Fragmente antologice" ("Anthological Fragments"). Selection and translation by Radu Bogdan. Pp. 148–160, in *Secolul 20 (The 20th Century)*. 128(9). Bucharest: Writers' Union of the Socialist Republic of Romania.

French, Richard A. 1995. *Plans, Pragmatism and People: The Legacy of Soviet Planning for Today's Cities*. London: UCL Press.
French, Richard A., Hamilton, Frederick Edwin Ian. 1979. "Is there a Socialist City?". Pp. 1–21, in *The Socialist City. Spatial Structure and Urban Policy*, edited by R. A. French and F. E. Ian Hamilton. Chichester: John Wiley & Sons.
Friedmann, George. 1952. "Sociologie et filmologie". Pp. 226–227, in *Revue internationale de filmologie*, 11.
Friedmann, George. 1955. "ProblProblèmes sociologiques". Pp. 35–40, in *Revue internationale de filmologie*, 6.
Friedmann, George, Morin, Edgar. 1952. "Sociologie du cinéma". Pp. 95–112, in *Revue internationale de filmologie*, 10.
Friedmann, George, Morin, Edgar. 1955. "De la mDe la méthode en sociologie du cinéma". Pp. 79–80, in *Bulletin de psychologie*. Tome 9 No. 2.
Friedmann, Georges, Morin, Edgar. 1955. "Congrès international de Filmologie, Paris, 19–23 février 1955. De la méthode en sociologie du cinéma". *1895. Mille huit cent quatre-vingt-quinze. Revue de l'association française de recherche sur l'histoire du cinema (1895. One thousand eight hundred and ninety-five. Journal of the French Association for Research into the History of Cinema)*. [on line] 75 | 2015. https://journals.openedition.org/1895/4967.
Garçon, François. 1992. "Cinéma et histoire: autour de Marc Ferro". *CinémAction* No. 65/ 4. Paris: Éditions Corlet – Télérama.
Gardies, René. 2007. *Comprendre le cinéma et les images (Understanding Cinema and Images)*. Paris: Armand Colin.
Geiger, Jeffrey, Rutsky, R.L. 2005. *Film Analysis. A Norton Reader*. New York London: W.W. Norton &Company.
Gheorghiu, Manuela, Saizescu, Geo. 1976. "Cinecluburile și cultura cinematografică" ("Film Clubs and Film Culture") in Ioan Cantacuzino and Manuela Gheorghiu (eds.). Pp. 194–199, in *Cinematograful românesc contemporan (1949–1975) (Contemporary Romanian Cinema (1949–1975))*. Bucharest: Meridiane Publishing House.
Godelier, Maurice. 1980. "Language and History. Work and Its Representations: A Research Proposal". Pp. 164–174, in *History Workshop Journal*. Vol. 10, Issue 1.
Goffman, Erving. 1956. *The Presentation of Self in Everyday Life*. Edinburg: University of Edinburg.
Goldmann, Annie. 1971. *Cinéma et société moderne*. Paris: Éditions Anthropos.
Goldmann, Annie. 1976. "Quelques problèmes de sociologie du cinéma". Pp. 71–80, in *Sociologie et société (Sociology and Society)* 8(1).
Goldmann, Lucien. 2013. *The Hidden God*. London and New York: Routledge.
Gorz, André. 1982. *Farewell to the Working Class. An essay on Post-Industrial Socialism*. London and Sydney: Pluto Press.

Gorzo, Andrei. 2009. *Bunul, răul și urâtul în cinema* (*The Good, the Bad, and the Ugly in Cinema*). Bucharest: Polirom Publishing House.
Grady, John. 2001. "Becoming a Visual Sociologist".Pp. 83–119, in *Sociological Imagination*. 38(1/2).
Gramsci, Antonio, Forgacs, David (ed.). 2000. *The Gramsci Reader. Selected Writings 1916–1935*. New York University Press.
Gramsci, Antonio, Bellamy, Richard, Cox, Virginia. 1994. *Pre-Prison Writings*. Series: Cambridge Texts in the History of Political Thought. Cambridge University Press.
Gurvitch, Georges. 1964. *The Spectrum of Social Time*. Dordrecht-Holland: D. Reidel Publishing Company.
Haferkamp, Hans, Smelser, Neil Joseph. (eds.). 1992. *Social Change and Modernity*. Berkeley: California University Press.
Harte, Verity. 2007. "Language in the Cave". Pp. 195–215, in *Maieusis. Essays in Ancient Philosophy in Honour of Myles Burnyeat* edited by Dominic Scott. Oxford University Press.
Hauser, Arnold. 2011. *The Sociology of Art*. New York: Routledge.
Herbert, Thomas.1968. "Remarques pour une théorie générale des idéologies". *Cahiers pour l'analyse* (*Notebooks for Analysis*). No. 9. Paris: Le Seuil. http://cahiers.kingston.ac.uk/contents.html.
Herseni, Traian. 1974. *Sociologie industrială* (*Industrial Sociology*). Bucharest: Didactic and Pedagogical Publishing House.
Horkheimer, Max, Adorno, Theodor W. 2002. *Dialectic of Enlightenment*. Stanford, California: Stanford University Press.
Jarvie. I. C. 1970. *Towards a Sociology of the Cinema. A Comparative Essay on the Structure and Functioning of a Major Entertainment Industry*. Routledge and Kegan Paul. London.
Koch, Gertrud. 2000. *Siegfried Kracauer. An introduction* (translated by Jeremy Gaines). Princeton: Princeton University Press.
Kracauer, Siegfried. 1995. *The Mass Ornament. Weimer Essays*. Harvard University Press.
Kracauer, Siegfried. 1997. *The Theory of Film: The Redemption of Physical Reality* (with an introduction by Miriam Bratu Hansen). Princeton: Princeton University Press.
Kracauer, Siegfried. 2004. *From Caligari to Hitler. A Psychological History of the German Film*. Princeton and Oxford: Princeton University Press.
Kracauer, Siegfried. 1998. *The Salaried Masses*. London: Verso.
Krasnaseschi, Vladimir. 1971. *Orientări în științele muncii* (*Orientations in Labour Sciences*). Bucharest: Scientific Publishing House.
Lefebvre, Henri. 1991. *The Production of Space*. Oxford UK and Cambridge USA: Blackwell.
Lenin, Vladimir Ilici. 1963. *Collected Works. Volume 19. March-December 1913*. Moscow: Foreign Languages Publishing House.

Lenin, Vladimir Ilici. 1972. *Materialism and Empirio-Criticism*. Peking: Foreign Languages Press

Lenin, Vladimir Ilici. 1976. *Collected Works. Volume 38. Philosophical Notebooks*. Moscow: Progress Publishers.

Lipovestky, Gilles, Serroy, Jean. 2008. *Ecranul global (The Global Screen)*. Iași: Polirom Publishing House.

Martin, Marcel. 1981. *Limbajul cinematografic (The Language of Cinema)*. Bucharest: Meridiane Publishing House.

Marx, Karl. 1904. *A Contribution to the Critique of Political Economy*. Chicago: Charles H. Kerr & Company.

Marx, Karl. 1906. *Capital. A Critique of Political Economy*. New York: The Modern Library.

Marx, Karl. 2006. *Wage-labour and Capital and Value, Price and Profit*. New York: International Publishers.

Marx, Karl, Engels, Friedrich. 1976. *Collected Works. Volume 5*. New York: International Publishers.

Marx, Karl, Engels, Friedrich. 1978. *On Literature and Art*. Moscow: Progress Publishers.

Marx, Karl, Engels, Friedrich. 1987. *Collected Works. Volume 25. Dialectics on Nature*. New York: International Publishers.

Marx, Karl, Engels, Friedrich. 1998. *The German Ideology*. New York: Prometheus Books.

Marx, Karl, Engels, Friedrich. 2008. *The Communist Manifesto*. London: Pluto Press.

Mazierska, Ewa. 2011. *European Cinema and Intertextuality. History, Memory and Politics*. Palgrave Macmillan.

Mazierska, Ewa (ed.). 2013. *Work in Cinema. Labor and the Human Condition*. Palgrave Macmillan.

Mănoiu, Alice. 1976. "Decorul – o poartă către stil (Décor – a Gateway to Style)" in Ioan Cantacuzino and Manuela Gheorghiu (eds.). Pp. 139–150, in *Cinematograful românesc contemporan (1949–1975) (Contemporary Romanian Cinema (1949–1975))*. Bucharest: Meridiane Publishing House.

Measnicov, Ioan, Hristache, Ilie, Trebici, Vladimir. 1977. *Demografia orașelor României (Demography of Romanian Cities)*. Bucharest: Scientific and Encyclopedic Publishing House.

Mennel, Barbara. 2008. *Cinema and the Cities*. London: Routledge.

Metz, Christian. 1974. *Language and Cinema*. The Hague: Mouton Publishers.

Mihăilescu, Vintilă, Nicolau, Viorica, Ghiorghiu, Mircea, Drinovan, Gabriela. 1993. "Snagov – Trei proiecții asupra sistematizării (Snagov – Three Projections on Systematization)". Pp. 18–32, in *Sociologie românească (Romanian Sociology)*, Year IV, No. 1. Bucharest: Romanian Academy Publishing House.

Mills, C. Wright. 2000. *The Sociological Imagination*. Oxford: Oxford University Press.

Miroș, Liubomila. 1977. *Echitate și dreptate (Equity and Justice)*. Bucharest: Scientific and Encyclopedic Publishing House.

Mitry, Jean. 1997. *The Aesthetics and Psychology of the Cinema*. Bloomington and Indianapolis: Indiana University Press.

Morin, Edgar. 1956. *Le cinéma ou l'homme imaginaire. Essai d'Anthropologie*. Paris: Les Éditions de Minuit.

Morin, Edgar. 1977. *Starurile. O privire istorică, sociologică și estetică asupra stelei de cinema (Stars. A Historical, Sociological and Aesthetic Look at the Movie Star)*. Bucharest: Meridiane Publishing House.

Morin, Edgar. 1978. *Le cinéma ou l'homme imaginaire. Essai d'Anthropologie Sociologique*. Paris: Les Éditions de Minuit.

Murgescu, Bogdan. 2010. *România și Europa. Acumularea decalajelor economice (1500–2010) (Romania and Europe. Accumulating Economic Gaps (1500–2010))*. Bucharest: Polirom Publishing House.

Murray, Pearse, Szelényi, Iván . 1984. "The City in the Transition to Socialism". Pp. 90–107, in *International Journal of Urban and Regional Research* 8.

Nemoianu, Virgil. 2013. *Structuralismul. Calmul valorilor (Structuralism. The Calm of Values)*. Bucharest: Spandugino Publishing House.

Park, Robert E., Burgess, Ernest W. 2019. *The City*. Chicago and London: The University of Chicago Press.

Parsons, Talcott. 1991. *The Social System* (Preface by Bryan S Turner). London: Taylor & Francis Routledge.

Pasti, Vladimir. 1995. *România în tranziție. Căderea în Viitor (Romania in Transition. Falling into the Future)*. Bucharest: Nemira Publishing House.

Piaget, Jean. 1970. *Structuralism (Structuralism)*. New York: Basic Books.

Pickvance, Chris. 2002. "State-Socialism, Post-socialism and their Urban Patterns: Theorizing the Central and Eastern European Experience". Pp. 183–203, in *Understanding the City. Contemporary and Future Perspectives*, edited by John Eade and Christopher Mele. Oxford: Blackwell Publishers Ltd.

Pivniceru, Constantin. 1971. "Mihai Viteazul în fapte și cifre (Michael the Brave in facts and figures)" in *Cinema* No. 1/1971.

Poster, Mark. 1975. *Existential Marxism in Post-War France. From Sartre to Althusser*. Princeton, New Jersey: Princeton University Press.

Potra, Florian. 1970. "Cinematografia românească în căutarea propriului chip" ("Romanian Cinema in Search of Its Own Face"). Pp. 74–81, in *Lupta de clasă (The Class Struggle)*. No. 9 (September).

Powers, Stephen, Rothman, David J., Rothman Stanley. 2018. *Hollywood's America. Social and Political Themes in Motion Pictures*. New York: Routledge.

Programul P.C.R. de făurire a societății socialiste multilateral dezvoltate și înaintare a României spre comunism (Programme of the Romanian Communist Party: for the building of the multilaterally developed socialist society and Romania's advance toward communism). 1975. Bucharest: Political Publishing House.

Propp, Vladimir Iakovlevici. 1983. "Transformările basmelor fantastice" ("The Transformations of Fantasy Fairy Tales"). Pp. 662–683, in *Ce este literarura? Școala formală rusă* (*What Is Literature? The Russian Formalist School*). Anthology by Mihai Pop. Bucharest: Univers Publishing House.

Reiner, Thomas A., Wilson, Robert H. 1979. "Planning and Decision-Making in the Soviet City: Rent, Land and Urban Form". Pp. 49–71, in *The Socialist City. Spatial Structure and Urban Policy*. Edited by R. A. French and F. E. Ian Hamilton. Chichester: John Wiley & Sons.

Rokeach, Milton. 1973. *The Nature of Human Values*. New York: Free Press.

Rönnäs, Per. 1982. "Centrally Planned Urbanization. The Case of Romania". Pp. 143–151, in Geografiska Annaler. Series B, *Human Geography*, Vol. 64, No. 2 (1982). http://www.jstor.org/stable/490668.

Sadoul, Georges. 1961. *Istoria cinematografului mondial* (*The History of World Cinema*). Bucharest: Scientific Publishing House.

Sandu, Dumitru. 1987. *Dezvoltarea socioteritorială în România* (*The Socio-territorial Development in Romania*). Bucharest: Publishing House of the Academy.

Sartre, Jean-Paul. 1968. *The Communists and Peace with a Relplay to Claude Lefort*. New York: George Braziller.

Sartre, Jean-Paul. 1986. *L'imaginaire*. Paris: Gallimard.

Simmel, Georg, Frisby, David, Featherstone, Mike. 1997. *Simmel on Culture: Selected Writings Theory, Culture and Society*. Sage Publication.

Sobchack, Thomas, Sobchack, Vivian C. 1987. *An Introduction to Film*. Second Edition. New York: Longman.

Sorlin, Pierre. 1977. *Sociologie du cinéma*. Paris: Aubier.

Sorlin, Pierre. 2005. *European Cinemas, European Societies, 1939–1990. Studies in Film, Television, and the Media*. London: Taylor & Francis Routledge.

Steriade, Ștefana, Câmpeanu, Pavel. 1985. *Oameni și filme* (*People and Films*). Bucharest: Meridiane Publishing House.

Szelényi, Iván. 1996. "Cities under Socialism – and After". Pp. 286–317, in *Cities after Socialism. Urban and Regional Change and Conflict in Post-Socialist Societies*, edited by Gregory Andrusz, Michael Harloe and Iván Szelényi. Oxford: Blackwell Publishers.

Thompson, Edward Palmer. 1966. *The Making of the English Working Class*. New York: Vintage Books.

Trebici, Vladimir, Hristache, Ilie. 1986. *Demografia teritorială a României* (*Territorial Demography of Romania*). Bucharest: Publishing House of the Academy of the Socialist Republic of Romania.

Tudor, Andrew. 1974. *Image and Influence. Studies in the Sociology of Film*. London: George Allen & Unwin Ltd.

Tyler, Parker. 1960. *The Three Faces of the Film*. New York: Thomas Yoseloff.

Tyler, Parker. 1972. *The Shadow of an Airplane Climbs the Empire State Building – A World Theory of Film.* New York: Doubleday & Company, Inc. Garden City.

Weihsmann, Helmut. 1997. "The City in Twilight: Charting the Genre of the "City Film" 1900–1930". Pp. 8–27, in François Penz and Maureen Thomas (eds.), *Cinema and Architecture: Méliès, Mallet-Stevens, Multimedia.* London: British Film Institute.

Wright, Terence. 1999. *The Photography Handbook.* London and New York: Routledge.

Zhdanov, Andrei A. 1950. *Essays on Literature, Philosophy, and Music.* New York: International Publishers.

Zukin, Sharon. 1978. "The Problem of Social Class under Socialism". Pp. 391–427, in *Theory and Society.* Vol. 6, No. 3 (Nov.). Springer. https://www.jstor.org/stable/656759.

Index

Abel, Richard   6
actuality film   3, 12, 15, 149, 152–155, 157, 158–160, 188, 195, 198, 202–204
Adorno, Theodor W.   100–103, 106–107
Altenloh, Emilie   7, 86
Althusser, Louis   117, 130–133, 209–210
always-already subjects   133
Arendt, Hannah   27, 30
Aristarco, Guido   11, 138
Arnheim, Rudolf   71–72
artistic criticism   126
Aumont, Jacques   83

Balázs, Béla   106
Balibar, Étienne   133
Banks, Marcus   14
Bazin, André   8
Berger, Peter L.   18, 20–21
Blumer, Herbert   85
Bourdieu, Pierre   210
Bremond, Claude   81
Bresson, Robert   89
Brooker, Peter   11

Căliman, Călin   149, 152–154, 164, 169, 269
Câmpeanu, Pavel   83, 164–168
Casetti, Francesco   94–97, 103
Caudwell, Christopher   137
Chatman, Seymour   80–81, 83
cinematic images   4, 9–10, 16, 72, 79, 89, 110, 271
cinematic reality   22, 93, 104, 209
cinematic representations   4, 9, 12, 14–15, 64, 90, 104, 174, 178, 186, 251, 266
class relationships   35
class struggle   31, 36–37, 118, 133, 155
Colin, Michel   87–88
condition of work   13
content analysis   15, 86
convergent theories   43
counter-analysis of society   13, 109–110, 113, 275
critical method   107
cultural artefact   90, 105
cultural industry   95, 97, 99–104

cultural production   1, 68, 72, 121, 146, 149, 241, 279

Dahrendorf, Ralph   31–32
Deleuze, Gilles   18, 22, 23, 72–73
Diken, Bülent   18, 90
divergence theories   44
division of work   11, 27, 30, 117–118, 271
dominant ideology   117, 130, 211, 219, 227, 252
Duma, Dana   154
Duvignaud, Jean   89

economic system of production   14
Eisenstein, Sergei   75, 138–139
Elsaesser, Thomas   11
empirical ideology   87
Engels, Friedrich   9, 28–31, 50, 117, 120, 124, 134–135, 142, 146, 176
Enyedi, Georgy   38, 43, 45, 47–48, 50–51
Establet, Roger   133
evaluation of work   14
external narrative   14

Faure, Élie   8, 9
female identity   189, 194
Ferencz-Flatz, Christian   92
Ferro, Marc   109–113
film as social document   11
film criticism   13, 152
film economy   171–172
filmic construction   13, 103, 114–115, 159, 197, 261
filmic image   73–74, 76–77, 79
filmic narrative   83, 113, 154, 159, 187–188, 198, 265
filmic organization   83
forces of production   30, 60, 65, 69, 118–119
Forgacs, David   126–130
frameworks of the city   11
Francastel, Pierre   25, 116
Friedmann, George   86–87, 94–95, 97, 104
functions of work   10, 14, 279

Garçon, François   113
Gardies, René   77

Geiger, Jeffrey   71, 77, 91
Godelier, Maurice   26–28
Goffman, Erving   93
Goldmann, Annie   83, 88
Goldmann, Lucien   72
Gorz, André   34–35
Gorzo, Andrei   95
Grady, John   85, 87
Gramsci, Antonio   117, 124–130, 143, 209
Gurvitch, Georges   69–70

Hauser, Arnold   91
hegemonic attitude   129
hegemony   117, 128–129, 211
Herbert, Thomas   87–88
historical bloc   128
historical materialism   36, 66, 117, 122, 134–135, 143
homogeneity of cultural products   101
Horkheimer, Max   100–102
human body on film   11

ideological apparatus   132, 209
ideological control   68, 140, 268, 279
ideological meanings   12, 195
ideological structures   91
ideology   2, 13, 36, 38, 46, 69, 87, 91, 100–101, 110, 113, 118, 120–122, 124, 128, 130–133, 138, 140, 143, 149–150, 163, 187, 195, 204, 210–215, 218–219, 227, 232, 243, 245–246, 252–253, 255, 265, 272, 274, 276, 279
ideology of work   13, 195, 255
illusion of reality   75
images of work   4, 9–10, 16, 61
inconspicuous surface-level expressions   106
Individualization   10, 108, 136, 187, 241
industrial bureaucracy   186–188
industrial technocracy   188
industrialization   5, 39, 44, 50, 52, 56–58, 60–61, 101, 186, 228, 233, 236, 240
inequalities   31, 49, 98, 218, 243, 250, 263, 271
institutional hierarchies   63
institutional structures   63, 192
internal narrative   14, 24
interpellation   117, 130, 133, 209–213

Jarvie. I. C.   99

Koch, Gertrud   107–108
Kracauer, Siegfried   68–69, 105–108, 115

Laustsen, Carsten Bagge   18, 90
layer of a autonomous significance   81
Lefebvre, Henri   46
Lenin, Vladimir Ilici   50, 121–122, 135, 138
Lipovestky, Gilles   89
Luckman, Thomas   18, 20–21

Macherey, Pierre   133
Martin, Marcel   73–74, 76–78, 87, 100
Marx, Karl   9, 28–31, 50, 69, 117–121, 124, 128, 130–135, 142, 146, 209, 277
mass culture   6, 9, 100–101, 103, 137, 161, 171
material conditions of existence   117, 119, 128, 274
material existence of a ideological apparatus   132
material frameworks of work   14, 202
material ideological apparatus   132
material objects   117, 121, 175, 247, 252, 279
material rituals   132
Mazierska, Ewa   9, 115
mechanism of dramatization   24
Mennel, Barbara   7
mental maps   18
method of dramatization   18, 20, 22, 24
methodological thinking   108
Metz, Christian   115
Mihăilescu, Vintilă   53, 54, 59
Mills, C. Wright   17–20
Mitry, Jean   84
mode of production   60, 117–121, 133, 142
modern urbanity   9, 11
Morin, Edgar   4, 86–87, 92–95, 97–99
multiplicity of urban spaces   11

narrative material or content   16
narrative messages   81
narrative structure   82, 233
nature and function of work   28
non-visible through the visible   110

object of knowledge   14
object-image   109
objectivated human activity   20

party bureaucracy 186–187, 193, 230, 231–232, 234, 262, 269
perceptual apparatus 107
physical realities 107
physiognomy 147, 232, 264, 106
Piaget, Jean 82–83
political bureaucracy 185, 187, 199, 232
political discourses 11
political economy 26
political physiognomies 9
popular education 11
professional category 13, 188, 193, 221, 228, 234, 242, 262
Propp, Vladimir Iakovlevici 80, 81

Rancière, Jacques 133
re-enactment of a social experience 113
reflexivity 10, 100, 214
representational structure 24, 83
representations of the social 90, 95, 104
representations of work 4–5, 9, 12–13, 15, 59, 64, 174–176, 211, 243, 253–254, 270, 279
representative systems 113
Romanian cinema 152, 157, 160, 163, 167, 169, 260, 269
Rutsky, R.L. 71, 77, 91

Sadoul, Georges 6
Sartre, Jean-Paul 35–36, 71
sense of reality 74, 79, 105, 265
Serroy, Jean 8, 89
Simmel, Georg 12
Sobchack, Thomas 85, 88
Sobchack, Vivian C. 85, 88
social change 10, 12, 33, 36 50–51, 93, 134, 137, 207, 233, 235, 241
social competence 188
social conditions and institutions 9, 15
social consciousness 21, 33, 69, 118, 122, 134, 136, 143, 149, 266, 274
social construction of reality 18, 20, 24, 237
social critique 1, 175, 219, 238
social differentiation 31, 32, 46
social experiences of work 9
social groups 12, 116
social history 25, 88, 219, 229
social imaginary of work 9, 14
social institution 1, 9, 61, 82, 97–99, 227

social mobility 205
social order 33, 60, 147, 207, 210, 218, 224–225, 233, 236, 246, 258, 271
social prestige of work 14, 256
social processes 13, 45, 89, 175
social representation 7, 12, 15, 31, 86, 97, 104, 176, 209, 272, 278
social status 28, 42, 46, 91, 94, 195, 229, 235, 238, 240, 244, 250–251, 261, 264, 266–267, 270, 272, 274, 276
social values 28–29, 97, 103, 224, 240
socialist cities 40–42, 47
socialist modernization 1, 61, 235–236, 241, 274
socialist realism 1, 4, 5, 13, 65, 67–69, 129–130, 134, 137, 139, 143, 146, 150, 160, 201, 211, 219, 259, 261, 266, 270
socialist urban policies 45
socializing agents 93
socio-economic processes 29
sociological analysis 3, 12, 32, 85, 87
sociological concepts 15
sociological ideas in film 14
sociological imagination 2, 13–15, 17–20, 22, 24, 198, 271
Sorlin, Pierre 75, 83, 93, 114–115
specialization of roles 33
speculative ideology 87
sphere of action 20, 274, 276
star-system 98
stereotypical symbols 9
Steriade, Ștefana 83, 164–168
structuralist theory 80
subjective experience of work 4, 14
suburbanization 38–39, 43, 52
superstructure 36, 118–120, 122, 128–129, 132
symbolic form 8, 206, 274
system of authority 32, 263
system of values and norms 17
systematization policy 53
Szelényi, Iván 37–43
technical bureaucracy 69

technical division of work 30
terminal and instrumental values of work 10
theory of cultural hegemony 117
theory of interpellation 117, 130

theory of reflection   117, 121–122, 135, 143–144
Thompson, Edward Palmer   33, 34
total social fact   115
Tudor, Andrew   85
Tyler, Parker   75

urban infrastructure   11, 59, 244
urban population growth   39, 55–57
urban proletariat   30
urban sociology   1, 15
urbanization   1, 5, 13, 31, 33, 36–39, 41, 43–53, 55, 58–61, 68, 203, 212, 251, 273, 275

value of culture   126
value system   2, 7, 88, 175, 207, 213–215, 218, 233, 235, 239–240, 247, 257, 263, 249
virtual reality   14, 22, 23, 25, 88
visual and auditory images   15, 24

visual culture   3, 11
visual paradigms of work   9
visual perception   8, 71
visual research   12
visual sociology   1, 3, 15
visual thinking   3, 8, 92, 95

Weihsmann, Helmut   9
work hero   196, 276
work system   14, 61–64, 177, 187, 194, 198, 223, 276
work system morphology   14
working class   5, 11, 30, 33–34, 39, 43, 45, 61, 67, 69–70, 121, 127, 129, 133–134, 137, 142, 148–149, 155, 170, 215, 223, 225, 230–232, 247, 265–268, 270
working communities   12, 68
working subjects   13

www.ingramcontent.com/pod-product-compliance
Lightning Source LLC
Chambersburg PA
CBHW070612030426
42337CB00020B/3764